By Ved Mehta

Face to Face
Walking the Indian Streets
Fly and the Fly-Bottle
The New Theologian
Delinquent Chacha
Portrait of India
John Is Easy to Please
Mahatma Gandhi and His Apostles
The New India
The Photographs of Chachaji
A Family Affair
Three Stories of the Raj

CONTINENTS OF EXILE
Daddyji
Mamaji
Vedi
The Ledge Between the Streams
Sound-Shadows of the New World
The Stolen Light

CONTINENTS OF EXILE

THE

STOLEN

LIGHT

VED MEHTA

CONTINENTS OF EXILE

THE

STOLEN

LIGHT

W. W. Norton & Company

NEW YORK / LONDON

First published as a Norton paperback 1990.

Printed in the United States of America.

Parts of this book appeared in The New Yorker.

The text of this book is composed in Garamond #3.

Library of Congress Cataloging in Publication Data
Mehta, Ved Parkash, 1934–
The stolen light.
Continues: Daddyji, 1972; Mamaji, 1979; Vedi, 1982;
The ledge between the streams, 1984; and Sound-shadows of the new world, 1985
1. Blind—United States—Biography.   2. College
students—California—Biography.   I. Title.
HV1792.M4A3   1989   362.4′1′0924   {B}   88-15102

ISBN 0-393-30673-9

W. W. Norton & Company, Inc.
500 Fifth Avenue, New York, N.Y. 10110

W. W. Norton & Company, Ltd.
37 Great Russell Street, London WC1B 3NU

2 3 4 5 6 7 8 9 0

To Sage

I conceived this series of autobiographical books nearly thirty years ago, and, between writing many other books, I've been working on it ever since. Quite early, I had in mind an omnibus title, but I wasn't sure that I would have the physical and emotional stamina—or, indeed, the means—to keep on with the project. In any case, at the start it was mostly a private vision. With the publication of this, the sixth book, I feel that the series has a manifest architecture, and am therefore emboldened to give it the name I have carried so long in my head: "Continents of Exile."

At different times during the writing of this book, I was especially helped by Georgine Maniscalchi Edwards, Alexandra Alger, Laura Mosedale, and Amy Clyde. As with my other books, I benefitted from Eleanor Gould Packard's reading and rereading of the proofs at every stage. I can do no more here than simply thank all of these, who, for lack of a better word, are called amanuenses. I know no way of describing the nature and the extent of the professional but intimate, dedicated but lively editorial help they gave me. In fact, they worked so closely with me that it is no exaggeration to say that each amanuensis became almost an extension of my hand. Finally, I wish to acknowledge the ineffable help of my wife, Linn.

V.M.

New York
October 1988

CONTENTS

PHOTOGRAPHS

CONTINENTS OF EXILE

THE

STOLEN

LIGHT

I

JOHNNIE'S
VOICE

IT WAS FRIDAY, THE DAY THE RESIDENCE HALLS OPENED for new students at my college, in California. All day, sophomore men had been weighing and measuring— "sizing up"—the freshman women as they were about to enter their dormitory. The "sizing-up" ceremony for women was one of a series of initiation rites for all incoming freshmen, men and women. I was a freshman myself, and, eager not to be left out of anything, I had a "dink" (a green beanie) on my head and, in my pocket, the student "Bible" (a handbook that listed the college organizations, set forth the college rules, and gave the words of the college songs and yells). Each of us "greenhorns" was required to wear a dink and carry the Bible at all times on the campus and in town, on pain of court-martial by the sophomores. With a great many other men, I was pushing and shoving to get near the front porch of the dormitory, where a scale had been set up. Sophomore men were milling about up and down the street, to direct the stream of cars in which the women were arriving, with their parents, and to help unload and carry luggage, and escort the women to the scale.

During a lull in the general hubbub, there was clapping and cheering as a new arrival was swept up onto the porch, laughing and mildly protesting. The men pressed closer to the porch to get a better look.

"Step back, gentlemen, you're crowding the lady," a smooth-sounding man said. He was one of the Ghosts, who, I had just learned, were members of the most illustrious male honorary society on the campus, restricted to fifteen upperclassmen. They policed all the activities connected with our initiation.

"What's your name?" someone asked the young woman.

"JoAn Johnstone," she said.

"O.K., Johnnie, up on the scale."

There was a clink as she stepped on the scale, still laughing, and a rattle as its measuring rod was adjusted to the top of her head.

"Johnnie's weight?"

"A hundred and fifteen!"

"Johnnie's height?"

"Five feet four inches!"

"Arms up, Johnnie! We have to get the measuring tape around you. It'll only take a second."

Several sophomore men of the campus-leader type were doing the weighing and measuring. As her statistics were shouted out, one of the sophomores recorded them on a list of the incoming freshman women. (The list was to be circulated through the men's dormitories.)

"Johnnie's bust?"

"Thirty-four!"

"Waist?"

"Twenty-four!"

"Hips?"

"Thirty-seven!"

There was clapping, cheering, hooting, and laughing all around.

From the perspective of the nineteen-eighties, the sizing-up rite seems sexist and degrading, reminiscent of slave markets and cattle auctions, but in 1952, the year I was a freshman, the whole ceremony was conducted in a spirit of innocent fun.

"Hey, what do you think of your new nickname, Johnnie?" a man near me called out.

"I like it," she said.

"It's better than Mud," a man at my elbow said. Maud Ching, a freshman who had arrived earlier, had received the nickname Mud.

"It certainly is!" Johnnie called back over her shoulder as she disappeared into the dormitory.

"That girl is going to be a homecoming queen," someone said.

Another new arrival was escorted onto the porch.

The air was fresh with the scent of eucalyptus, which made me think of childhood colds back home in India and the eucalyptus leaves crushed in a handkerchief which my mother would press against my nose. No matter how stuffed up my head was, it seemed, I could always smell the pungent, overpowering fragrance of eucalyptus. Johnnie's voice is just like the eucalyptus scent, fresh and heady, I thought. I'll never be able to get it out of my mind. It has a note of forced cheerfulness, as if she were always making the best of things—just like me.

It seemed I could hardly turn around without running into Johnnie, in classes and in the library, on college walks and in the quadrangles. She was always surrounded by friends, men and women, but she always greeted me as we passed. She had a sweet, singsong voice, was quick to laugh, and came across as an All-American girl. Johnnie was immediately elected a freshman-class officer, and she was featured in the "Frosh Show," where she danced the Charleston. She went to dances and football games and fraternity parties, to beach barbecues and ski weekends—all the things I would have liked to go to but somehow felt I couldn't. And she was smarter than practically all the other students who took part in such glamorous activities. In classes, when the professors asked questions she gave just about the best answers, and not in a pushy, forward way but tentatively and discreetly. Like most of the smart women, it seemed, she didn't want to show that she was smarter than men. She was also unusual among us freshmen in knowing her own mind. She was planning to major in English literature, had taken an exam offered by the English Department, and, unlike the rest of us, had been allowed to skip the first semester of the freshman-composition class. In fact, it was obvious that the department rated her one of the freshman students most likely to do well.

I came to believe there was something special even about her nickname, Johnnie—something independent, mature, and serious, just as there was about the "Johnnies" who had spent two years fighting a war in Korea and were now freshmen with us. They and Johnnie had the same forced cheerfulness in their voices, but their cheerfulness just sounded strong and manly, whereas Johnnie's cheerfulness sounded as if she were trying to hide some sadness that had touched her life. I found that sadness heartrending, and wanted to gather her up in my arms and comfort her. I felt that I alone sensed her sadness, and I secretly identified with it and thought of it as a bond between us. There was another, more apparent bond between us as well: like me, and in contrast to most of the other students, she seemed to be in want of money. She had no car, no strings of pearls or necklaces that she fingered noisily in class.

In the years that Johnnie and I were in college together, I never stopped thinking about her—almost to the exclusion of everybody else. Whenever I read a novel, I saw her as its heroine—most of all as Catherine Earnshaw. I felt that if I had her at my side I could do anything—cut quite a figure in the world. But although we came to be friends I never had a proper boy-girl date with her, never even kissed her on the cheek. And I never declared my love for Johnnie. Once or twice when I hinted at my feelings, she tactfully brushed them aside.

After college, we went our separate ways, and for thirty years I scarcely saw her. Now and again, I would hear something about her—that she had got a Ph.D., had married, had got divorced, had remarried, was tutoring law students in writing at Stanford. In the meantime, I had found my vocation in writing in New York City. I, too, had married, and I had a child. Then, in the autumn of 1985, I found myself in San Francisco, and I looked her up. Though so much time had passed, so much had happened to us, and we were living so far apart, we were able to rediscover the friendship of our college years. We spent a day together, sitting in the house of a friend in North Beach (where I was staying), and walking around, and going out to lunch. We had never talked so freely before.

At one point, I told her what she had meant to me in college. "I remember that time we went to see 'Uncle Vanya' at Show Boat," I said. "But I never got anywhere with you, JoAn. I mean, I was in love with you, as you probably knew."

"As a matter of fact, until that moment I wasn't particularly inclined to know," she said. "I knew you liked me a great deal, but I didn't put it to myself in terms of romantic love."

"Really? Why not?"

"I always hoped you would form a romantic attachment with someone like Anne Lockwood. She always seemed to me an appropriate companion for you, because she seemed—here's this silly word—an 'intellectual,' not only intelligent but devoted to the life of the mind, whereas I was always a highly ambiguous figure in that respect. It didn't take much to really impress me in those days. Once, Anne and I were having hamburgers at a restaurant. It was someplace where they had a jukebox with classical music, and she said, 'Oh, the "Brandenburg."' I've missed that record so much. I must hear it.' And I didn't know a 'Brandenburg' Concerto from anything, so I thought, Well, here's a really serious intellectual. I always looked up to women like that. But I also thought that you got along with her very well—that she could be your girlfriend.''

"But she seemed mostly interested in politics—in social work instead of social life," I said. "I wanted someone who was very literary and also very popular. I wanted to be a Ghost, and have the kinds of girls the Ghosts got to go out with, and she certainly wasn't one of those girls."

"Oh, those Ghosts! Yes, those Ghosts. Remember how public-spirited they were?" Her quick laugh erupted, and she said, a little tongue-in-cheek, "They were, oh, so friendly, genuine, enthusiastic, and sincere."

"If I could have become a Ghost and married you, a belle of the campus, I would have been in seventh heaven—that was the ultimate achievement. I was doing all these intellectual things, like trying to become a writer, and get to Oxford, just because I couldn't become a Ghost and couldn't marry you—the things I *really* wanted to do."

"And I had the same vision of the ultimate achievement, of course. I wanted to marry someone who would be not just a Ghost but the head Ghost, the lead singer in the 'Torchbearers.' " The "Torchbearers" was our college anthem, and one of the qualifications for becoming a Ghost was the ability to sing it stirringly. "I was looking for someone who was a leader of men, who could carry himself well in a well-cut suit and also had a certain degree of athletic ability—that mixture of sincerity and prowess—and had a good handshake, a good smile, and a lot of enthusiasm for outdoor life, and who was going to make a whole lot of money, too. Clearly, the future with you was not going to be a future with a lot of money. This, I think, was why you had trouble getting girls to go out with you. In fact, you were almost a scourge of that sort of future. I remember your being contemptuous of the secret dream of so many of our college classmates, the secret dream of all of us in Southern California (mine, too): to have fun at the beach, with everybody good-looking and properly tanned, to run free in the hills and drive a pickup truck across the desert, or perhaps an open-topped car, as fast as the wind on the freeway, but, no matter what, with a lot of laughter, and a lot of money right around the corner. I guess that swept us all up. Then what would you and I have done next? Live in Southern California in a ranch house?" Her laughter was coming faster and faster.

"I never got that far. You had that social side I wanted, because you would have been an ultimate form of success, almost as if I weren't blind." I have been blind since the age of four, as a result of meningitis. "And you had that other side, too, which was apparent to me from discussions with you about stories—books we were reading for class. I remember talking about Lawrence's 'The Blind Man' with you. Both of us were put off by his heavy prose. You tried to explain to me that this was a particular kind of style, but I didn't have the patience for it. I was quoting sentences to you, or adjectives, or phrases, or something, and you were laughing. I remember talking about 'Portrait of the Artist as a Young Man,' and reading about it in your senior thesis. I could see that you had not only a social side but also a powerful intellectual side. As for Anne, she was very outgoing and adventurous but basically she was melancholy. Even her laugh was subdued. I felt that with Anne I'd be dragged down. With you, I thought, I'd be flying high, I'd be up on a trapeze."

"You and I would be world-beaters—beat the world at its own game," she put in. "We could do anything we wanted. I think I represented a lot in the way of excitement, and vitality, and 'let's go.' A lot of self-confidence."

"You laughed very easily. It was as if your whole body were caught up in it in some way. Not convulsive, but it expressed your whole self."

"Well, you made me laugh. We had some good times together—good talks. It was so much fun discussing books with you. In retrospect, that was really one of the nicest things I did in college. I look back and think about sitting quietly and talking over the stories with you. You always had good things to say, and you used to think funny, humorous things. That was our version of about the best time we could have in college, you and I. But you just didn't seem to have all those other things, those college trappings. For a lot of people, including me, that was collegiate success—that façade of masculinity. Some sense of—I can't say a sense of direction, because those Ghosts didn't really have a sense of direction. Still, they could bring a presence to bear on a situation. The masculine presence. The masculine promise."

"Did you ever have any deeper feeling for me?"

"I had very deep affection for you. You could say that, in my way, I loved you—there's no reason not to say that. I think by our junior year I even recognized your feelings for me. They made me very uncomfortable. They worried me. I thought, Oh dear, if he has *those* feelings . . . Oh dear, what shall I do? Gee, there just isn't going to *be* any kind of— There's *no* sexual relationship between us possible. I will not *have* that. Our visions were in a way the reverse of each other, in that I was devoted to securing my future by marrying someone who would go to the Stanford Business School and make a lot of money. I wanted to live in a ranch house and have four or maybe six children, like my girlfriends. Somehow, I didn't picture the private life between my husband and me at all. I imagined that most of the time I would just be a rich housewife, but that every once in a while I'd go off by myself and read, or write poems, or something. A ridiculous image, but it was what I pictured. But I also had a contradictory vision, which I thought at the time was a hopeless one, of falling in love with an intellectual, a kindred spirit, who might—who knows?—become a writer, a professor, a teacher, or something like that. But that was a dream too impossible even to contemplate."

"I once met somebody who knew you during your first marriage, and he told me that your husband was an intellectual," I said. "So you did find someone who you had thought would be impossible to find. In fact, the man I met said your marriage was just like the marriage in 'Portrait of a Lady.' "

She was silent for a moment, and then said, "It's true. It was. But at our age, Ved, when we were in college together, I could not reconcile demands of friendship with demands of the heart. I very seldom had the luxury of being friends with any of the fellows I thought were my proper sexual partners. I don't mean that we were having sex—no, I wasn't doing that with anybody. Too risky. But I grew up thinking that it's better not to love someone who belongs to a different church, a different Protestant sect. That's how provincial my upbringing was—how darned American it was. The American culture dictated that what you were supposed to do was to go out with boys of a certain mold, and all of us girls were supposed to be of that mold, too. For one of us to go out with someone who didn't fit into that mold, which was athletic, Waspish, very materialistic— What I mean is that you, Ved, just didn't rate. And, besides, you were"—she took a deep breath—"Indian!" I was born in India, and came to this country at the age of fifteen. "You were Indian—think of that! That seemed so unreal, alien. You were so exotic. You came from a different culture. The difference between us was just so great—I thought it was insuperable."

"How did you view me? What picture did you have of me? I mean, if I was so unreal to you, what kinds of things struck you about me?"

"Well—" She paused, as if she were reaching back into her memory. "You were so thin, Ved. You were just so thin. That was very touching. And along with that great slenderness there was a great poise. My image of you was of someone standing, very nicely balanced, on slightly larger, slightly outsize feet, and then tapering up to a very, very slender waist and slightly curving back. The contrast was these big, solid shoes and a very delicately poised curve atop the shoes. What size shoe do you wear? I see now, not that big. Maybe it was that you wore dress shoes and the others wore tennis shoes, loafers—whatever. But there was a contradiction between the size of your feet, marching along very firmly—as though you were, in fact, not exactly *in* your shoes but *on* them—and your backward curve, as though you were sailing along in your shoes. Perhaps it was because you stood up so straight that when you walked you almost seemed to be leaning back. You walked so erect that we were afraid if you relaxed, if you let down your guard, you would break—simply fall apart. Other boys could be very clumsy, rough in their movements and their walk, but you never were. You were a much more delicate person. It was a more androgynous image, partly because you were put together more the way the girls were. And, perhaps because of your blindness, your movements were more circumscribed, more confined, and so, in a way, more feminine. And, with your great poise, you proceeded with such confidence. It was one of the strongest impressions I had—an impression other people had—that you were so brave."

I said to myself, *Not brave, really. Just trying to go about my business—get through the day—like everyone else.*

"You always seemed to be in danger, from the point of view of the rest of the world—to be in an enormous amount of physical danger. Everyone who saw you walking from a class upstairs to a class downstairs or from building to building, or, sometimes, running like a madman, thought something terrible was going to happen to you at any moment. As far as we could see, you were always going to walk into a bush or a puddle, run into a lamppost or a tree. It was always remarkable that you got through all right. However well we got to know you, however often we saw you avoiding obstacles, never falling down, we would stand and watch. We'd think, Is he going to run into something? Is he going to miss a step? Is he going to make it, or is he going to go down the stairs headfirst? And if he makes this one will he miss the top step of that little flight going down to the door? Actually, we saw you guiding other people around. You know, it was like being with someone who was set very far apart, in some very different realm, and who could yet be— 'Condescending' is the right word but has the wrong connotations. Who could yet extend his own graciousness to bridge the distance between the two realms. What I'm saying is that it was you who had to help other people over the distance of their fears for you and their sense of your differentness. It was obvious—at least, to me—that, without knowing it, you were creating a wonderful tension around yourself and then crossing over it. It was a little bit like watching a king, or some member of a royal family. We think, If he makes a mistake, what a terrible thing that will be. What if he drops his glove? He can't pick it up. He can't admit to doing anything wrong. You carried yourself so independently, seemed so aloof, that people were afraid to approach you, to help you in any way."

Not a king—just afraid of seeming like a helpless blind beggar. I must have used dignity as a shield.

"And then to find that this person who is in such a risky position is able to be outgoing, gracious, and so on, and is not really bothered by the situation that seems so desperate to everybody else. Not desperate because it's pitiable but desperate because this person is so open to danger—so vulnerable."

We stopped at an Italian restaurant for lunch.

"I remember you eating," she said. "I remember that you spilled more than other people did—things fell off your fork. But it wasn't so much that you were sloppy, because there were people whose table manners were worse—you know, they ate with their mouths open, or bent over their food, or shovelled it in. I think the reason it was hard for us to watch was that it made us nervous. Is the fork going to get to his mouth all right, and what's going to be on it when it gets there? Some things we were served in the dining hall were so hard to manage. There was chicken to cut up, chops—things with bones in them—and all that kind of thing. It seemed to us that every food that was served to you presented some kind of problem. But you probably didn't see it that way. If you'd been eating in the West Point style— raise the fork straight up, bring it straight across to the mouth—

I think the effect would have been the same, because we'd have thought, Is he going to be able to make the turn of the fork at the right moment? What I'm trying to say is that your eating in the dining hall, like your walking around the campus, created psychological problems for us.

"I also remember being aware that you didn't like the things you were eating, so perhaps it was partly a question of: The poor guy, he's here all the way from India—why does he have to eat this food? Why can't he have something that he would eat in India? It used to make me self-conscious about how funny our food must seem to someone who wasn't used to it. It had probably been a long time since you'd had any Indian food, but even so it seemed that the diet was not natural to you."

Parathas cooked with sugar on them, kofta curry, pea pilaf, mint chutney, and a hundred other foods not tasted or smelled in all my high-school or college years.

"It would have been the same if you'd been Chinese. I had the impression that in China they ate very different food."

A girl who was born and raised in a small town in Oregon, then moved to Washington State, who had met hardly any foreigners, never once eaten Indian food, and here I'd been dreaming of dating her, taking her home to India, making her a member of my family. No wonder she ran in the opposite direction if I as much as hinted about what was in my heart.

"I would have felt sorry for somebody from China who was sitting down in the dining hall to mashed potatoes, gravy, peas, and a breaded veal cutlet. What a sorry thing! What I'm trying to say is that I remember you as extremely foreign, completely out of context. That is what was striking, what was distancing. If it had been just your blindness, I think we all might have handled it. I don't mean to say that your blindness didn't set you apart. All those special activities, like signing your name against the edge of a piece of cardboard, keeping track of your notes and papers, figuring out which book was which—these uncanny ways might have been interesting, might have piqued our curiosity, if we had been older, but, oh, we were all so young, so young. Now that I think about it, there was still another thing that set you apart—the purposeful, determined way you did everything, the purposeful way you walked, went about your work. Yes, the purposeful way you got through your food, and even the way you listened to—concentrated on—lectures and conversations. You always knew what the next thing you were going to do was. It always seemed to me that you had some plan to fulfill. I never stopped to ask what plan, whose plan. It was just the impression of being purposeful that you gave. But just to use the word 'purposeful' sounds funny. It somehow doesn't fit anybody else. There can't have been very many other people who were purposeful in our day."

We finished our lunch and were back out on the street. "You were also remarkable because you talked. Other people didn't complete their sentences, and you did. You could talk about public affairs. You talked about history—things you were studying. I remember that you could carry on a conversation, present a whole different point of view. You had a whole background of information, ideas, values in your brain. All this set you apart. You did have some funny sides to you, you know. You were capable of getting on a number of high horses. One was the religion high horse, of attacking the absurdities of Christianity. And I believe you had a diatribe or two against the materialism of American culture."

We spent the rest of the afternoon walking and talking. I told her how I had pictured her, and asked her questions about her family, about what she was doing. We talked about how different her life had turned out to be from her college expectations of it—how much fuller and happier. Then I walked her to her car. We lingered, reluctant to say goodbye, overwhelmed by our meeting, by the past.

"I remember you as such a gentle person," she said. "But the gentleness was often combined—again, like the big shoes and the slender body—with a real anger inside, an enormous anger, almost a frightening irritability. These two things were at odds. I myself thought it very charming, because a person never knew whether you were going to be angry and fierce or get to laughing and be sweet. So there was a lot of variation of moods in you. I didn't know anybody else whose feelings I could chart the way I could yours: 'Now he's very angry. . . . Now he's very kind. . . . Now he's very sweet. . . . Now he's happy.' I think it's because most other people didn't have such strong, almost palpable emotions. It seemed to me that you had more emotions than we had. You were different in that way, too—as though you had come from a place in which people had stronger feelings."

Now, after the passage of thirty years, we could comfortably kiss each other goodbye on both cheeks. I waited for her to drive away, and then walked back to the house where I was staying. She had started the process of thawing my college past for me; her warmth had started a flow of associations that had been frozen in some benumbed part of my mind. The return of feeling to that mental numbness was already beginning to hurt.

How many of us ever have the chance to know how even one other person really sees us, I thought. We both yearn for and dread such knowledge, and rightly so.

II

AT A RICH MAN'S GATE

WELL DONE!" MY FATHER SAID TO ME. ALL AROUND, AIR-
planes seemed to be taxiing or refuelling, taking off or
landing. The air was so thick with rumble and thunder,
fumes and heat that I thought I had arrived in a place on
fire. It was 10:20 A.M., and I was standing on the tarmac
beside the airplane I had come on, not knowing which
way to turn my face.

This was the summer after my last year of high school, and I
was at Los Angeles International Airport. I was eighteen years
old. I'm going to be with Daddyji, I thought, and then felt a
little embarrassed. "Daddyji" was what I'd called my father all
my life, but somehow the word now made me uncomfortable, as
if I had outgrown it. I wondered what changes he would notice
in me. Since the day he walked me to another plane, in New
Delhi, three years before, when I was bound for America, I had
been living more than ten thousand miles away from my fam-

ily—at the Arkansas School for the Blind, in Little Rock. Though my father had been in America for the past three months, I hadn't seen him. Would he think that my three years in an enclave of the blind in an American backwater had made me unfit for his normal world, I wondered. The idea pained me, and I pushed it to one side and thought instead about home. I recalled the religious violence that had accompanied the Partition of India and had forced our family to flee from the newly created Pakistan with little more than the clothes on our backs, and take shelter in independent India, with millions of Hindu and Sikh fellow-refugees. We were all scarred for life by the memories of that violence, but no one in Arkansas, it seemed, had even heard of the Partition. When I left home, the country had been independent only two years, and was unsteady on its feet, like my little brother Ashok, I thought. Now the family was boasting that he could ride a bicycle, getting on and off it himself. What strides might India have taken?

I switched a flight bag I was carrying from my right hand to my left as it struck me that I needed my right hand for a handshake. Handshake? Well, my father and I were in America, after all, and not in our native Punjab, where we would have embraced, like two good Punjabis. My heart began to beat faster, not from excitement but from apprehension, as if I were going to meet a stranger to whom I had to prove myself a well-adjusted blind person. My own father might as well have been the principal of a residential school. Being away at school makes you independent, just as they say, I thought, but it also makes you wary.

In a moment, I'll be speaking Punjabi with my father, I thought. Will I stumble? Can I have forgotten any of it? But the prospect of speaking Punjabi was also pleasant. I looked forward to speaking like an Indian again. Then, too, I was relieved to think that I wouldn't have to reveal to my father right away that I now spoke English perhaps like an Arkansan; the aspiration of us colonials had been to speak English like Englishmen.

I felt my father's large hand on my shoulder through the cloth of my shirt, his arm around me in a half embrace. My concern over how we would greet each other dissolved, and I put my arm around him.

"Well done!"—those were my father's first words, and they were in English. I wasn't sure if he was referring to how I had stepped off the airplane or to how I had got myself from Little Rock to Los Angeles or to the completion of my high-school education after three years of determined study, which had involved fighting off loneliness and depression. Whatever he had in mind, his praise, in the voice as well known to me as my own childhood, filled me with shy pleasure.

He dropped his arm, and we set off, the back of my thumb almost imperceptibly touching his little finger. Since leaving India, I had grown to almost his height. As we walked, we exchanged some Punjabi small talk about the flight and the weather. Just hearing Punjabi made me throw off my adolescent reserve. I found myself babbling on and laughing as I hadn't—or felt I hadn't—since I left home.

"You will be meeting Vivian Thind soon," my father was saying. "She has a wonderful, sweet nature, and when it comes to doing things for people the word 'no' is not in her vocabulary. She is an American married to a Sikh gentleman who has been in this country since 1912—he must have been one of the first Indians to settle here. It's her second marriage, but she is much younger than he. They are members of an Indo-American community—it is quite strong here in Los Angeles. They live a little in the Indian style. Almost since the time of their marriage, her parents have lived with them, and the children—Rosalind and David—honor and respect their grandparents exactly as you children respect Bhabiji." Bhabiji was our paternal grandmother.

We were now in the baggage-claim area, and my father switched to English and introduced me to Mrs. Thind. The last thing I wanted was to have a third party there, but Mrs. Thind greeted me in such a gentle, kind manner that I could return her greeting with a smiling face.

We three walked to a parking lot. I noticed that Mrs. Thind called my father Dr. Mehta and he called her Vivian. There is a touch of the Indian about their friendship, I thought—the man in the saddle and the woman walking behind. But the car we got into in the parking lot was Mrs. Thind's, and it was she who got behind the steering wheel, with my father on the passenger's side, where my mother generally sat. I sat in the back. In all my life, I had never ridden with my father without his being in the driver's seat. Even when he was given an official car with a driver, he would have the driver take the back seat, and drive the car himself. He had brought us up to think that he was the best driver in the world—that with him behind the wheel we were as safe as we would have been at home in bed.

My father, as if reading my thoughts, was saying that a lifetime of driving on the left had made him fear driving on the right. There was always that one-per-cent chance of turning into the wrong lane. Moreover, this was California, where people called roads "freeways," as if drivers could do anything they pleased on them. I don't like to know that he's afraid of anything, I thought. Now, in the speeding car, I concluded that there was something American about my father's friendship with Mrs. Thind, for the woman seemed to be in the saddle.

How I wish that my father and I were alone, I thought. But then I recalled that without Mrs. Thind's car we would have had to pay limousine and taxi fares, and we were poor. My father had written me a memorable letter soon after he arrived in America. In it he said that he had only one change of shirt and had to wash the other by hand every night. (I myself had only a couple of changes of clothes.) Every week or two, he had to carry the rest of his laundry—sheets, towels, and the like—to a laundromat. "And this is California, which they used to say was a land 'rich in gold and precious stones,' " he had written. Although he was a visiting Fulbright professor at the medical school of the University of California at Los Angeles, it was only for a term, and the position was essentially an honorary one. (The Fulbright paid little more than the cost of his transportation to California and back.) In any event, the exchange rate for the rupee was so low that thinking in Indian money here was little better than playing with Monopoly money. "Five hundred rupees at home goes almost as far as five hundred dollars here," he had concluded. "But when rupees are converted into dollars they lose four-fifths of their value. When I go out and spend dollars, I try to forget that I'm earning in rupees and spending in dollars, or I wouldn't be able to buy anything at all." I recalled that when I was at home he had never given a thought to money. Even after the Partition, if I asked him for five rupees for something, he would give me ten. But then he had a monthly salary, and in Indian terms was as rich as a king. Now he was retired. I sat back in the car, feeling sad.

"Vivian has very kindly asked us to lunch at her charming house in Hollywood," my father said, from the front seat.

"Dr. Mehta says he can't even cook an egg," Mrs. Thind said, with a girlish laugh.

"You know the famous story about Newton," my father said. "It is said that he tried to boil an egg, but he boiled his watch and looked at the egg."

We all laughed, my father most of all. Daddyji never tires of laughing at his own stories, I thought. He has told this one ever since I can remember. I suddenly felt quite at home in Mrs. Thind's car.

"You have a house in Hollywood, Mrs. Thind?" I asked, leaning forward.

"Hollywood is not what people think," she answered. "Doctorji is always having disciples visit him, and they want me to show them Hollywood. They won't believe me when I tell them that I've lived here for years and never seen a movie star. People expect all of Hollywood to be a movie set, but it's just a big suburb of Los Angeles."

I asked who Doctorji was and what kind of disciples he had.

"My husband, Dr. Thind, isn't a medical doctor, like your dad. He's a famous Sikh teacher, with disciples all over the country."

My father conspiratorially squeezed my hand, which was resting under his on the top of the front seat. He seemed to be signalling to me that Doctorji wasn't all that Mrs. Thind had made him out to be. Sharing this secret in the car made me feel very close to him.

When we arrived at the Thinds' house for lunch, we asked after Rosalind and David. "They're both in bed," Mrs. Thind said, with an apologetic laugh. "Rosalind was out with her college friends until this morning. She came home after Doctorji got up. And now that school is over even Doctorji can't get David out of his bed until two or three in the afternoon."

I was shocked. At home, such behavior would have been unthinkable. It was certainly unlike the Indian style my father had spoken about at the airport.

"Sleep is God's gift to the children," said Dr. Thind, a burly-sounding Sikh, coming into the room.

Mrs. Thind's parents were out. Only the four of us sat down to lunch. My father was impressed by the whole establishment, and remarked how much he liked the Mediterranean style of the house. "It has a little of the flavor of India, Doctor Sahib, with, of course, the richness of America."

"Doctor Sahib, God has been bountiful in giving me students all across the country," said Dr. Thind. There was something comical about their addressing each other as Doctor Sahib—one a doctor because he had gone to medical school, the other a doctor because he used the honorific title as a man of God. "In Milwaukee and in Tacoma, in Detroit and New York and Boston, students flock to my lectures to tune in to the airways of God."

I couldn't control a snicker, and, pretending that I was about to sneeze, felt in this pocket and that pocket for a nonexistent handkerchief.

My father came to my rescue, saying, "That's very interesting, Doctor Sahib. I would like to know more about your lectures."

"Doctorji is hardly ever here," Mrs. Thind said ruefully. "He spends one week at home and then two months out lecturing. He's so much in demand. If Dad and Mom weren't living with us, I would go nuts."

"As a matter of fact, I myself prepared several lectures, on our religion and culture and politics and constitution, and a few on tropical medicine, before I came here," my father said. "I collected quite a few slides and filmstrips to illustrate them. I thought the lectures would be a good way to earn some dollars to help pay for Ved's education and keep the home fires burning. But I've been in California over three months now and nothing has come of it. What is your secret?"

"My secret, Doctor Sahib? The secret is God. God, who controls all the airwaves in Heaven and on earth."

"That may all be true, Doctor Sahib, but how do you go about getting a lecture hall? How much do you charge for tickets?"

"Oh, Doctor Sahib, I never charge for tickets. No one will come to any lecture anywhere if you charge for tickets."

"Then how is money to be earned by lecturing in this great country?" my father asked.

"Not money, Doctor Sahib, but offerings. At the end of my lectures, I pass a plate and people make offerings. That's plenty to keep this wireless set going."

"How do you get people to come, Doctor Sahib?" my father asked.

"When I arrive in a city, I take out advertisements in the newspapers," Dr. Thind said.

Mrs. Thind left the table and came back with some sample advertisements. She handed a couple of them to my father.

Dr. Thind picked one up and started reading it out loud, in an ingenuous voice—no doubt for my benefit: " 'Come with an open mind, Minds are like Parachutes, they function only when they are open. Master Meditative Science of Knowing God. Class Every Tuesday and Friday, 8 to 10 P.M. One God, One Life, One Cosmic Brotherhood, One Truth and Only One Way of Knowing Him. All sincere seekers of the True Science of Man's Nature invited to join this class . . . Secure the Seven Meditational Manuscripts, the priceless text-lessons. We Put Order in Your Kingdom of Chaos.' "

"There is more," my father said, with a smile in his voice, and he read, " 'Noon Hour Radiant Health Class, Breathing and Gland Exercises Daily from 12 to 1 Noon except Saturday and Sunday . . . Breathe and stay above ground. . . . If your nose is not mortgaged to any one, let us teach you how to demonstrate Radiant Health by working with Nature's Laws. . . . Breath is the Flywheel of Life, Its Dynaspheric Finer Forces Sanely Used Add Years to Life and Life to Years.' "

"Doctorji always mentions the titles of his books in his advertisements, and people send in checks from all over the country," Mrs. Thind said. "There is a stack of letters over there that just came in this morning."

"Have you written a lot of books?" I asked.

"Enough to do God's service. You may have heard of some of them, Doctor Sahib." He intoned the names of the books, as if he were reciting a litany: " 'Soul Celestial—The Darling of God.' 'The House of Happiness.' 'Overcoming Old Age.' 'Glands and Gladness.' 'Vitamins and Vitalizers.' "

"Who publishes them?" I asked.

"I publish them myself, from right here—1466 Queens Road, Hollywood 46," he said.

"I'm the one who packs them and mails them out, since Doctorji is hardly ever here," Mrs. Thind said.

The Guru, The Knower of God . . . Is the Ferry-Man across the Ocean of Life. . . .

When there is an unaccountable lack of zip and zest in life for things which ordinarily interest him, it shows that soul energies are blocked and choked. . . .

Analyze yourself, be your own critic, your own chemist and your own crucifier. . . .

Many a small Fry has stretched and inflated himself: and the multitudes have hailed him a hero, a world-teacher, a great man, but what good a bag of wind can do: a few Pin-Pricks, and lo its wind comes out at last and it falls flat to the ground.

The manuscript of a book in preparation was passed around, and the above passages were read aloud as if they were the intellectual course of our meal. I was still rattled by my plane ride, by the shock of being in a totally new place, by finding myself among strangers. I felt like a person in a dream. But never more so than when I heard Dr. Thind reading out the "small-fry" passage. His voice sounded very profound, perhaps because it was filtered through his beard. And yet what he read seemed simple-minded and inane.

I remember that I was relieved when my father gave a slight turn to the conversation. "I don't know that if I advertised my lectures anyone would come."

"You have spoken the truth, Doctor Sahib. You are not a man of God. You see, God is a radio station. He is broadcasting day and night. I am only one of the wireless sets through which he lectures to the people. Reception in this blessed country is especially good, and reception here in Southern California is the best. But you have taken a different path. You are not in the Science of the Saviours."

"WHAT an odd duck Doctorji is," I said, fanning the pages of the manuscript and advertisement that Dr. Thind had pressed on us. My father and I were finally alone, in front of 683½ Levering Avenue, in Westwood Village, where he lived.

"Well, as the good Doctor says, we are in Southern California," he said, and he added, "In your letters to me you're still spelling 'Daddyji' in the old, British way—j-e-e. There has been an official change in the Roman spelling of Punjabi. The suffix 'jee' is now spelled j-i, and 'ghee' is spelled g-h-i, and 'gulli' is now spelled g-a-l-i." He's really a schoolteacher at heart, I thought, and that's why he wasn't a good father to Brother Om—he was always pulling him up and correcting him, like a taskmaster. The thought was so subversive that I felt frightened; my heart raced, and I quickly decided that my father was only trying to be helpful to Brother Om—just as he was now trying to be to me. He has probably been signing letters to me "Daddyji" with an "i" the whole time, I thought, but I didn't know it, because his letters were read to me.

"If I read the word 'gali,' I wouldn't know whether it was the word for 'abuse' or the word for 'narrow street,' " I said. "The changes seem silly."

"They certainly are not silly," my father said. "Englishmen spelled words as foreigners would spell them, and we are now spelling them as we think they should be spelled. You may have a point about 'gali.' But then you would know which it was from the context. Anyway, the word for 'abuse' should be spelled with two 'a's—g-a-a-l-i."

We were soon mimicking the funny way Englishmen pronounced Punjabi words and the funny way Punjabis pronounced English words, and we were laughing together as we opened the door to his apartment. It was a bachelor's apartment, one room, at street level.

Once we were in the apartment, my father put his hands on my shoulders. I could feel him looking at me. "How you've grown in three years!" He ran his hands slowly down my upper arms, pressing them and sizing them up. "You must weigh a hundred and ten pounds now."

"A hundred and five," I said, shrugging his hands off my arms. I felt guilty, but told myself that part of growing up was not liking to be examined and petted like a child.

"You still look very thin, but you're at least an inch taller," he said warmly, as if he understood why I had needed to rebuff him. "But it is not just that. It is the confident way you walk, and the way you hold your head. I wish your mother could see you. But then if she were here she'd be after you to eat butter." He laughed.

When I was small, I was sick a good part of the time, and my mother used to force-feed me gobs of butter in a spoon, thinking that it would build up my health. I had come to loathe butter, and had fought off her attempts whenever I could. But now I found myself saying, "What do children know? Parents know best." I realized with a shock that I was expressing views in Punjabi that I no longer held when I was speaking English. Still, in the warm flow of Punjabi the awkwardness I had been feeling with my father was being washed away. I didn't realize how lonely I was in Little Rock, I thought. Punjabi words linger in the ear, like the sweet notes of the violin after the bow has been drawn across the strings. How I long to go back home and fill my soul with the music of Punjabi!

"I was talking to Surinder on the telephone the other day," my father was saying. Surinder, my first cousin, was a year older than I was. He had come to America for his education a year before I had. "I spoke to him in Punjabi, and he replied in English. Surinder seems to have forgotten his mother tongue. But you are talking Punjabi as if you had never been away."

In a surge of emotion, I felt like a grateful small child praised by an all-loving parent.

My father sat down in the only chair and started untying his shoes. "Would you like the mattress or the box spring?" he asked. He had taken the mattress off the box spring of the daybed and made two beds out of one.

I offered to take the box spring. Books, papers, and clothes were everywhere. The hundreds of slides and files he had brought along to help him give talks were spread out on a small table and on the beds and on the floor. The apartment had the disorderly feeling of a student's quarters. At home, Mamaji would pick up after him, I thought. There would be a servant to make things fall magically into place. But here there seems to be no place to put anything away—not even a dressing gown. I thought of our three-story house in pre-Partition days in Lahore. Now here we were in a depressing little one-room apartment in a section of a vast, anonymous city with, as far as I had been able to tell, neither a center nor a discernible boundary. I felt a pang for my father, a pang for myself. Yet while I was having these feelings my father was pointing to the apartment's comforts, like hot running water and a refrigerator. (In our house in Lahore, we had only a small *hammam* for heating water and an ice chest to keep food fresh.) He seemed genuinely proud to have his own place where we could both stay.

"Would you like a cup of tea?" he asked. At home, we children were not allowed to go near tea or coffee—drinking either was considered a bad habit. Chachi Subhadran, Surinder's mother and my aunt, drank sixteen cups of tea a day to my mother's two to three, and people in the family spoke of her as if she were an opium addict. I had never tasted hot tea. Iced tea, which I had tried for the first time in Little Rock, didn't seem to count, because it was served to us in the summer with meals, like cold milk.

"Yes, please," I said. He put the kettle on to boil.

There was no kitchen, just a hot plate on top of a waist-high refrigerator. My father made me some weak tea with lemon, and we sat down and had tea together.

I asked him how his teaching was going.

"There's not much teaching as such," he said. "Just occasional lectures." He tried out on me an idea for a lecture, "Longer Lives in India Through Modern Medicine," that he was planning to give at the medical school. We started talking about the many changes that had taken place in India since I left. It all made me feel very grown up.

I was amused when after tea, to save his hands, my father,

whom I had never known to wash dishes before, stuck a cake of soap on a fork and applied it to the cups and saucers. I tried to take over the job, but discovered that his method didn't work for me: without feeling the dishes I had difficulty knowing whether I had got the soap off them, and that defeated the whole purpose of the fork.

After the chore was finished, my hands felt wet and empty. I sat down on the box spring. I stood up. I walked back and forth between the front door and the bathroom door, along the foot of the beds. I tried out the mattress and sat down again on the box spring.

My father picked up a pamphlet and started reading me a passage about the new Five-Year Plan for India.

"You know, I applied for admission to Columbia," I blurted out, interrupting him. "Well, they've rejected me." I had trouble getting the word "rejected" out, but I knew that the longer I waited the harder it would be to own up to my failure. I've been getting rejections from schools in England and America since I was seven, I thought. Why does this rejection rankle so much? It must be because it puts in doubt the quality of my Arkansas education and its value, after all the money my father has spent on it. Counting transportation from India, he must have already spent more money than he ever earned in a year—more money than he spent on my three big sisters' education from kindergarten through college. "The school has appealed to the admissions authorities to reconsider, and they said they would," I added, trying to take the edge off the bad news.

"I took your Columbia admission for granted—I was hoping for a scholarship for you," my father said. "What happened?"

"I think it was mainly my scores on the Scholastic Aptitude Test," I said. "I wasn't prepared for it, and the testing people didn't send me a Braille copy. But now they say there's no point in my retaking them."

"Oh," he said, sounding like my discouraged heart. But, as always, he was quick to rally. "When the Columbia people meet you and talk to you in person, they'll admit you right away, and give you a scholarship, too," he said. "You can take it from me. I went off to London without an admission, against all advice, and got myself admitted to University College just by going around and calling on a couple of people. We Mehtas make an excellent personal impression."

He doesn't know what it's like here, I thought. He's still thinking in terms of the British Raj, where it was a matter of getting in touch with this person, pulling that string. I had always looked up to him, felt inferior to him, but I now savored—if fleetingly—a sense of superiority. Still, I recalled that I was in America on a student visa. I had to attend college or leave the country. I calculated that the cost of a year in college for me would be three thousand dollars—two thousand for tuition, room, and board, and a thousand to pay readers, since most of the books would have to be read aloud to me. The B.A. degree, therefore, was at least twelve thousand dollars away, and that didn't take into account board and lodging for summer vacations. A year or so earlier, after he passed the age of fifty-five—the age of mandatory retirement in the government service—my father had been forced to retire from the post of deputy director-general of health services in India. He now had no foreseeable prospect of work, and I wondered whether I might not have to go back home.

"Do you think my training in Arkansas would mean something in India—I mean if I were to go home today?" I asked.

"Bahali Ram is a high-school graduate, like you, and look at his fate," my father said. Bahali Ram was his first cousin. I had always been afraid of ending up a permanent poor relation, like him, cadging cups of tea and old, discarded razor blades from well-to-do family members. "Our country is full of Bachelors of Arts and Masters of Arts who have their sight, and they can't even find jobs as stenographers. Anyway, your American training in mobility would be useless in India, and without that ability to get around by yourself you'd feel frustrated and miserable."

He was right. At home, there were hardly any traffic lights, there was little order or plan to the streets, and the movement of traffic and pedestrians was chaotic. The streets were a free-for-all of cars, motorcycles, tongas, oxcarts, bicycles, rickshaws, cows. Such sidewalks as existed were crowded with people, sitting or squatting, milling about or sleeping; were littered with cooking utensils, fire pots, whatever; and ended in open drains or steps. Everywhere, one had to watch out for manure and rubbish. There was no way any blind person could get around without an attendant constantly at his side.

"But I don't think I could ever create a home in America," I said. "I'd like to go back to India and establish a home there that I could permanently call my own, and where I could be close to the family. Being happy is more important to me than being very successful." I felt self-conscious about my accent, but he didn't seem to notice it.

"You don't realize how grim your living conditions in India would be," he said.

"But how can I possibly stay in this country? Even if I got admitted to some college, we don't have the wherewithal."

"Of course, it sometimes looks discouraging," he said. "But things have a way of working themselves out."

My father was about the only person from home who had written to me regularly in America, but over the last year or so his letters to me in Arkansas had grown sketchy. He was used to dictating letters to a shorthand typist in his office, but on his retirement he had lost the use of office and staff, and had to write everything by hand. Instead of long typed letters I had lately received brief aerograms, containing only tantalizing morsels of information. Once, he simply wrote, "I'm thinking of building a house for us in New Delhi." I was thrilled, but wondered how he could possibly afford it. Then he got my hope up by writing, in an aerogram, "If I succeed in getting a Fulbright grant, I can come and visit you in America," without explaining exactly what the Fulbright grant was, which American city it might take him to, or when that might be. But soon an aerogram came saying that he was definitely not coming, because he didn't have the money to buy a ticket to America, but saying nothing about what had happened to the Fulbright grant. Then, suddenly, he was writing from Geneva on his way to Los Angeles, and giving me a date when he would visit me in Little Rock. And then, just as suddenly, he was in Washington, D.C., but was completely tied up, and soon he headed off to Ceylon, leaving me more curious and frustrated than ever. His changes of plan, his saying one thing and doing another, his lack of explanations were all very uncharacteristic.

"Every time I got one of those brief, wretched aerograms from you in Little Rock, I wondered what, exactly, was going on," I said later that first afternoon, as I was stuffing our dirty laundry into a pillowcase. "I thought I would never get to see you. I thought there would be a third world war, and you would be stuck somewhere on the other side of the world and I would be stranded in America."

My father's laugh came through the open door of the bathroom, where he was changing into street clothes from pajamas, which he had put on for an afternoon nap. "You're just like me—being carried away by your own imaginings."

"I suppose I've never got over how Pearl Harbor ruined your original plans to send me to America for my schooling when I was seven."

"Man proposes, but God disposes," he said, emerging from the bathroom. He picked up his felt hat, I picked up the laundry, and we set out.

"I want to know everything—what the family is living on, just when you retired, how you can possibly think of building a house," I said. "I want to know about Geneva and Ceylon—what you were doing in those places. I can't tell you how cut off I've felt in Arkansas."

My father and I were on the street, walking side by side, his arm straight and firm beside me, the back of my thumb touching his little finger. Walking with him like this, in step, made me feel confident and normal, almost as if I could see.

"Well, as you know, we have to retire at the age of fifty-five, regardless of how fit we are."

"But when did you turn fifty-five?" I realized that I didn't know exactly when my father was born.

"I reached the dreaded age in December, 1950. Early that year, however, the government had notified me that my service had been extended by a year. The government does this in very special cases, when it thinks the services of a particular officer are 'indispensable.' But I had six months' accumulated leave, so I was able to stay on in my job only until May, 1951—just a year ago."

"Did you get your provident fund?" I asked as we walked quickly to catch the green light, with the laundry bag bumping against my leg.

"After thirty years of service, with bonuses, it amounted to only fifty thousand rupees—only ten thousand dollars in American terms. Still, it would have been a lot of money for us if we hadn't had to start over again after Pakistan."

"Did you get the money in one big check?"

"The new, post-Partition rules gave us government servants the alternative of converting the lump-sum provident fund into a life pension. But people in our country think so negatively that practically everyone I talked to advised me against that. 'Who can guarantee you a life of eleven more years?' they said. That's the time it would have taken to get back the fifty thousand rupees."

My father live for only eleven years more? I couldn't imagine his being gone—in fact, I couldn't imagine the world at all without him.

"Don't worry—I'm not about to die," he said, guessing my thoughts. He took my hand and pressed it. "I feel as fit as a fighting cock. May I live to be a hundred. If we hadn't had to start building the house, I would have converted the whole blessed provident fund into a life pension. As it is, I took two-thirds of it in a life pension of three hundred rupees a month and the rest in cash."

We reached the neighborhood laundromat my father used. It was a stuffy little hole of a place, with three or four machines whirring and spinning and giving off infernal heat. Its lone attendant, a Chinese woman, took the laundry from me and put it on the scale.

"As always, no folding, Madame," my father said, with a twinkle in his voice.

"Only a quarter extra for folding, Doctor," she said mechanically.

"But, Madame, as you know, we are refugees."

"Customer always right, Doctor."

The good-natured exchange was carried on like a movie routine, my father speaking loud and clear, as if he were lecturing, and the Chinese woman speaking so softly that she could hardly be heard over the din.

Back on the street, my father said to me, "Every time I think of spending money here, in my mind I can't help translating it into rupees. The good lady wanted only a quarter for folding our clothes. Yet for that—a little more than a rupee—our washerman would hand wash and hand iron, pick up and deliver the clothes, and salaam in thanks. One really has to earn here in order to spend here. Otherwise, America seems like a country for kings or robbers."

We laughed, and continued walking, this time to another Chinese establishment to pick up some take-out food.

"Where, exactly, is the family living now?" I asked. At retirement, my father had had to surrender his official residence.

"Luckily, none of you children are with us at the moment. Your mother and I are carrying on as best we can at Dwarka's."

Uncle Dwarka was my mother's brother. He, Auntie Santosh, and their three daughters lived in Old Delhi, in a dilapidated rented house, which had been put up as a temporary structure for the festivities of the Durbar of 1911 but had escaped demolition because of the housing shortage created by the First World War and its aftermath. My father's letters had often mentioned the deficiencies of the house. Its roof was in such disrepair that during the monsoon buckets were placed on the floor to catch the rain water, and shards of lime dropped as a matter of course off the walls and ceilings. But Uncle Dwarka was one of our few relatives who had settled outside West Punjab. He had therefore escaped the ravages of the Partition; he and his family were lucky to have a roof over their heads at all. My maternal grandparents and another maternal uncle, Lakshman, and his wife and their two sons—all refugees, like my family—had already taken permanent shelter with them. No matter how crowded the house got, Uncle Dwarka and Auntie Santosh seemed always to be able to welcome one more person. Their generosity seemed to have no limit.

"Where does everybody sleep at Uncle Dwarka's?" I asked. "If I remember, the whole house has only three or four bedrooms."

"We Indians somehow always manage," my father said. "That's the beauty of it all."

I waited for a truck to thunder past and then asked about the house he was building.

"The house has an interesting background. Some time ago, the government began giving refugees like us compensation of ten to twenty per cent in kind for property lost in Pakistan. I became eligible for a two-hundred-square-yard plot in a new refugee colony in Nizam-Ud-din. Allocation was by a lottery system, but the government was also accepting tenders for larger plots, provided that one could come up with some cash. I had a run of good luck at the poker table at the club, and I was also able to get a little loan against my provident fund. So I put in a bid of eleven thousand rupees for one particular open corner plot, facing East Nizam-Ud-din Park, that was listed as three hundred square yards. My tender was the highest, and I got the plot. When I had it measured, it turned out to be four hundred square yards. We Mehtas are really lucky. I got Romesh to draw up the plans"— Romesh was my father's architect brother—"and when I left, last July, the walls had already started going up. Your mother and Romesh have been looking after the construction in my absence. We were allowed to build on only part of the plot, so the house will be small, but for us it will be a palace. Here we are at my Chinese-food haunt."

We walked into a small, crowded, smoke-filled kitchenlike place. I had all but forgotten that we'd come out to get some food. Now that I remembered it, I was ravenous. But I couldn't help coughing—choking from the smoke.

"It's wretched here," my father said in Punjabi, "but I come here because it's about the only place in the whole of Westwood Village where no tip is expected." At home, he leaves double the tip of anyone else, I thought.

Like the laundromat, the kitchen had only one attendant—a Chinese man, who seemed to be taking food orders, cooking behind a counter, packing the food for take-out, and ringing it up on the cash register, all at the same time.

My father read me the short menu on the wall, and when our turn came we asked for one egg roll, one order of vegetable fried rice, and one order of chicken with cashew nuts and bean sprouts.

"Two fortune cookies," the Chinese attendant said, throwing them into the bag, ringing up the order, and turning back to the stove in one quick motion.

My father counted out nickels, dimes, and pennies, and laid the exact change on the counter.

"O.K.?" he asked the Chinese attendant.

"O.K., you leave there," the man called over his shoulder.

"Please count the money for yourself," my father said.

He wants to make sure he won't be taken for a thief, I thought, suddenly feeling ashamed. In my heightened sensitivity, I felt that even though we were building a house of our own our whole way of life was now diminished. My father and I had to hole up in one cramped room, carry our laundry through the streets, save a quarter by folding it ourselves, eat take-out meals on the cheap—count nickels and dimes. Even the life at the state school in backward Arkansas seemed luxurious in comparison. At least there, after the tuition, room, and board had been paid, I didn't have to think about how the laundry got done, how much the food cost. Since the money came in the form of bank drafts, I had been shielded from knowledge of how it had been got together, at what sacrifice. But now there would be daily reminders that my father had become a pensioner at an early age, with four children still to support, and that we belonged to the world's population of impoverished refugees.

"Just leave there," the Chinese attendant repeated. I picked up the bag of food, and we left. On the street, walking with my father, touching and not touching his hand, being close but independent revived my spirits a little.

In the apartment, my father sat on the chair, I sat on the box spring, and we ate our dinner, mostly in silence. At the end, I broke open one of the fortune cookies and gave my father the little slip of paper to read. "Like you, I'm not at all superstitious," I said, "but before you go on with the story of your retirement I want to hear my fortune."

"Of course. I'm eager to know my fortune, too. You might say we are two professed atheists in a foxhole under fire, saying our prayers just in case." He read, " 'It is foolish to be poor and wise to be rich.' " The fortune was so uncannily on target that we both broke into uncontrollable laughter. He barely managed to take a breath to read out his own fortune: " 'One hand can't clap.' "

BEFORE my father retired, Dr. George Leiby, of the newly established U.C.L.A. medical school, who was in India working with my father on the control of venereal diseases, had introduced him at a club in New Delhi to a Mr. Horace Poleman. Mr. Poleman, also an American, was in charge of Indian Fulbrights, which, thanks to Senator J. William Fulbright, had been set up with the rupees that America had received from selling to India, at low prices, surplus war matériel. The rupees had been earmarked for a regular exchange of students, research scholars, and teachers between the two "sister democracies."

My father told Mr. Poleman of his pending retirement. "In the West, a man of my age would be considered still at the height of his powers," he said. "If I could somehow get across to your great country and explore avenues of work, I could remain in harness some years longer and keep the wolf from the door." (As I listened to him tell the story, I could imagine the whole scene: the three men sitting on the lawn at the club, drinking lemonade and eating chicken patties under the tropical sky, with bearers hovering in the background; and my father seeing in the American whom he had barely met a promise of a whole new life, and telling him about his seven children, his long government service, his degrees and awards, the deep wound of Partition, and many other things, in the typical manner of conversation in India, where one's family history and accomplishments are the main way of separating oneself from the mass of one's compatriots.)

Mr. Poleman took, as my father saw it, "a personal interest" in his problems and suggested that he apply for a Fulbright to teach in America, saying, "In that way, you'll get your air passage paid, and once you finish your assignment you could look around for something else to do."

My father was eventually awarded a Fulbright with an honorary visiting professorship at Dr. Leiby's medical school for the semester beginning in September, 1951. He converted ten thousand rupees, most of his savings, into two thousand dollars and flew out of India in late July. He had arranged for stops in Geneva, London, and New York to scout around for future job possibilities.

As soon as he reached Geneva, he called on the director-general of the World Health Organization.

"There is no staff opening with us," the director-general told him, "but, as it happens, the International Bank for Reconstruction and Development needs a public-health adviser. The bank is hiring short-term advisers on public health, agriculture, transport, industry, and so on, for a mission it's sending to Ceylon. The mission will evaluate Ceylon's application for a development loan of twenty-five million dollars. It will study all aspects of Ceylon's economy and advise the bank whether the loan will be productive and whether Ceylon will be able to pay it back. A bank representative from Washington is expected here in a week or so. If you're interested in being a public-health adviser, I can recommend you and he can interview you on the spot."

"That's very kind of you," my father said. "I am very much interested." He had planned to stay in Geneva for only two or three days, but he put off his departure.

As he was looking through his papers, back at the hotel, he came across an old newspaper clipping he had saved. It said that a Watumull Foundation, based in Los Angeles, was sponsoring an essay competition on population control in relation to food production in India, and that the three best essays would be published for wide distribution in poor countries. The clipping listed Margaret Sanger, the renowned founder of the planned-parenthood movement, as one of the judges, and announced a first prize of six hundred dollars. The contest must be an important one if Margaret Sanger is involved, he thought. If I can win first prize, I can increase my dollar reserve by almost a third.

As it happened, since taking his post with the central government, some years earlier, he had been pressing for a campaign for family planning. His efforts had been blocked by his Minister of Health, Rajkumari (Princess) Amrit Kaur, who was a devout Christian and believed that any form of birth control other than sexual abstinence was against the will of God. As he took leave of her at retirement, he had consoled himself with the thought that "time and tide wait for none"—that one day her antiquated belief would be washed away by the tide of history. In the Watumull Competition, he now felt, the tide might finally be turning in his favor. He became fired with the spirit of competition, just as he used to be when he was playing in cricket and hockey matches at college. He had nothing else to do—no friends, no family in Geneva to divert him—so he immediately sat down at the hotel-room desk and started on an essay. "India has been having bumper crops—of babies," he wrote. "India is rich—very rich—in people." Two days later, he was still at the desk, writing, with his papers scattered all around him. He argued that in earlier times nature had controlled population growth in poor countries like India through disease and famine but that modern medicine and modern methods of agriculture had changed the balance; that as a result India now had fifteen per cent of the world's population but only two per cent of its land area; and that none of the many kinds of contraceptive devices were proving very effective as a means of birth control in India, because the devices were expensive and were often made of rubber, which deteriorated quickly in tropical heat. He concluded that perhaps the best hope of controlling population growth lay in making use of a combination of methods—training ancillary medical staff, establishing family-planning clinics, promoting public education, disseminating various types of contraceptive devices, and teaching self-restraint.

After he had the essay typed, he glanced at the clipping again and found that entries were restricted to three thousand words. His was almost twice that length. He stayed up all night, as he used to do when he was a college student, and cut his essay by half. He then got it retyped and sent it off under registered cover, not knowing whether it would get there in time. The date was August 4th, and the contest closed on August 8th.

He had barely recovered from writing the essay when the bank representative arrived in Geneva. The representative interviewed him at the offices of the World Health Organization and offered him the job, saying that if he took it he would have to report for work on September 1st at the bank's headquarters, in Washington, D.C., and that he would receive a salary of seven hundred dollars a month, tax-free, for six months, along with fifteen dollars per diem and all his travel and living expenses.

Seven hundred dollars a month—that is almost twice my government salary, he thought. Over six months, it will come to a total of four thousand two hundred dollars, or twenty-one thousand rupees—almost half the amount of the provident fund. With all my living expenses paid, I'll be able to save most of the money and use it to put a second story on our house. The rent from that will at least keep the lentils and chapatties on the table. And once I get my foot in the door of the international world, who knows what other doors might open up? In India, I'm a dead duck, but here in the West I'm still considered valuable.

"The mission should be reaching Ceylon by the middle of October, and if your wife wishes to join you there the bank will foot the bill," the representative was saying.

My father could imagine my mother's reaction. But there was a hitch—a big hitch. He had already used the Geneva portion of his Fulbright ticket, and he was due to arrive at U.C.L.A. medical school at just about the time the bank wanted him to begin the job in Washington.

"How long do I have to think about your offer?" he asked.

"A week—but no more. We are already into the second week of August, and Sir Sydney Caine, who is leading the mission, would like to know as soon as possible who the members of his mission will be."

My father thanked him, and went back to his hotel and telephoned Mr. Poleman, in New Delhi, and Dean Stafford L. Warren of the U.C.L.A. medical school, in Los Angeles. As it turned out, they both agreed that he should take the bank job and postpone going to U.C.L.A. until the spring semester. They didn't mind how he used his Fulbright ticket as long as he got himself to Los Angeles. My father at once informed the bank that he would accept the job.

❦

MY father and I cleared away the cartons of Chinese food and started getting ready for bed. "What a big telephone bill we ran up between Washington and Little Rock when I arrived in America," he said.

"I wish we had really been able to talk, as we are doing now," I said, and he continued with his story.

"After some preparatory work in Washington, the mission flew to Colombo. I'd cabled your mother, and she joined us at the stopover in Bombay. You can imagine her sensations at being in a plane for the first time, flying over an ocean, and going to a new country."

"She must have had the time of her life in Ceylon," I said. I had learned this expression in Arkansas, and used it at every opportunity.

"Yes, she certainly did. She thought she had never seen such a beautiful and comfortable place as the Galle Face Hotel, where we stayed in Colombo. Our rooms overlooked the Indian Ocean, and the bathroom was stocked with every imaginable cologne and soap."

"How did she fit in? Did the other members of the mission have their wives with them?"

"There were only two other wives, and I don't know how, but your mother managed to talk to them in English—especially when I wasn't there. But I think she found it a little upsetting at first to see everyone else eating beef in the dining room. Then she hardened herself. If chicken or fish was not on the menu, she contented herself with several helpings of pudding or ice cream."

I marvelled at her adaptability. At home, she wouldn't have gone near anyone eating beef. "What did she do all day? Without the family around her, she must have been completely lost."

"Not at all. The Ceylon government had provided me with a car and a driver, and every day I visited various hospitals and clinics. I toured the whole island. She usually came with me. She enjoyed seeing coconut groves, rubber plantations, and whole gardens of cardamoms and tea. The tea gardens interested her especially, she being a connoisseur of tea. I finished my work in Ceylon by Christmas, and took your mother back to Delhi. She still talks about the trip. And she stands out among her friends, who have neither flown nor crossed an ocean. From Delhi, I flew back to Washington alone to write my report, and I flew here early in March, soon after the beginning of the spring semester at U.C.L.A."

"Did you ever hear from the Watumull people about your essay?"

"Ah, yes, that's another very interesting story. The prizes were to be announced at the end of December. I told the family to watch for the announcement in the papers, but January came and passed and I heard nothing. I began to wonder if the whole contest might have been a hoax. But early in February I received a cable from your mother saying that she had just heard the news that I had got the first prize. Apparently, the number of essays submitted was so large that the results had been delayed. Your mother said in her cable that on the day she got the news Nandini was born in the new house. How very propitious!" Nandini, the second child of Sister Pom and her husband, was my parents' first granddaughter, born on the first of February.

"Is the house completely finished, then?"

"Only the first story. But I was able to save and send home my entire salary from the bank job, so we are now building the second story."

That night, before I went to sleep, I tossed and turned on the hard box spring, thinking that I was seeing my father almost for the first time not just as a parent but also as a person, a person like me—going for interviews, writing essays, worrying about his abilities, trying to impress people and win their confidence, straining to make ends meet. At the same time, I thought about what a good storyteller he was. Even when I knew the outcome—about his getting the Ceylon job, for instance—he held my attention as closely as if he were telling a suspenseful tale. I can't be a doctor like him, but maybe I can learn from him how to tell good stories, I thought.

❧

"I HAVE approached many Indian government officials and foundation officials, pleading with them to give you financial aid on humanitarian grounds, but the pity is that our country is so poor, with so many needy people, that nobody has time for the problems of any one person," my father said one evening. "Our best hope is right here in America."

"But there is no time to get me a scholarship before the colleges open in September. How will we manage?"

"You leave it to me—I've always managed," he said, as cheerfully as if he were anticipating a big win at the card table. "After all, people who come to America do extremely well. Look at Dr. Thind—or, for that matter, at Mr. Davies, Mrs. Thind's father. Mr. Davies' father was a Welsh coal miner, and Mr. Davies started out as a coal miner, too, when he was only eleven years old. But somehow he managed to get himself over here when he was a young man, and he made good. Mrs. Thind tells me they speak very well of him at the Southern Pacific Railroad, where he worked for many years. Maybe, like Dr. Thind, I'll make some money lecturing to Americans. Maybe I'll get a medical job in America, and even build up some capital. Maybe I will meet a rich American. Maybe I'll do something in India. Maybe I will start a practice in England."

I had heard him talk like this for years. His letters to me in America had been full of such talk. As a child, I had unquestioningly believed him, but now, to my grownup ears, the talk sounded like just dreams, pure dreams. I wanted to point out that it would take some years for him to build himself up as a lecturer, if he could do it at all; that to get a job in America he would have to immigrate, and only a handful of Indian immigrants were allowed in any one year; that in India he was considered an old man; that he had never done private practice, and, anyway, would need money to establish a practice anywhere. But something in me stopped me from saying anything.

That night, I stayed awake on my box spring worrying. I heard my father toss and turn on his mattress. I pretended to be asleep, breathing deeply and listening for his loud, regular snoring, for which he was famous among us children. I recalled what a rare treat it had been to sleep in the room with him, because his snoring always had the effect of lulling me to sleep. I waited, but there was no sound from his mattress. He's awake, I thought. He's pretending, like me.

We had gone to bed at ten, and some four hours later he said abruptly, as if we had been talking the whole time, "Three years ago, who would have thought that we two would be in the States together, sleeping in our own apartment? In India, the average life expectancy of people is little more than thirty. Here I am, almost twice that age, planning a new career. How fortunate we are!"

I was struck yet again by his optimistic nature. He has always had a way of carrying us along with him, I thought. I felt reassured in spite of myself.

"Your daddy has always been solvent," he was saying. "Besides, as Bhabiji used to say, 'money is dirt of the hands.' The sooner it's got rid of the better."

I thought of all of us children who were still dependent on him, and would be for many years to come. I could have wept for my father. I turned my face to the wall.

"One must have faith in the future, and not think too much about money," he said, turning to the wall on his side. "It's only dirt of the hands." Soon he was snoring, and I, too, was fast asleep.

Years later, I asked my father if he had ever felt despondent in those days about not having money. "Not for very long," he said. "Whenever I did, something would happen that would give me a lift." He said he remembered once writing a letter that ended on a despondent note to an old college friend famous for irrepressible high spirits. He read me his friend's reply, in Urdu, which had made him feel his lighthearted self again.

My Beloved Friend,

Thanks immensely for your kind letter. My excitement at perusing it, however, turned into pain at the close, when you hinted at the ebb of your happiness. No, my friend, life is not as good as the poets sing it to be, but then it isn't as sordid as the cynics say it to be, either. You and I had superb training in the school of poverty, and our penurious background ought to make us smile in derision at fools who attach value to goods of this world. Lakshmi, goddess of wealth, is a faithless hussy, constant only in inconstancy, now jilting this one and now making up to that one. I tell you, the aids to our living are all within us. We should hitch our lives to a star and have nothing to do with the filth at our feet. Cheer up, my friend, and acquire your old resilience of youth. In 1911, 1912, and 1913, you were one of the most buoyant of lads up north, and a little bit of that tensility and springiness ought to see you through the remaining years of your worldly existence.

So, my friend, let me not hear any more doleful notes from your lips, always known for their enchanting smiles.

Much of the first month I was with my father in Los Angeles was spent trying to obtain scholarship money for me from local foundations, state agencies, or individual philanthropists. This involved filling out endless forms picked up from the offices or homes of various people we met or were introduced to. The forms wanted my father to list the years and make of each of his automobiles, his stocks and bonds, his real-estate holdings, his insurance policies, the addresses of his banks and brokers and his account numbers with them, and the sources of his spouse's income. They wanted to know the amounts of his first-mortgage payments, second-mortgage payments, and alimony payments, the taxes he owed, his Social Security number. They wanted him to set out his assets against his liabilities, his total income against his total expenditures, in order to determine our exact financial need. He and I would struggle over the answers, fearing that if we filled up all the columns of cramped blanks following dollar signs with "Not applicable," or "Nil," or "These questions are meant for Americans, and we are Indians," we would jeopardize my chances of obtaining financial help. And yet the questions seemed as appropriate to our circumstances as vulgar jokes in a tragic play. Still, they did make us laugh, providing us with some comic relief from our plight.

Fortunately, many of the forms invited the applicant to "attach letter if necessary," and my father took full advantage of the opportunity. " 'So long as I remained in service and an earning hand, I continued to pay for the education of my blind son,' " he read out to me when he had finished a draft of one of the first letters. " 'His educational expenses from 1949 to 1952, taking into account the devaluation of the Indian rupee which occurred soon after he came to the U.S.A., have amounted to no less than Rs. 35,000, an equivalent of about seven thousand U.S.A. dollars. It has been a joy to pay for his education. He made the best of his opportunity and finished four years of high school in three years. But now I find myself unable to give him any support. I pity myself for that. I do hope and pray that you, sir, will recognize his merit and give him the opportunity of higher education which he so well deserves.' "

He sat in the chair, at the small table, while I sat on the box spring, listening with the ears of the hypercritical teen-ager that I was, squirming at practically every sentence. "I don't want you to harp on my handicap, and things like that," I said. "It's never been in our character to play on people's pity." Worrying that there might be a note of disrespect in my voice, I added, "It all sounds too fatherly, when they probably want cold facts."

"As a father, I'm only taking pride in your achievement. And we have to get them to take a personal interest in you."

I sat there burning with embarrassment but not knowing how to write a better letter.

He went on reading from the draft: " 'It may not be out of place here to give you a background picture of Ved's family—the rest of my children. I have seven children (four daughters and three sons), ranging from the age of twenty-five to eight years. The eldest and the third (both girls) are now married; the second, also a girl, has just taken an M.A. degree in social work and has found a job as a medical social worker in the steel town of Jamshedpur, in Bihar, with a salary equivalent to fifty U.S.A. dollars per mensem. I am glad she will be self-supporting at least for the time being, but I still have the responsibility of providing her with a dowry and marrying her off. My oldest son, nineteen, is in Bombay studying marine engineering, my youngest daughter, fifteen, and youngest son, eight, are at boarding schools up in the hills, and they and my wife are entirely dependent upon me.' "

The entire paragraph seemed to me somehow wrong, but I fastened on the point that seemed most obviously wrong, out of place, and asked my father why he had to tell them so much about Sister Nimi and her degree and her job in Jamshedpur.

"It's a feather in the cap of our family."

"But *she's* not applying."

"Take it from me, Nimi is a good advertisement for the kind of stock we come from. They have to know what a good, progressive family we are—that you're a chip off the old block, that you're a good investment."

Feeling that perhaps I was in the wrong and he knew best, I tried to make a joke. "It looks as if I were applying for a loan from the International Bank."

He laughed. "But philanthropists are no different from the International Bank. They want to know that the person they might give money to is deserving, that he will be productive, make a contribution to society—reflect well on them."

I held my tongue, and he read on: " 'As a result of the painful Partition of India, my family and I became refugees, also known as "displaced persons." If I had ever envisaged the Partition of India, I would certainly have taken good care not to raise such a big family. Nor would I have put all my eggs in the same basket in the shape of a very valuable house—now in Pakistan—-which we had to leave with very little compensation. However, one has to submit to such historic events in the life of nations and to gracefully accept God's will. But the truth is, we find it really hard to make the two ends meet.' " He paused, and said, "Perhaps I should mention my first prize in the population-essay contest here."

"Oh, no, not that!" I burst out. "I don't think you should apologize for the number of your children, either."

"In a way, I agree, but in countries with a higher standard of living people go in for smaller families, and the question of why I have so many dependents is bound to come up, especially if the philanthropist should get to know about my interest in population control. They have to be reminded that you children were all born in a different time, when conditions of life were very different."

I thought maybe he was right, and said so.

He took time to write in a sentence about the Watumull essay, and read on: " 'I had a distinguished academic career as a medical student. I was awarded honors, certificates, and medals for standing first in surgery, forensic medicine, and toxicology. I took the degree of M.B., B.S. from Punjab University in 1920. It is registrable in the United Kingdom. I followed this up with postgraduate studies in England. There I received a Diploma in Tropical Medicine and Hygiene from the School of Tropical Medicine at University College, London, and a Diploma in Public Health from the Royal College of Physicians and Surgeons. In 1921, I returned to India to join the newly created public-health department of the Punjab, my home province. Early in my service, I was selected as one of the first fellows of the International Health Board of the Rockefeller Foundation, and that gave me an opportunity to visit the U.S.A. and various European countries and study public-health problems. I served the government for some thirty years, during which I was selected for various other honors and posts of responsibility. My most recent assignment was a short-term paid appointment with a mission of the International Bank. Our study and report on Ceylon will be published in the form of a book, "Economic Development of Ceylon," and will be available in this country from the Johns Hopkins Press, at the price of seven dollars and fifty cents, and in England from Oxford.' "

"It sounds as if *you* were applying for something."

"But they have to know what kind of people we are—what kind of stock you come from," he said, repeating the familiar theme.

Thereafter, every application we sent out was accompanied by some version of that letter.

MANY of the people who played host to us were Indian men with American wives, and many of these Indians spoke English so badly and had such rustic manners that it was hard to imagine that they could have done well in an Indian city. Yet in Los Angeles they all seemed to be rich and prominent. They all had two or three cars. I couldn't get over the fact that one had only to touch a button in a car like theirs and the window would automatically glide up or down. Their houses were on many levels. They had special, built-in rooms for bars. I couldn't imagine how there could be so many kinds of drinks that people needed a whole room for them. The rugs were so thick that one practically sank into them. And they had vacuum cleaners, something I had never heard of before. (At the Arkansas school, there were no rugs, and we had used brooms and mops.) Many of them seemed to have American social secretaries and live-in European servants. The idea of Europeans waiting on Indians seemed odd.

We had been brought up to think that dignity and respectability and reputation were worth more than all the money in the world. Whenever we children admired a friend who lived in a bigger house, was better clothed, came to school in a chauffeur-driven car, our father would say, "No amount of money can buy the respect that goes with government service." We felt almost sorry for children whose parents were not in government service—whose parents were building contractors or cloth merchants. Now, in Los Angeles, my father paid no attention to the trappings of money all around us, but I was intimidated by them and felt like an unwanted poor relation. I couldn't forget that their pin money would be enough to see me through college. Some of them had family foundations, and I always imagined they were scrutinizing me for a grant, especially since my father never failed to bring up the subjects of my financial need for college and my various achievements. I felt a little like a Hollywood child being paraded by his parent in front of talent scouts. On such occasions, I would feel first humiliated, then angry, then hopeless—loving my father for putting himself in what I considered to be demeaning situations for my sake, and, at the same time, hating the fact that such situations were part of our lot. I was continually amazed by the fact that my father didn't share any of my feelings, and conducted himself in the richest of rich houses as if he were a maharaja and I a prince. As far as I was concerned, the only thing to be said for these outings was that we were fed sumptuous meals, whereas when we were left to find our own meals we generally picked up Chinese take-out food or hamburgers and ate them sitting on our makeshift beds, with the problem of disposing of the wrappings and leftover condiments looming large in my head. Wherever we put the bag of garbage, it was in the way.

I remember that on one of my first days in Los Angeles I

happened to mention to a neighbor of my father's that I very much missed listening to music; my radio-phonograph combination, along with a few records and some other things I owned, was being kept for me back at the school until I knew where I would be living. The neighbor immediately lent me his old phonograph and presented me with a recording of Offenbach's "La Vie Parisienne." I played it again and again—I had no other record, and we couldn't afford to buy one. I think that at first I waited for my father to tell me to switch off the machine. But he said nothing. He read and I daydreamed, or we talked, but the record played on, automatically repeating itself, the lively melodies pouring out into the little apartment all day long, like the cascading bells of some supernatural clock telling me that I was marking time, that, as so often before, I was being left behind like a pair of discarded party slippers while the world danced merrily on.

DR. Jacobus tenBroek, who lived in Berkeley, was one of the best-known blind people in the country in the nineteen-fifties. He had made it possible for dozens of blind students in California to go to college. There was no person I could think of who could better help me get a scholarship. When my father and I got an offer of a ride to Berkeley, we called Dr. tenBroek, were given an appointment, and, one cool, rainy June afternoon, arrived on his doorstep.

I had often come across facts about Dr. tenBroek in Braille publications, and I had been inspired by them. It seemed that his family and mine were somehow alike in our struggles for independence and education. Dr. tenBroek's father had run away from his native Holland as a ship's cabin boy and for some thirty years had sailed the high seas. Then, after arranging a marriage to a California woman of Dutch descent, whom he saw for the first time on their wedding day, he had settled as a farmer in Alberta, Canada. He had acquired six hundred and forty acres of rugged prairie land there under the Free Land Homestead Act, and in time he cleared and developed the land and won the right to own it. In 1911, his son Jacobus was born on the homestead, in a log cabin, with a dirt floor, that his father had built with his own hands. When Jacobus was seven years old, he and a friend were playing with a bow and arrow, there was an accident, and he eventually lost the sight in one eye. Good medical attention was apparently not available in rural Alberta, and by the time he was fourteen he had lost the sight in the other eye through sympathetic ophthalmia. His parents moved to California, so that Jacobus could attend the California School for the Blind. He graduated from there and went on to receive a bachelor's degree and a couple of law degrees from the University of California at Berkeley. Later, he earned an S.J.D. from Harvard. The most successful blind people were known to be lawyers, and I myself had often thought of studying for a law degree. But tenBroek had never practiced law. Instead—disappointingly, I thought—he had devoted his energies to rhetoric (he was now a professor in the Speech Department of Cal, as the state university at Berkeley was called) and to work for the National Federation of the Blind, an organization he had helped to found, in 1940. By the time I came to know of him, he had been president of the federation for some years, and he was a frequent contributor to its literature. He wrote as if he were at war with all other organizations for the blind, contending that they raised money in the name of the blind and did welfare work for the blind but carried on their activities only in the spirit of "custodial care," while his organization was "of the blind, by the blind, and for the blind," in the American democratic tradition. He no doubt had a point, but I thought that if I were in his place I would have aspired to be King of the Mountain rather than King of the Valley of the Blind. After all, Roosevelt had not passed up the chance to be President in order to dedicate his life to polio victims. But when I mentioned my reservations about Dr. tenBroek my father pointed out, "He's only human."

Now my father was gazing up incredulously at the tenBroek house. Standing boldly on a hillside, it loomed four stories high, and looked like a fortress. It was hard for me to imagine that a blind person could be so prosperous in the first place, and then flaunt his prosperity in such an unapologetic, almost aggressive way.

The door was opened by a sighted woman of about forty—Mrs. tenBroek. She led us up some flights of stairs.

My father remarked on how impregnable the house seemed.

"Our foundation walls are thick because they used to house a rock-crushing machine," she said. "We live near a quarry."

"How did you come to live in this house?" I asked.

"We lived in an apartment for ten years, but Chick, my husband, got tired of it," she said. "He wanted elbow room, and he discovered this house." The idea that Dr. tenBroek was nicknamed Chick and that he had picked out a four-story house for "elbow room" made me want to laugh out loud.

A blast of heat from a huge fire hit us when we entered the living room, as if this were the dead of winter instead of just a wet summer day. It was a long walk to the fireplace, where the big fire snapped and crackled, and which seemed to be as tall as I was, and I almost stumbled, because I hadn't realized that the room was on two levels.

"Here is Chick," Mrs. tenBroek said, having led us to a chair at the side of the fireplace.

Dr. tenBroek stood up and found my outstretched hand with an assurance that I associated with well-adjusted blind people, confident in mobility. He towered over me, and seemed big and vigorous, like a lion.

Mrs. tenBroek excused herself, saying that she had to attend to their baby. Dr. tenBroek pushed a couple of chairs in our direction, and we sat down in front of the fire. "This fireplace eats up logs faster than I can chop them," he said. "But I like sitting by it—or, rather, under it." He chuckled. Turning to me, he asked me to tell him a little bit about myself.

I sketched out my background for him and told him that I wanted to go to college.

"You say your father has money problems, so Cal is the place for you," he said, without hesitation. "It's a state university, and tuition here is free. For you, since you're not a resident of California, there will be a small tuition charge. But I can fix that. And, given your record, you don't have to worry about getting in. Admission for you will be automatic. I'll see to it."

My father mentioned the problem of my vacations. Where would I stay? What would I do with myself with no classes to go to and with no money to enable me to go home to India? Additional money would have to be found to cover my living expenses during the summers. "That's one area in which I can't help you— I don't think anyone can," Dr. tenBroek said. He went on, "But did anybody tell you that California has the best state educational system and the best state education for the blind in the country? It's about the only state with a special law permitting any resident blind student in any college to receive state aid of seven hundred and fifty dollars a year for readers. Readers generally get seventy-five cents an hour. That means that each blind student in California gets a thousand free hours of reading per academic year. How can you be so foolish as to think about going East—going to Columbia?"

He had a big voice, and as he talked he ran his fingers through his beard. I had what in retrospect I can only call an attack of envy—envy of his house, of his fireplace, of his voice, of his beard— and a feeling that I couldn't have any of these things, even when I grew older, because I wasn't born in the West, and because I would never have a wife to raise my children (the tenBroeks had three), to look after the house, to trim my beard. I had met married blind people before, but never a blind family man. And Dr. tenBroek radiated power and successful social adjustment—

the ultimate goal of education for the blind.

But he was talking on, the words tumbling out of his mouth; he seemed a born rhetorician. "Here at Cal, you could do some important work for the National Federation of the Blind," he was saying.

I had another attack, this time of fear—fear of being in somebody's shadow. I didn't want to be anybody's acolyte, and certainly not a blind man's, however brilliant and generous the blind man might be. I wanted to be free of blind people, free of their organizations and schools, free of their special cares and special-interest groups—indeed, free of the very word "blind," of my own blindness. Getting involved with the blind in any way seemed like a backward, almost degrading step. In hindsight, this reaction strikes me as childish, adolescent, perverse—how could I ever have hoped to be free of my own blindness? But at the time I was in the grip of a fantasy that I would be done with blindness if I could only join an ordinary college, in the ordinary, sighted world. I longed to compete with sighted students as if I were one of them, without any special dispensation, and prove that I could beat them on their own terms.

"Cal is too big for me," I said, fastening on one of many objections that rose within me. "I'd rather go to a smaller, private, residential college, like Stanford or Pomona." I had heard that these were two of the best private colleges in California.

All the schools I'd ever gone to had had a hundred or so students at the most, and I had heard that the University of California at Berkeley had a student body of almost twenty thousand. The mere thought of sitting in a classroom with hundreds of other students, whom I didn't know and with whom I would have no social contact, as I might at a private, residential college, was repugnant. I imagined that state universities were chaotic, whereas private, residential colleges were complete, distinctive communities, where people ate together, played together, worked together. I imagined that private, residential colleges were cozier, more personal—that they developed the whole person, gave a polish to manners and character. My brothers and sisters had gone to private schools and private colleges. I had always wanted to go to Perkins, a private school for the blind. But I had ended up in a state school in Arkansas. I was determined to go to a private college.

"I have no patience with private education," Dr. tenBroek said. "Public education is the backbone of democracy. If you go to a private college, you'll have to go it alone."

To my horror, I found myself saying, "Then I'll go it alone." My father reached over and pressed my hand, as if to say that I should hold my tongue.

The fire was so hot that I pushed my chair back a few inches. Mrs. tenBroek came back into the room. "I've just made a fresh pitcher of iced tea," she said. "Would you care for some?" She had the baby in her arms, and was trailed by a seven-year-old boy, introduced as Dutch, and a four-year-old girl, Anna Carlotta.

We all accepted her offer, and when she returned with the tea my father asked her the question that had been at the top of my mind from the beginning of our visit—how she and Dr. tenBroek had met.

"It will sound strange to you, but we met on a blind date," she said, with a laugh. "We were both about twenty-five. We were married six months later to the day."

"It was love at first sight," Dr. tenBroek said, with a chuckle. The jokes about a "blind date" and "love at first sight" irked me. I felt I was back at the school for the blind, where people often cracked such inside jokes, as if jokes could mitigate the pain of blindness.

"Hazel has been my right arm ever since," Dr. tenBroek was saying. "I don't know what I would do without her. She reads to me every morning before the children wake up."

"As the children came along and we had more and more to do, we've had to get up earlier every day to get all the reading done that Chick needs."

As we were leaving, Dr. tenBroek repeated, "If you come to Cal, I'll do everything I can for you."

"I'll think it over," I said.

On the street, I felt oddly lightheaded, as a man might who had been inside a lion's cage and come out unmauled.

"He should be a great example to you," my father said. "He's a remarkable man."

"He is," I said. "But I'm different."

To my relief, my father dropped the subject of Dr. tenBroek, and said, "I agree with you that you would be lost in a big, anonymous university. All the people I've consulted feel as you do—that at a big university you would be swallowed up by the masses, but at a small college you might become a leader." From the time the question of my going to college first came up, people at the Indian Embassy, at the American Foundation for the Blind, and at the Arkansas school had been advising us that we should think more of my happiness than of my academic success, and should apply to an easygoing college. Some of them had urged that I go to "a junior college in a rural community." My father was now saying, "We should make personal visits to Pomona and Stanford and see if they'll take you there. That is aiming higher than our advisers wish us to. But then aiming high is in our character."

❧

MRS. Thind drove my father and me to Claremont, a small town some twenty-eight miles east of Los Angeles, to visit Pomona College. The town's population couldn't have been more than a few thousand, and I remember that we were both much impressed by the feel of the place—by its quiet atmosphere, by its eucalyptus and pepper trees, by the inscriptions on the college gates, which we felt might have been written with us in mind: "Let only the eager, thoughtful, and reverent enter here" and "They

only are loyal to this college who, departing, bear their added riches in trust for mankind."

While my father and Mrs. Thind waited in the outer office, I went in to see the dean of admissions, J. Edward Sanders.

"What are your interests? What do you plan to do after college?" Dean Sanders asked, rather mechanically.

"I don't know. I'm interested in journalism—I want to write my memoirs one day—but maybe I will have to become a lawyer to earn my living. All successful blind people seem to end up as lawyers. But that requires a lot of study and money. Without a scholarship or a loan, I could never acquire that profession."

"I should tell you right away that the formal deadline for filing admission applications was in March," Dean Sanders said. "All the freshman places have already been filled up. I wish we'd heard from you earlier. The competition is keen. We have to turn away three applicants for every one we admit. Along with Swarthmore and Reed, Pomona is known as one of the top small coeducational liberal-arts colleges in the country." I had never heard of Swarthmore or Reed, but, again, I was impressed. I'd never seriously entertained the idea of ending up at Pomona, but now that Dean Sanders seemed to be telling me I couldn't I wanted to go there more than anything. I had only to sense hurdles and I became determined to jump them.

"You should know that I was rejected by Columbia, because of my scores on the Scholastic Aptitude Test." Even as I said this, I feared that I was jeopardizing any chance I had. But I told myself that any place I applied to would find out about the rejection sooner or later, and it was better for me to own up to it.

"I got my doctorate from Columbia, and I know the people in the admissions office right well. I'm surprised they gave any weight to your S.A.T. scores. I've been an officer of the College Board, and I've served on their committees and panels. I can tell you that in your case your test scores couldn't amount to a hill of beans. Foreigners don't test well, and I know for a fact they'd never tested a blind Indian before."

I listened to Dean Sanders in utter astonishment. He seemed to be arguing my case better than I could have argued it myself. I was also struck by something familiar about his accent. It seemed to me he spoke like someone from Arkansas, though with a trace of an accent I associated with radio programs originating in New York.

"What school did you go to—Arkansas School for the Blind?" he asked now. "Wasn't your superintendent a Mr. Woolly? I think I taught his brother, John, when I was in the Education Department of Hendrix, in Arkansas. The Woollys seemed like decent, intelligent people."

I told him that Mr. J. M. Woolly was indeed the superintendent of the Arkansas School for the Blind, and asked him if he himself was from Arkansas.

"I'm from Arkansas as sure as I'm sitting here."

Dean Sanders picked up the telephone and asked a Mrs. Morrison to place a long-distance call to Mr. Woolly for him. A moment or so later, he was saying, "Hello, Max, this is Sandy Sanders, out at Pomona. How are you? . . . Good to hear your voice, too. I have Ved Mehta here, who wants to come to Pomona. What can you tell me about the young man, Max?"

I don't know what I'd expected from the interview, but I certainly hadn't imagined that Dean Sanders and Mr. Woolly would be talking to each other with me in the room. I was at once fascinated and frightened, and so overwrought that I didn't take in much of the conversation.

Dean Sanders hung up and turned to me. "Mr. Woolly tells me you have good habits, you get along with everybody, and you're diligent. He can't say enough good things about you. You sound like just the kind of young man we want to have at Pomona. Besides, we've never had an Indian student, and it would be educational for our students to have you around. Of course, you'll need to write an essay on why you want to come to Pomona, and get Mr. Woolly to send us your transcript and two letters of reference. Then I'll have to put your application before our admissions committee. But I've never known them to turn me down if I really want someone. And, boy, I'd like you to come here. Do you think you'll be able to pay your way here? Pomona is a pretty expensive place. We can't possibly give you any financial aid, at least in the first year."

"I think my father will be able to manage it," I said boldly. I was now counting on my father's being able to make some provision somehow, and anyway I didn't want to jeopardize my chances for admission by dwelling on our financial need.

"Are you going for interviews anywhere else?" Dean Sanders asked.

"I'm planning to try for admission to Stanford."

"It's a good university, but the student-faculty ratio at Stanford is not nearly as good as ours." He went on to give me what I can only term a sales pitch for Pomona. "Pomona, Scripps,

Claremont Men's College, and Claremont Graduate School are known as the Associated Colleges of Claremont. They are modelled on the Oxford system. They are all residential and independent, each with its own dean of students, admissions office, and teachers—they're just like the colleges at Oxford. And, as at Oxford, a student enrolled in one can take courses at any of the others. That means that even though we are small we have all the advantages of a big university. In fact, we are generally known as the Oxford of the Orange Grove. Of the four, Pomona, which is coeducational, is the largest and the best. It has almost as many students as the three other colleges put together, and we provide a single room, with a telephone, for practically every student who wants one. There is one teacher to every ten students, and all the Pomona faculty live in houses around the campus. The atmosphere here is very much that of a happy family."

Years later, I came across Dean Sanders' pencilled notes of our interview at the beginning of my admissions file:

Interest in journalism. Seems poised and mature under the circumstances. Did poorly on SAT but seems administrator of it was inexperienced and did not follow instructions. *Candidate says finances are not a problem* but I have some doubt of this. Wrote Woolly for report.

Back in the car with my father and Mrs. Thind, I began to have doubts about going to Pomona. Dean Sanders' eagerness to have me made me feel that perhaps I didn't want to go there after all. As always, I was challenged by a steeplechase but balked at the bridle path. Mrs. Thind and my father, however, dwelt on the advantages of Pomona and Claremont. Claremont seemed small, friendly, and self-contained, free of the industry and heavy smog that burdened Los Angeles, and yet it could call on the cultural riches not only of Los Angeles, with its Hollywood Bowl, but also of Pasadena.

"I'm all for your going to Pomona," my father said. "There's a lot of pioneering spirit in Southern California. Look at how well all our Indian friends here are doing. People tell me that it may be America's last frontier, where people like us can still make good."

"But to me Pomona seems small and provincial, like the Arkansas school. I think I would be happier in a somewhat bigger, more cosmopolitan place."

"But Southern California is a wonderful place," my father said. "It's pleasant here the year round. In the winter, you don't even need to wear a jacket."

"But I don't like the idea of going to college and not wearing a jacket. What is it like to live in Northern California?"

"They have seasons up north," Mrs. Thind said. "Not seasons like New England, but it gets down to forty in the winter. And they also have a lot of fog."

"Then it's like your London," I said to my father.

"But Southern California is certainly the best place for you from the health point of view," my father went on. "I saw a lot of t.b. patients during my service, and although we don't have a family history of t.b. you are certainly very thin for your age."

Perversely, the thought of living in the cold, foggy climate of Northern California and getting t.b. appealed to me. It seemed romantic.

"Rosalind says Stanford is the best university in the whole world," Mrs. Thind said. Rosalind was a year or so older than I was, and was attending Stanford. The thought of being at the same university as Rosalind and maybe getting to know her excited me.

"I really want to go to Stanford," I said.

❦

"I HAVE found a cure for cancer, Dr. Mehta," said Mr. Vidya (that's not his real name) as he was driving us to meet Rixford Snyder, the director of admissions at Stanford. Mr. Vidya, who was a graduate of Stanford and a teacher there, was a fellow-

Punjabi to whom we had had an introduction. He had helped me get an interview with Mr. Snyder.

"Then you are bound to get the Nobel Prize—it will be a feather in our country's cap," my father said.

"No, it will be a feather in Stanford's cap," Mr. Vidya said. "Everything I have in my coconut I learned at Stanford. You will see—when my cure for cancer gets to be well known, this will be the most famous university in the world. Harvard and Oxford will bow to it, as our disciples of old bowed to their gurus."

As we were driving around the campus, my father observed that Stanford reminded him partly of a Western-movie set and partly of a little Mediterranean town. "It's very different from Pomona, but it has a charm all its own," he said.

"It's the charm of brainpower," Mr. Vidya said.

As soon as we had been shown into the admissions director's office and had shaken his hand, my father withdrew, saying, with a wide smile in his voice, "Mr. Snyder, he's all yours." My father tried to get Mr. Vidya to follow him out, but Mr. Vidya sat down and made himself at home.

"Stanford is a private university, and since we're able to pick and choose our students the competition here is very tough," Mr. Snyder said. He talked about Stanford much as Dean Sanders had talked about Pomona. "Even the top students from the best schools often just scrape by with a C average here."

"And *they* can see," Mr. Vidya put in.

"I think I will be able to average better than a C," I said. "I can work very hard, and can put in long hours."

"Mr. Snyder, we Punjabis are not intellectuals," Mr. Vidya said. "We are known the world over for our practical nature. But what we lack in intellect we make up for with social finesse. Some of us, though, can work very hard. Some mornings, I get to the laboratory at six o'clock and am there until midnight—burning the midnight oil, so to speak."

In the course of the interview, Mr. Vidya butted in frequently. Sometimes he seemed to be arguing for my admission, and at other times he seemed to be suggesting that perhaps I was overreaching myself. More than once, I had the impulse to tell him to be quiet, and not interfere in my interview, but I remained on my best behavior. Mr. Snyder, too, showed no sign of exasperation. This struck me as all the more remarkable later on, when I learned that people at the university did not take Mr. Vidya seriously and dismissed his claim of a cure for cancer as a hoax.

Like Dean Sanders, Mr. Snyder told me that although applications had formally closed months earlier he would consider an application from me, and asked me to apply. The requirements were more or less the same as those for Pomona.

"IT says here in the paper that a man has made his fortune by selling real estate on the moon, which no one owns in the first place," my father said, reading the morning newspaper. "It's wonderful. This kind of thing can happen only in America—in California."

"How was it possible for him to do that?" I asked.

"He advertised for people to send in a dollar for an acre on the moon. All he offered in return was an executed deed for the acre, along with a map of the moon showing where the acre was situated. Tens of thousands of people sent in their dollars."

"Isn't that fraud?"

"No, it isn't. He made no false promises. It's no different from Sarna bells."

Whenever we walked in Westwood Village and happened to go past Bullock's department store, we would laugh and shake our heads, thinking of the "Sarna" bells for sale inside. At home, these bells—cheap, rustic, handmade ones—were as common as the cows around whose necks they were hung. One could hardly cross a street or pass a field without hearing these bells clinking. But no one in America had seen or heard of them until one Sajjan Sarna, who was an Indian living in the United States, got the inspired idea of importing them and marketing them as home decorations. After he exhibited them at the New York World's Fair of 1939, the bells had sold like hotcakes. As a result, he had become perhaps the richest Indian in America. My father had always spoken of America as a land of opportunity, "God's own country," where people with ambition, optimism, and intelligence (or with one inspired idea, like Sarna's) invariably walked off with the prizes. My temperament was less sunny than my father's. Like my mother, I dwelt on disasters. I had, however, accepted my father's view of America as a blessed land. I could never hear a radio program like "Queen for a Day," in which some poor, wretched woman told her sob story and won her heart's desire in worldly prizes, without thinking that it was indeed just a matter of knowing where to look—where to prospect, as it were—to find gold in America.

"If we could think of a good gambit, like the acre on the moon or the Sarna bells, all our financial problems would be solved," my father said. "You would have the money to go to Stanford or Pomona, and I would have the rest of the money I need to put the second story on our house. My years of retirement would pass in comfort. I might even be able to bring all our family here." As always, we had a good laugh over our daydreams.

I think it was on this same morning that we stood in a grocery store in Westwood Village while my father read out the brand names of different soaps arrayed on a shelf. "Dial is the best soap," I said. Although we didn't know about Dial soap at home, I had been using it almost from the day I arrived in Arkansas—ever since I had heard a persuasive advertisement for it on the radio, saying that doctors recommended it as the best soap for the skin.

My father picked up a cake of Dial and studied the packet. "But it costs almost five times what the other soaps cost," he said. "And soap is soap. Now, here is a soap we have in India— Lux soap." His voice had a satisfied air, as if lighting on the familiar had given him a boost. We bought a cake of Lux soap— our single purchase—and walked out of the grocery store.

In the apartment, I stood at the bathroom basin and washed my hands with the new cake of soap. The bathroom was the kind that might be found on a boat—so small that I couldn't imagine how the fixtures had been fitted in. As I was thinking about the wonderful Lux theatrical productions I used to listen to on the radio in Arkansas, I heard a whistle of amazement from the other room.

"What is it?" I asked.

"If we can say in twenty-five words or less why Lux soap is the best, our money problems will be solved. It says right here on the packet that Lux is holding a nationwide contest for the best descriptions of its product in twenty-five words or less. The judges will select many winners, and the top winner will get a big cash prize and a Cadillac. We Mehtas are known for walking off with prizes in contests. We can submit as many entries as we like. The only hitch is that we have to send the wrapper from a cake of Lux soap with every entry, so we will have to be careful and send in only our best efforts."

I soaped and resoaped my hands, concentrating on the texture of the soap, inhaling its fragrance, touching my hands all over after washing the soap off them, to see exactly how they felt different, and at one point even biting off a small piece of soap to get an idea of its taste—all the while trying to compose in my head a paean to Lux that might hit the jackpot.

After that, my father would sit down every day with pencil and paper in hand. I would dictate some choice words about the soap to him. He would read them back, we would revise them, he would count the words, and we would add and subtract. I remember that one entry went: "Lux soap has the texture of Kashmir silk and smells sweeter than tea roses. It makes skin feel soft, fresh, and baby-new." Every time we sent off a submission, we would feel that we had come up with the winning entry, only to be bedevilled by doubts a short time later. We would go to the grocery store and buy yet another cake, in order to make yet another submission.

Our bathroom became a Fort Knox of unwrapped Lux soaps, and the apartment smelled as if we were in the soapmaking business. But when the winners of the contest were announced we didn't get so much as an honorable mention. We were dumbfounded. We felt that the entry that took first prize could have applied to any old soap. None of the winning entries seemed to us immortal, poetic, or even memorable. Our hoard of Lux, freighted with our dreams of gold and silver, suddenly smelled noxious.

I don't remember how we disposed of all the cakes, but I do remember that we had merely to mention Lux to each other and we would dissolve in helpless laughter, like two children, as if in some part of our minds we had known all along that the whole enterprise was foolish.

In the meantime, following up leads for financial aid which friends and acquaintances gave us, my father and I visited many small private foundations and civic clubs. My father would do most of the talking, and then I would perform—tell how I'd got myself admitted to the Arkansas school, how I'd come to America alone, and how well I'd done at the school. Nothing came of our efforts. Sometimes I was disqualified from receiving aid on technicalities: the local Rotary Club sponsored only foreign students who were not already in the United States. Sometimes I was reprimanded for wanting too much: why did I have to go to a private college, which cost a lot of money, when I could have gone to U.C.L.A., like ordinary people, for much less? And then there was the question of how I would spend my vacations, and who would pay for those. Asking for so much money was hard for me to justify purely in terms of basic needs.

❧

ONE afternoon, my father and I went, by appointment, to see a well-known elderly philanthropist who had made his money in cattle feed. When we arrived at his house, we were horrified to discover that a party was going on, and people were toasting him on his eightieth birthday. We tried to slip away, but he wouldn't let us go until we told him why we had wanted to meet him. We managed to half stammer and half whisper the purpose of our visit, trying to somehow keep the guests from overhearing us.

"That's a lot of money you want," he said. "I don't think it's worth it. I don't think you need a college education to make good in life. Look at me—I never finished high school."

Unlike us, he had spoken out vigorously, and the guests gathered around had heard him. A few of them joined in.

"It's initiative you need."

"With enough spunk, you can do anything."

"Everyone can see that you're not lacking in spunk. You've both got plenty of that."

As the old man showed us to the door, he reached into his pocket and rattled some change, as if he were considering something. I stuck out my hand for him to shake. Before I knew what was happening, I felt something cold and hard in my palm, and realized that he had pressed a fifty-cent piece into it. "Here is a little contribution for your taxi," he said. The sheer surprise of the gesture—the shock of it—left me speechless. The coin scarcely touched my palm—it fell out of my hand and rang and rolled down the front steps—but my hand burned with humiliation.

Long, long ago. A beggar follows us, whining like a child. My mother: "Give him something. He's blind." . . . *The high-school gym teacher: "They think the world owes them a living. They give us all a bad name—the beggars, the blind beggars! I'd shoot them all dead!"* Old memories and fears opened up, like so many tender wounds in my soul. I am a beggar at a rich man's gate, the gate of my nightmares, I thought.

"He's an old man who probably didn't know what he was doing." It was my father's voice of reason speaking to me out on the street.

❧

"HERE is a letter from Mr. and Mrs. Watumull inviting us to dinner tomorrow evening," my father said, bringing in the mail. "The Watumull family foundation gives some scholarships to postgraduate students from India who they think will go back to India and contribute something to the country. You are only a high-school graduate, but they might make an exception."

Oh, not again, I thought. Not another humiliating interview to be gone through. But then I recalled that it was the same foundation that had sponsored the memorable essay contest on population control, and I decided that perhaps the Watumulls were genuinely interested in helping others. I asked my father how they had become so rich that they could have their own foundation.

"Mr. Goma Watumull is not only rich but famous—he's been written up in the *Reader's Digest*," my father said. "His father was a very humble brick contractor in Sind. Some of our shrewdest businessmen come from there. When Mr. Watumull was eight years old—he is now sixty-one—his father was thrown from a camel and crippled for life. He had a large family to support, and one of his sons, Jhamandas, went to Manila and opened up a shop selling handmade Oriental knickknacks, just as you and I used to dream about selling ivory curios. Unlike us, he was a real businessman, and he did some business in other Asian cities, and finally started a shop in Honolulu. He sent for Mr. Goma Watumull, who began managing the Honolulu shop. At the time, I think Mr. Watumull was twenty-five or twenty-six years old. He's never had to look back."

"And Mrs. Watumull?"

"She is an American, of equally humble origins. But they are the good sort of philanthropist. When I met them here in Los Angeles and told them a little about you, Mrs. Watumull, especially, was impressed by your independence, by the way you have overcome your handicap. She herself lost an index finger when she was fifteen or sixteen, and wasn't able to pursue her career as a pianist. They may be our best hope. But a lot will depend on their meeting you. By the way, I should mention that the decision about your scholarship will probably be made by Mrs. Watumull, because Mr. Watumull is a typical Sindi shopkeeper type. He takes his orders from Mrs. Watumull—she is 'His Master's Voice,' you might say. One thing I must warn you about—under no circumstances are you to get into an argument with her over teeth or toothpaste or drinking water."

I laughed, in spite of myself. "Teeth, toothpaste, and drinking water would never have occurred to me as fit subjects of conversation with anyone. But why not?"

"There is a big controversy going on here about putting fluoride in the water supply. Dentists want to put it in to protect the teeth of children, but Mrs. Watumull thinks it's a Communist plot. I can assure you that she will tackle you on the question of fluoridation, but you must duck it, change the subject—do whatever you think best. Do not express any opinion on it. It's like a red rag to a bull."

When we arrived the next evening at the Watumulls' house, which was also in Westwood Village, it was full of people drinking, munching canapés, and talking boisterously, their voices rising like the crescendo of a brassy march. Why is it that these philanthropists are always having a party when they call me for an interview, I wondered. I had assumed that we were going to be the only guests.

My father walked ahead of me, introducing me, and introducing himself to the few people he didn't know. I was impressed all over again by his amazing capacity for making friends with all kinds of people. In the short time he had been in Los Angeles, he had got to know almost as many people as he knew in Delhi, it seemed. How I wished I had his gift. The only people in the room whom I already knew were Dr. and Mrs. Thind.

I shook hand after hand, and marvelled at the happy voices and big handshakes of so many people who sounded as if they had always known plenty of money, good food, and clear skies. And yet, oddly, only the women were American. The men all seemed to be Indians, and, like me, I thought, must have been born and brought up under the bleak, brutal Indian sky, and must have developed these voices and handshakes only after finding gold in America. For my part, I felt like a shrinking Indian teen-ager, as small as one of the party canapés.

"This is my blind son. . . . He came here for his education because he had learned all that the Indian schools for the blind could teach him. . . . He came alone to this country at age fifteen. . . . He has just graduated with flying colors from the Arkansas School for the Blind. . . . He's brilliant, you know."

Why is he doing this to me, I thought. These guests are not interviewing me for a grant. Why can't he just introduce me as his son? Why does he have to boast about me? In private, I had often implored him not to embarrass me in this way, and he had often promised to refrain. But in public he seemed unable to stop himself. It seemed to be his way of trying to win respect and admiration for me. It was as if he felt that because of my blindness people discounted me—didn't treat me as an equal, tended to patronize me—and he wanted to show them their mistake. Yet the effect of his boasting, as I saw it, was to elicit pity, which I hated above all.

At the back of the room were Mr. and Mrs. Watumull: Mr. Watumull had a retiring voice and an almost furtive manner, while Mrs. Watumull had a commanding voice and a no-nonsense, businesslike manner. Mrs. Watumull seated my father and me between her and Mr. Watumull on a sofa and started interviewing me.

"What are your goals?" she asked.

"Education," I said tentatively, realizing that it was a weak answer.

"Uh-huh."

"I think Mrs. Watumull wants to know what you plan to do after finishing your education," my father said.

"Uh-huh," Mrs. Watumull said.

"I don't know, but I'd like to get as much education as I possibly can first," I finally said.

"Uh-huh." She seemed to use "Uh-huh" alternately as a period and as a question mark, but it was hard to know which she meant this time.

"Doctor Sahib," Mr. Watumull said, speaking as quietly as a discreet salesclerk in a good haberdasher's, "let him go back and be a teacher in a blind school in India. He's already had three years of American education. He already has so much to offer to our blind people. Our country is crying for boys like him. Our country needs her sons."

By now, much of the company was listening to us, and men from various parts of the room clinked the ice in their glasses, slapped the arms of their chairs in satisfaction, and made approving remarks.

"Watumullji has hit the nail on the head."

"Watumullji has spoken like a true patriot."

"Watumullji has expressed our thoughts exactly."

I didn't doubt that Mr. Watumull and the other Indians in the room were doing a lot for our country—sending money home, bringing relatives to this country for their education, and carrying on charitable work for India, perhaps on the model of the Watumull Foundation. Still, they were all settled in America. And yet they wanted me to go back home without getting the education I came for. I could just barely stand Dr. tenBroek's urging work for the blind on me, but what business did these sighted people have? What did they know of any of it? I wanted to strike out on my own, do something different, have a normal career—like a sighted person.

"I'm not going back until I have received all the education I need," I said truculently. "I don't think I ever want to go in for work for the blind, either."

"Uh-huh." I couldn't tell from Mrs. Watumull's "Uh-huh" whether she was pleased or displeased—whether I sounded to her determined, as I thought myself, or selfish, as I feared that Mr. Watumull must think me. My hands were trembling, and my father put one of his large, reassuring hands over one of them.

Mrs. Watumull asked me whether I knew what I wanted to do with my education if I didn't go into work for the blind, and whether I could tell the friends gathered there how I managed to travel alone and get around everywhere by myself, as she had heard. Her questions were pointed and crisp, and, with everyone listening, eyes fixed on me, I couldn't explain as readily as I had to Dean Sanders and Mr. Snyder exactly what I wanted to do or could do—become a lawyer or a journalist, teach in a college, go into foreign service. After all, I didn't even know where I would live—in India or in America. As for getting around, it was hard to put into words the various techniques and knacks that blind people develop—that I had developed. An explanation of facial vision as a sort of perception of "sound-shadows" sounded especially murky to my ears as I gave it. But the guests around the room didn't seem to mind.

The attention mercifully shifted from me to my father. Someone asked him if he thought India would go Communist. Someone else mentioned the "Communist campaign" for fluoridation, and everybody started talking at once. Soon I was talking about the Communist threat in India, along with everyone else, and was being listened to. I started having a good time, feeling that I was an adult at a party with lively people who were interested in my opinions.

We went in to dinner. Mrs. Watumull put my father on her right and me on her left, and while she was talking to him I surreptitiously felt the heavy starched-linen tablecloth and napkin and the flatware, which seemed to be weighted down with bars of silver. A plate was filled and brought to me by a servant. I heard the clatter of forks and knives as people around me started eating, and I picked up my fork and in a gingerly fashion explored my plate. On one side was something soft and grainy. I took a forkful, and ate it. The dish was new to me, and I felt I had never tasted anything more delicious. (It was wild rice.) On the other side were some slippery slices. I speared one of them and put it in my mouth. Again, the dish was new to me, and, if possible, it was even more delicious. (It was pickled watermelon rind.) I felt that the foods were a sort of ambrosia. In the middle of the plate, however, was something hard and unyielding, and I listened for some clue from the people around me that would indicate what it was without my having to ask—I regarded that as a "blindism." But all I heard was people cutting this thing and picking at it. Mrs. Watumull was concentrating on my father, and everyone seemed to be preoccupied with his or her neighbor. I circled and skirted the thing. I finished both the side dishes.

"Isn't this squab delicious?" I finally heard someone observe to his neighbor.

I had eaten the bird at home once, using my fingers and teeth, and even then I had had great trouble getting any meat off the bones. The table linen, the dishes of ambrosia, the knife and fork set up a hubbub in my head: "If you can't eat Watumull squab, you'll never get to a private college." My forehead felt exposed and wet.

I picked up my knife and fork and felt the outline of the bird, found a spongy bit, and tried to cut it out.

"Can I give you a hand?" It was Mrs. Thind, addressing me in a voice that was hesitant and full of feeling. I had been so preoccupied with the food on my plate and with my sense of being under scrutiny for a Watumull scholarship that I had almost forgotten that seated on my left was Mrs. Thind: the nice, good Mrs. Thind, the ever-ready driver, the ever-helpful person—the Mrs. Thind whose name we always filled in on forms that asked for the name of the "next of kin" in America to be notified in case of emergency.

"Yes, please." I pushed my plate over. While she worked on the bird, I sat there, the tablecloth in front of me naked without the plate, my hands empty.

"Here it is," Mrs. Thind said softly, putting the plate back in its place.

"I went from Hawaii all the way to Portland, Oregon, my home town, to get married," Mrs. Watumull was saying to the table at large. "But my parents wouldn't hear of my getting married to an Indian. So Goma and I went to San Francisco, and we couldn't get anyone to marry us there. We had to go to Redwood City to find somebody who would marry us. Then, in 1923, the Supreme Court handed down a decision that in effect took away the citizenship of those of us American women who had married Indians, and it was eight years before the law was amended, and then I had to be renaturalized. Goma didn't get his citizenship until 1946, almost twenty-five years after we were married."

"Let bygones be bygones," an Indian man with a Muslim name said. "We are all a hundred per cent American now."

"Do you think you'll marry an American?" Mrs. Watumull asked, turning to me.

I could feel myself flushing. It almost seemed as if she had the power to read my secret thoughts and divine my hopes for the future.

There was general laughter.

At last, my father and I were in Mrs. Thind's car, being driven home. "Things couldn't have gone better," my father said, in Punjabi. "You can take it from me that the Watumull scholarship will come through."

Mrs. Thind hummed to herself, as if she understood our need to talk in a language that excluded her.

Perhaps my father was right, but I couldn't get the squab out of my mind. I felt like a surgeon who had botched an operation after performing many successful ones.

❧

WITHIN a few days, I had letters of acceptance from both Stanford and Pomona; a letter from Dr. tenBroek saying that even though I wasn't yet officially a California resident he had spoken to the officials in charge, and I could draw on the readers' fund of seven hundred and fifty dollars a year wherever I went to college, as long as it was in the state; and a letter from the Watumull Foundation granting me an annual scholarship of fifteen hundred dollars for two years, to cover room, board, and tuition during the academic year. That left an annual shortfall of perhaps seven hundred and fifty dollars, not counting expenses for summer and other vacations. My father was sure that we would somehow be able to make up the difference, especially since both Stanford and Pomona intimated that if I did well there my first year they would consider my application for financial aid. My father thought that I owed my good fortune to personal meetings. "We Mehtas always make a good personal impression." I thought, however, that my good fortune was due to the American spirit of generosity—that I must be a beneficiary of it, as my father was of the Fulbright program, and India of American foreign aid.

Both Stanford and Pomona wanted to know almost immediately whether I would "accept" their offer of admission, and I was worried about making the wrong choice.

"Climate—you must think about climate," my father said, harping on his old theme. "You are so thin for your age, and there is nothing like the Southern California climate for putting flesh on the bones. People from all over the world come to live here—Aldous Huxley and Christopher Isherwood are settled here. Mrs. Watumull is certainly of the opinion that you should accept

Pomona. She says it will give you a well-rounded liberal-arts education. Everyone says it's small and friendly, and the professors
will take a keen personal interest in you."

"I don't think I'd like to go to Pomona," I said. "It sounds
too provincial. I think I'd rather accept Stanford." I had never
heard of Pomona before coming to California, and I imagined
that it was as little known to the world at large as the Arkansas
School for the Blind. I was tired of explaining to people why I
hadn't gone to Perkins Institute for the Blind, and had ended up
in Arkansas. Secretly, I had a very low opinion of myself, and I
felt that the world was more likely to think well of me if I went
to a well-known university, like Stanford—it would add lustre
to me.

"But people say that Stanford has a country-club atmosphere,
which may not suit someone of your serious temperament," my
father said. "It may have a lot of rich students, and you might
not be able to keep up with their social life. Here people seem to
attach a lot of importance to money—just money."

The whole idea of my "accepting" Pomona or Stanford, when
I stopped to think about it, was funny. I had got twenty-nine
rejections from English and American schools before the Arkansas
school accepted me. That was the only school in the English-
speaking world that would have me. It seemed I had never had a
choice about anything before, and the two admissions would have
felt like a great luxury had I not been besieged by so many contradictory feelings. I wondered how anyone reached a decision.

"Why don't you sleep on it?" my father said. "There will be
plenty of time in the morning to let Stanford and Pomona know."

But that evening, as my father was looking over the literature
on Stanford and Pomona, he observed aloud, almost to himself,
"Here is an interesting fact: there are three men students at Stanford for every woman student, while at Pomona it's almost one
to one. The proportions of coeducation even in California seem to
vary from place to place."

This chance remark settled everything for me. At Pomona,

I'll be three times as likely to find a lifelong companion as I would be at Stanford, I thought. Perhaps walking with a sighted companion through life is a better way of winning acceptance than going to a well-known university. For some reason, I thought of that companion as some beautiful, universally desirable creature, whom everybody would want, and whom I would have to win in a competition that pitted me against the sighted. Until I proved myself in such a competition, I felt, I was unworthy of any sighted girl. Yet I also felt that in any real race with the sighted I was bound to lose, like a donkey running against horses. The fact that the odds at Pomona favored me more than the odds at Stanford made the competition there seem less threatening.

I wouldn't announce it to my father until the next morning, but I had already decided that I would be a Pomona man—that I would go there for at least two years, and then maybe get a girl and transfer to a well-known university. In the years to come, I would give many lofty reasons for choosing Pomona, such as its ideal size, its favorable student-teacher ratio, and its intellectual excellence, but the real, base reason was girls, sighted girls, my bursting wish to storm their citadel—a reason I was as scared to voice as I was to admit to the throbbing, ugly desire that kept me awake at night with lascivious, silky imaginings, all the more urgent and excruciating because I did not have one, not one, real experience to set them against.

The next day, I sent off a letter to Mr. Snyder declining his offer of admission to Stanford and a letter to Dean Sanders accepting his offer of admission to Pomona. Just the idea of my having the power to reject and accept made me feel that I was on my way to being in control of my destiny, like any ordinary, sighted person.

III

THE MARKLESS
WILDERNESS

Y OUR FIRST READING ASSIGNMENT FOR THIS CLASS WILL
be 'The Bear,' " Mr. Mulhauser said, opening the fresh-
man-level English class in Holmes Hall. It was the end
of June, and I was back in class only a month or so after
leaving the Arkansas school. This was the first day of
Pomona's six-week summer session, which I had enrolled
in as soon as my arrangements for attending the college were
completed. I was taking one course, in the hope that it would
help me familiarize myself with the campus, learn how to go
about hiring and using readers, and work out a general system of
living and studying at college, before it formally opened. "The
story is by an important American writer named William Faulkner. As you read 'The Bear,' ask yourselves what the bear is a
symbol of. Can anyone tell us what a symbol is?"

People shifted in their desks, and the wooden floor creaked.

"Young lady in the second row?" Mr. Mulhauser said, apparently acknowledging a raised hand.

"It's a sign," a girl said. She had a lovely, confident voice, and I thought she would say more, but she stopped, as if she didn't know how to go on.

"Sign for what?" Mr. Mulhauser pressed. He was talking and smoking at the same time, and sounded as if his cigarette were hanging from the corner of his mouth and about to drop off.

No one volunteered an answer. Whether the members of the class were shy or ignorant or were slow students taking summer school to catch up I never found out. Still, as I write this I wonder how we could all have been so ignorant or inarticulate about things we should probably have learned in elementary school.

"Well, can anyone tell me what a metaphor is, then? What about a simile? Someone must know what that is. Come on— this is something you must have learned in your high-school English class." I had the impression that he would have liked to make fun of us but was too good-natured and indulgent to actually do it.

I like his voice and manner and his way of teaching, even though he's putting us on the spot, I thought. I remember, however, feeling overwhelmed by the thought that I knew nothing, that I was an ignoramus. I felt that I had wasted my time learning useless things in high school, that I would probably not be able to keep up with the demands of college work, that I didn't deserve to be in a college at all. The fact that everyone else appeared just as ignorant didn't console me; for once, I didn't compare myself with anybody. I just felt crushed by my own deficiencies.

"Let's take these definitions one at a time," Mr. Mulhauser said, getting up from his chair on the platform, writing on the blackboard, and talking quickly—still with the precarious cigarette in his mouth—over the tap and screech of the chalk. "When something stands for something else {tap}, like the cross for Christianity {screech}, that's a symbol. When something is compared to something similar {tap, screech}—'Your eyes are like stars'—that's a simile. When something is compared to something else in such a way that it is said *to be* that thing—'Your eyes are stars'—that's a metaphor. A conceit is a very farfetched metaphor; for example, 'Your eyes are the stars. Our love is the firmament. We are the universe.' " As he talked, he paced back and forth on the platform, taking puffs on the cigarette between sentences. He seemed so absorbed in what he was saying that as I heard his footstep near the edge of the platform I feared he would forget to turn back, and would fall off, but he never did.

People sitting around me were writing, their pens and pencils racing lightly across their notebook pages in accompaniment to the tap and screech on the blackboard. I sat there, tense, my hands idle, feeling anxious because Mr. Mulhauser might write something on the board and not say it aloud, and straining to remember every word. But the more I strained the more I feared that I was retaining little. My mind is a sieve, I thought. The others will have the lecture safely preserved in their notebooks, for ready reference, and I—I will have nothing. How will I ever pass an exam?

Mr. Mulhauser went on, pacing the front of the room, "Similes, metaphors, and conceits are figures of speech, and figures of speech, along with images, which are pictures in words of things, are used by writers to build up symbols. They are sometimes used consciously, at other times unconsciously. Can anyone here tell me why a writer would use a symbol—or, for that matter, a figure of speech or an image?"

"They want to make money, and so they dress things up to hook readers," a boy said.

"Some writers may only want to make money, but not good writers. And in this class we're only concerned with good writing. Any other ideas? Anyone else?"

"Writers like to play with words," a girl said.

"That could certainly be one reason. By the way, are you all noticing that as we are talking we are using images? 'Dress up,' 'hook,' 'play' are common verbs, but they also give you a mental picture. They help to make your statements vivid. As it happens, though, the answers miss the point of what writing is—at least, what literature is. Does someone else want to take a shot at the question 'Why do writers use figures of speech'?"

"Writers just don't like to tell the truth," a boy said.

"On the contrary, writers try to get at deeper, spiritual truths by using symbols," Mr. Mulhauser said. "A symbol works on many levels. Take the sentence 'Eve ate an apple.' There is the literal truth *{tap, screech}*. And there is the deeper truth *{tap, screech}*. In the second instance, the apple is a symbol of man's fall, his expulsion from the Garden of Eden, his burden of Original Sin. One little fruit that you and I eat in our salads every day symbolizes so much—the appeal of the forbidden fruit, our suffering on earth, man's conflict with God, free will versus determinism." He paused, as if inviting comment from the class.

I wanted to speak, to participate, to hear the sound of my voice, but I could think of nothing to say, except that I was in awe of Mr. Mulhauser and his explanations, and excited by the power of the apple—the power of literature.

"In this course, we'll be studying some examples of literature which I hope will inspire you to read literature for the rest of your lives, whatever your majors." He wrote down on the blackboard the names of some of the things we'd be reading for the course—in addition to "The Bear" they were Sherwood Anderson's "I Want to Know Why," Stephen Crane's "The Open Boat," Lytton Strachey's "Queen Victoria," and Jonathan Swift's "Gulliver's Travels"—and observed that we would be studying the genres of the short story, biography, and satire, and that the works could be bought in a couple of omnibus editions from the college bookstore. "As you read your first assignment, ask yourselves, 'What is the author's governing intention in writing "The Bear"? What are the figures of speech and images he uses to realize his governing intention? How does he handle the development of character and plot?' "

By the time the hour was over, I thought I had never attended a class in which I learned so much so quickly—a class that stirred me up so much. I thought that Mr. Mulhauser was some kind of paragon, with stores upon stores of marvellous knowledge. I wanted to be his most passionate student: to give up eating, sleeping—everything—to read and reread his assignments and win his praise. I wanted to commit the text of everything he assigned to memory, to know it better than anyone else, perhaps better than the author himself. But how was I even going to read "The Bear"—the assignment for the next day? (It was a matter of general knowledge that practically everything required for college work in those days was unavailable in Braille or on Talking Books.) Who would read it to me? How was I going to set about finding a reader in less than twenty-four hours? How would I take notes? Using Braille was so slow that it was out of the question; typing raised the problem of who would read the notes back to me—the problem of finding a reader all over again—and anyway it would disturb the class.

The bell rang, and the people around me stood up, audibly stretching and yawning, shuffling notebooks and tucking them under arms. I sat paralyzed in my chair, dreading the walk by myself back to my room in Clark Hall, the main residence for men.

I had arrived at the college just that morning—Mrs. Thind had driven me there, along with my father. My father had wanted to show me around the college, or, at least, walk with me from Clark Hall to the classroom and back a couple of times. He knew as well as I did that I needed to walk a route a few times with someone, so that it would become fixed in my feet and I could go back and forth confidently. But people were milling about, and I didn't want them to watch me being taken around the place, however discreetly. I was impatient, as usual, and made my father and Mrs. Thind think that I would be able to find my way, like anybody else. Actually, I imagined that I could. (Years later, I realized that almost from the time I lost my eyesight a fiendish fantasy that I could see had remained fixed in my head.) I practically pushed Mrs. Thind and my father to leave, to go back to Los Angeles, when they had barely shown me the way from my room to Frary Dining Hall, and before I had stopped to think about how I would get anywhere else.

As it turned out, I had been able to get to class easily. Mr. Mulhauser had come to my room and walked over with me. His kindness flabbergasted me. Walking in the exalted company of a professor made me feel shy, like a child. All the same, I shrugged off his hand on my arm and walked beside him, as if I didn't need his help—and in certain respects I didn't. He kept on irritatingly pointing out steps and doors, which I could recognize by myself, by means of sound-shadows.

Now two or three students were standing around Mr. Mulhauser, asking him how long "The Bear" was, whether the reading assignments for the course were going to be heavy, what the last day was on which people could switch courses. I waited, in panic, wondering what I would do with myself when I somehow did get back to my room.

"Would you like to come with me to my office next door?" It was Mr. Mulhauser, addressing me from above my head. I jumped up.

"How are you going to read the story?" Mr. Mulhauser asked as soon as we had sat down in his office. Then he lit a fresh cigarette. He sounded as if he were gazing at me intently.

I was so encouraged by the interest he was taking in me that I found myself sketching out a plan for him that until then hadn't occurred to me. "I have to find readers," I said. "I think the best way of finding them is for you to announce in class that I need readers and that I'm able to pay seventy-five cents an hour. I think some students might like to do it, because they would be getting through their assignment while they were earning money reading it to me. If it's a boy, he can read to me in my room. If it's a girl, we could possibly read in an empty classroom."

"It's wonderful," Mr. Mulhauser said. "You have it all figured out. I wish we had had this talk before class, because now I can't do anything about it until tomorrow. Do you know how to find your way back to Clark Hall, or do you want me to walk back with you?"

"I know my way," I said, trying to sound confident, and I stood up.

Although I was unsure of the route, I didn't so much walk as run to Clark Hall, as if to prove to all the people I passed along the way that I was independent and self-sufficient. I felt that if someone even lifted a finger to help me I would hit him. Once in my room, I slammed the door shut and slumped into a chair, feeling weak and lost. Most of the day and the night were ahead of me. I had no Braille books or Talking Books, no radio; the idea of my attending summer school had come up so suddenly that there hadn't been time to get in touch with the local library or to arrange for my things to be sent from Arkansas. I tried to busy myself by arranging my clothes, but it took hardly any time to hang up what I had—a couple of old discarded suits of Mr. Watumull's that he had given me as a present, and that had been altered for me in a hurry. My room had a campus telephone on the wall, but I could think of no one to call. I had, however, brought along the phonograph and "La Vie Parisienne." I put the record on and collapsed on my bed, an arm under my head, wishing that I had eyes—that I could find the college bookstore without asking for help, buy the book, and read "The Bear" myself. The record played through and repeated itself again and again, but I scarcely heard its happy melodies.

I had been needing to go to the bathroom for some time. I half raised myself, then thought, I can wait a little longer, and slumped back. I am finally not at an institution for the blind but at a proper school, an ordinary college for normal people, I thought. This should be the happiest day of my life. Here I am at the destination that, in a sense, I've been waiting to reach ever since I was five years old and was put on the train for that wretched boarding school for blind orphans in Bombay. Yet I feel utterly miserable. The inside of my head feels like a school bell without a clapper, like the wheels of a car spinning on a road without traction. I am a dunce, going nowhere.

ON the second day, Mr. Mulhauser opened the class by asking if anyone could tell him what the author's governing intention was in writing "The Bear." As in the previous class, his tone was conversational, his voice amiable; in fact, he radiated amiability. He gave the impression of someone who had spent all his life in comfortable surroundings, among congenial people, in pleasant climes.

"There are many intentions," a girl said.

"Is there one overriding intention?"

"It's very confusing, especially the second part. But when I was reading the first part I thought maybe the theme was education."

"Good—but education how? Certainly not with books."

"Well, the boy sort of learns most when he completely gives himself over to the woods, without teachers, without a gun— when he tries to be completely independent and self-reliant," she said.

Mr. Mulhauser tried to draw out other students, but didn't seem to get anywhere. It was hard for me to gain from their answers any idea of what the story was about. To my relief, Mr. Mulhauser, perhaps deciding that everyone needed coaching in how to read a story, soon gave us his own interpretation, step by step, but talking quickly. "Note the repetition of words like 'humility,' 'patience,' 'courage' in the story," he said. "The boy has to learn these values before he can be worthy of the bear, worthy of the wilderness in which the bear roams, which no man can own or tame or overwhelm—before he can establish a mature relationship with the bear."

I sat there listening to the pencils racing all around me, like encircling bees manufacturing the honey of knowledge, which would later nourish the sighted students, sustain them through the study and examination of the story. My fingers twitched for a magical pencil with which I might be able to write, too. It is one thing to want to be among the sighted, one among equals, and quite another to *be* among them and come up against one's limitations with each of their pencil strokes, I thought. Before this class, I could never have imagined the importance of a little thing like a pencil.

"Note the contrast in the story between the town and the wilderness," Mr. Mulhauser was going on. "The town represents civilization and corruption. It's where people go to gamble and buy whiskey. The train that takes people to town is an engine of destruction. The wilderness represents self-reliance, fortitude, natural forces, balance. Note how the boy is instructed in the school of the wilderness, season by season, year by year, from the time he is ten, and has neither a gun nor the most rudimentary skills of the woodsman, to the time he is sixteen, and has acquired a gun and all the hunting skills he needs in order to meet the bear."

Mr. Mulhauser paused. There was a clack as he opened a book on the desk. He had the air of being very much in control of his students and of his material. He said he was going to read a key passage from the story, and began to read aloud in the manner of a minister clinching an argument in a sermon by quoting a Biblical text: "If Sam Fathers had been his mentor and the backyard rabbits and squirrels his kindergarten, then the wilderness the old bear ran was his college and the old male bear itself, so long unwifed and childless as to have become its own ungendered progenitor, was his alma mater."

The pencils, if anything, raced faster. I tried to repeat Mr. Mulhauser's words in my head, so as to remember them—hold them in my mind until later in the day, when I might be able to note them down somehow, on a typewriter or in Braille, at my own speed. *I am in the college of the bear. A bear likes honey. Honey is dripping onto their notebooks. . . . Aren't these conceits?* But he was reading on, and I wasn't listening; my mind was drifting. How would I remember anything? I could feel the waters of desperation rising inside me.

"His teacher is Sam Fathers," Mr. Mulhauser was saying some time later. "Note the name Fathers. And Sam Fathers is part Negro and part Indian, Chickasaw Indian. As you must have gathered, the story is set in the late eighteen-seventies and the eighties, and at that time Negroes and Indians were looked on as peoples who had never been tamed or civilized and therefore had closer ties to the wilderness. Sam Fathers' lesson is this: The boy must meet the wilderness not on the terms of his civilization, of buying and selling land, of cutting down the woods, of building the railroad—of commerce, of expanding and despoiling—but on those of the bear. I'd like you to open your books and read along with me. I'm going to be skipping around a bit, but I think you'll have no trouble following." He mentioned a page number. All around me were the sounds of books opening and pages turning and people picking up pencils, all making me feel more self-conscious than ever because I had no book and no pencil, and hadn't even read the story. "This, you will remember, is the scene where the boy goes in search of the bear by himself for the first time. You will remember that he is eleven years old and already knows more about getting around in the woods than men two or three times his age, and they recognize it."

He read:

He left the next morning before light, without breakfast. . . . He had only the compass and a stick for the snakes. . . . Sam had said: "Be scared. You cant help that. But dont be afraid. Aint nothing in the woods going to hurt you if you dont corner it or it dont smell that you are afraid. . . ."

By noon he was far beyond the crossing on the little bayou, farther into the new and alien country than he had ever been, travelling now not only by the compass but by the old, heavy, biscuit-thick silver

watch which had been his father's. He had left the camp nine hours ago.
. . . He had already relinquished, of his will, because of his need, in
humility and peace and without regret ["He's talking about the gun,"
Mr. Mulhauser said], yet apparently that had not been enough, the
leaving of the gun was not enough. He stood for a moment—a child,
alien and lost in the green and soaring gloom of the markless wilderness. Then he relinquished completely to it. It was the watch and the
compass. He was still tainted. He removed the linked chain of the one
and the looped thong of the other from his overalls and hung them on
a bush and leaned the stick beside them and entered it.

The idea of surrendering the stick resonated in my head as if
the author had in some mysterious way had me in mind when he
chose the stick as the last act of surrender before the boy could
realize his ambition. Practically every blind person I had ever
known carried a stick or a cane to guide himself through the maze
of streets and traffic. I had long since got rid of my stick. Everybody said I was reckless, but I was only trying to be self-reliant
and independent—independent just like the boy, I now thought.

"So we see that he has entered the wilderness to all intents
and purposes as naked as the bear," Mr. Mulhauser went on.
"And it is only then that he realizes his ambition to come face to
face with the bear—the bear that has filled his dreams for six long
years, but that until this moment of complete surrender to the
wilderness he's never seen." He put down the book and continued, "We have already seen that the bear is a recurring challenge,
a natural force, which the hunters—old General Compson, Cousin
McCaslin, Major de Spain—encounter every year on their hunts.
But they are not serious hunters—they go through the ritual,
they play at it, they somehow don't get around to the bear until
the last day of their annual hunt. For them, it remains elusive,
mysterious, year after year. They don't understand its meaning,
they don't know how to go about finding the bear, go about
coming to terms with the challenge it poses. Among the hunting

party, Boon—Boon Hogganbeck—stands out. He is described in animal terms, as if he were, in a sense, a child of the wilderness. The boy and Sam Fathers are also of the hunting party. They are portrayed all along as the most serious hunters. The boy is serious and single-minded, passionate." Mr. Mulhauser went over to the window and started fingering the cord of the blind. Perhaps he's making a hangman's noose, I thought. He certainly has the manner of an intellectual executioner. "But note: now that the boy has come face to face with the bear he doesn't kill it. Note also that the boy observes but does not participate in the eventual killing of the bear—that is done by Boon Hogganbeck. Faulkner seems to be saying that the hunt is more important than the prize. Again, note that when the bear dies Sam Fathers dies. It's as if Faulkner were saying that their function was to teach the boy and they have fulfilled that function. The last picture we have of the boy is of him watching Boon, now gone mad, destroying his gun. But this vast theme is only one of two themes of the story. The other has to do with inheritance, with ownership of the land, with property rights—with the question of who can possibly have the right to own and to spoil the wilderness, lay claim to the ownership of nature. I want you to think about this question. Study the second part of the story in the light of it. For that is what we'll be discussing in class tomorrow." How will I ever read any story again without Mr. Mulhauser to interpret it, I thought. I have read stories for years, but I had no idea that they had symbols and deeper meanings packed inside them, like Chinese boxes. I read stories as just stories; now it is as though I hadn't read them at all. I will have to read them all again, asking myself at every juncture what various things symbolize, what it all means. In my childish enthusiasm, I began daydreaming of Mr. Mulhauser as Sam Fathers.

In my reverie, I'd almost forgotten that Mr. Mulhauser was going to make an announcement about readers, and now it startled me to hear him saying, "Ved Mehta, the blind student in our class, would like to find people to read to him. He is able to pay seventy-five cents an hour. Anyone interested should see him now."

I rose and stood at one side of the classroom waiting for people to come to me, the blood rushing to my face. No one will come up to me, I thought. What will I do then? How will I read the assignments? I'm not as independent and self-reliant as the boy in the story after all. I'm just a helpless blind person.

"I'd like to be a reader." It was a girl's voice, a little on the heavy side, but with good volume—and she was applying for the job. "I've never read aloud before, but I think I would like to learn."

"There's not much to learn," I said, sounding more offhand than I felt. She was the only applicant, and the first reader I had ever hired. "Speed is all I care about."

"I'd like to try."

I arranged to meet the girl on the steps of Holmes Hall that afternoon, when she would have a few free hours.

As I was hurrying out of the classroom, I heard Mr. Mulhauser calling me from his office. "Ved, I saw you crossing College Avenue yesterday from this window, and I was horrified just watching you," he said, showing me to a chair. "You know, you could easily get killed. You shouldn't cross streets without a stick."

Although College Avenue was one of the main streets of Claremont, it had very little traffic on it. Anyway, Claremont was a quiet town, with practically no rushing wind, so I could hear a car coming blocks away. Still, he has a clear view of the crossing from his window, I thought. Now I'll always get nervous and flustered, feeling that I'm crossing the street under his eye. He probably thinks he's being kind and caring, and yet, without knowing it, he's patronizing me, telling me things I've spent years thinking and learning about. I wish I could tell him not to meddle, but I don't want to offend him. I don't want to be disrespectful.

"I don't need one," I said. "I've crossed much busier streets than College Avenue without using a stick." My heart was practically jumping out of my chest from fear. I'm in the right, so why should I be afraid, I asked myself. Why is it that my insides churn whenever I speak up for myself? I wish I were like the boy in the story, unafraid.

"If you are shy about the stick, just use it when you're crossing College Avenue. There are hedges on both sides of the street, and you can simply hide it once you're safely across."

"I'm not ashamed of my blindness," I said quickly, feeling my face redden. I was at once moved by his thoughtfulness and troubled by his persistence. "That is written all over me in large letters. It just so happens that I don't need a stick."

Here he is, I thought, teaching a story about a boy who leaves behind not only his watch and his gun but even his stick when he enters the wilderness, so that he'll be worthy of it—the wilderness, with snakes and bears—because the boy has taken to heart Sam Fathers' advice that he would be safe as long as he didn't panic, wasn't afraid. And yet here is the same teacher telling *me* to carry a stick just to cross the street. He understands the boy in the story, and yet he doesn't understand me. Doesn't he understand that I might want to be as self-reliant as the boy?

"I'll never carry a stick," I said petulantly. "I should be trusted to know what I can do."

"But the college authorities are responsible for your safety. I should tell you that a lot of people besides me are concerned about the way you're going around without a stick, and Shelton Beatty, who is our dean of men, has already spoken to me about it. I think he'd like to see you."

I was furious. I felt I would have to prove to Mr. Mulhauser—to all the sighted Mr. Mulhausers all my life—what my capabilities were, and somehow make it clear that I could develop them only by stretching them to the limit.

"I'll talk to Dean Beatty if he insists," I said. "But I think you'll see after a while that I'm better off relying on my own senses than on the drivers' looking out for me."

Whether it was the tone of my voice or the look on my face, Mr. Mulhauser allowed the subject to drop.

Later that morning. Dean Beatty accosted me in the quadrangle. "A stick, man, a stick. Why won't you carry one of those white sticks with a red tip? You're going to get yourself killed and give the college a bad name."

He fell in step with me and let loose a torrent of words, in the manner of a failed preacher. He had a Southern accent, and he spoke fast, as if he wanted to cover it up. I shut him out. "White stick with a red tip . . . white stick with a red tip" was about all I took in. The meddling, interfering busybodies, I thought. Why can't they leave me alone? Can't they understand that whether I carry a stick or not—whether I live or die—is *my* business? "When school starts in the fall, a lot of the students will be here with their cars, driving around as if this were a freeway. You might get by now without a stick, but, I assure you, you'll need one then."

I've got to let him have it, I thought. I've been deferential, mealy-mouthed, and afraid. "I don't want to hear about a stick," I said. "I know my capabilities best. It's my business how I get around."

"Hey, wait a minute. I'm the dean of men. It's my business. It's the college's business. As long as you're a student here, you're under our care."

He attached himself to me like a shadow, and I couldn't get away from him. I explained to him about facial vision, and he didn't believe it. He wanted me to prove to him that I had any such thing. I walked along, pointing out places where there were hedges and where there were none, where there were lampposts and where there were none. He seemed to be impressed and interested, and suddenly left me, as if he had remembered an important appointment or an errand.

Back at Holmes Hall after lunch, my reader and I sat in an empty classroom and started reading "The Bear." We read for hours. I had never had anything read to me for that long, and I felt transfixed, as if I had learned a whole new language in a matter of a day.

❧

I DREADED going to meals. I would enter Frary Dining Hall, where all the men ate, and start purposefully walking along the line that snaked around the hall, listening to the voices, so that I wouldn't bump into people and could gracefully take my place at the end, but a hand would reach out and grab me, as in a scary dream. Either I would be pulled willy-nilly into the line wherever the stranger who had grabbed me was standing, as if my blindness exempted me from waiting my turn, or some officious fellow would propel me to the end, as if I were a cart of dishes that had to be got out of the way. If I somehow managed to get to the end of the line by myself, without such indignities, and was allowed to proceed, unmolested, to the counter where the trays were stacked, someone was sure to pick up a tray for me and jab it into my ribs. Or, if I escaped that indignity, too, someone was sure to try to get my food for me, although I was perfectly capable of pushing my own tray along the cafeteria rails and getting my own food, since the student workers who served up the food behind the rails always called out the fare. Instead, I would have to walk along the rails empty-handed. Once the food was on the tray, there would be much to-do about directing me—or misdirecting me—to a table: "Take my arm. Hold on to me." "Follow me. Left—no, right." Once at the table, I would reach for my milk or my salad only to discover that the person who helped me had forgotten to get it. I couldn't go back for it without creating a fuss. Once I was safely stowed away in my seat, no one would have anything more to do with me, as if I were an object of interest only when people thought I needed assistance.

I felt both angry and guilty. I wanted to hit out at everyone and everything, but was also overwhelmed with guilt at the thought that all these people were only trying to be helpful—that they were nothing if not well-meaning. I would resolve to initiate a conversation, but didn't know how to go about it. I would sit there envying my easygoing blind-school friends, who, I imagined, would have butted into the conversation of their neighbors, told jokes, forced themselves on people's attention, and gradually got people to accept them on their own terms. How I wished I had the common touch, so that I, too, could joke and laugh, could make friends. Instead, I retreated into my shell, ignored the people around me as they ignored me, and felt as soft inside as I must have appeared severe outside. Any word of warning ("Watch out! You're going to get gravy on your sleeve") would raise my hackles, and I would strike back ("No, I'm not. Mind your own business") and then feel sorry but not say I was sorry, leaving the impression that I was abrasive and arrogant, when actually I ached with the wish to be loved.

Sometimes, on the street, students would walk up to me and ask "How do you know when you get to a curb?" Many students, it seemed, thought that I counted steps, that I had had the whole town of Claremont paced out, measured out, so that I always knew when I was coming to a step down or a step up, to an obstacle or an open area. And a fellow said to me, "I saw you walk around that parked car as if you could see it. How much can you really see?" Later, a friend told me, "Dauphin thinks that you can see, and that you're only keeping it a secret because you want to impress everyone—that you're a wily Oriental." (Dauphin was nicknamed after the memorable character in "Huckleberry Finn.") I knew that these erroneous notions were commonplace among the sighted; we used to laugh at them at school. I took pains to explain facial vision to everyone, but misconceptions about my ability to see persisted.

In the first few days, without knowing it, I developed a manner that made people fearful of offering advice or help. I was allowed to do everything myself from start to finish in Frary Hall. Even the furor over the stick died down. When I automatically stepped up to or down from a curb, crossed College Avenue, or put my hand on the doorknob as I reached a door, people in the vicinity might hesitate for a moment, as if reassuring themselves that I was all right, that I knew what I was doing. I could feel them staring at me, as if they were awestruck, as if they thought my getting around was some kind of mysterious feat. In my hearing, they would exclaim, as if I were deaf, things like "He must have a sixth sense," "He has ESP," and "He must count steps." But a few weeks into the summer session people stopped making such remarks, as if my doings were of no consequence. Now, perversely, I regretted not having the little exchanges I'd had in the days when people tried to help me on the street or in Frary Hall. That help, however embarrassing and nettling to my pride, at least gave me contact with the people around me. But to be held in exaggerated respect, endowed with abilities I did not have and could not have, to be thought superior to everyone—a view to which I might have contributed by shrugging off people's help— made for a kind of isolation that seemed to me worse than the isolation I felt when I was surrounded by oversolicitous people. Now people passed me on the street or sat down next to me in Frary Hall without so much as a word of greeting. I would try to greet people first, try to start a conversation. But my attempts would be either faltering or unproductive. I might elicit a solemn exchange, but then the person would walk on or turn to someone else and laugh and joke. It was as if people couldn't be natural with me.

I realized that except for one summer in Little Rock which I'd spent out in the world doing a summer job I had been sheltered nearly all my life, in schools for the blind or in the circle of my family and relatives. I had therefore come to assume that people had an automatic understanding of my capabilities and deficiencies, without my having to explain anything, and the result was that when I arrived at college I was ill-prepared to adjust to my new circumstances, ill-prepared to face the fact that I was probably out in the world for good. My difficulties mounted when, toward the end of the summer session, I had to make arrangements to stay on in Claremont until the opening of the college: take a room at Miss Marsh's lodgings; familiarize myself with the route from her house to a cheap café called the Sugar Bowl, where I would be having all my meals; and order Braille and Talking Books from the library, so that I wouldn't be totally friendless when all the students had left Claremont.

Although I hadn't seen much of my father since I came to Claremont, it was comforting to know that he was only a couple of hours' bus ride away. But by June he had completed his Fulbright term, and he had so far not found any other work to keep him in America. I had to face the prospect that he would soon be homeward bound, and I would be all alone in my new, alien, sighted surroundings.

❧

ONE morning, just after I had crossed College Avenue I felt a light hand on my arm.

"Ved—I'm Anne."

Despite myself, I stiffened, thinking she was trying to help me, but she didn't let go of my arm. "You know me?" I asked.

"Everyone knows you," she said. I was annoyed that she knew me when I didn't know who she was. Then she asked, "Can I walk with you"

"Sure—it's a free country," I said.

She didn't say anything, and we walked in silence for a little while. I wondered if she thought I'd been rude. I'm developing a carapace, I thought. Everything I say seems to have a hard edge. I've lost my chance to make my first real friend at college. I felt sad, because I had somehow concluded that she was attractive, was just the right height and age, and was going to be a freshman, like me. (I could pick up such things about people without exactly knowing how.)

"Can you come to dinner tonight?" she asked forthrightly,

without any preliminaries. I listened to her sandals squeaking and scraping along the path. They gave her a summery air.

There was nothing I would have liked better, and I would have liked to say "Sure" and to ask what time and where. But I felt a little apprehensive. It would mean going to a house or a restaurant, since men did not eat meals with women on campus. How would I get there? How could I afford to pay for her? Would she have to escort me, when it was I who should have been escorting her?

"Thank you very much," I said, "but I've already paid for my dinner in Frary Hall." I felt a little lightheaded. If I had gone to dinner with her, I might have had to go to the bathroom in the middle of the meal. The very thought was excruciating. I would rather die than have to be taken to the bathroom by a girl—by a young, desirable, sighted girl—as if I were a helpless little boy. Who knows? She might insist on showing me the toilet. That would be so humiliating.

"Maybe another time," she said. She slipped her hand out from under my arm and walked away.

I speeded up. I wanted to get to a sink as quickly as possible and hide my hot face in cool water. But when I had almost reached the steps of Clark Hall I heard her running after me.

"Tomorrow night?" she asked. "I'll ask my mother. Maybe she could have you tomorrow night." She seemed to have interpreted my statement about having paid for dinner as the lame excuse that it was.

I wanted to say yes—that little word. (It's about the hardest word to get out, when it should be the breath of life.) She didn't wait for my answer. She was gone. I couldn't imagine how I would find her the next day to say yes, or how she might get in touch with me.

That evening, the wall phone in my room rang. "It's Anne—Anne Lockwood." She took it for granted I was coming, and said she would meet me on the steps of the Sophomore Arch at Clark Hall and walk with me to her parents' house. I hung up, thinking that she had taken all the initiative, that I was passive, just as people imagined all the blind to be.

I MUST have gone to the bathroom half a dozen times before I went out to wait on the steps of the Sophomore Arch. I had on a pair of Mr. Watumull's trousers, which I was wearing for the first time. They had been altered badly. Mr. Watumull's tailor had apparently taken in the waist, which must have been six or eight inches too large for me, from the back, because as I walked the side pockets rode to the rear and the creases at the knee came almost out to the side, making the trousers like a clown's pantaloons. I wanted to take them off and throw them away, but they were the only lightweight dress trousers I had—the only ones I felt I could wear with a white shirt and a tie, which I thought were required if I was to go to Anne's parents' house. As I waited on the steps, I felt as self-conscious as a bridegroom, because, deep down, I had decided that I was in love with Anne, that she had a perfect reading voice, and that she would be just like Mrs. tenBroek, who read books to her husband early in the morning, who took his dictation in shorthand, who typed his papers, who walked with him to unfamiliar places until he got used to the way and could go by himself. At the same time, I thought, a little contradictorily, If I can just show Anne how independent I am—how, given half a chance, I could be just as good as a sighted man—she might love me back. She must already have fallen for me in some way, or why would she have taken the initiative, run after me to invite me again, arranged for me to meet her parents? After all, people at home got married virtually sight unseen, and Dr. tenBroek had met Mrs. tenBroek on a blind date. The thought of marrying Anne within six months, as the tenBroeks had, gave me pause, however. I couldn't imagine how I would go about studying if I had a wife around all day long.

I recalled that this was Saturday night, when all magical things happened in America. I stood there on the steps, pulling my trousers this way and that way, as alert as a fox for the sound of Anne's footsteps, so that I could greet her before she greeted me, and greet her in a normal, calm, grownup way. But people were constantly going up and down the steps, in a sort of thunder of footsteps, and she sneaked up on me. I jumped at the sound of her voice.

We set off along Sixth Street, her hand on my arm. I stumbled over a curb, and I never really regained my balance. My wretched trousers, which seemed to pull across my front every time I took a step, kept me off guard. I would start crossing a street before a car had quite gone by. Even her hand on my forearm, which I could feel through my shirtsleeve, and which gave me a pleasant sensation all over, seemed somehow to be badly placed—it was too close to my elbow and kept slipping down—and I didn't know how to tell her that she should hold my arm firmly in one place. Then, abruptly, she took hold of my hand. I noticed with pleasure that she slipped her hand inside mine from behind, as if *I* had taken hold of *her* hand, instead of grabbing my hand from the front, as people did when they tried to lead me. Her arm was just the right length. We walked comfortably hand in hand, almost as if we were sweethearts.

"You were born in India, and I was born in China," she was saying. "You should know something about my parents. They worked for the Y.M.C.A. and were missionaries in China. There are a lot of retired missionaries settled in Claremont, in Pilgrim Place, and a lot of them spent their lives in the East. Having an Indian student in the Associated Colleges has created quite a stir among them."

I felt pleased that I was one of a kind, and at the same time felt a little depressed that, after Arkansas, I had ended up in another parochial place.

"Did I tell you that I spent some time in India?" Anne was

saying. "I went to Woodstock School, up in the hills, for a year and a half. My parents sent me there from China to get away from the war."

"So you know India?"

"I feel more at home in the East than in the West."

Oh, God, I can't believe my good luck, I thought. We share a background. Then I thought, Why would any parents prefer me to a normal fellow for their daughter? But they're Christians. Maybe Christians would disregard my disability. My father always said that Christians, who believed in personal salvation, had compassion in a way that Hindus, who were fatalists, did not, and that, ultimately, only a Christian girl could make me happy. But how would even Christian parents in their right mind approve of a blind person for their daughter if they knew all the disadvantages? I felt suddenly crushed, flattened, as if someone had knocked me down from behind. "What do your parents do now?" I asked.

"My parents? Oh, they're retired."

I thought I felt the pressure of her hand on mine. How independent she is, I thought. Maybe she wouldn't pay any attention to what her parents said. I wonder if Mrs. tenBroek's parents objected, and how she got around them. After all, Anne is walking hand in hand with me, for all the passersby to see her love for me. The thought of it—the reality of it—made my spirits soar.

We walked along Seventh Street, between College Avenue and Harvard Avenue, and stepped into a modest house with a screen door, which slammed behind us, *BANG-a-bang-bang*— perhaps the most familiar sound of my own home. Anne took me to the kitchen. The tap was running, something was sizzling on the stove, and Anne's mother was chopping what smelled like onions. Nervously, I stuck out my hand to shake hers—a "blindism," I realized even as I did it, since I knew that her hands were busy and messy.

"My hands aren't fit to shake a dog's paw," she said. "But it's nice to meet you. We've heard a lot about you."

I stiffened. We had been taught in one of our social-adjustment classes in Arkansas that to say "heard a lot about you" was a faux pas, because it left the other person wondering what you'd heard.

"Nothing bad, I hope," I said stupidly.

The thing on the stove sizzled very loudly.

"What did you say?" Anne's mother asked.

I couldn't bring myself to repeat it.

"He said, 'I hope nothing bad,' " Anne said, and rushed to the stove.

"No, all good," Anne's mother said. "People say you're a marvel, the way you get around."

Because of the kitchen sounds, normal conversation seemed impossible. I stood there, not knowing what to do with my hands, taking a couple of steps one way and then the other, wondering what kind of impression I was making, and hoping that my face didn't wear the stony expression associated with blind people, while at the same time feeling more and more that it did. I had somehow got it into my head that if I weren't talking or listening I looked asleep (that stony expression). The skin under my eyes certainly felt tense. Why has Anne left me standing here, I thought angrily. Why doesn't she show me to a seat in the living room? I longed to be in my own room in Clark Hall, to look the way I did without worrying about how I looked to other people, to let my face relax and look as dead as it would, to be near the bathroom just down the hall from my room. That got me wondering what it would be like to be with Anne twenty-four hours a day, to have to stand around the kitchen while she cooked, and to have to go to the bathroom when she was around. The prospect, instead of being enticing, was terrifying. I wanted to bolt from her mother's kitchen, to hide—to do anything but have dinner with her and her family.

Anne's father came in and shook my hand a little loosely. It could have been his normal handshake, but I imagined there was disapproval in it. "Let's go in and sit down," he said. "Dinner looks ready." He took me into the dining room.

There was a lot of awkward maneuvering as he tried to lead me by holding on to me and I tried to follow him moving independently, in my usual fashion. Throughout the dinner, I continued to feel a little out of sorts. I remember that at one point we played a guessing game. Each of us had to decide which famous person we would most like to be, and then give five clues. I chose Tolstoy; Anne chose Florence Nightingale. After each of us had guessed the other's idol, Anne and I got into a heated argument, which I provoked, about whether it was better to be a novelist or someone who did good works.

"Anyone who saves even a single life is a thousand times as good as someone who spends his life trying to entertain other people," Anne said passionately.

"What nonsense!" I said. "Without art, we'd be little better than animals."

During the argument, it emerged that Anne was going to major in political science and do social work. She's not literary, I thought. She's just a social worker. She won't be interested in reading to me or helping me improve my English, my writing. She's not lighthearted—she's depressing.

After dinner, Anne accompanied me back to Clark Hall. We walked in glum silence, her hand in mine feeling practical and heavy. It's terrible to be dependent, I thought. I hate not knowing my way all around Claremont by myself yet and having to be taken home, like a child.

I was probably no more confused than the young usually are about being dependent and wanting independence, but because of my special situation I was more demanding of others and of myself, and therefore more liable to feel disappointed in others and easily saddened. I should note that in time Anne Lockwood and I became good friends, and enjoyed drinking coffee together to the sound of a Brandenburg concerto on the jukebox, but I was never able to summon up my original romantic feelings for her, and, as it happened, she had no use for romance. She made fun of women who went to college to find husbands.

That night, I went to bed feeling disenchanted, bitter, as if I had been married and gone through a divorce within a few hours.

IV

PROMETHEAN LIGHT

THE COLLEGE HAD FORMALLY OPENED, AND WE FRESH-men had been going through an orientation program for five days. After lunch, there was a battle cry. It may have been a call to battle by the Ghosts. It may have been a single Ghost beating a metal tray with a spoon, or just men shouting "Mudhole! Mudhole!" I no longer remember the exact signal, but I vividly remember that the moment it was given I stripped naked, pulled on a cheap pair of trousers that my father had picked up for me in an Army-surplus store in Los Angeles, and ran outside as fast as I could. Other men—freshmen and sophomores, a hundred or maybe two hundred of them—were also running out of their rooms, shouting, cursing, calling to each other: "Bill Seelye!" "Come on, Summit!" "Where in the hell is Dick?" "These sophomores are pushovers! They're just like a bunch of Indians with war paint on!"

The mudhole was a ditch in the middle of an empty dirt lot

the size of a football field, a few yards west of Clark Hall. A hose had been left running in the ditch for a couple of days, to turn it into a veritable bog.

Generations of Pomona freshmen had fought the sophomores in the mudhole, in order to prove themselves worthy of attending the college—of sharing the turf. The mudhole was both the culmination of the orientation program and an initiation into the life of the college, and now it was our turn. I couldn't wait to get into the mudhole and prove myself worthy.

As it happened, though I probably looked like a hooligan my head was full of lofty notions about the important place that Pomona occupied in the world and in history, in higher education and in Christian civilization, in dedicated service and in Christian fellowship. These notions came directly from the speeches of the college authorities during the orientation program. My head was also full of their remarks on the New England origins of the college (it had been founded by the Congregationalists, the same denomination that founded Harvard, for instance) and on the combination of New England-like intimacy and cosmopolitanism in Claremont. Pomona had the advantages of Southern California and the Pacific Coast, and also the rich heritage of New England—even of England and Oxford. Many of our professors and administrators held graduate degrees from Ivy League universities, and some of them, including the president, had been Rhodes Scholars. The authorities had told us that, in the best tradition of New England and England, we Pomona men and women were expected to uphold certain ethical principles and certain standards of intellectual excellence and physical vitality, for we were nothing less than "torchbearers" of our generation.

I was finally at the edge of the mudhole and ankle-deep in mire, under a sun that burned with the desert heat of nearby Death Valley. It was all I could do to keep my balance in the press of sweaty freshmen, all trembling with nervous energy, who were crowded on one side of the ditch. But I swelled with new-found college spirit, even as I felt a little vulnerable and out of place, thinking that I was probably scrawnier than any of the other men.

"Get back, you'll get hurt! You blind man, get to the back!" men shouted at me, but I managed to squelch forward. I was suddenly in the front rank, raring to go, like a hunting dog that has caught the scent of its prey. Then I was in the mudhole, thrashing about in eight or ten inches of soupy, gritty mush, my chest, arms, and legs burning and feeling raw. Someone—a sophomore—had me clamped in his grip. I rose up and wrestled him to the floor of the bog and sat on him so hard that I thought he was going to beg for mercy. At that moment of triumph, the mudhole was for me college, California, the baptismal font—the place in which my murky future lay buried. Within seconds, I was thrown, almost hurled, clear of the bog, as if by a volcano under me, and lay panting on the bank, wiping with the back of my hand the salty mixture of sweat, blood, and mud on my face and wriggling my toes to try to shake loose the scratchy mud caught between them. Over the sounds of the mob surging all around me I heard the clicks of a camera. (The battle was being photographed for *Metate,* the college yearbook.)

The mudhole was the first in a series of freshman raggings— some for men, some for women, and some for both—that were part of the highly formalized, college-sponsored state of war between freshmen and sophomores. (The war lasted almost until Christmas.) It included such events as a pie-eating contest, a wheelbarrow race, a tire-pulling battle, and a scrimmage with a six-foot rubber beach ball. As it turned out, the mudhole was about the only part of the war that I was able to fight in, because after that I became absorbed in my studies, and anyway the other contests seemed to call for the kind of outgoing nature that I didn't really have—not to mention sight. And even the recollection of the mudhole—however thrilling the battle was at the time—came to fill me with repugnance. I seem to recall that at least two men were taken to the infirmary from the scene of the battle, without our ever being told exactly who they were or how badly they had been hurt. (The college authorities must have had second thoughts, too. Some time after I left, they changed the fight over the mudhole to a gentler tug-of-war, and eventually paved the mudhole and made it part of Clark Hall parking lot.)

❦

I WAS at the freshman-orientation dinner at Frary Hall. About a half-dozen of us new students got our trays and sat down at a table with our sponsor, a sort of big brother. (Perhaps because of my participation in activities like the mudhole, people had stopped trying to help me do things like get my tray.)

"Can each one of you say a little about yourself?" our sponsor said.

The fellow next to me began, hesitantly, "I have a difficult name—Kaizo Kubo—so people generally call me K. I am twenty-four years old. I'm a junior at Pomona. I'm a transfer student from Reedley Junior College." He paused, as if considering something, and added, "I'm a Nisei. In case some of you don't know, Niseis are Americans of Japanese parentage."

I was immediately taken with him. He was older and seemed different. He spoke with intensity and simplicity. I even detected a certain eagerness in him, suggesting that, like me, he was trying to make up for things he had missed out on.

After the introductions, the conversation was nervous and desultory until our sponsor observed, "Do you all like the mural of Prometheus, on the back wall here? In my opinion, it's our most prized possession."

People looked toward the mural as if they had just noticed it. They exclaimed over the massive thighs of the gigantic, crude naked figure and the striking blues and reds.

"Who in the heck is Prometheus?" K asked. "Who is the painter?"

"According to Greek mythology, Prometheus was a Greek hero who stole light—or, rather, fire—from the gods and brought it to man," our sponsor said. "In mythology, fire symbolizes knowledge. Has anyone heard of the painter Orozco?"

No one had, and our sponsor went on, "José Clemente Orozco is one of Mexico's leading artists, and he wanted to cover all the walls of Frary with figures of Greek gods and giants. But when he finished the mural the college trustees were so scandalized by the naked figure that they wanted to plaster it over. The students organized a protest and saved it. The other murals he planned for Frary ended up in a library at Dartmouth. That was in the thirties, but even today the administration doesn't seem to know what it's got. Even today, ignorant students throw food and salt shakers at it."

It was odd to hear our sponsor, who I'd assumed represented the authorities, disparaging them. But then it occurred to me that the mural might be a symbol of community in Frary Hall, where the men had their meals three times a day throughout their college years, and that our sponsor might be initiating us into that community.

"I AM very fortunate in having met John Zeigel," I wrote home early in the first semester. "We are rooming together. We've got an excellent suite in Clark Hall, with a study, a bedroom, and a bath, and our own phone. Every room or suite in the college has its own phone. John and I have enough things in common to be good friends—he is also a freshman, and his father is also a doctor. We have enough things not in common to improve our natures—he likes Bartók, and I like Offenbach. He has been selected to be a violinist in the college orchestra."

I had met John during the summer session, but we had decided to room together only after attending an orientation lecture at which we happened to sit next to each other. The speaker used a Latin phrase, and I felt frustrated, because I didn't know Latin. John turned to me almost at once and said, "That means 'City of

God.' That's a famous book by St. Augustine." He had been studying French at the summer school, but I had no idea that he also knew Latin. I had never heard of anyone my age who knew Latin. When I asked him about it after the speech was over, he said, "I had four years of Latin at St. Andrew's. Many boys there took Latin. It's a boys' school in Tennessee run by the Episcopal Order of the Holy Cross. In fact, I'm a postulant for the priesthood."

It all sounded unbelievably exotic. He's better educated than I'll ever be, I thought. I'd give anything to know Latin. But even if I started learning Latin right now I'd never catch up with him. Maybe I should room with him. Being around such a person will be ennobling. It will be an education in itself.

John and I had already been assigned separate single rooms. It seemed that for as long as I could remember I had slept in rooms with relatives or in dormitories with a lot of other boys. The thought of having a room of my own, where I didn't have to fret about how I looked—the fear of looking stony-faced in front of others was a constant preoccupation—and could play my Talking Book machine, my phonograph, or my radio any time I liked, was very appealing. All the same, I found myself saying, in a small voice, "What about sharing a suite?"

I was sure he would reject the suggestion out of hand. He had so much to offer me, and I felt I had nothing to offer him. To my surprise and delight, he said, "That's a swell idea. Let's try to change our assigned rooms." It's his charitable nature, I thought. It's his religious self that has made him accept me.

We went together to see Dean Beatty and got ourselves a suite. One of our first nights there, I got into bed and started reading a Talking Book—using my earphones, so as not to disturb John—and John, who had been getting ready for bed, suddenly knelt down in the space between the beds, opened a book, and started half chanting, half singing, "*Credo in unum Deum, Patrem omnipotentem, factorem caeli et terrae, visibilium omnium et invisibilium.*"

I let my earphones drop and lay there, hypnotized. He has such a beautiful singing voice, I thought. I fancied I smelled the wafting incense and melting candle wax of the chapel at my sisters' convent school, where I had once heard such a prayer. Then, as now, I thought I heard an answering echo from above, but was no more sure of what it was saying than of what the words it was echoing had said.

"Genitum, non factum, consubstantialem Patri: per quem omnia facta sunt."

John's prayer came across as a wail, at once repetitive and fresh, yearning and satisfied. The mysterious long words seemed to express my own vague, wordless yearnings and hopes for fulfillment, and the prayer had the ring of an Eastern melody, but with a Western cadence, as if it were set to some higher, universal music. Indeed, it seemed to speak to all my different selves.

"Qui propter nos homines, et propter nostram salutem descendit de caelis."

When John had finished, I asked him if all the boys at his school said their prayers in Latin.

"Not at all. I was just saying them from a Roman Catholic service book because I like the sound of Latin."

I wished that I had gone to a high school that offered Latin. I wished that I'd been born an American. I wished that I were a violinist in the college orchestra, that I had a beautiful voice I could raise to God. I wanted to know Latin, possess it—as if it were a thing, as if it were the Meccano set I used to play with as a child. In fact, I wished that I were John.

IT was registration day. We had all been furnished with the college's annual catalogue—a thick softcover book—and told to study it, choose our courses, and register accordingly. I imagined that everyone else had long since mastered the catalogue, while mine had been sitting on my desk in the study for the last couple of days, because I hadn't figured out how to get it read. Now the day was at hand, and I simply had to put, as it were, a voice in it and make it speak to me—make it tell me what the course offerings were and how I was to proceed. Often, I had thought of asking John, but just as often I had rejected the idea. I felt that my relationships with readers should be independent of my friendships. In that way, I would avoid imposing the special problem of my blindness on my friends, and anyway I would get more work done with my readers, who, after all, were people I had to pay for their time. John was first of all my friend, and my wish to be on an equal footing with him—one of my first sighted friends—was so strong that in front of him I felt embarrassed that I had special needs, that I was blind at all. Yet, paradoxically, the person I immediately thought of for reading the catalogue to me—perhaps becoming a regular reader—was Johnnie Johnstone. And that was because getting her to read to me was about the only excuse I could think of for getting to know her—for having some contact with her, even if it was during paid reading time.

I had barely met Johnnie, but I couldn't get her voice out of my head. It was buoyant, it was considerate, it was careful in its choice of words. Above all, it gave the impression of discriminating intelligence. But I knew I didn't stand a chance with Johnnie; as a friendly, vivacious, outgoing person, she was already on the way to being a very popular girl in the college. I was sure she was going to be a campus figure, a student officer, a cheerleader—one of the girls most sought after by men. Still, during the various orientation events I had discreetly maneuvered to sit near her—to be within the range of her voice, her laughter, the very rustle of her clothes. On the college paths, I had already learned to pick out her practical, no-nonsense step. Unlike many other girls, she walked as if she were wearing sensible walking shoes, and there was a spring to her step which made me imagine that her hair must bounce when she walked. But I didn't want her to know that I had mastered her step—that I was smitten with her—so I never greeted her first. Johnnie, however, never failed to call out "Hi, Ved!" even when she was chattering and laughing with other people. In this and in many other little ways, she seemed exceptionally understanding. Other people slipped by me without a word of greeting, even when they were walking alone; they didn't realize that I knew their steps. Even though I felt that almost anyone who could see had much more to offer Johnnie than I did, I longed to be one of the people she laughed and chattered with. I felt I simply had to find a way of spending some time with her and having her take notice of me. As in the case of John, I thought that association with Johnnie could somehow exalt me, complete me. I was always being led on by visions of greener pastures, which arose from my sense not of envy so much as of inadequacy. Indeed, I was oblivious of other people's inadequacies—alert only to my own, as if the injured body, the injured self, were longing to be made whole.

While I was walking on College Way, mulling over the problem of engaging Johnnie as a reader and getting her to help me register, I heard her step and her voice behind me. "I wish I were like those rich girls, and didn't have to work," she was saying to someone in parting. "But I've just got to get myself a job, before they're all gone. The problem is that I don't know what courses I'll be taking yet, what my schedule will be."

Sensing her just a few steps behind me made me want to run away and hide, as if the mere act of my imagining any connection with her had violated her. I was certainly invaded by a feeling of shame for my longing for her, for my need for help, for any kind of dependency—shame for my blindness.

"Hi, Ved!" Johnnie said, catching up with me.

I was terrified. The top of my head tingled under my dink.

"Have you registered yet?" Johnnie asked. "What courses are you taking?"

"Well, I don't know yet," I said, my throat dry. "I have to go through the catalogue before I can register."

"You mean you haven't even done that yet?"

"Not really—there's been no way for me to really read it." I must not get tongue-tied, I thought. It's now or never. "When I took a course this summer, the way I got my reading done was to pay someone in the class to read the assignments out loud to me. Now that college is starting, I'll need readers again." I tried to control my trembling. After all, it's a job I'm proposing—not a date, I thought. I must sound businesslike. "Would you be interested in being a reader? We are bound to be in some of the same classes. I pay by the hour—seventy-five cents."

"That sounds great." I couldn't believe my ears. I was still shaking from the effort of having broached the idea, but her reaction was quick, direct, and actually enthusiastic. "I've never read aloud, but I think I could do it. Reading would certainly be better than waiting tables or sitting behind a checkout counter in the library, and it pays just as well. But—" She paused. "But I couldn't accept money from you, especially if I'm just sitting and reading my assignments to you."

"The money doesn't come out of my pocket. It's the state that pays—the state has a readers' fund for college students in my situation." I wasn't able to get out the word "blind."

"I don't know my schedule yet. When will you need me to begin?"

She is going to be my reader, I thought. I'll get to be with her on a regular basis, hear her voice, maybe daily. I'll have her to myself, speaking only to me. A date can be a one-time affair, but a job—it goes on and on.

"Well, I have to go through the catalogue today to register."

"I can help you after lunch, if you like."

Throughout lunch, I fretted over the problem of getting Johnnie to sign a loyalty oath to the State of California. The state agency in charge of payment for my readers had instructed me that every reader had to sign a loyalty oath before his or her application for payment could be processed, and had sent me a whole ream of cyclostyled loyalty oaths for the purpose. I'd heard that several professors in the state-university system had refused to sign the oath, and I called up the agency and protested to a harried-sounding woman. I asked her what I was supposed to do if some readers refused to sign the oath. "Then they're Communists, and you should have no truck with them," she said. "Just look for new readers. You might be hiring them, but we're paying for them. They're state employees."

Writing this today gives me pause, but I was living in the California of the early fifties, when anti-Communism was virulent, and people seemed almost to be getting ready for an atomic war. For instance, in the front of the student telephone directory, which every student was furnished with, was printed this admonition:

When and if an Atom Bomb falls:

1. Try to get shielded—bomb shelters listed below. If caught outdoors, seek shelter alongside a building or jump into any handy ditch or gutter.

2. Drop flat on ground or floor.

3. Bury your face in your arms.

4. Don't rush outside right after a bombing.

5. Don't take chances with food or water in open containers.

6. Don't start rumors.

Appended to it was a list of more than a score of bomb shelters—halls and basements of practically all the college residential and classroom buildings.

Now, at lunch, I couldn't eat my Waldorf salad, even though it was my favorite food, for worrying over Johnnie's reaction to the oath. At Cal, people are state employees and at least know what they're getting into, I thought. But this is a private college, and no one seems to know anything about the oath. At summer school, I had discovered that none of my readers had ever heard of it. Though they had all signed it, I knew that I myself wouldn't have signed it—and if I had had the choice I wouldn't have had anyone else sign it. And I was no Communist. I was afraid Johnnie would refuse point-blank. She seemed so bright and independent.

The first thing I did when Johnnie and I met to read the catalogue was to hand her the loyalty oath and ask her if she would mind signing it. We were sitting on the steps of Big Bridges Hall, the only quiet spot we could find without wasting time. (Since the beginning of summer school, I had been talking to the authorities about finding a fixed place where I could work with women readers—men and women were not allowed in each other's rooms under any circumstances—but they hadn't yet been able to come up with anything.)

"What in God's name is this?" she asked, and she read the oath aloud as if her voice were on tape, and the tape and the tape recorder were in fast-forward mode. " 'I, blank, do solemnly swear (or affirm) that I will support and defend the Constitution of the United States and the Constitution of the State of California against all enemies, foreign and domestic—' " She paused long enough to exclaim "Heavens to Betsy!" and then read on: " 'That I will bear true faith and allegiance to the Constitution of the United States and the Constitution of the State of California; that I take this obligation freely, without any mental reservation or purpose of evasion; and that I will well and faithfully discharge the duties upon which I am about to enter. And I do swear (or affirm) that I do not advocate, nor am I a member of any party or organization, political or otherwise, that now advocates the overthrow of the Government of the United States or the State of California by force or violence or other unlawful means; and within the five years immediately preceding the taking of this oath (or affirmation) I have not been a member of any party or organization, political or otherwise, that advocated the overthrow of the Government of the United States or the State of California by force or violence or other unlawful means except as follows . . .' " She looked up from the paper and burst out laughing.

"Hadn't you heard of the loyalty oath?"

"Not me, I swear—or should I say affirm?"

"I'm afraid I have to get you to sign this oath. All my readers have to, as state employees."

She laughed again. "Let's see—five years ago, I was thirteen. What did I belong to? Girl Scouts? No one would say *they* were Communists." She read the rest of the oath: " '(If no affiliations, write in the words "no exception") and that during such time as I am a member or employee of the (name of public agency) I will not advocate or become a member of any party or organization, political or otherwise, that advocates the overthrow of the Government of the United States or of the State of California by force or violence or other unlawful means.' "

"Then you don't mind signing?"

"Why should I?"

"Do you think other readers would mind?"

"Why should they? No one here at amiable Pomona could be plotting to overthrow our government."

She signed the loyalty oath with a lot of crackling of the paper and scratching of the pen, and handed the sheet back to me, saying jokingly, "Cross my heart and hope to die, I'll read nothing to you that will make you want to overthrow the government."

I was relieved, but also disappointed at the thought that Johnnie—and, by extension, Pomona—might be politically asleep. Johnnie had already turned to the catalogue.

"Can you read me the requirements for courses?" I asked.

"The first requirement I think you ought to know about is that we all have to take phys ed every year, because, the catalogue says, Pomona believes we should have 'knowledge of the structure and functions of the human mechanism; understanding of the hygienic practices which promote physical, mental, and social health; reasonable skill in developmental and recreational activities of a physical type which will promote the individual's well-being during college years, and in later life; and a disposition to make such knowledge and skill essential elements in effective living.' They really go in for some puffery, don't they?"

I tried not to think about Johnnie, her voice, her breathing by my side, and the movement of her lips around the big words. I gritted my teeth and channelled all the powers of my concentration into what she was reading—into the catalogue.

"And here is something else that everyone has to be careful about. You're a foreigner, so your English is very good, because you learned it properly, but it says here, 'In the evaluation of all academic exercises the quality of English used by the student will be weighed together with the soundness and completeness of his thinking. Faculty members are expected to report—' Blah, blah, blah. 'A student whose English is persistently unacceptable' may be asked to leave. Get this: 'Habitual and flagrant misspelling is considered a deficiency in English to which this regulation applies.' "

I found Johnnie's manner of reading the catalogue exasperating. She would skip around, dip into paragraphs and move on, read aloud little snatches, paraphrase, begin something and stop to make a comment. But I suppressed my irritation, for fear of losing her as a reader. It's probably very irritating for her to have to read it aloud, I thought, trying to see things from the other person's point of view—something my father had drummed into the heads of all of us children. If you're intelligent enough to take in a page at a glance, it must be very tedious to have to say it all slowly aloud. I moved closer to Johnnie on the step, touching ever so lightly the hem of her skirt.

"The catalogue says that the college is here to give us a good, liberal-arts education," she was saying. "Therefore, all Pomona students must take seven required courses, each lasting a full year." She looked up from the catalogue and said, "The girls in the dorm call these courses the Seven Pillars of Wisdom." She read—or, rather, talked—on, and, from what I could gather, the Seven Pillars were an English course consisting of reading and writing, a course in a biological science, a course in a physical science, two courses in the social sciences, a course in literature, art, or music, and a course in philosophy or religion. "These pillars, as you can imagine, are the foundation of our curriculum, of our liberal-arts education, which is to prepare us, it says here, for 'leadership in diverse roles and offices, humble or great,' and 'a life in which professional achievement is accompanied by personal happiness, cultural balance, and social responsibility.' That's really putting a lot of weight on those poor pillars!"

She's being a little offhand, I thought. But then she's a woman. It is the man who has to carry the burden of the world on his shoulders. It is he who has to provide for her; to be a leader among men, like the Ghosts; to succeed in his profession; to buy a house; to create the kind of world the catalogue is describing, in which she will be safe and will be able to raise a family. Even as I thought this, I couldn't think of myself as that man. I had no confidence that I would ever be able to provide for myself, let alone for her.

"We have to be done with the pillar courses by the end of our junior year," Johnnie was saying. "But it says here we should probably also start taking some courses in our major in the first two years."

I looked at my watch. We had already spent about an hour's reading time, and hadn't even got to the descriptions of specific courses. "What do they say about specific courses? Can you find that quickly?"

"They list all the departments here in alphabetical order, and it tells you all the courses and majors, or concentrations, that the college offers."

"Please do read them out." I feared I was sounding impatient and peremptory in spite of myself.

"There are a lot of them."

"I know, but I'd like to get some idea."

"Well, if that's what you want. But I'll just read a course or two in each department. Otherwise, we'll be here past registration, and until midnight. Most of the courses are probably too advanced for us to take anyway. 'Art . . . History of Art. Mr. Slive. A study of the historical development of art with special

attention to an analysis of the works examined. . . . Astronomy
. . . Celestial Mechanics. Mr. Whitney. A short course in the
application of the laws of mechanics and gravitation to the mo-
tions of the heavenly bodies, with problems on the prediction of
eclipses and occultations and on the computation of the orbit
of comets. . . . Biology . . . Genetics. Mr. McCarthy.
This course considers modern developments in the study
of heredity and evolution and their general application to
plant and animal breeding and to eugenics and race questions.
. . . Geology . . . Introduction to Geology. Mr. Shelton.
A survey of geologic principles and processes, and of earth
history.' "

At the Arkansas school, we had had no choice of courses. The
curriculum for the ninth through the twelfth grades was fixed, as
was the daily schedule of classes and activities, and it had taken
me a year of campaigning and petitioning to get the school
authorities to introduce one new course—elementary French, the
first foreign language that the school had ever offered. But here
there were courses not only in art, astronomy, biology, and geology but also in botany, zoology, music, history, economics, government, chemistry, mathematics, psychology. There were
language offerings in Greek and Latin and German and French
and Spanish and Russian and Chinese. I felt like a man starved
since childhood who had finally been led up to a table laden with
every kind of delectable food. I felt like a know-nothing, who
would have to sit at the feet of a professor—an expert—in order
to learn anything at all. I wanted—I thought I needed—to learn
everything the college had to offer, even if it took twenty, thirty,
maybe forty years.

"I think I'd like to take that course in Celestial Mechanics
with Mr. Whitney," I said.

Johnnie put the catalogue down on her lap. She was silent,
and then she laughed, in her rather forced way. "But you can't
possibly take astronomy," she said. "How could you manage the
telescopes and such?"

"History of Art, then. Genetics. Introduction to Geology." I realized I was almost shouting.

"Didn't you tell me you wanted to become a lawyer or a journalist? Why are you interested in these courses?"

She had a point. Even when I was shouting, I knew that History of Art, Genetics, and Introduction to Geology were no more available to me than Celestial Mechanics. It seemed that sight was an unwritten prerequisite for the courses in many departments. If it wasn't observing through a telescope, viewing paintings, dissecting frogs, or charting chemical reactions or rock formations, then it was dealing with complicated graphs, symbols, and characters, beyond the capacity of Braille. There are so many subjects I can never major in, I thought. If I take any of those subjects, it will have to be only the most elementary courses, to fulfill the Seven Pillars requirements. The lack of sight is an obstacle to studying the subjects that attract me, just as it is to getting Johnnie to think of me in a romantic way—to getting a date at all. I felt deficient, frustrated, as if my high ambitions—to get the best education I could at college, and to find there a life's companion—were crashing around me. The sun suddenly seemed very hot, pressing me down, shrivelling up my soul.

"Besides," Johnnie was saying kindly, "I thought you said before that you're on a scholarship. You want to take courses in which you'll do well—get good grades."

She's so smart, I thought. She knows so much about the world.

She was saying, "I forgot to tell you, the catalogue lists times and days for all the courses. But you tell me what pillar courses you'd like to take, and I can rough out a schedule and see if the times work out."

Whatever my ambitions, four short years are all I have at college, I thought. I must make the most of my opportunity. "I think I'll have to take mainly courses in things that basically involve reading, like history and philosophy," I said. Above all, I wanted to add English, but her remark about the scholarship and good grades made me have second thoughts. I became afraid that as a foreigner who had really been speaking English for only three years I wouldn't be able to do well in English courses—compete successfully with Americans, for whom English was a first language. I recalled that Johnnie thought my English was better for my having learned it as a foreigner, but I was sure that she—and the world—would think English courses were best suited to girls. I associated subjects like history with masculine pursuits, with leadership, diplomacy, worldliness, and associated subjects like English with feminine pursuits, with motherhood, enjoyment, personal fulfillment.

It turned out that because of the anticipated size of the freshman enrollment in certain pillar courses each of those courses had been divided up among different professors in the department, and were taught at different times on different days, including Saturday. Johnnie and I consulted the front of the catalogue, which listed the faculty members by rank, with their titles, years of arrival at the college, and degrees, along with the names of the universities they had attended, and I eventually settled on History of the Development of Western Civilization, with John Gleason (professor, 1939; B.A., Ph.D., Harvard; B. Litt., Oxford); the History of European Philosophy, with W. T. Jones (professor, 1938; B.A., Swarthmore; B. Litt., Oxford; Ph.D., Princeton); Elementary French and Elementary French Conversation, with Robert F. Leggewie (assistant professor, 1951; B.S., Loyola; M.A., University of Southern California; A.M., Ph.D., Harvard); Introduction to Music, with Daryl Dayton (associate professor, 1938; B.Mus., Oberlin College; graduate study in Berlin and New York with Artur Schnabel, Leonard Shure, Dalies Frantz, and Guy Maier); Fundamentals of Speech, with Benjamin Scott (professor, 1923; B.A., University of Southern California; S.T.B., Ph.D., Boston University; graduate work, Brown and Harvard); and two physical-education courses. I was especially pleased with my choice of philosophy and history professors, because I had grown up hearing that Oxford was the mecca of the academic world. (Johnnie, like me, had chosen History of Western Civilization and French, and she was also signing up for introductory courses in geology, government, and poetry.)

By the end of registration day, Johnnie and I were walking around to various tables set up on the grass of Marston Quadrangle, picking up forms, filling them out with the code numbers and meeting times of the courses I wanted to take, and handing them in, all in a certain mysterious order. All through this time with Johnnie, the only physical contact I had with her was to touch the hem of her skirt, yet now and again my heart would beat fast, as if we were out on a real date—as if I were having a romantic tryst with her on the secluded steps of a building, as if I were dancing around with her on the grass, showing her off to the world. The only thing was, our "date" had to be kept a secret—especially from her.

ONE evening, in our suite, I was singing, along with the opening bars of a recording of Mozart's "Haffner" Symphony, "Eisenhower is a dumbhead, President Truman come back, come back!" In practically every class of my Introduction to Music course we had a new symphony to learn, and we all made up silly mnemonics to fix the music in our heads. For that day's class we had been assigned the "Haffner" Symphony.

"What in heaven's name are you doing?" John asked.

"I'm trying to do my homework for music class." I felt chastened. Next to him, I considered myself a musical ignoramus. In class, I was hearing many symphonies, by Mozart, Haydn, and Beethoven, for the first time, and was just learning to tell one from another. He listened to and knew by heart works not only by these composers but also by modern composers I had never heard of, like Shostakovich, Stravinsky, and Bartók.

"Putting such horrible words to Mozart is an abomination, a desecration!" he said, sounding pained.

"What is desecration?" I asked meekly. John was always using fascinating big words whose meaning I didn't know.

"Desecration? It's an insult to the sacred nature of something. It would be like painting a clown's nose on a picture of Jesus Christ."

I revered Jesus Christ, with Buddha and Socrates, as one of the greatest men who had ever lived. I didn't want to do anything to insult him, so after John's reprimand I tried very hard to learn the music without resorting to mnemonic devices. I could never think of using one without feeling bad—without calling up the image of Jesus Christ defaced with a clown's nose.

❧

I TRIED never to have a reader in the suite when I thought my roommate might be around, because I felt embarrassed and also because I didn't want to disturb him. One afternoon, when I knew that John had orchestra practice, I arranged to read a philosophy assignment with Eugene Rose in the suite. I felt very lucky to have found Gene as a reader. His own work was so well organized that he seemed to have plenty of time to give to me, and he read with such clarity that I almost had the illusion that he was explaining things. The assignment was hard and I was concentrating on it. Suddenly, the door opened and John walked in. Gene broke off his reading.

"John, I thought you were at orchestra rehearsal," I said sheepishly.

"The rehearsal was cancelled," he said, setting down his violin. He went over to his desk, pulled up his chair, and started shuffling papers, as if he intended to settle down to study. I felt I couldn't ask Gene to stop. He had saved the time for me and was counting on being paid for it. Yet I felt mortified at the thought of doing my work in front of John. The study was mine as much as his, and he often studied with music pouring out of the phonograph or practiced his violin in the room. But somehow, in my state of heightened self-consciousness, my reading seemed more of an intrusion in the room than his music ever had. Still, I didn't say anything to Gene—just hoped that John would either go into the bedroom or leave the suite. He resumed reading, and I felt flustered and distracted.

When I proposed living with John, I hadn't stopped to think that there might be occasions when I would want to read in my room. Later, when I did realize that, I thought that John could read in one room and I in the other. But the bedroom was very small. There was no desk or chair in it—just two beds and a night table cramped together. I couldn't imagine reading in it with a reader. And John was the kind of person who had to be sitting at a desk with a proper light from a lamp falling on his book. He said that when he read in bed he fell asleep.

"John, would you like us to move?" I asked after a while.

"Well, a friend is coming over," he said, without looking in my direction, as if he were upset with me. "I don't want to force you out, but we have to do our Latin together."

I felt annoyed. I wanted to say that I had as much right to the study as he did, and that I had started working in it first, and to ask why he and his friend couldn't study in his friend's room. At the same time, I was afraid that if I took a position that was within my rights as an occupant of the suite he would mistake it as a plea for special consideration. And that was the thing I most wanted to avoid. I didn't want him to feel that sharing a suite with me was a burden in any way. So I told Gene we'd have to leave off reading.

"I've been reading only a few minutes," he said, standing up. "I won't charge you for this session."

I wanted to protest. I wanted to insist that he charge me. Readers generally put aside chunks of two hours' reading time for me, and if they turned up to do the job I felt that they should be paid. But I said nothing. I didn't want to get into a discussion with him about all that in front of John.

That day was the beginning of my realization that I couldn't comfortably room with John, or perhaps with anyone—that I had to sacrifice my overwhelming need for companionship for the greater need, as I saw it, to get my work done. I needed to retreat with my problems within the four walls of a room of my own. I dreaded the prospect of living alone, of having to make an arrangement every time I wanted to be with someone, instead of just coming home to my suite and finding a roommate there, but I felt I had no choice. In due course, John and I agreed to room separately, and put in our requests to Dean Beatty for single rooms, and an awkwardness settled over our friendship, perhaps because neither of us ever discussed what had gone wrong. I now realize that if I had been a bolder, more self-confident person I might have confronted John with my needs and problems and battled it out with him, and, if sharing a suite with him didn't work out, found another roommate. For all I know, that would have been a better, "healthier" way. But that was not my way at the time. I did plenty of battle in areas that involved only me, but when they involved someone else—someone sighted—I tended to withdraw into my shell.

FOR the first time, I was on my way to Honnold, the main library for the Associated Colleges, which had just been completed and inaugurated. I wasn't familiar with the path, and I was forced to walk slowly. I felt anxious, because I didn't want to keep Jane di Stasi, my second reader from my philosophy class, waiting. Usually, Jane read to me in any empty classroom we could find; that was the arrangement I had worked out with women readers during the summer. But that morning Mr. Jones had assigned us some pages from Windelband's "History of Philosophy," which, he said, he had put on reserve at Honnold. That meant that the book had to be read in the library and returned to the reserve desk within two hours of being checked out. I wondered whether the library authorities would find us a spot at Honnold where Jane could read aloud. If not, would they make an exception for me and let me take the book out? But Honnold was off the beaten path of the Pomona campus, and I feared we would lose valuable reading time looking for a classroom. I picked up my pace, stumbled on a step, regained my balance. Finally, I was inside the library's two sets of double doors. I snatched the dink off my head and stuffed it into my pocket.

Jane was waiting for me at the reception desk. We wasted a good hour going from person to person, from desk to desk, trying to work out some arrangement for me to read the book, only to be told that I could not take the book off the premises and that there was no private spot where Jane could read aloud to me without disturbing other students. Maybe I should have gone to Cal after all, I thought. The university has graduated dozens of blind students and must have separate cubicles for them—maybe a separate library, where they can work with readers. But here I must make a plea for special consideration. I didn't want to get a reputation for doing that, but there seemed to be no help for it. I called Dean Beatty, and, with his intercession, Jane and I were permitted to sit with the book on a window ledge in a corner of the stacks on the third floor and read.

"The assignment looks a little dense. How do you want me to read?" Jane asked. There was an irritating buzz from the fluorescent light, and we had scarcely half an hour left of a two-hour reading session.

"Just read," I snapped. Then, feeling guilty, I added, "Would you like to get a drink of water before we begin?"

"I'm fine," she said.

"Do you have a pencil for underlining? Later, I'd like to be able to go over the pages and type out some notes."

"But this is a library book, and anyway there's no place to type here."

"Oh, I forgot." I'll have to underline in my head, I thought. But this will never do. I really must press for a room of my own in the library. It must have chairs and a desk, a place for my typewriter, an electrical outlet for my tape recorder.

Jane was reading, " 'That, however, a single cosmic matter, or world-stuff, lies at the basis of the entire process of nature, appears in ancient tradition as a self-evident presupposition of the Ionic School. The only question was to determine what this elementary matter was. The nearest course was then to seek for it in what was given in experience, and so Thales declared it to be water; Anaximenes, air. To this choice they were probably determined only by the mobility, changeability, and apparent inner vitality of water and air.' "

As I came to write this scene, I remembered the passage quoted here only vaguely. I had to look it up. Even reading it now, I had to puzzle out the meaning. At the time, I must have found the passage opaque and brain-numbing. The book was a translation from philosophical German. I wonder how Jane's reading could have made any sense of it, even though she was a sophomore, and what, if anything, I could have got out of it.

" 'It is evident, too, that the Milesians thought little in this connection of the chemical peculiarities of water and air, but only of the states of aggregation concerned,' " she continued. " 'While the solid appears in itself dead, moved only from without, the liquid and volatile make the impression of independent mobility and vitality; and the monistic prepossession of this first philosophising was so great that the Milesians never once thought of asking for a reason or ground of this ceaseless change of the cosmic matter, but instead assumed this as a self-intelligible fact—a matter of course—as they did all change or occurrence; at most they described its individual forms.' "

On top of everything else, I had trouble taking in the words because of the music of Jane's voice. Her voice was like a clarinet. I wanted to listen to it without a time limit. I wanted to have it to myself—take it home and play it at will. In fact, I was conscious only of Jane sitting next to me on the window ledge and of my overwhelming desire to put my arm around her, to embrace her. I kept my arm at my side by sheer force of will. If I so much as touch her with the back of my hand, she'll quit as a reader, I thought. Word will get out. People will think I'm a letch. I'll have no one to read philosophy to me—no women readers at all. I'll fail. I have to be purer than a man who's taken a vow of celibacy. If I am to become a scholar, I'll have to suppress all desire. I'll have to become deaf to the voices, and listen only to the words. "Listen to Windelband, forget Jane. Listen to Windelband . . ." I kept repeating to myself, somehow thinking that, like abracadabra, the incantation would bring about what I wished.

" 'The reason for this lies probably in the fact that in the school, which for a time was widely extended, various trends of thought ran side by side,' " Jane was reading. But reason for what? Which school? " 'And that among these the general fundamental thought, first brought forward perhaps by Philolaus, was worked out in different ways. It would be of great service to attempt such a separation.' " She looked up from the book, and said, "This is a good place to stop. I have to go to phys ed."

My heart sank. I wanted to review. I wanted to read on, ask her for the spelling of this name or that proper noun. But I asked matter-of-factly, "How many pages have we read?"

She turned some pages. "A little less than five."

"How long is the book?"

She flipped the book over. "Six hundred and eighty-one pages."

My God, we've read only five pages in half an hour, I thought. At this rate, a book that costs a few dollars to buy will cost me many times that sum to read.

"I really have to go," Jane said.

"Thank you very much," I said, standing up. I sounded as cold and formal to my ears as a viceroy.

"Do you want me to show you the way down?"

"No, I know my way," I said. "I'll return Windelband. You go—go."

She picked up her handbag and was gone.

I was often bedevilled by lustful thoughts when I had a woman reader or any kind of brush with a woman. My desire seemed to roam and prowl and reach out in every direction. Jane di Stasi, Johnnie Johnstone, Anne Lockwood—it seemed that it almost didn't matter who the object of my desire was. From my present perspective, this indiscriminate interest in women suggests an emotional promiscuity, but it was precisely because my desire remained unsatisfied, was not nourished by a single romantic involvement in which my feelings might have been reciprocated—might have found a voice, an expression, a home, an attachment—that I was desperate, frustrated, wild. One pretty-sounding girl—perhaps any compassionate woman—would have done as well as the next.

This lovesickness, I now feel, may have stemmed from homesickness. I had left home at fifteen, in the bloom of adolescence, and so had been abruptly separated from all the people who loved me and whom I trusted. Somehow, at the Arkansas School for the Blind my homesickness had been in some measure supportable, because I was in the familiar world of the blind and was able to make friends on an equal footing. But now, at college, I found myself, for the first time—and, it seemed, for good—in the cold world of the sighted. The predicament was challenging but also frightening; heady but also isolating. Every day, I felt more inadequate, because I had to live and study—socialize and learn—by standards that were not set with the difficulties of the blind in mind. Yet, of course, I wanted to raise myself to those standards, prove myself worthy of them, live by them. But I was too different to fit in, not only because I couldn't see but also because I wasn't athletic, I didn't have money, I didn't have a car, I wasn't a Southern Californian—I wasn't even an American. There were a hundred reasons for feeling inadequate. So, naturally, I imagined that if this sighted girl or that sighted girl accepted me it would be a sign that I had met the standards, that I had made the grade. Being connected with just one girl would light up not only the pages of the book she read to me but also the path to social acceptability, and would make me a participant in events at which I was only a wistful bystander—would almost restore my sight.

❦

AROUND the time I got my single room, I was also given an office in Honnold Library—an office all my own, with its own door and lock, to which I had the key. It smelled of fresh paint and new furniture, and was so spacious that I could almost have held conferences in it. No other student had an office in the library, and my special status embarrassed me at first. But no one seemed to take any notice of it, and I soon got used to going in and out of the office, in and out of the library, as if it were as natural for me to have an office of my own and do all my studying out loud with readers as it was for other students to sit communally in the library and read silently to themselves. From eight o'clock in the morning, when the library doors were unlocked, to ten at night, when they were shut, unless I was in class or at meals I was in my office, working with a relay of readers, getting them to read fast, and to tape-record key passages from the books, or from notes I had typed out on the books, or from notes they had taken on lectures. At the end of the long day, I would cart the tape recorder to my room and stay up late into the night reviewing the material. Yet I was steadily falling behind in my work. Even though I spent practically every waking minute reading, and constantly urged my readers to read ever faster, I seemed never to catch up. To compound my frustration, my ear took in information at the crawl of a tortoise, while my mind was ready to absorb it at the pace of a running Achilles. With the passing of each week, the backlog of reading grew—exponentially, it seemed. At night, I would feel like a spent force, without the mental energy even to read a novel on a Talking Book record. Yet I couldn't fall asleep. The pressure of assignments unread would build up in me like the water in a sealed kettle on top of a lighted burner, and I would seethe and boil until I couldn't stay in bed. I would creep out of bed, drink water, take aspirin, take a shower, put on music. When I did get back into bed and fall asleep, I would wake up a few minutes later with a heavy head. Sometimes I would slip out of my room, take the first unlocked bicycle I could find standing in an archway, and go riding in the empty streets—along Sixth Street, down College Avenue, along Third Street, up College Way, making a sort of tour of the main arteries of the campus. I would pedal hard, breathe in the eucalyptus- and pepper-scented air, wonder how I would get through college: how I would survive midterms and finals, college semesters and years; how I would get the grades necessary to continue obtaining financial aid; how I would ever get a college degree. I would return to the room dead tired, with the childish certainty that Mehtas didn't fail, that it was all a matter of hard work, that I would somehow manage. I would fall into such a deep sleep that an earthquake probably couldn't have awakened me.

The pressure of getting reading done was combined with the pressure of having to write papers on what I read. One week, I had to turn in three papers: one for Mr. Gleason, on how Charlemagne helped to make Europe safe for Christianity; one for Mr. Jones, on the Milesians' theories of cosmic matter; and one for Mr. Dayton, on the style of Mozart's symphonies. Each of the courses relied mostly on one standard textbook—in the case of Mr. Jones' philosophy course, a textbook he himself had written—and the lectures parroted what was in the textbook. All I had to do, therefore, was repeat back to the professor, in summary form, the relevant pages of the textbook or the relevant bit of his lecture. Nothing could have been simpler, in theory. But in practice I was stumped.

The first of the three papers due was the one on Charlemagne, and I got one of my history readers, Jay Wilcoxen, to read me the pertinent pages in the textbook, R. R. Palmer's "A History of the Modern World." After Jay left, I sat down at my typewriter, fidgeting with the keys. I inadvertently pressed a key a little too hard, and a letter jumped out and struck the paper. I backspaced, hoping to go over the mistake when the right word came to me, only to have another letter jump out. Whatever I type, I won't be able to read over, correct, revise, I thought. It has to be perfect on the first go-round. I tore the piece of paper out of the typewriter and inserted a new one. To keep my restless fingers still, I put my hands under me, but without the keys beneath my fingers, without the clicking sound, I felt blocked, as if I needed physical contact with the typewriter to write at all. I put my fingers back on the home row.

At the Arkansas school, I had reviewed material in Braille and written most of my themes in Braille, so I was able to read, revise, and rewrite them. Later, at Pomona summer school, I had somehow got along without being able to review and revise on my own—perhaps because I was taking only one course, whose assignments consisted mostly of reading stories, and those were easy to retain and regurgitate. But the material in my history course was so full of unfamiliar names, dates, and concepts that I felt that even with my tape-recorded notes I couldn't write anything half decent. I felt I needed to read along what I was writing, to be sure that it was coherent and made sense. I felt I needed to flip through the pages of Palmer on Charlemagne, check things in the index, look at a map.

"Charlemagne won back northeastern Spain for Europe," I wrote in my head, and realized with a sinking feeling that, because the material had been read to me, I didn't know how to spell "Charlemagne"—or, for that matter, "Pyrenees," "Aix-la-Chapelle," "Carolingians," and many other proper names that I had encountered in Palmer for the first time and knew only by sound. I should have got Jay to spell the words for me, I thought, but then it occurred to me that even if I had interrupted his reading every time we hit a new proper name, and had risked losing the thread of the narrative in order to have him spell the word for me, I probably wouldn't have retained it as well as if I had read the word with my fingers. There was something about reading a word for myself that helped me to visualize it, to make its configuration of dots almost automatically imprint itself on my brain. *I'm going to misspell, muddle everything in this paper.* Get Jay to read the chapter over to you and look things up for you. *But he's already read the material once. I can't afford to have him read it again and again.* Do it this once, and in future tape-record more carefully when you need material for a paper. *But I still won't know how to spell things.* Then type the paper first and ask Jay to correct the spellings afterward. *But I'll feel embarrassed. He'll think I'm stupid.* You are working yourself up into a lather. Where there's a will, there's a way.

My legs felt as if they were in irons, but I somehow walked over to Jay's room, in Smiley Hall. He was busy writing his Charlemagne paper, but I interrupted him and got him to come back and tape-record some of Palmer's text on Charlemagne. Alone again, I reviewed the taped material and typed a few sentences, not caring how I spelled proper nouns, how I said what I said. Then I got stuck again. I'm stupid, I thought. I don't deserve to be at college. I went and lay down on my bed. My head felt full of cobwebs. I eventually fell asleep.

I woke with a lightning thought: I will dictate my paper—I will get Jay to take it down. Then I can ask him to look things up—even pick up direct quotes from the book. He can read the paper back to me and I'll be able to go over what I wrote and correct it. By composing aloud, I may even be able to make my papers better than anyone else's. I'll write by the sound of the words, by the rhythm of the language. By God, I'll make my papers sing! Every cloudy sky has a bit of blue. I'll turn my disadvantage to advantage.

I felt exhilarated, light-headed, almost heard my unwritten paper singing in my head. But Jay is a busy student, I thought, sobering up. He doesn't have that much time. Anyway, Jay was a forceful, critical, cut-and-dried sophomore. The idea of his sitting poised to take my dictation frightened me. Suppose the words don't come to me on demand in front of him, I thought. Suppose

I dictate gibberish to him? He will know how incompetent, how stupid I am. The word will soon be out that I am a dumbhead. I'll lose face. I'll be done for. I have to find someone who is not a fellow-student, someone who has not read the same book, someone who is not writing the same paper, someone with whom I am not in competition, someone who has endless time, endless patience—someone who has the understanding of a woman. And then I remembered Miss Harriet Rietveld.

Early in the school year, Miss Rietveld had stopped me on College Way, taken my hand, and introduced herself. "I hear that you work with readers," she had said. "If you ever need additional help, please think of me. The only problem is, you'll have to come to me at Kenyon House." She had gone on to say that she was the head resident of Kenyon House, where a dozen or so girls who liked to practice speaking Spanish lived; that her duties there were light; that she had no family; and that the only thing that took her out of the college was Quaker meetings, so she had plenty of free time available and enjoyed doing volunteer work. I thanked her and told her I would call her if I needed her. I liked her manner—it was apologetic and gentle. But I had dismissed her from my mind as a lonely lady, a well-meaning, do-gooder type, who was probably not very well educated, when what I needed was young, enthusiastic, crackerjack college students who had to earn money and would read with almost automatic comprehension, so that I could comprehend in the same way. In any case, it was clear to me that Miss Rietveld wanted to be a volunteer reader, and I generally avoided volunteers, because I had heard that they tended to be undependable. Good will wore thin, but the need for an income was as solid as a rock. Then, too, Kenyon House was the last of the residence halls for women, at the far southeast end of the campus. The idea of walking under a whole block of windows, through which women in who knew what stages of dress and undress might be looking down at me, and then going into a house in which women actually lived and breathed was intimidating. I imagined that wherever she and I sat down to work girls would be constantly coming and going. But now my need to get my paper written swept aside my qualms. Perhaps Miss Rietveld is just the person to help, I thought. It was late evening, but I got up and walked over to Kenyon House as if it were the most ordinary thing to do.

"What would you like to dictate to me?" Miss Rietveld asked after I had explained the purpose of my visit and told her that I must insist on paying her for the work.

"My papers. Do you know typing?"

"Yes. You would talk to me, and I would take it down on the typewriter?"

"Well, not really. The noise of the typing would get on my nerves. Maybe in pencil, and type it later, in your own good time."

"But I don't know shorthand."

"That doesn't matter. I think very slowly. Sometimes I can't think of the right word for five or ten minutes. Would you mind that?"

"I could go and attend to something else while you're thinking."

"Oh, no. That would break my concentration. I'd like you to stay there and be ready for the word when it came."

"Maybe you should talk into a tape recorder."

"That won't do. I have to look up spellings and quotes, look things up in the index—not only that but in the dictionary, in Roget's Thesaurus."

"Oh. So you will want me to read to you, also."

"Well, yes—some. It will be a combination of a lot of things—reading, taking down dictation, typing."

"But I couldn't charge you when I'm just waiting."

"Oh, no, I couldn't think of not paying. You'd be on duty. You would have put aside the time for me."

"How much time would you need?"

"I don't know, but a lot. Whenever I had a paper to do."

"But you know I couldn't work after ten-fifteen in the evening—that's when we lock the doors."

"I know. I can't get anyone to work after ten, even in the men's dormitories. Do you agree? Will you try?"

"I don't mind trying, but I still don't know exactly what is involved."

"I don't know myself. We will have to experiment, just work things out. By the way, where could we work?"

"Right here, I suppose."

"But this is the sitting room."

"But the girls are mostly out or in their rooms. I don't think we'll be bothered. When would you like to begin?"

I wanted to say "Tomorrow" or "On the weekend," to give myself time to adjust to a whole new set of circumstances. Until then, I had composed only with a Braille stylus in my hand or with a typewriter under my fingers. I had never dictated. I would now have to write in a totally different way. I felt like a man who had always typed his thoughts and was suddenly forced to compose with a fountain pen on an unlined pad. But the papers were due that week. Moreover, I was worried that if Miss Rietveld had time to think about the plan she might change her mind, back out.

"Now," I said.

"You don't mean right now?"

"Yes, right now." I made my voice sound as emphatic as I could.

"It's nine-fifteen. We'll only have an hour."

"It'll be a start."

With foresight born of desperation, I had brought along my Palmer and my American College Dictionary. And so it was that Miss Rietveld (she was always Miss Rietveld to me) became my first amanuensis.

"It . . . is interesting to think . . . that before Charlemagne the Muhammadans were vanquished—no, stopped—the

Muhammadans were stopped at the Pyrenees. Otherwise, he could not have made Europe safe for Christianity, as he did."

"How do you spell 'Charlemagne'?"

"I'm not quite sure. Could you look it up in the index of this Palmer book?" I was able to spell "Muhammadan" for her, but she had to look up "Pyrenees." There was a lot of stopping and starting. I would lose the thread of what I had written. She would have to read the sentence back to me. As soon as I heard it, I would start rewriting it.

By the end of the hour, I was telling her to spell the unfamiliar proper nouns any old way, perhaps phonetically, and we would look them up later; to take a new sheet of paper when I rewrote a sentence, so I would have both sentences to choose from; to cut out a sentence from the top of the page and Scotch-tape it in at the bottom; to look for this or that passage in the book. She fumbled, I worried. The hour was over before I had one satisfactory paragraph.

I returned the next day and the day after to dictate to Miss Rietveld. In fact, every time I had to write a paper I repaired to Miss Rietveld at Kenyon House, with a load of books that I had previously underlined and marked with the help of a reader. I became a fixture in the sitting room, almost oblivious of the girls who were coming and going, shouting to each other, or singing in the shower, as they were wont to do. I concentrated only on the paper I had to write. I would dictate something, Miss Rietveld would read it back, it would sound so awful that I would start again. My competence at English and English grammar was comparable to that of a child who sits behind the steering wheel of his father's car thinking he is driving when all he is doing is turning the steering wheel back and forth.

"It sounds fine," Miss Rietveld would say after reading something back to me. "The professor will like it."

"No, it sounds terrible," I would say. We'd begin yet again.

What education she'd had, how much she knew about what she was taking down, how accurately she could tell whether a

draft was better than the one before it I never found out. For she was to me like a wailing wall, to whom I could go to cry out my struggles with words, cry out my tortured sentences and tortured opinions until I somehow became calm for having them written down on paper. I would leave them for her to type out, and somehow, magically, they would get done.

ONE afternoon, as I was going in through the Frary Hall door for lunch, I brushed against someone. I stopped to apologize.

"It is I who should apologize to you." It was K. "I was looking at the mural of Prometheus and hadn't noticed I was blocking the doorway."

"What do you think of the mural? What does it mean to

you?" I asked, trying to prolong the conversation.

"The mural has such rich, earthy tones—you know, I was just reading that Prometheus made men out of clay. Just imagine—men out of clay!" He went on to describe, in a somewhat convoluted way, what he thought the philosophy behind Orozco's mural was, dwelling on Prometheus as an abiding symbol of man's aspiration for knowledge and enlightenment, and on the powerful, vivid colors. His description was a little incoherent but passionate.

K and I soon became fast friends, and we began spending a lot of time together. Students generally studied in the library until it closed, at ten. By that time, many of us were famished—supper was served to us at five-thirty—but there was no place open in Claremont to get a snack. K had a rickety old car, and I often met him in front of the library for a drive to the nearest take-out place, a few miles away. We would pick up hamburgers and Cokes and go back to my room and eat and talk.

Although K was reluctant to talk about himself, I gradually learned some things about him. His parents had come to America from Japan in steerage in the twenties. They had found work in California as day laborers, picking and packing fruit. K was born in San Diego, in 1928. A few months after Pearl Harbor, when he was fourteen, he, his parents, and his three sisters—along with many other people of Japanese descent—were "evacuated" and interned in a temporary restriction center in Santa Anita. From there they were moved to a relocation camp in Poston, Arizona. K didn't like to talk about this time, except to explain why his education had been interrupted. "Sure, we had classes, at Parker Valley High School, in the camp," he told me. "But they were mostly out in the open, and we never did very much. We couldn't—the atmosphere was so bad. I don't remember anyone in the camp who was sympathetic to the Japanese side, but because we had Japanese blood in us we were all suspect. I actually used to think the Americans would kill me, but I prayed for their victory. I don't bear any grudge against America—if the Japanese had been in the Americans' shoes, they would have been much crueller." In 1946, K was separated from his family, and went to work as a houseboy for an American family, the Lundstroms, in Monticello, Indiana. They eventually arranged for his schooling, entering him in the twelfth grade at New Trier High School, in Winnetka, Illinois. He never spoke about Mr. Lundstrom, but he used to refer to Mrs. Lundstrom as his "American mother." "She saved me from starvation," he once said, but didn't explain further. He went on, though, in a tone of surprise mingled with enthusiasm, "Can you imagine? Mrs. Lundstrom was as much devoted to my education as my own mother was, and even though I came to her as a houseboy she wanted me to go to college, and finish it, too, and maybe teach afterward. That was such a happy time. It's strange—when I dream about my mother, I dream about her, too, and I get them mixed up."

After finishing high school, K went to Reedley, a city in the fertile San Joaquin Valley, where his family had settled. For the next six months, he worked alongside his father, picking tomatoes under the hot sun. Then, because he hated manual labor, he ran away. For the next year or so, he wandered around the country doing odd jobs—washing dishes, hawking newspapers, setting up pins in a bowling alley. He ended up at McPherson College, in McPherson, Kansas. After a semester there, he returned to his family in Reedley, and he worked there as a day laborer for two and a half years. In 1950, soon after his father died, he resumed his studies, this time at Reedley Junior College. To help pay for them, he had many part-time jobs, in the fields and on the campus. "In America, there's dignity to manual labor," he told me. "And here I was able at least to go to college. In Japan, with my family so poor, I would probably never have been able to finish high school." At Reedley, K found a mentor in Ridgway Shinn, a young teacher, who himself was only a college graduate but who taught virtually all the courses offered there in history, political science, economics, and sociology. Shinn inspired K to throw himself into his studies and campus activities, so that after finishing Reedley he could go on to a four-year college and earn a B.A. degree. K became the editor of the college literary magazine, the vice-president of the World Affairs Club, and the toastmaster of the school's annual spring banquet.

In 1951, K went to Stanford as a member of his college's delegation to an annual Model United Nations, organized by colleges and universities in three Western states to teach students about the workings and ideals of the United Nations. There he was so dazzled by the performance of the delegation from Pomona— a college he had never heard of before—that he decided to apply to it as a junior-year transfer student. In his application for financial assistance he gave thirty-six hundred dollars as his family's total annual income, made up of his mother's income as a fruit packer, an older sister's income as a secretary in the Psychology and Philosophy Department of Fresno State College, and his own part-time and summer employment. He received a full-tuition grant of six hundred and fifty dollars. He had to come up with as much again for room and board, but he somehow managed.

"JOURNAL" is perhaps too lofty a term for what follows. It consists of short entries on fleeting feelings, thoughts, events, typed out whenever I was alone and had a few spare moments. Inexplicably, sometimes there are college rules copied out verbatim. I probably never thought of the exercise as a proper journal. If I thought of it as anything at all, it was possibly as notes for writing letters home, as talking points for a return home one day, or as a silent friend—someone I could talk to when my feelings overwhelmed me. Indeed, the entries have been sifted from such a chaotic mass of material that I had to edit them in order to reproduce them here at all. I've generally selected entries dealing with things that I don't write about at length elsewhere. Certainly the entries chart, as nothing else does, my hopes and fears, my highs and lows, my soaring dreams for tomorrow and petty frustrations of today. Reading them over has made me realize my essential differentness from the people in that college of the fifties. The entries have been selected from my freshman year:

September 18

Daddyji left Los Angeles yesterday. He must be in Chicago by now—or would it be Lawrence, Kansas? After visiting Boston, Washington, and New York, he will head back to India. Then I won't have him in the country at all anymore. Though I daresay he has enjoyed his stay in the States thoroughly and has rested a good deal, his plans for his future are just as uncertain as mine, and it is uncertainty that deprives him and me of peace of mind.

September 19

Just thinking about the Arkansas school last night brought on a flood of tears. Why did I cry—because I missed the school? If so, it means that I am a sentimental person. If being sentimental is a mark of immaturity, then I am also an immature person. Perhaps I am only frightened because I don't know what's going to happen to me in college.

September 20

Three hundred freshmen have arrived, and the place is swarming and buzzing like a beehive. What a contrast this hurly-burly of humanity is to Miss Marsh's lodgings and my solitary meals at the Sugar Bowl.

September 22

Today starts a new phase in my life. It will write a chapter all its own in my memoir, for, you see, it is registration day. Hence I am no longer merely a high-school graduate but a college man.

September 27

The Saturday-night mixer is even now probably going on full swing. But it seems to me that the mere act of holding a woman on the dance floor would publicly advertise my most urgent secret desire.

September 28

We get less smog than Los Angeles, at least quantitatively, but qualitatively—well, I get different opinions from different people. Some say it's so bad that even the alley cats' eyes water. Mine don't, but that ain't saying much.

September 29

The college food is better than any food I've ever had at any other institution. In fact, it's even better than what we ate at home. Huge salads and fresh-fruit plates, and as much as you can eat. Coats and ties are mandatory for dinner, which is served to us by student waiters. All this is part of what is called "gracious living" here.

September 30

I am the only handicapped person at Pomona, and the only Indian.

October 2

The smog did make my eyes water today. It was a hot, close day, which always brings in a lot of smog. People said they couldn't even see Mount Baldy.

October 4

Balboa Island, Newport Beach, Hermosa Beach, Manhattan Beach, Palos Verdes, Malibu. When I asked a fellow who was going to Newport Beach what that was like, he said, "Oh, you wouldn't be interested. It's very expensive—you know, a fancy sailing club."

October 6

The word "sophomore" comes from the Greek, and means both wise and foolish.

October 8

I need to hear Edward R. Murrow every day. For me, politics is that apple which keeps the doctor away.

October 9

I have to fill out a form every quarter, and send it in to notify Mrs. Watumull of my progress. I must somehow make sure I don't forget, or I might lose my scholarship.

October 10

Pat Corbitt told me that she'll have to cut down on her reading, because she's busy designing and sewing our class banner. She said she might be able to read more once the men "spring" the banner. When that might be she couldn't say, because the banner has to be sprung in front of a lot of people and then raced to Dean Beatty's office without the sophomores' pinching it, so it has to be a surprise. The pity is that my reading time with Pat is now going to be cut down, and I won't be able to participate in the banner-springing, either. But, as Daddyji used to say, "what cannot be cured must be endured."

October 11

Jane told me that her class name is Ahuramazda, but she didn't know that that is the name of a Parsi god. I felt proud to know just this one thing that she, a sophomore, didn't know.

October 12

President and Mrs Lyon asked me to bring along slides of India to the frosh tea. I didn't have any, but the tea was fun anyway. The Lyons are very sweet but very conservative. Mrs.

Lyon said that divorced professors should not be allowed to teach in this college.

October 16

A lot of high jinks, and not just between freshmen and sophomores. K was thrown in the Frary Courtyard fountain.

October 18

At the Arkansas school, I would have been part of the waterdumping from the Sophomore Arch and tire-pulling and pieeating as a matter of course. But here . . . Well, I'm left out. How can I then hope to be a Ghost?

October 22

"Cars, trucks, or any motor vehicle, including airplanes, helicopters, etc., shall not be used in interclass rivalry, including abductions."—Handbook.

October 27

No Braille books are for sale, and even those few that I could borrow from the library I can't keep for more than two weeks at a time. In class, there's no way I can take Braille notes. Even if I weren't made extremely self-conscious, as I am, by the *click-click* of punching dots, no matter how frantically I tried there would be no way I could take down even a cursory summary of the lecture.

November 1

Now I know why so many blind students never go near a college—why they prefer to spend their lives in sheltered workshops. Life in the sighted world for us must be all tooth and claw. But even if only one blind person had succeeded in completing college, then I should be able to do it. I will have to work twice as hard as any other student, and keep up my determination and self-confidence, but always appear modest of demeanor, despite my secret vaulting aspirations.

November 5

Adlai Stevenson lost. The like of him will never be seen. His simple speech conceding defeat, about stubbing his toe, made me convulse with sobs.

November 6

I need readers more than ever, but except for Jay and Jane all of them have stopped coming. They want to study for their own tests. I must get some townspeople as backup readers, or I'm going to fail my tests.

November 10

I have been seriously considering of late becoming a lawyer, and I doubt if this is a passing whim.

November 12

Our class banner has finally been sprung, and my dink is off for good. The banner's background is orangey-gold, and the centerpiece is brick red. The design shows some kind of a curving thing, like a rainbow, and some other little lines, like the teeth of a comb, extending from it, for rain clouds and rain. Our class name is Dekanawida. Dekanawida is a red-Indian rain god. Everyone says that Doug Grayson is sure to become a Ghost. [Grayson is not his real name.] He led the springing of the banner. The Punjabi saying goes, "Seeing another's buttered bread, don't let your mind be disturbed; eat dry and nonwheat bread and drink water." Still, I am disturbed.

November 13

Anita has lived in France, and she has a perfect French accent. I spent half an hour today trying to learn how to pronounce the French "r" from her. I'm so lucky to have her as my French reader.

November 14

I'll have to wait now until I can again be with Daddyji so that he can select a suit for me. I have never bought a suit by myself and lack the confidence to do it. Since I've been in this country, I've had to buy almost every piece of clothing by myself, and I've had to rely on the judgment and sales talk of salesmen. But a suit is such a big item, and I want to buy a good suit that will give me long service.

November 15

My worries about being at college are lightened by the fact that I am a student among Americans, who, as a people, have a real generosity of spirit. They might be immature in their enthusiasms, but they are also sincere. They tend to see the good points of people before their bad points. This in itself creates an encouraging environment for me to live and study in.

November 17

My tape recorder is proving of aid to me every day. It's very helpful for taking notes, and Anita has been reading French into it, and I am learning good French pronunciation because of it. The only difficulty I am having is in lugging the tape recorder from my room to the library and back, but I am not sure yet whether it is imperative for me to have a second tape recorder.

November 18

I had a constructive correspondence with Daddyji about writing my memoir. I believe I should be able to spare two hours a week to devote to such writing, especially if I got a second tape recorder, with a foot control. But what's the use of even thinking about the features a second tape recorder should have, when I can't afford one?

November 21

Another torchlight parade passing outside the window of my room:

RAH!-RAH!-RAH!
P-O-M-O-N-A
P-O-M-O-N-A
FIGHT TEAM FIGHT FIGHT
FIGHT TEAM FIGHT FIGHT
FIGHT TEAM FIGHT FIGHT
FIGHT!

November 23

I hope to take a swimming lesson today for stroke improvement.

November 25

Some readers, when they read, yawn a lot, as if they were starved for oxygen, or the drone of their own voice were putting them to sleep. Other readers seem to find that when they read aloud they don't take in the material themselves. It seems they are so busy enunciating and reading with expression that they can't absorb the material. These are but two of the many problems I am having in getting my work done.

November 30

What comfort is contained in our Indian couplets, which our father used to recite to us when we were growing up. Whenever I get angry with somone, I recite to myself a couplet of Tulsi's and feel better: "In the world, there are different and still more different people. Sit and mix with everyone, the way a boat joins the river."

THE letters I wrote home during the first part of my freshman year suggest that I felt isolated and was reaching out for someone with whom I could share my new experiences. That someone was naturally my father, who was the only one in my immediate family to have been in the West, and who therefore might have at least an inkling of what I was going through. (A few years before his death, in 1986, at the age of ninety, he gave me all his papers to help me with "Continents of Exile," and among them were the letters I'd written to him.) Yet, at the same time, I was wary of telling him too much and so worrying him. I wanted to protect him from me, keep him in the dark about my problems. Rereading my letters now, I find them reserved and distant—filled with philosophizing, generalizing, rationalizing, hemming and hawing. Their sentences are often in the passive voice, the words abstract and formal-sounding. Between the lines, however, is a *cri de cœur*. Before Christmas break, I wrote:

December 9, 1952

MY DEAR DADDYJI,

Please forgive me for not writing you a detailed letter until now. I did not delay writing to you because of my failure to realize my duty or because of any unthoughtfulness on my part. To be honest, there were two reasons that governed my postponement. The first is that our first impressions usually prove unreliable. This is especially applicable in my case, for it takes longer for me to adjust and acquaint myself with new situations and new people. The second is that the strain of finding new readers and of getting used to new situations and methods of studying made me, at first, a little irritative and depressed. I have gone into this long explanation not in vain. You see, this letter will treat some subjects that might be rather hard for you to understand, since you are not here to experience the situation itself. If, therefore, you find a note of pessimism here and there and then a contradictory note of optimism scattered across the pages, please refrain from drawing any conclusions, as my college life is still in its infancy, and perhaps the views at present may be immature and may experience a change as time goes on.

I had considered not writing to you at all about my feelings, as they may cause you worry and concern. But then this would have been failure of my duty. The feelings, be they optimistic or pessimistic, must both be shared with you, for you are the only person who can guide and direct me as to how I can best solve my problems. I admit that perhaps I have sometimes shown hesitancy in accepting your advice. This, of course, was a sign of immaturity. And, as you often remarked, I later returned to your advice, and was thankful for it once I had had the experience for my own self. The desire to experience everything for ourselves varies from individual to individual, and I envy those who are fortunate enough to be able to learn from the experiences of others. Alas! My nature is not constructed in that manner and of that substance. I have the undeniable adventurous streak in me that forces me to live an experience *for myself,* and then, and only then, can I learn from it. If I were writing to someone besides you, I might concern myself with limiting the length of this letter. But I do not have this feeling in writing to you, since I feel you should know me thoroughly.

At the Arkansas school I lived among the people who suffered the same type of handicap as I did. Those who were not handicapped in this manner understood the capabilities of people such as us. Even there I had my ups and downs, as I guess we all must at one time or another. But when we look back on our past we recall only the happy memories and the memories that we cherish and the ones that we would like to relive.

As you know, there I had established myself well. I had the confidence of the students, who honoured me with the presidency, the highest honour they could bestow upon me. I received a medal for having the highest grade in the whole school, from kindergarten to and through the twelfth grade.

It is true that my office as school president took a lot of time and hard work, but my grades did not suffer, because I could do my work myself. I was not dependent for it on anyone else—no one was. In other words, I was not forced to do all of my studying in the daytime with readers. I was the master of my own will and time. To be honest and frank with you, I find none of these elements existing in my present situation. It is important that this fact be made clear, for the rest of the letter will fall back on it time after time.

In summary about my school life in Arkansas it can safely be said that I had friends in whom I had confidence and who in turn had confidence in my abilities; I was intimate with my teachers and spent long hours in learned discussion; I was completely independent and I had conquered my handicap, even if it was only for that period of time. I had completely forgotten my handicappedness and had become a normal, self-sufficient, and self-reliant individual.

The Arkansas school became my second home, and I chose Pomona because I thought that here I would find the same type of homey atmosphere I knew there. My present impressions are that I was wrong in anticipating this. In order to lead the same type of life as I did in Little Rock, it is necessary for me to be accepted without any prejudice on account of my handicap. In order to have that, it is imperative that I cultivate friendships and continually make an attempt to fight the prejudice here. Were you to be skeptical about my use of the word "prejudice," I may say this in answer: the prejudice of which I speak is not a conscious prejudice in the minds of those with whom I live here. No, rather, this could not be true, for they see me go to any corner of the campus and into the town of Claremont, and are well aware of the fact that I am independent. They compliment me on my courage and independence over and over again, professors as well as students. The prejudice of which I speak is in their subconscious: their hesitance in being themselves when I am present. It is hard to put into words what I mean. I am not a part of them, accepted by them, as I was in Little Rock: students there talked about petty things and discussed problems with me, all the while perfectly at ease. Here, on the other hand, it seems that whenever I happen to be present the conversation can only pursue a general course, that being politics, India, America, or studies. I hasten to add that this is not true of all my friends. I have, indeed, cultivated some good friends among the students that live in my dormitory. They see me as I am and accept me as such. You may dismiss the whole situation by saying that it all exists in my mind alone. If it is so, I am unaware of it at this time. As soon as I learn this, I shall be the first one to admit it.

When I see some people who are active in college government, I am all the more convinced of my inability to be in there with them. This is due to the fact that these students spend their day working on their various projects and leave their studying until late at night. I can't do that. I have to do my studying in the daytime, for the readers cannot be expected to read to me after ten o'clock at night. I was given an assignment to cover the Associated Colleges' meeting for *Student Life,* the college newspaper, but I had to refuse it, because the time of the meeting conflicted with an appointment I had with one of my readers. And I had wanted to cover that meeting so very badly.

All these moments of temporary depression are compensated by the intellectual side of the life here. I thoroughly like the courses in which I am now enrolled. This inspires me to study hard for them. The intellectual atmosphere is serene and subtle and breathtaking, such an atmosphere as could not be found in any country other than the United States. Their unregimented manner of education, which, though it seems easy, ends up being a hardhitting program, leaves a foreigner gasping, and Americans are the last to appreciate it. This lack of appreciation may be attributed to their easygoing nature, to their immaturity in some respects—they are curious about new things at the expense of old institutions.

We may then conclude that college has its own charms, which are intangible. In order to be accepted socially as I had been in Little Rock and be one of them, it is necessary that one be like them in most respects or one is forever a stranger to that society which is not his.

Please excuse me for ending this letter abruptly. Perhaps later on, when we meet with each other, I will be able to discuss in greater detail my thoughts and feelings.

With all my love.

Affectionately yours,

Vedi

(Vedi was my childhood nickname, which I had generally avoided since adolescence.) My father's replies were as ambivalent as my letters. If my conflict was "Yes, tell him everything. No, don't," his conflict seems to have been "Yes, sympathize with him. No, leave him alone—he will manage." His letters were short and sweet, and ended with sayings he had brought us up with since childhood: "Think for yourself." "Learn to be independent." "A person grows only in the school of hard knocks." "What can't be cured must be endured." Even before I heard from him, I felt comforted, as though relief from my frustration were all I needed, and that was provided by the opportunity to correspond with him. Yet the relief was temporary. I didn't know how to go about sitting and mixing with the people, the way a boat joins the river, as the poet counselled.

ONE Friday in my freshman year, I went to see my Ghost. Each freshman had a Ghost assigned to him *in loco parentis*. The Ghosts were our advisers, our big brothers, symbols of dedicated service and rectitude—tapped by the college authorities as most likely to succeed. "Hi, feller," my Ghost said, shaking my hand when I called on him in his room. "What can we do for you today?" He had a deep voice and a big handshake. He sounded full of good spirits and good manners. Like most of the Ghosts, he was a "Nappy"—a member of Nu Alpha Phi, the most illustrious of the college social fraternities.

"I think you are my Ghost."

"That's right—you're certainly one of my bunch. You're the blind Indian fellow from Arkansas."

"I'm an Indian from India."

"But I'm sure you're from Arkansas."

"I just went to high school there."

"Well, I'm glad we got that straightened out. What's on your mind today?"

"I'm having a lot of trouble getting through the weekends." I didn't know how to go on, and added foolishly, "I can't get any work done. I can't find any readers on Saturdays and Sundays."

The truth was more complicated. On weekends, other men

went with their dates to football games, tennis matches, college dances, or fraternity parties, or drove off in their cars to church retreats, beach parties, or road races, or to ski slopes or, if their parents lived close by, their homes. But every Saturday, after my morning classes were over, the weekend stretched ahead of me like a two-day sentence to solitary confinement. (I wasn't able to see much of K. He spent the weekends studying.) When there were no important sporting or social events at the college, the whole town seemed deserted, like a docked cruise ship whose passengers had gone ashore, and when there were such important events the academic side of college appeared to shut down on Friday afternoon, and the campus would swarm like a country fair. The deserted weekends, when even Miss Rietveld was tied up with Quaker affairs and couldn't help me work, I would spend walking or bicycling on the familiar paths I knew, going round and round, like an automaton, and longingly imagining the warm California waters, in which I had never dipped a toe, or the California mountain snow, which I had never felt scrunching underfoot, or one of a hundred other weekend pleasures from which I felt excluded. On the busy weekends, I would be afraid to venture out, in case I was noticed and pitied for being on my own. I would try to study with the tape recorder, but my mind would wander. I would find myself wishing that there were sports I could take part in, wishing that I knew how to dance well—or, at least, that I knew a girl well enough to walk out onto the dance floor with her, boldly ignoring all the sighted people who might be watching me—and wishing that I could have glamorous friends with whom I felt equal and who would accept me as an equal.

My Ghost put his arm around me in brotherly fashion and took me for a stroll around Frary Courtyard. Somehow, being with him out in the open, with the fountain in the middle of the courtyard gurgling, and men merrily whistling, singing, greeting each other up and down the steps of Frary Hall on their way in to an early Friday supper, made me feel even more awkward, even more hesitant to talk about my problems.

"Don't you know all work and no play makes Jack a dull boy?" my Ghost said. "If you spend your weekends studying, you'll miss out on the great college experience of being at Pomona. I'm sure you have plenty of interests. Many people have marvelled at the way you tear around on a bicycle."

"But I don't have a car."

"Well, that's a serious problem, all right, but you can still go out and make friends with people who do have cars. Also, what's stopping you from joining a church and participating in Christian fellowship—going on weekend retreats?"

"But I'm a Hindu."

"Well, then, what's stopping you from going to a football game and cheering for the Sagehens, or taking a girl out to the Wash?" The Sagehens were the Pomona football team, named after the sage grouse in the area, and the Wash was a piece of wilderness with shaded roads and lanes, a Greek theatre, and an observatory, where couples went for romantic walks and to "park" in their cars.

I wanted to say that I didn't know the first thing about football and I'd be bored by it, and ask why a girl should go out with me in preference, say, to him, since it was every man's dream to be a Ghost and every girl's dream to marry a Ghost. I wanted to say that I simply had to use my weekends for reading, because reading aloud took longer. But I didn't say any of that. Somehow, he seemed awe-inspiring—above it all. I thanked him for his help and went in for a quick supper and then back to my room to face another weekend. I tried to review taped material or read a novel on a Talking Book, but I had trouble concentrating. I slumped down on my bed and thought about the fun that everyone else seemed to be having. My room was near the Sophomore Arch, where rowdies and rabblerousers congregated, especially on weekends, and both my room and the Sophomore Arch looked out on Sixth Street, which was part of the route of all campus rallies and parades.

I roused myself, opened the French doors overlooking Sixth Street, and sat behind the curtain, out of view, my ear alert to catch every last happy sound that streamed in. I imagined I heard the *plonk, plonk* of tennis balls, halloos from the Wash, distant notes of the dance band in the Coop (the student-coöperative building). The idea that all these sounds could be floating around at the same time, I realize even as I'm writing this, was absurd. But I went as far as to fancy that I heard, above everything else, Johnnie—cheering, shouting, laughing. And not only that but I was sure I also heard Laurie Glass, Doug Grayson, and Rich Hungate abetting the merrymakers. Laurie Glass, Doug Grayson, and Rich Hungate—all freshmen—had all, at one time or another, dated Johnnie.

The sounds I did hear loud and clear were the cheers from the football field, where the ritual pep rally was in progress around a bonfire:

S-s-s-a-g-e-H-h-h-e-n-s,
S-a-g-e-h-e-n-s,
Sagehens, Sagehens, Sagehens!

Suddenly, there was silence. Then men's voices, deep and strong, rose from the football field. The lower basses chanted, like a distant thunder, "Drumbeat, drumbeat, drumbeat, drumbeat." It was the opening strains of the most beloved college song, "Torchbearers." The ralliers moved out of the football field, the percussive sound gathering force as more male voices—more drums, as it were—joined in: the upper basses, the lower tenors, the upper tenors, one after another. The "drumbeat, drumbeat" throbbed like a heartbeat under the melody. No doubt it was the usual rally procession, in which the adoring women followed the singing men, and in which the front runner carried a flaming torch.

> (Drumbeat, drumbeat, drumbeat, drumbeat)
> Drumbeats rolled o'er the silence profound
> Far above Pomo-ho-na, above Pomo-ho-na.
> Chanting braves making echoes resound
> Far above Pomo-ho-na, above Pomo-ho-na.
> Garbed all in feathers, each ghostly frame
> Loomed 'gainst the embers while soft there came,
> Borne through the gloom like a feather of flame,
> He ne ter-ra-to-ma, ne ter-ra-to-ma.

I had no idea what that last line meant. The ralliers moved along the parade route and passed under my window. I felt like the "ghostly frame" hovering in the gloom, shut out from the warmth and light of the procession passing outside. Johnnie must be passing under my window now, I thought as I skulked behind the curtain. She'll marry one of the braves. She'll marry Laurie Glass or Doug Grayson or Rich Hungate. She'll make a home for him, have his children, cheer him on to victories. I will always be left at the window, behind the curtain.

> (Drumbeat, drumbeat, drumbeat, drumbeat)
> Southland slopes in their sunlit repose
> Lie around Pomo-ho-na, around Pomo-ho-na.
> Soft winds, breathing of poppy and rose,
> Sigh around Pomo-ho-na, around Pomo-ho-na.
> Stern was the promise our fathers knew,
> Pineclad ranges of misted blue,
> Scent of the sagebrush and yucca that grew
> High around Pomo-ho-na, around Pomo-ho-na.
> He ne ter-ra-to-ma, ne ter-ra-to-ma.

The ralliers passed the Sophomore Arch. They turned down College Way. Of course, they are the ones to go to the football games, to Coop dances and beach parties and ski parties, I thought.

They have the looks and the confidence. They are not afraid that the women of their desire will see them.

> (Drumbeat, drumbeat, drumbeat, drumbeat)
> Ours be the faith of the builders whose dream
> Raised our fair Pomo-ho-na, our fair Pomo-ho-na.
> Bear we the torch of their honor whose gleam
> Blazed o'er fair Pomo-ho-na, o'er fair Pomo-ho-na.
> Where bleak and barren the sagebrush rolled
> Rise green orchards of fruited gold.
> Glory to those who with vision of old
> Gazed o'er fair Pomo-ho-na, o'er fair Pomo-ho-na.
> He ne terra-toma, He ne terra-toma,
> He ne terra-toma.

The men sounded farther and farther away, until their voices were just an eerie echo in my head. They deserve to become Nappies and Ghosts and marry the pretty girls, I thought. They deserve to become the patriarchs of society, torchbearers for Christian civilization in the outer world, while people like me won't amount to anything. They will harvest golden fruit in green orchards—my life will take root like sagebrush in bleak and barren land.

My letters and journals of the period bear witness to this somewhat melodramatic, self-pitying boy of eighteen—in love, for instance, with the idea of Johnnie rather than with Johnnie herself. From my present perspective, I can see only comedy in the spectral representation of the boy I once was—a thin little Hindu, looking almost consumptive, speaking English with a mixture of Raj and Arkansas accents, whose most prominent feature, according to Johnnie, was his big feet, in shoes that seemed too large for him. What a clown I must have been to want to belong to the car culture of Southern California, to aspire to be, of all things, a patriarch, a torchbearer for Christian civilization, when happiness for me obviously lay in marching, in my big shoes, to the beat of a different drummer.

❦

MORE selections from my journal from my freshman year:

December 3

Marvin just read words on the page, for a whole hour. Half the time, I had no idea what he was reading. Thank God, he's quit. Anita reads as if she were acting in a play. Jay reads faster than almost anyone—that's especially good, because he reads history to me. Yet it's frightening to think that he would be no good at reading philosophy, and Jane, who is so good at puzzling out abstruse philosophy passages, would be no good at reading history.

December 5

I'm terrified of Jay. Any time I ask him to go back and reread a passage, he makes me feel very stupid. I'm frightened of asking him to reread anything.

December 8

I don't have enough money to pay all the readers I need. This is an extra worry, from which I was free at the Arkansas school, where everything was done in Braille and we were all in the same boat. But, then, now I can go to an ordinary library and read any book I like—theoretically, at least. As long as I want food for my mind, I'll always have a hole in my pocket. But whatever the state of my pocket I will never let my reading suffer.

December 10

I wrote my first story for *Student Life* on a French student here, the beautiful Natalie. "We, the French, are better equipped to understand and appreciate the value of a college education," she says. "Our conversation is more a discussion of art, politics, and current events and is not limited to talk about boyfriends, calories, and clothes." Many other foreign students also feel that the concerns of American students are superficial.

December 15

Lately, I keep falling asleep when people are reading to me. My ears must get tired.

January 3

To attain my independence seems like an unending life struggle. I have the fear that once I compromise on my independence, allow myself to be helped, I will appear helpless, just as people imagine the blind to be, rather than every bit as self-reliant as the sighted, as I think myself to be.

January 5

Suddenly, lots of cars—people are coming back from Christmas vacation. I'm struck again by the wealth of many students. Their fathers do things like own the main General Motors dealership. But money is understated—most students seem to have old cars.

January 6

I have a new reader, Mr. William Rattenbury. He's an old man, and a volunteer. He is such an eager reader that he sometimes arrives an hour early and waits. But the trouble with him is, if I stop him reading and ask him to reread something he gets all confused and can't find his place. I can really only use him for reading novels.

January 16

How could I ever have dreamed that Johnnie could take any romantic interest in me? I have no car. Besides, she's now going out seriously with Richard Hungate—wholesome, positive, tall, a real flat-crewcut type.

January 24

My social life is made up mostly of solitary walks from one end of campus to the other, exchanging a few words along the way with people who greet me, and whose voices I recognize, because they are fixed in my mind and ring in my head like bell notes.

January 28

I keep on being surprised at the good grades I'm getting. My acquaintance with the better students makes me realize how deficient I am, but I'm working hard to catch up. Mr. Jones is right in calling me "a hothouse plant."

February 10

People here have silly nicknames. Betty Peterson's friends call her Boob.

March 6

A dinner was held for electing the president of the International Relations Club of Pomona, Claremont's Men's College, and Scripps. Eighty members and guests came. Dean Beatty, Dean Walton, and President Lyon were present. After dinner, President Lyon gave a short address, and then each of the five of us who were running for president was given eight minutes to make a speech. The four other candidates were upperclassmen, but I was elected, even though I was a freshman, by a two-thirds majority. Dr. Darby, the government instructor, commented that it was my speech that secured me this position. I must have acquired some skill in public speaking since arriving at college. If I had realized the possibility of my election, I might have withdrawn my name, for the club is going to require much of my time.

After my election, I learned from President Lyon that in the autumn our college is going to be host to the national organization of the International Relations Clubs. Three hundred members will be coming from all over the country, most of whom will be foreigners. I will be responsible for finding accommodations for them in private homes and on the campuses of the three colleges. I will also have to preside at this conference. This experience of working with people will stand me in good stead in later years.

I wish I could write more but I am very sleepy. It is about 2 A.M. and I have not yet studied my French lesson for tomorrow.

March 10

I'm making my best friends from the executive committee of the International Relations Club—Herb Garelick and David Shapiro. We are planning a tri-college I.R.C. dance, a showing of a foreign movie, a monthly newsletter, and fortnightly teas at Kenyon House. We will also be regularly having dinners and panel discussions, and will engage speakers.

March 13

Have joined the staff of *Student Life* and written a feature story on Fahid Tobaishi, who landed at LaGuardia Airport on March 20, 1952, not realizing that eleven months later he would land among the élite Pomonans. Fahid is a 23-year-old native of Saudi Arabia. He says he finds our "tribal" customs, from wearing shoes, socks, well-creased slacks, and cravats to being served dinners in Frary Hall—customs sparsely spiced with scholastic pursuits— all too good to be true.

March 24

President Lyon and the faculty have selected me to lead the college's delegation of ten to the third annual Model United Nations Conference. It's going to be held at the University of California at Berkeley, and students from sixty colleges and junior colleges from six Western states and Alaska will be included. Anne Lockwood and Laurie Glass will be in my delegation. We'll be representing Cuba, and I don't know Cuba's position on any world issues. I'll have to bone up on it.

April 15

Registration for the Model U.N. today at Eshelman Hall Auditorium. The conference has the atmosphere of a student festival.

April 16

Very exciting day. I wish we were representing India (assigned to U.C.L.A.) or the United Kingdom (assigned to Stanford), but our delegation made a lot of noise and speeches in the General Assembly session—made Cuba into almost a major power.

April 18

We had a very heated discussion about the seating of Communist China. The Secretary-General ruled that Red China leave the assembly and remain only as an observer. I was for the admission of China, but I had to take the Cuban line, toadying to the American position against it. Our delegation also took an active part in the discussion of a solution to the Korean War, Tunisian independence, and self-government for territories.

Excellent banquet—we were served shrimp cocktail, filet mignon, baked potatoes, mixed vegetables, hot rolls, ice-cream roll, and cookies.

May 15

I.R.C. used to be a defunct club but now has sixty-three paid members and almost forty-five more who haven't paid dues but are active in club functions.

May 31

It turns out there are many kindred souls here who I didn't even know existed until I became active in the I.R.C. These people are not particularly well off. They don't have cars. They tend to be Jewish, or children of missionary parents, and are very serious.

❧

IN 1987, thirty-five years after I was a freshman at Pomona, I found myself at Berkeley, giving a talk. Afterward, Doug Grayson came up to me and caught me by the sleeve. "I'm sure you don't remember me," he said, with an air of bonhomie. "I was in your class at Pomona."

"Doug Grayson! How could I forget you?" I cried. Unlike me, he was never alone—never without his group. Everywhere he went, the group went, too, as if he and the members of his group were one being, some mythical creation with many heads and voices. They gave the impression of having long since learned to make themselves at home irrespective of where they happened to be and who else was around. Over meals in Frary Dining Hall, they seemed always to be talking loudly or laughing at some private joke—carrying on as if they owned the place, as if no one else were there. I would have given anything to have them call across Frary to me to come and sit with them, as if I were one of the group, even though I knew that if I should ever find myself sitting among them I would be so intimidated that I wouldn't be able to open my mouth.

I asked Doug now how life was treating him.

"Things couldn't be better," he said. "I'm a full professor here at the university. My two children from my first marriage have graduated from Pomona."

Doug Grayson sat next to me at a lunch the university had arranged, and afterward I walked back with him to his house and he showed me a vast amount of the Pomona memorabilia he kept stowed away in cardboard cartons in a closet in his study: a framed diploma; a moth-eaten blue Pomona jacket; a letter man's sweater; a sort of puppet of Cecil the Sagehen; old catalogues; old college calendars with spiral bindings; copies of *Metate,* of *Student Life,* and of *MSS* (the college literary magazine).

I asked him how he had happened to go to Pomona.

"Well, I came from a long line of distinguished Yale graduates. My father's father was a Wall Street stockbroker, and his father was an Episcopal bishop in New York. After Yale, my father went to a music school and became a Broadway director-producer, and by the time I was born he was a successful Hollywood movie director. I grew up among the so-called lights of Hollywood in the Golden Age, spent a couple of miserable years in a military day school in North Hollywood, and then, against my will, was shipped off as a boarder to the Webb School, which, you'll remember, is a prep school in the hills above Claremont. At Webb, I modelled my personality as best I could on the rich-kid, playboy group I attached myself to. I threw myself into athletics—for three years in a row I was a letter man in tennis, and my last year I was the most valuable player in football. I expressed my creativity by editing the school paper, and fanta-sized about the time when I would get to college and become an intellectual or a writer, or some such. I figured that being an intellectual or a writer would be socially acceptable at college."

"I'm still not clear about how it was that you ended up at Pomona."

"My parents urged me to apply to Yale, but I refused to go there or to any other Ivy League school, out of sheer obstinacy. And Pomona was next door, and sounded safe and tolerant." Doug picked up a college calendar and started leafing through it. "But I see from the entries in this college calendar from our freshman year that in those days I was still trying very hard to live up to the image of a playboy. The calendar is scrawled all over with things I was doing, and clever little drawings of myself."

Every freshman was given a school calendar like the one Doug had in his hand. It had photographs of college landmarks and scenes from college life. I remember getting my calendar and trying to imagine the photograph that went with the caption

"College Avenue, with its great eucalyptus trees, fills hourly with students as they change classes." But I must have thrown the calendar away. Anyway, if I had managed to save it, it would have remained as pristine as when I got it, since my life was devoid of any calendar-worthy events. Now I wanted to know exactly what Doug's life at college had been like—the life that I thought at the time I would have led if it had been in my power. I asked him to read out the entries in his college calendar.

"There are no entries for September and October," he said, turning the leaves. "I guess I was so caught up in all those orientation activities and battles with the sophomores that I didn't have time to even write them down. The first entry is in November—'November 12th: Harwood Open House.'"

"What was that?"

"It was just the freshman women playing house—under supervision, of course—trying to prove to us men what good wives and mothers they would make."

"Was Johnnie there?"

"Oh, of course. She was already a very sought-after girl."

"You went out with her, didn't you?"

"Oh, yes, but it wasn't a heavy date. I think she was more interested in Rich Hungate. He was the perfect crewcut middle-class Nappy type, and went on to become a Ghost."

"Didn't you become a Ghost?"

"Oh, no. I was sort of a gentleman-middling student—I failed Spanish. I wasn't the kind of person the authorities would naturally take a shine to." He continued reading the calendar, in a bemused tone, as much to himself as to me, and pausing to fill in, to explain, to answer my questions. "'November 14th: Oxy Frosh Here.' I played in that game with Occidental College—I'd gone out for freshman football. But that turned out to be my last game ever. We lost, and I hung up my bad knee for good. 'November 15th: Santa Barbara Game.' I remember I just went along to Santa Barbara for the ride. The game was at night, and a group of us stayed over in a motel and got premeditatedly and grossly drunk. 'November 16th: San Dinas Drive. Ghost Party, 7–8. November 18th: Pint to Blood Bank. Steak Dinner. November 19th: Artist Course. November 20th: Ski. Guard Bonfire.' "

"Who was it you were guarding the bonfire from?"

"We'd laid this very big bonfire—I think some of the logs were broken telephone poles we'd found around—to be lit the next night for the football rally, a sort of war dance, a truly pagan ritual. The reason for guarding the pile was the fear that Oxy—or, more likely, those villainous and diabolical scientist types from Cal Tech—would set it off in advance and ruin the ritual. The guarding must have been successful, because I see here that the rally took place on Friday night and the Occidental-Pomona game on Saturday afternoon. 'November 25th: F.B. Banquet.' The end of the football season was celebrated by a banquet for all us players. 'December 5th: Dean Beatty, 1:45.' You remember Dean Beatty."

"Sure. He had a preposterously high voice." We both laughed, as if that high voice would never cease resonating in our heads.

"You probably never got a note from Dean Beatty saying he wanted to see you," Doug said, "but the notes were an indication of being in some kind of trouble, and, boy, did I ever get my share." He read on: " 'December 6th: A.W.S. Formal.' "

"What was A.W.S.?"

"A.W.S.? Let's see—Associated Women Students. It was a women's student organization for all the Associated Colleges. An A.W.S. dance was one of the big events of the college social season. I think we men wore tuxes. I know the women dressed to the nines, in strapless gowns with tulle skirts sticking straight out. Everyone wore a boutonnière or a corsage."

"Didn't people get dressed up for all the dances?"

"Certainly not. Didn't you ever go to a Friday night Coop dance?"

"No, never."

"Oh. Well, they were free-for-alls in the Coop ballroom. There were records instead of a live band, you didn't have to get dressed up, you didn't even need a date. They were basically mixers. Do you still want me to go on with my calendar?"

"Yes, of course."

" 'December 8th: 3rd low grade.' This is a reference to the custom of the dean's sending out a notice in the campus mail to anyone getting below a C in any class. You probably didn't get any."

"No, I didn't."

"I got a number of them in my frosh year, since I cut classes frequently, and found that my prep-school training wasn't all that much better than the training of the average Pomona frosh coming from the public schools." He continued reading. " 'December 12th: Go to play. December 13th: Scripps Formal. December 14th: Torrey Pines Road Races. December 18th: Xmas Vacation Begins.' So much for 1952. 'January 5th: Back. January 7th: Frosh Party, Harwood. Poverty Prom, Coop. January 8th: Go skiing, also to movie at Pomona High School. January 10th: Joe College Dance. January 14th: Plug Ugly, Coop Dance.' You must have gone to a Plug Ugly."

"I think I did once, but I don't remember it."

"It was always an interesting affair—a satirical play on student fads and fancies, on movie stars and politicians, and on the idiosyncrasies of particular professors and administrators, who were expected to come and laugh at themselves. 'January 17th: Interfrat Formal.' The fraternities must have given this dance, but non-frat members must have been invited, since I went, and, as a frosh, I couldn't have been in a fraternity. 'January 24th: Party, Stoddards Canyon.' "

Some of the entries in his calendar, like "Torrey Pines Road Races," I could guess the meaning of, and I let him slide over them. Others, like "Stoddards Canyon," were totally mystifying. I asked him, "What was Stoddards Canyon?"

"Stoddards Canyon was a private club up in the mountains north of Claremont. Since drinking was illegal on the Pomona campus, and in the town of Claremont, too, we frosh sometimes rented the club for a big booze-up. I remember the Stoddards Canyon party well, because we all played the sophisticate to the hilt. Laurie Glass arrived with a bottle of gin. He was a shrimp of a fellow, but, boy, could he drink! Do you remember him?"

"Yes. I remember him as a very engaging, intense fellow who wasn't afraid of making a fool of himself. He had a certain flash and dash."

"Yes, he was the kind of fellow who made things happen. He was by then my best friend, and became one of the most influential people in my life."

"So you were saying Laurie Glass arrived at Stoddards Canyon with a bottle of gin."

"Yes, and a Lang twin on each arm." Ines and Lilo Lang cut quite a figure in the college. They were bright, intelligent women from Argentina, and in my casual meetings with them around the campus I had always found them warmhearted and talkative. They had husky, sexy voices. "After the party at Stoddards Canyon, the Lang twins, Laurie, and I had a very dangerous drunken drive down the canyon to Claremont. The next day, I penitentially went on the wagon. In fact, here in the calendar I have a little stick drawing of myself sitting in a wagon—the kind children pull behind them." He resumed reading. " 'January 28th: History Final, 8. January 30th: Spanish Final, 8. January 31st: English Final, 8.' I remember we partied right up to the last minute. Looking back on it, I'm amazed at how compulsive—and, for a freshman, seemingly compulsory—all this socializing was. 'February 3rd: Speech Final, 9.' That was a gut course called Interpretive Reading, in which we got up and declaimed things. 'February 6th: Semester Break Begins.' I remember I went skiing. I was a terrible skier then, but I persisted, because I imagined that skiing was the thing to do. 'February 11th: Classes Begin. February 20th: Whittier.' 'Whittier' here, I think, means a tennis tournament with Whittier College. 'February 21st: 8 College Dance.' This dance must have involved colleges beyond Claremont—perhaps Occidental, Whittier, Pepperdine. 'February 27th: Cocktail Party, L.A. February 28th: Scripps Formal. March 6th: Tennis Match. Cal Poly, Here. March 7th: Jazz Concert—Shearing, Christy, Brown. Party, Legion Hall.' We hired the Claremont American Legion Hall for a post-concert party, because it was a major event, what with three big-name jazz stars—George Shearing, June Christy, and Les Brown, with his Band of Renown, playing in Big Bridges. You must at least have gone to that one."

"I remember I thought of going, but I was struggling with a philosophy paper on Francis Bacon and the Scientific Method, and the only time I could get Miss Rietveld to take dictation conflicted with the time of the concert."

" 'March 8th: Field Trial, Newport.' My dad had the hobby of training Labrador retrievers and entering them, with other trainers, in field trials. 'March 15th: Drags.' 'Drags' means the drag races at the fairgrounds in Pomona. 'March 17th: Sports Night. March 22nd: Palm Springs Road Races.' The road races at Palm Springs were an elegant affair, with ritzy sports cars and a European flavor, in contrast to those drag races at Pomona, which were very much what would now be called a redneck event, with junky hot rods. 'March 28th: Monte Carlo Dance. Won $1.70.' This is a very interesting entry. The Monte Carlo Dance was a pseudo gambling club, installed in the Coop lounge, where you could play roulette with scrip between dances. I think that at the time I thought of it as a really silly idea. But the calendar tells me otherwise, recording my pride at winning a dollar-seventy! 'April 4th: Spring Vacation Begins. April 21st–25th: L-o-a-f.' I was recovering from an appendectomy. 'May 10th: Beach Party, Dana Point.' As soon as spring weather set in, this Compleat College Playboy put away the skis and put on swimming trunks and got an instant tan. By the way, did you ever go to a beach party—do you know what they were like?"

"I hate to admit it, but I never did. I would love to hear about it." I added, a little self-consciously, "I enjoy experiencing things vicariously almost as much as experiencing them myself."

"A beach party involved us couples cavorting in the waves and working on our tans all afternoon, sipping quarts of illegal beer from bottles in paper bags. At dusk, we'd build a fire to roast hot dogs and marshmallows, which we'd wash down with more beer, until it was dark enough to pair off and 'make out,' with the sound of the waves and the blessing of the stars." He resumed his calendar. " 'May 12th: Class Election Speeches, Frary.' One of my specialties was ghostwriting such speeches for candidates who were politically more palatable than I was. I liked my ghosting role, and even imagined I might practice it one day on the national level. 'May 13th: 2 P.M. Government Makeup Test.' Some more tests. 'May 16th: Supper-Dance, Scripps, 5:45.' Scripps dances were always preceded by heavy-duty drinking, so they began early—usually in some dorm room at Claremont Men's College, where drinking was condoned. 'May 17th: Frosh Class Beach Party. Little Corona Yacht Club.' Little Corona Beach was in Corona del Mar, near Balboa. A very chic location for body-surfing. Board surfing in those days was an esoteric rarity, practiced only by some muscle-obsessed super-athletic types. Shall I continue?"

I said yes.

" 'May 20th: Sing, 8 P.M.' This was our spring sing. As you probably know, it was held outdoors, on Marston Quadrangle. I remember we sang things like the Fred Waring arrangement of 'Bye Bye Blackbird.' 'May 21st: Selective Service Test.' That was an S.A.T.-type test to determine which of the current college students should retain their deferments and which should be drafted for the Korean War. I remember getting a barely passing mark. I also remember that in those days there was not so much as a peep of dissent over the draft—just a pragmatic investigation of all the ways of avoiding it. Getting married was one of the more drastic options. 'May 23rd: Dean Beatty, 11:15. Starlight Ball— Carousel.' Why I would be seeing Dean Beatty at eleven-fifteen on a Saturday morning is anybody's guess. More important matters lay ahead that night, at the Starlight Ball. 'Carousel' was probably the theme of the dance—dances always had to have themes. 'May 24th: Beach Party. May 26th: Sports Banquet, Harwood, 6.' This was the last week of classes, so it signalled a flurry of social events. 'May 27th: Frosh Final Full Moon Fling, 4, Rembrandt Quad. May 28th: Room Drawings.' You must have taken part in the room drawings, after dinner in Frary Dining Hall. Laurie Glass and I both drew low numbers, and so we had our choice for the following year. We chose rooms next to each other. 'May 30th: French Test. Last Class. Harwood Court Formal.' You won't believe it, but although I never missed a dance I was a dreadful dancer. Nevertheless, projecting my playboy image for all I was worth, I danced on, stepping on various feet as I went. 'June 1st: Finals Begin. Get typhoid shot.' I celebrated the official beginning of finals by getting my typhoid shot for my upcoming summer trip to Europe. 'June 4th: Jack W. arrives.' He was one of several old prep-school friends who were arriving in Claremont for a reunion of the gang. 'June 10th: 8— History Final. June 16th: Leave L.A. TWA Flight 20.' That concludes my academic year—if you could call it that—of 1952–53. I was airborne for the East Coast to catch a nine-day boat across the Atlantic and see the world with seven other Associated College kids, escorted by my Western Civ. professor, Vincent Learnihan. Shall I tell you about that trip?"

"Thanks. Your school year was fascinating, but I'm afraid I should think about getting on the road."

Talking about the college with Doug Grayson had made me feel closer to him than I could ever have imagined feeling. After all, we had rediscovered something we shared, however differently we had experienced it. But he was still capable of relishing his experiences there, while I had tried to forget mine, to put the pain of them behind me—that is, until I started thinking about college with a view to writing something about it. We now sat for a few minutes longer in his study, silent, like two companions approaching the end of a long journey who wish to be alone with their private thoughts but don't want to part just yet.

"You remember that talented writer in our class, Charlie Stivers?" he asked after a while. "He tragically killed himself with drink. Laurie Glass— Even today, I can hardly speak about it. During our junior year, Laurie transferred to U.C.L.A. In a way, he was a mama's boy, and wanted to be closer to home. His father practiced medicine in Los Angeles. But his leaving Pomona didn't affect our relationship one whit. The summer between our junior and senior years, he and I went on an incredibly farflung and politically reckless trip through the assorted dictatorships of Central and South America. We got to see Batista's Cuba, Trujillo's Dominican Republic, Perón's Argentina, where we dropped in on the father of the Lang twins in Buenos Aires, and the Haiti of the pre-Papa Doc autocracy of some other tyrant, whose name escapes me. We also managed to travel to Machu Picchu, and go a thousand miles up the Amazon by ship. After U.C.L.A., Laurie spent a year at the London School of Economics and then started working in television. His ambition was to be another Edward R. Murrow. In 1961, when he was still in his twenties, he went on a deep-sea-fishing trip in Mexico with his fiancée, a British airline hostess. While they were driving back, he fell asleep at the wheel, and they were both killed."

"Oh, I never knew that. I am sorry."

"You know, when I look back at our college years I can't help feeling that Laurie and Stivers were as gifted as any Pomona people of our day who are so famous now—I mean people like Richard Chamberlain, Bob Towne, Kris Kristofferson. But now, except for those of us who knew them, no one will remember them."

I left Doug thinking what a charming man he was, what a surprisingly pleasant time we'd spent together. He seemed to be at peace with his past in a way that I perhaps could never be. At college, I envied him his group, and possibly, without knowing it, he might have envied me my purposefulness (after all, at prep school he had aspired to be an intellectual, and I, in spite of my early anxieties, by dint of hard work excelled as a student), but for the most part we had been, as it were, invisible to each other,

blind to each other's potentialities—indeed, to our own potentialities. For all his youthful antics, he was now a serious person.
He had a capacity for friendship, an open, outgoing nature, an
ability to laugh at himself. He was gracious, spirited, self-depre-
ciating. But it had taken me years of maturity to appreciate him
for what he was and to accept myself for what I was: to view the
life of fruited gold and the life of rolling sagebrush and see in
each of them its own justification.

V

THE
BENEFACTRESS

E VEN NOW, I HAVE MERELY TO THINK OF THAT SUMMER
in 1952 when my father and I were going from one rich
man's house to another in Los Angeles, trying to get
money for college, to feel the pain all over again. If it
had been anyone but my father who was parading me in
front of potential benefactors, I would rather have died
than subject myself to the humiliation of what I perceived as
begging. But the sweep of his confidence and optimism carried
me along. Indeed, I so venerated him that I couldn't imagine
that anything he did could compromise his pride and dignity—
compromise *our* pride and dignity. Among the papers he gave me
was a letter he wrote that summer to Mr. Watumull, and reading
it made me realize, with a shock, how much my father must have
had to humble himself for my sake, how much of his own pain
he must have kept from me, and how obtuse and self-absorbed I
must have been not to discern it on my own. The letter reads:

UNIVERSITY OF CALIFORNIA
Department of Medicine
School of Medicine
University of California Medical Center
Los Angeles 24, California

July 17th, 1952

MY DEAR WATUMULLJI,

May I express my gratitude for the privilege you gave me of calling you a friend the very first time we met. You have been a friend indeed and the poet (Sheikh Sa'di) could not define it better:

Dost aan baashad keh girad dast-e-dost
Dar pareshaan, hali-o-darmaandgio

[A friend is he who catches hold of a friend's hand
in times of anxiety, illness, and misfortune.]

I cannot find words to express my gratitude for all that you and yours have done for Ved and myself.

My own life is that of a floating leaf—and a dead one at that—in the waves of a stream (of life) entirely at the mercy of the flow. It's not even a green leaf which may hope to touch the shore before it disintegrates!! It is a brownish yellow leaf which will perhaps disintegrate long before it is washed on to the shore!!!

Being an unemployed and a freelance at that, I know not when and where I will be next. I may hibernate here or somewhere else in this great country, or may find some employment somewhere to keep the wolves away from the door. But wherever I may be my best wishes will be for you and yours and all that you are doing for Ved. With kindest regard,

Sincerely yours,
Amolak Ram Mehta

There was, of course, no way for me to tell if my father had aged physically—if his hair had turned white, if lines had begun to crease his face—and his talk was beguiling. But the letter gave me a glimmering of what a burden my education must have been for him. I can't help wondering now whether if it hadn't been for the pressure of my education, of getting me on my feet—however long that might take—and saving me from the fate of becoming a beggar, my father would have allowed himself to get into the situation I'm about to describe, or, if he had, whether he would have allowed it to continue as long as it did.

LATE in November, I received a letter from my father saying that he had been in India for a month or so but was coming right back to America and hoped to see me soon. I was staggered. There was no hint in the letter of where he would get the money, what job, if any, he had landed, how he could think about flying from continent to continent as if he were a maharaja.

On the heels of my father's letter came another letter from India, this one from a Mrs. Ethel Clyde. She said that my father had been travelling with her as her "court physician" and was taking her back to New York in early December, and that she would like it if I joined the two of them in Miami over my Christmas vacation. She added that I could travel by plane or train, whichever was convenient, and she would cover all the expenses, because I would be her "guest." She said I could write to her at 52 Gramercy Park, New York City. The letter had a few words scribbled on it by my father, saying that he whole-heartedly approved of the plan.

I was overwhelmed. I had never met Mrs. Clyde, or even heard of her. The terms "court physician" and "guest" in the senses in which she used them were totally unfamiliar to me. Until her letter came, I had dreaded the approach of Christmas—dreaded battling the onset of depression as the routine of classes was broken, the residence halls emptied out, and I was left to walk around the echoing halls by myself. That is what Christmases at high school had been like for me, and I had had no reason to suppose that anything would be different at college.

Over the next few days, I must have written a hundred different letters of thanks to Mrs. Clyde in my head, but none of them sounded quite right, and before I managed to get one off to her a parcel from her arrived in the post, with a card saying that to help me with my studies she had picked up a little present for me in Switzerland, where she and my father now were. I tore open the parcel, and could scarcely believe what I found. It seemed like a toy typewriter, but it turned out to be every bit a real one, and more. Made in Switzerland, it was light, compact, and small, it had French-accent signs, and it responded to my fingers as if it had been specially made for them.

I typed out the following note to Mrs. Clyde on my new typewriter:

December 9, 1952

Dear Mrs. Clyde:

It was indeed a delightful and pleasant surprise to receive your very sincere letter and your practical gift. For you see this new gadget will have a two-fold purpose. It will aid me in my studies, and—sentimental and foolish though it may be—provide me with a constant reminder of the greatness of a person whose thoughtfulness and generosity could extend itself to an individual she hadn't even met, and place such faith and confidence in him. I hope I will prove worthy of this confidence, and thus endeavor, in my little way, to show my overflowing gratitude. Words actually fail me in expressing my thanks to you, so please excuse this futile attempt.

Surprises never cease. Because I had been expecting to spend a rather dull, yet perhaps studious Christmas, now seeing you along with Daddy will be to me a great lift and will act as a stimulus to my work.

Hoping with keen anticipation to see you. With my very best compliments for the season and kindest regards.

Very sincerely yours,

Ved Mehta

After I posted the letter, I heard from Mrs. Clyde again, this time from London. She wrote that, as it turned out, she had to spend Christmas Day itself with a very sick friend, Ben Marsh, in Winter Park, Florida, so could I meet my father and her a couple of days later? I had planned to fly to Florida, but I now decided to take the train, as a way of having something to do on Christmas Day.

On the eighteenth of December—I remember the date because it was when college let out for the Christmas holidays—I got a telephone call from my father in New York. He and Mrs. Clyde had just arrived on a transatlantic flight. I started asking him questions about Mrs. Clyde, but he put me off, saying that there was a lot to tell—too much to tell on the phone—and that we'd have plenty of opportunity to talk when we met in Florida. Mrs. Clyde came on the line. I remember I groped for words, but she, although she restricted herself to amenities, was very fluent. I listened to her voice for some clue to her, to her life. It sounded ebullient, expansive, amused, almost boisterous, as if she were intoxicated by surprising me, talking to me for the first time, meeting me on the phone, making plans, putting them into effect. I remember hanging up and thinking that, compared with hers, many voices sounded stunted, shrinking.

The travel agent who was handling my reservations got me a roomette on the train. I didn't know exactly what a roomette was, and even when the porter showed me to it I couldn't take it all in. It seemed to contain within its four walls, in a space exactly the size of a single bed, a world of comforts—a sofa, a washbasin, a toilet, a table, a bed, all fitted snugly together. When the bed was folded up into a wall, it became the back of the headrest of the sofa. When the tabletop was lifted and folded back, it revealed the toilet and washbasin. But the space was used so economically that the only way one could climb into bed was by stepping out into the corridor, and a stationary heavy curtain hung over the doorway, so that fellow-passengers wouldn't see one getting in and out of bed. The same curtain also helped to muffle corridor sounds once the sliding door was closed. The roomette was perfectly heated, and the windows were sealed against the soot and detritis that flew into Indian trains. In fact, it was as sanitary and well fitted as an American dream house.

"America . . . America . . ." I found myself mindlessly repeating the word, to the padded clackety-clack of the train, as I kept getting up from the sofa, moving out into the corridor with the curtain behind me, pulling down the bed, climbing onto it, getting down from it, folding it back, and sitting down on the sofa again—all the while trying to imagine how the rich passed the time in their cocoons, if this was how they travelled, and what my new-found benefactress was like.

That night, Christmas night, I changed into my pajamas and hopped into my bed. *America . . . America . . .* No sooner had I closed the door and got comfortable between the sheets and under the blanket than I felt that I wanted to use the toilet again. I slid back the door, got down between the bed and the curtain, folded up the bed and the tabletop, used the toilet, put the tabletop and the bed down, and got back into the bed. The bed must not have locked into place properly, because just as I was dropping off to sleep it slipped out of its lock and sprang almost shut, sandwiching me, head down, between bed and wall. I remember the blood rushing to my head, and my arms and legs, though actually paralyzed with fear, twitching frantically with violent phantom movements. One false move and the bed will snap shut, I thought. I'll suffocate. I'll be buried alive. In fact, I was sure that a mere jolt of the train would finish me off. (Whether or not it was actually possible for the bed to snap shut with me inside I don't know to this day. There certainly seemed to be enough space between the wall and the upended bed to seal in my thin body.)

Although I had no leverage, gradually and painfully, like a worm inching and feeling its way, I somehow slowly shifted my weight toward the top end of the bed, and at last I got the bed down far enough to jump out of it. Thereafter, I sat up on the sofa, benumbed, my heart thumping every time I thought of getting into the coffinlike bed, with its lid about to shut on me, and my pride keeping me from asking the porter for help. *America . . . America . . .* We travelled on and on, pulling into anonymous stations—I had no way of knowing what they were and where I was. I ran out of the little Braille material I had brought to read. Once or twice, I walked to the dining car and back, in the hope of striking up a conversation, but I didn't meet anyone. I looked at the hands of my watch again and again, trying to hurry them on. As we approached Tampa, where my father and Mrs. Clyde had arranged to meet me, I grew more and more worried that she would be disappointed in me.

ON the day of our meeting, Mrs. Clyde wrote in her diary:

We drove to Tampa and met Ved, who arrived from Pomona by train at 1:10. He has fitted right into our little group. What tragedy and what courage! Poor Ved and poor Mehta. It is a heartbreaking business!

She must have mistaken my fright for courage, because I remember that I was scared as I stepped off the train, carrying my suitcase and trying to force my eyes open, so that I would look as independent and normal as I could. Suddenly, a familiar arm was around my shoulder, and my father was introducing me to Mrs. Clyde. I put out my free hand to shake hers, and that caused some awkward confusion, for it turned out that she had to shift a cane from one hand to the other. (I learned later that she was seventy-three years old.)

Outside the station, her car and a driver were waiting for us. I remember that it was a big Packard, that Mrs. Clyde got in the front seat next to the driver, whom she introduced as Bruce Sweetland, and that my father and I got in the back.

"Bruce is from Huntington, Long Island, where I have a farm,"

Mrs. Clyde said. "He helps out with driving whenever I hit the road."

We drove toward Miami, Mrs. Clyde doing most of the talking, my father mostly murmuring agreement, and Bruce scarcely opening his mouth. She spoke of examples of meaningless suffering she had come across in the morning's newspaper. Someone's operation had been botched, and he had been left paralyzed. Someone else had starved. Each time, she asked rhetorically, almost provokingly, "To what end?" She mentioned Ben Marsh, the sick friend she had just visited in Winter Park. He was the founder of an organization in Washington, D.C., called the People's Lobby, which fought against social injustice, and which she had been supporting for years. He had a severe case of pleurisy, she said, and was on his deathbed. "To what end?" she repeated. "If your God exists, Mehta, he must be a fiend."

My father didn't rise to the bait. Instead, he said to me, "You see, Mrs. Clyde is a vehement atheist."

"But do you believe in God?" I asked him, remembering that he used to make fun of my mother for her superstitious religious beliefs.

"Not as such, but I certainly think there may be a power higher than we."

"But to what end, Mehta?" she asked, and then, turning to me, "Do you think such meaningless suffering could exist if there was a God?"

I wanted to say that I thought it could, but I wasn't sure of my ground. I couldn't make out exactly who Mrs. Clyde was and whether my father would have me speak freely with her. I kept silent.

"I think the best thing all the statesmen in the world could do would be to make one big bomb and blow the world up," Mrs. Clyde said.

I could hold back no longer, and, like the college freshman I was, jumped into the debate with both feet. "You can't possibly mean such nonsense. You're voicing a sort of death wish. A person may have the right to wish death for himself but not for the whole world. Even people who are miserable and suffer a lot would rather live than die." And so on. I liked the sound of my voice, and thought that my arguments were very impressive—the more so because she seemed to be giving me her full attention.

"But horses manage their affairs much better than we humans do," Mrs. Clyde said, with a laugh. She had a distinctive, hearty laugh. It erupted, and went on for a long time. She seemed to throw her whole self into it. I suddenly became aware that I wasn't getting anywhere with her, and felt crestfallen.

"The greatest compliment Mrs. Clyde can pay anybody is 'He has horse sense,' " my father said, as if to console me—to say that no one else could get anywhere with her, either.

"Horses don't have war or poverty or crime, and they live in harmony with nature, without clothes—without shame and guilt—as we human beings were surely meant to do, but don't," Mrs. Clyde said. "Can you tell me why we wear clothes?"

She laughed, and my father joined in, as if they had had this conversation before.

"To be decent, I think," I said.

"What's decent about clothes? Aren't horses decent? Aren't all animals decent? Would you be surprised if I told you I used to go to a nudist camp?"

I said I was surprised.

"You know, I've always been known as the black sheep in my family." She laughed and laughed.

"Mrs. Clyde believes that none of us should feel any more guilty than horses," my father said.

"My philosophy is that we do what we do because of our heredity, environment, and experience," Mrs. Clyde said. She asked me, "Can you improve upon it?"

I was nonplussed.

"Your father told me you're studying philosophy," Mrs. Clyde said. "You must have studied the problem of free will."

"Yes, I have. Different philosophers have different views on it."

"Well, I've got the answer in my book. Did you know I'd written a book?"

I said no, I hadn't known that.

"I'm not surprised—it's privately printed," Mrs. Clyde said. "The book is called 'Horse Sense in Poetry, Prose, and Song.' "

"There's a copy here in the car," my father said.

Mrs. Clyde went on, "It says, 'Man's actions are inevitably the same whether or not he believes in free will, since his actions are always and only the result of those things that make freedom of the will impossible.' "

"That's only one way of looking at it," I argued.

My father pressed my hand, and I desisted.

She laughed. "You can't help what you are. You are what you are. A criminal can no more help being a criminal than you can help being a student. That's why I think no criminal should be punished. He should be treated humanely and given a fresh chance."

"But what if he is a repeat offender?" I said. My father pressed my hand again, vigorously.

"I have an answer to that. Then he should be shot, so that society will be free of him."

I despaired of continuing the argument.

"Mrs. Clyde is really very tolerant," my father said.

"You should read him my poem 'Homosexual,' from 'Horse Sense,' " Mrs. Clyde said.

He turned the pages of the book and then read:

> Have you ever asked yourself this:
> What indeed it must mean
> To have been born with instincts
> That to most men seem obscene?

To be normally abnormal,
To be shunned, loathed and
 scorned
Though having been natural
When you did the things they
 mourned?

If the critics had been given
Those same instincts, are you
Certain they would be acting
Now just as today they do?

I wish that all men understood
That man cannot reject
Mother Nature's gifts to him
Although tragic their effect.

  I was struck by her pithy versification of complicated themes. It's all so strange, I thought. In one way, she comes out with rigid, sometimes shocking statements. In another way, she seems to be the most accepting, enthusiastic, tolerant person I've ever met. Although she's broadminded, she's insistent about her opinions. I can't make her out.

  "Feel free to speak Punjabi between yourselves," Mrs. Clyde was saying. "If I were in a foreign country, I would want to speak my own language. Go right ahead—don't mind us."

  Immediately, I turned to my father and asked in Punjabi, "Why didn't you want me to discuss the free-will question with her?"

  "You will see that the best policy is to agree with her, or, if you feel you can't do that, to be silent," my father said. "I know from experience that you cannot budge her from her view that everything is determined. You can argue the point with her until the cows come home, but she won't acknowledge any exception. If you don't agree that freedom of the will is impossible, you don't have horse sense, and if you don't have horse sense—well, you can't help it, because of your heredity, environment, and experience. Around and around the circle you go."

I had never known my father to be in any way hypocritical, and I felt a little uncomfortable talking about her in this way behind her back. I said as much.

"Then you'll have to learn by experience," he said.

"But why are we here with her, then? What are we doing here?"

"It's a long—a very long—story."

THAT night, we stayed at the Casa Grande Hotel in Coral Gables, on the outskirts of Miami. After dinner, as I lay on the edge of my bed in the room my father and I were sharing, I asked, "How long have you been together?" I had so many questions that I scarcely knew which to ask first. "How did you meet? She was in India with you, so you must have been together for over a month." I told him that I was struck by how he constantly tried to make his views chime with hers—how he agreed with her about nudist camps, for instance, when I knew he thought they were silly. "How do you stand it day after day, week after week? Ever since I can remember, all our relations have deferred to you, looked up to you, as if they expected you to give them the lead. I have never seen you defer to anyone before. But here you are agreeing with her about everything, saying yes to everything. And I can't get used to your calling her Mrs. Clyde, as if she were your employer, and her calling you Mehta, as if you were her employee. It irks me."

"Patience—have patience," he said. "I'll explain it all to you, but a step at a time."

The windows were open to let in the Florida breeze, and outside, against the night silence, the sound of the crickets seemed to recede. I lay very still, with my hand under my cheek, listening to my father.

The road to Mrs. Clyde began with the Watumulls, he was saying. In the summer, before he left Los Angeles, he had gone to a dinner party at the Watumulls' home and had met Margaret Sanger there. He had long admired her work for family planning, and she had wanted to meet him ever since she read his essay on population control and, by her vote as one of the judges, helped it win first prize. Mrs. Sanger and my father didn't have much of a chance to talk at the dinner party, but she invited him to spend a couple of days at her home, in Tucson, Arizona. On his way to New York, he stopped off in Tucson. She gave him an earful about free love, abortion, and the contribution of the suffragists. He had not often heard women talk so frankly about such matters. Then she told him that though she was in her seventies and in poor health she was determined to go to an international conference on population control to be held in Bombay from November 24th to December 2nd that year.

"Mrs. Watumull is going, and I'm very eager that you should also attend—in fact, take up the cudgels for our cause in your country," she added.

"I know about the conference," he said. "Mrs. Watumull, too, has urged me to attend. I myself am very eager to go and help wake India to the cause, but I am a retired man, and I am in no position to volunteer my services, like you and Mrs. Watumull. I don't even have the wherewithal to go to Bombay and stay in a hotel."

She lost no time in pressing into his hand a check for six hundred dollars toward his expenses, and then wrote for him letters of introduction to several people in New York: Mrs. Dorothy Brush, the secretary of the population-control conference; Miss Georgea Furst, the private secretary to the Doris Duke Foundation, which had been contributing money to the cause for years; and Mrs. Ethel Clyde, who had got the Doris Duke Foundation involved in it in the first place. "You should call on all three of them when you get to New York," she said. "They are all good friends of mine. But, of the three, Mrs. Clyde is the only one who might actually give you another check. She's been a big contributor to Planned Parenthood, to the Presidential campaigns of the Socialist Norman Thomas, and to a hundred other causes."

"I'm not in need of more money for my expenses at the conference," he said. "I'm looking around for a paying job."

"You'd enjoy meeting Mrs. Clyde—she's a friend of Mrs. Roosevelt's. Who knows? Maybe you can persuade her to come to the conference."

In New York, my father looked up Mrs. Brush and Miss Furst, and they filled him in on details of the population-control conference. Then he telephoned Mrs. Clyde. She told him that she was feeling abominably tired but would like him to come to tea that afternoon.

When he arrived at her apartment, on Gramercy Park, the door was opened by a large woman with brown eyes and plenty of silver-gray hair, done up in little curls, which came down to her nape. She had an expressive face and a pleasant smile. She was colorfully dressed—in a red dress, with flat shoes that exactly matched it—but the clothes looked simple. She introduced herself as Ethel Clyde and led my father into her living room, shuffling rather than walking.

He looked around. The apartment appeared to be two apartments made into one, but instead of seeming luxurious it had a homelike feeling. There was a lot of old, worn French-looking furniture, and innumerable objects apparently picked up all over the world. Above the piano hung a painting of a tall old man with a white mustache and a pointed beard. He had classic features and a broad forehead.

"That's my father, William Clyde," Mrs. Clyde said. "After I was widowed, I took back my maiden name—keeping the 'Mrs.' because I had two children. But I brought them up as Clydes."

"Your father is a very distinguished-looking man," my father said. "He must have been a banker or an important business executive."

She laughed, in her explosive, resonant way. He had never known a woman to laugh that way. She is brimming with more vitality than many young women in India, he thought.

"He was the president of the Clyde Steamship Company, which my grandfather founded."

"A very famous line," he said, and he told her that when Mahatma Gandhi first went to England he sailed on a ship called the S.S. Clyde.

"I don't know anything about that," she said. "I never took any interest in the business."

His eye wandered to some amateurish unsigned watercolors on another wall. "Oh, I did those," Mrs. Clyde said, with her laugh. "I do some painting."

He liked best a watercolor of flowers hanging between a snow scene and a landscape, and he complimented her on it.

"Oh, that—that one was done by my teacher," she said, with another laugh. She was quick to laugh, and seemed to laugh at everything. She had him sit next to her on a sofa, and asked him directly, the expression in her eyes turning noticeably hard, "What can I do for you?" She picked up a handbag from a corner of the sofa.

He remembered what Mrs. Sanger had told him about the ease with which she wrote checks. Fund-raisers must come calling on her every day, he thought. She probably gives each one a check and sends him away.

"What can you do for me, personally?" he asked. "Nothing. I am an old physician from India. I just completed a short assignment for the U.C.L.A. medical school. I'm harboring an ambition to settle in London and set up a medical practice there one day."

She laughed. "I took you for a fund-raiser," she said.

He thought that perhaps he had sounded too comfortable, so he told her about his straitened circumstances—about the Partition and his retirement.

She listened to him, sitting back and studying him, but with friendly eyes. "How do you happen to know Margaret?" she asked at one point.

He told her about the population essay and their common interest in birth control. "I was deputy director general of health services in India, and I could have done much for our population problem, but my hands were tied. My misfortune was that my Minister, who was a very powerful person in the government, was a devout Christian, and she didn't believe in birth control."

"What a terrible thing!" Mrs. Clyde said. "I thought Nehru was a good Prime Minister. You should have told him to get rid of her!"

"That's not the way things are done in our country," he said. "Anyway, she was a very special disciple of Mahatma Gandhi, and Gandhiji believed that children were gifts from God, and that while each child came with a mouth to feed he also came equipped with hands and feet, to work for his food."

"Which God?" She proclaimed, almost boastingly, "I am an atheist."

He was genuinely surprised. Except, perhaps, for Margaret Sanger, he'd never met such an outspoken woman. She had the manner and tone of a gracious, almost stately lady, but now he was seeing another side of her—that of a freethinker.

"How did they think you could stop people from reproducing like rabbits, then?" she asked him.

"You are right about the rate of reproduction. Even as we have been sitting here, hundreds of new mouths to feed have been born in India."

"I thought Gandhi was humane, and wanted to help your country. He must have had some notion of how to stop people from reproducing. Or did he want your people to die of hunger?"

"The only means of birth control that Gandhiji and his followers approved of was abstinence, and yet abstinence cannot work as a method of birth control in our country."

"Why not?"

"Frankly, sex is about the only diversion most of our poor people have."

Eventually, my father raised the possibility of her attending the population-control conference in Bombay. "Mrs. Sanger is going, and she wants me to attend," he said. "She thought you might like to go, too."

"I went to your country in 1925, and I never want to go near it again," she said. "There's so much poverty and misery there." He thought her reaction childlike and typically American, but she suddenly added, as if on an impulse, "Still, if Margaret is going I'll think about it."

"I myself am not a good example of the population control I preach," my father went on, with his usual twinkle in his eye. "I have seven children, and whenever my children complain that we have too many I ask them, 'Which one could we have done without?'"

Mrs. Clyde laughed. "But I'm a good example," she said. "I have only two sons, and they are now middle-aged, and between them they have just one child, my Toby."

They had a good laugh about the size of their families. Then he looked at his watch and, realizing that he'd stayed for almost two hours, got up to say goodbye. As he was leaving, she asked him where he was staying, and he told her the Commodore Hotel, on Forty-second Street.

"I enjoyed our talk," she said. "I hope we'll meet again."

He said he would like that very much.

Outside on the street, the light was fading fast, and he hurried along toward the hotel. If Partition hadn't happened, I might today still be in Lahore, he remembered thinking. I might be stopping by one of my clubs, playing a little tennis, seeing old friends, joining a table of low-stakes bridge—living the life of a retired man who has done well by his family and the government. Every little corner of his Lahore came back to him with a rush. A man is nothing but a bundle of associations, and an old man is best off passing his waning days among the landmarks of his childhood, he thought. What opposites were this New York and that Lahore! Who could have imagined that he would be made a refugee in his own country, like some human flotsam, cut loose from the moorings of his family and ancestors, who had lived in the Punjab for hundreds, perhaps thousands of years? As so often happened, an apt Urdu couplet came to him spontaneously:

Light of my memories, let them stay with me.
Who knows down which lane the evening of my life shall pass?

No sooner had he reached his hotel room than the telephone rang. It was Mrs. Clyde. "Tomorrow, I'm going to Old Fields, my farm, with my doctor, Coda Martin, and his wife, Kitty," she said. "If you're free for the weekend, I would like to take you along. The farm is in Huntington, Long Island."

Even before the phone call came, he had been telling himself that he was a lucky man to be out and about in the land of his dreams, healthy and vigorous for an Indian man of his age. He could never be sad for very long. Whenever he felt low, an optimistic thought soon swept over him. He had always dreamed of coming out to the West after retirement, and now here he was, in America, in New York, being invited for a country weekend. He began looking forward to the companionship of a new friend and also of a fellow-doctor, who might suggest some means of employment. Who knew where this acquaintance with Mrs. Clyde might lead? In any case, he had no plans for the weekend; he was just going to stay in the hotel, read, and write some letters—something he could do in the country as well as anywhere else. He accepted the invitation with alacrity.

"My doctor and I will be driving out there," she said. "We'll pick you up at seven in the morning at the back entrance of your hotel—that's on our way. Would you wait for us outside?"

"I'll be standing out there five minutes before seven." he said. "I'm one of those Indians who are punctual to a fault."

ON my second day in Florida, we drove to Miami Beach for a swim. In the car, Mrs. Clyde reopened the discussion about free will. I threw myself into it, arguing that we did have some kind of choice, however limited it might seem. "Look, I can raise my arm. That's my choice. That's free will."

"But the choice is made for you by your heredity, environment, and experience."

I went on trying to argue with her, saying that her schematic, generalized formulation almost seemed to preclude discussion, but I felt I was in a ring boxing with shadows. Besides, I felt constrained. She was the benefactress and I was the beneficiary. She was seventy-three and I was eighteen. Still, I persisted. "Can you give me an example of what you mean by heredity?" I asked. "Can you be specific?"

"Heredity is heredity. Don't you know what it is?"

My father pressed my hand and said innocuously, as if to change the subject, "The sky here is certainly nice and blue, but I myself thrive on the gray fog of London. I find that climate very bracing."

"How can you like the English climate?" Mrs. Clyde asked. "The English don't get any sun. I don't like England."

"Some of us like it very much," my father said.

"That's because you come from a hot country," she said.

He protested, saying, "Some of us like the English climate for its own sake."

Mrs. Clyde repeated his statement, worried it, challenged him to justify it, debated it, and would not rest until he had acknowledged that his view reflected his heredity and his experience of living in the environment of India.

"You always win, Mrs. Clyde," he finally said, laughing.

I had to laugh, too. For all his admonitions not to argue with her, he had fallen into the same trap I had.

"And would it surprise you to know that I never graduated from high school?" she asked me.

I said I was indeed surprised.

"I took some classes with my son Bill when he was going to Columbia. I took courses from John Dewey and Edward Hodnett, because I didn't want my sons to be so much smarter than I was that I wouldn't be able to talk to them. Can you imagine mother and son sitting in the same class? We created quite a stir."

She certainly is unusual, I thought. She doesn't fit into any mold.

"I never graduated, but one of my interests is 'educating the educators.' "

"Any time a cartoon, a newspaper story, or some fact Mrs. Clyde comes across strikes her as important, she sends it to a mail-order house with a note that every president of a college, or dean, or professor of history—whatever—should receive a copy, with her compliments," my father said.

I was much impressed, and felt that she and I shared a thirst for knowledge and a faith in education.

At the beach, Mrs. Clyde liked the looks of some beach shirts a vender was offering, and bought three, for Bruce, my father, and me. When my father and I went into a cabana to change into our swimming trunks and the shirts, I said to him, "I know these shirts are supposed to be salt-water-resistant, but I don't like their rubbery feel."

"I myself don't like them," he said. "They have pictures of sailboats and fishes on the back. They're something teen-agers and clowns would wear at home. But mum's the word."

The part of the beach we were on was fairly empty. Bruce rode far out into the sea. My father, an experienced swimmer, went beyond the breakers to swim. I wasn't much of a swimmer, and hadn't been in the ocean since I was a child, so I just waded in again and again, ran after the waves as they were going out, and ducked as I felt them coming in, to allow myself to be carried back. I was surprised at how warm and gentle the sea was, and in my heart I thanked Mrs. Clyde for bringing me to it.

❦

WHEN Mrs. Clyde's car pulled up in front of the back door of the Commodore Hotel at seven o'clock in the morning, my father was waiting. He slipped in beside Dr. Martin, who was behind the wheel. Mrs. Clyde sat in the back, alone. "I was looking forward to meeting your wife," my father said to Dr. Martin.

"My wife couldn't come," Dr. Martin explained. "She had to stay back to look after Jimmie, our dog, who's very old and sick."

Dr. Martin had a pleasant manner and bearing, and he was well spoken, but he was dressed in a gray suit and came across as a businessman. My father had trouble imagining him in the striped trousers and long white coat of an English doctor.

While Mrs. Clyde dozed, Dr. Martin drew my father out, quizzing him about his medical training. My father thought that Dr. Martin was trying to find out if his training was comparable with that of an American doctor, and wondered whether Dr. Martin might have a job for him up his sleeve.

"This was one of the first prefabricated houses to be built on the East Coast," Mrs. Clyde said when they pulled up to her country house an hour or two later.

"It could be a mansion," my father said, genuinely surprised. "This is a wondrous country, where such a house can be sold and bought, perhaps from a picture in a catalogue. The grounds, too, look very big."

"They're fields, not grounds," Dr. Martin said. "About forty acres' worth."

Mrs. Clyde told Dr. Martin and my father that they could do what they liked until lunchtime. A man called Berni, a German, who seemed to be a resident chauffeur cum butler, showed each of them to an upstairs bedroom with its own bathroom, while Mrs. Clyde went to sit in the sun on a glassed-in porch attached to her room.

My father went downstairs and knocked some balls around on a billiard table. He went out on the lawn and sat in a chaise longue and watched birds and rabbits dart about. He sauntered along a road, shaded by poplars, that seemed to lead into the village. He was used to doing things with my mother and the rest of us, and he missed our company, thinking how much fun the weekend would have been if we had all been there with him. He came back and went into the kitchen and made friends with the housekeeper, Mrs. Armer. She was a short woman with a plain but amiable face and a weak chin. What was most noticeable about her was a hearty working-class English accent.

My father asked after her husband.

"He's gone back to England to live, sir," she said. "He's always liked the English way of life better than the American. He's a private man, and now that he's getting on in years he likes his quiet. But I have to live here, because this is where my job is."

"My wife and I, too, have to live apart," he said. "I'm trying to make a living, and she's back home in India. And I, too, love England. I like its quiet and rhythm of life best of all. I would like to settle there." They commiserated with each other, and soon my father was telling her how to make *bhurji,* his favorite Indian dish, of scrambled eggs, onions, and chilies.

Mrs. Clyde came downstairs dressed in shorts. He was taken aback, but then reminded himself that, like Margaret Sanger, she was an outrageous rebel, even if she was also a gracious Victorian lady. "Let's go for a walk," she said, picking out a cane from a collection in a stand. "I'd like to see what's doing in the fields."

The day was crowded with many new impressions, but what he later remembered most clearly was that Mrs. Clyde talked to him and conducted herself with him as if he were an old, close friend rather than someone she had met only once before.

The next morning, as Dr. Martin and my father were sitting at the breakfast table and eating *bhurji*—Mrs. Clyde hadn't come down yet—Dr. Martin asked my father abruptly, "Would you be interested in travelling with Mrs. Clyde to India if she goes to the population conference?"

"I'm going to the conference anyway," my father replied. "I would be glad to accompany her and show her around."

"Well, she needs more than that," Dr. Martin said. "She told me that she would like you to take charge. If you're interested, we'll talk about her medical history when we get back to the city." He added, "I think she would make it worth your while to be her 'court physician.' She's very rich, you know."

" 'Neither their friendship is good nor their enmity,' as our Urdu couplet has it," my father said. Then, realizing that the couplet might be off-putting, he added quickly, "I would certainly be interested." He had never heard the term "court physician" before, and didn't know what that might involve, but the prospect of having a job, any job, and especially one connected with his profession, was tantalizing.

"She has the unmentionable disease," Dr. Martin announced. "You know what I mean."

My father didn't know what he meant, but decided to keep his own counsel for the time being.

"My opinion is she shouldn't travel without medical attendance, and she can well afford it," Dr. Martin said.

"Perhaps you would be interested in accompanying her yourself," my father suggested.

"It isn't easy for us American doctors to just pick up and go like that," Dr. Martin said, perhaps implying that Mrs. Clyde had told him about my father's straitened circumstances and that he took it for granted they would make my father willing to entertain such a proposal.

On the particular night of my Christmas holiday when my father told me about that conversation, it didn't occur to me to ask what "the unmentionable disease" was. Just hearing the words made my teen-age heart race. After Mrs. Clyde died, at the age of ninety-eight, in 1978, I asked my father if professional ethics would allow him to tell me what the disease was.

"Oh!" he exclaimed. "There is no great stigma attached to it nowadays. It was epilepsy." He went on to say, "But I have to confess that when Dr. Martin first volunteered the name of the disease to me, in New York, in those early days, I was thrown. My medical knowledge of epilepsy was very rusty. I don't think I'd read anything about it since the twenties, when I was a student—when it was indeed an unmentionable disease. I had to read up on it in the library. I learned that a lot of progress had been made. Dilantin kept it mostly under control. Mrs. Clyde took that medicine, but she must have had seizures in public when she was a child, before Dilantin was available, and she lived in constant fear that she might have a seizure in public again. You might say her doctors had to minister to her fear of the public manifestation of the disease rather than to the disease itself. The few seizures she had while I was with her were very easily taken care of. The picture was a little complicated, however, because she had a heart condition. She had to take digitalis. I remember at one point her fear of having a seizure in public started keeping her awake, and I consulted a specialist at the Columbia-Presbyterian Medical Center in New York, and added to the Dilantin a quarter of phenobarbital. This combination became her standby."

THE evening following the weekend that my father and Dr. Martin spent at Old Fields, Mrs. Clyde told my father that she wanted to have a serious talk with him. She had asked him to come and see her, and they were again sitting in the living room of her apartment. She had in her lap a legal pad, her diary, and her checkbook, and various papers were spread about her on the sofa. "I had the brain wave to go to India with you as my court physician when I realized you weren't a fund-raiser," she said. "Now that Coda has discussed the whole subject with you, let's get down to business." Her expression, usually pleasant and receptive, abruptly became hard and challenging. "I'd like to go a month or so before the conference and do a little travelling. I'll pay all your expenses when we're travelling. What salary would you like?"

He suddenly woke up to the fact that he was actually going to be paid a salary. So being her "court physician" will be an assignment, like the Fulbright and the International Bank job, he thought.

"My last real job was with the International Bank," he said. "I was getting eleven hundred and fifty dollars a month."

"Then I will pay you the same," she said, almost as if she were clinching a deal.

"But that included a daily allowance of fifteen dollars for expenses. My actual salary was seven hundred dollars."

"Well, then, I'll pay you seven hundred dollars, since I plan to pay both your travelling and daily expenses as my guest," she said immediately. The salary seemed very fair. It was even princely by Indian standards.

"But Mrs. Sanger has already paid me six hundred dollars toward my expenses in Bombay." He was prompted to volunteer this fact because, after all, Mrs. Sanger had given him the money for a designated purpose.

"Then I'll deduct that from your expenses—from the cost of your plane ticket," she said, noting down the amount. "In America, you will be my guest, like all my other friends, so I will pay you a salary only when you are travelling with me. Anyway, my tax people tell me that since you're not a citizen of this country and don't have a green card I can pay you only when we're abroad."

It never occurred to him to protest. She, of course, had her own doctors here, and technically he would be on duty only when they were travelling. He nodded.

"Hurrah!" Mrs. Clyde cried. "Then it's settled! The plan is very advantageous to both of us."

And my father recited to himself an Urdu couplet:

In this ocean of destruction, the boat of life sails along.
Whichever place the boat happens to run aground, that is
    your shore and home.

In the afternoon, my father and Mrs. Clyde went to 125 East 72nd Street, where Dr. Martin had his office. Mrs. Clyde got a vaccination against smallpox and injections against cholera and typhoid, all of which were required for travelling to India. Then she visited with Kitty in the Martins' apartment, which was in the same building, while my father stayed in the office and Dr. Martin filled him in on Mrs. Clyde's medical history. After telling him about various vitamins, sedatives, and medicines she took, he said, "She's no spring chicken, you know. You have to be careful that she doesn't fall sick. When she's travelling, she has to stay in first-class hotels and eat in good restaurants."

My father finally had an inkling of what it meant to be a "court physician": he was being asked to attend on some kind of American queen.

"What financial arrangements have you and Mrs. Clyde arrived at?" Dr. Martin asked, without any preliminaries.

My father told him.

"An American doctor of your standing might have asked for four or five thousand dollars a month, and got it," Dr. Martin said. "She can well afford to pay, and, after all, you're going to be on call twenty-four hours a day."

My father felt a pang for having been so open and spontaneous with Mrs. Clyde—for carrying his heart on his sleeve, as usual. "At least, it's all found," he said, laughing it off. "Seven hundred dollars a month is all that the services of a retired Indian doctor are worth."

"You certainly shouldn't allow her to deduct six hundred dollars from your air ticket."

Mrs. Sanger's six hundred dollars would have come in very handy, he thought, while it can make no difference to Mrs. Clyde. But he felt he had no choice, and said as much. The subject was dropped.

When Mrs. Clyde and my father left Dr. Martin's building, she suggested that they walk for a few blocks before getting a taxi. As they made their way along, people turned back to look at them, smiling a little. She had on her flat, comfortable shoes and was carrying her cane, and that day she was wearing a cape. It was cut very loose, and, draped around her, it emphasized her largeness. The shoes, which, she had told my father, were handmade for her on Cape Cod from the leather of cows that had died a natural death, seemed a little incongruous on the city sidewalk, and so highlighted her eccentricity. The cane was almost a practical necessity for her, but it also gave her walk a certain dignity, verging on imperiousness. And there was my father at her side, in complexion so light, in bearing so distinguished that he could have been taken for an Italian nobleman. She looked so old and he looked so young that they might have been a mother and son who had just stepped off the boat from Europe.

Without a preparatory word, she stopped on the street and pulled out of her bag a few ten-dollar bills and tried to press them on him.

He drew back. "What is that for?"

"I'm tired. Let's get a taxi."

"I have money. Anyway, a taxi ride is only a few dollars."

Right there on the street, she explained to him that whenever he was with her he was her guest. Wherever they went, whatever they did together, and even wherever he went alone on her behalf, she must pay. That had been her practice ever since she could remember, and everyone who was her friend knew and accepted it.

It will be one thing for me to settle our hotel accounts with money from her when we are travelling, he thought, but it's quite another thing to accept cash directly from her. The money was still waving in her hand, so that any passerby could snatch it, and he found himself saying, "I'll keep a record. You can give me the money later." He tried to hail a taxi.

"But I don't like carrying money," she said. "I want you to carry my money, and I want you to pay for everything, because you're the man. You ask Coda Martin. Whenever he and Kitty and I go out together, I give him the money and he pays for everything."

People were beginning to stare at them, as if they were having a family quarrel. He wanted to put an end to the argument, to hurry her along, get her into a taxi. He looked up and down the street, but no empty taxi was to be seen.

"While we are preparing to go, there will be many little expenses—passport fees, travellers' checks, restaurant bills—that you'll have to take care of," she was saying. "There may be times when I don't feel like going out to lunch, and you'll have to eat alone and pay for it. Since you're my guest, you should have money in your pocket. That's why everything will be so much easier if you'll just agree to be my banker. I make all my companions my bankers."

The term "banker" assuaged his feelings somewhat, but he saw his job with Mrs. Clyde in a new light. It wasn't like the International Bank job or the Fulbright at all. It was personal— that of a courtier. He took the money, emptied the inside left pocket of his jacket, and stuffed the bills in. From that day on, he treated that pocket as Mrs. Clyde's "bank."

Over the next fortnight or so, my father went with her in taxis or in her car, driven by Berni, to doctors' offices, to the homes of her friends, to shops, to her tailor, where she had herself fitted for a new cape. He accompanied her on expeditions outside the city, here to see a sick friend, there to investigate the efficacy of hypnosis or of the single-tax movement, and, on a longer trip, to drop in on her invalid brother, Will, and her sister, Mabel, who lived together in the Mayflower Hotel in Washington, D.C. He took most of his meals with her. Everywhere, he was her "guest," paying from her bank in his pocket. She told him that it would make her very happy if he would give up his room at the Commodore and stay in her guest room, but he resisted, clinging to a vestige of economic independence. Whenever he stopped to think about his new life, his new job, his new friendship, he recited to himself the Urdu couplet:

> God knows what happens after death.
> At least the present passes in tranquillity.

THE few days I was Mrs. Clyde's guest in Florida, I was bowled over by her restless energy. We would "hit the road" in the morning without knowing where we would be spending the night. She seemed to go anywhere, do anything that came into her head. We went from Miami to Palm Beach and on to West Palm Beach, St. Petersburg, St. Augustine, Jacksonville; from hotel to hotel, restaurant to restaurant, tourist attraction to tourist attraction, auto camp to auto camp.

I had never spent a whole day in a rich person's company, and I couldn't get over Mrs. Clyde's complicated attitude toward money. She would choose simple, unostentatious restaurants, and she balked at tipping more than ten per cent. Yet an extra zero on the check she was writing for our hotel rooms seemed to make no difference to her. It was as if she worried about pennies but didn't care about dollars. She booked into hotels without comparing rates with other hotels or asking what a room would cost. If something caught her fancy in a shop, she bought it, without stopping to think whether she needed it or could use it. She made long-distance telephone calls to her friends from hotel rooms without worrying about what the calls would cost. Indeed, just when a phone conversation seemed to be finishing, she would start it up again, not once but a dozen times, without seeming to be aware of the expensive seconds and minutes clicking away. We could never have dreamed of a life like hers.

All the time I was with her, I tried to persuade her that I didn't need a separate bed in my father's room—that I could sleep on the floor.

"Why?" she asked.

"You can save some money by having us stay in a single room instead of a double."

"And have you, child, uncomfortable?" She laughed and laughed. "You are my guest."

It seemed there was no way to recompense her except through talk and argument.

❧

MY father and Mrs. Clyde arrived in London on the way to India on the morning of October 21st, and he started telephoning hotels from the airport. It was part of his job to make all the travel arrangements, and before leaving New York he had visited the offices of Thomas Cook & Sons and American Express. He had found the task uncongenial, and, moreover, he had been staggered by the prices quoted to him, perhaps because on the few occasions when he stayed in hotels in London he had sought out cheap bed-and-breakfast places, and had often been able to use his personal charm to get the landlady to make additional concessions. The travel agents had assured him that rooms in London were plentiful at that time of the year, so he had put off making hotel reservations until he and Mrs. Clyde reached London and he could personally visit the hotels, thinking that that way he might be able to get lower rates. But now, when he telephoned, he discovered that he and Mrs. Clyde had arrived in the middle of automobile and agricultural exhibitions, and it seemed there was not a room to be had in the entire city. After a great deal of telephoning, he was able to secure two single rooms, without private baths, at the India Service Club, on South Audley Street, in Mayfair.

When they arrived at the club, it turned out that Mrs. Clyde was the only woman guest in the place, and he was able to prevail upon another guest to trade his single room with private bath for her room. When Mrs. Clyde was shown to it, she shrank back but bravely said aloud, "It will be fun." She seemed very sporting and understanding about his failure to make prior arrangements. "How could anyone possibly have known that all the hotels in London would be taken over by trade shows?" she said.

But the next morning, when she and my father started down to breakfast, they caught sight of the back of a big fellow walking out of his room in an undershirt and a pair of baggy drawers, and with hair hanging wildly down his back.

"What kind of place is this, where a half-dressed man with dirty long hair can walk around in full sight of everyone?" she asked. "I wouldn't object to him half as much if he were in the nude, and lived in the open, among birds and trees."

"He belongs to the martial religion of the Sikhs," my father said. "Ordinarily, his hair would be in a topknot under a turban, but he must have just got up."

"What is he doing wearing his hair like a woman? Hasn't he ever heard of a barber?" She laughed. Even when she was irritated, she saw the humor in things.

"Keeping long hair and a beard is part of the Sikh religion."

"Why haven't I heard of that religion? What is he doing living in England? He's not English."

"There are a lot of people living in England who are not English. They are immigrants."

In the dining room, the waiter came to take their order, and she ordered a sizable combination of Indian and Western breakfasts. She's wonderful, my father thought. She has a healthy appetite and is very adventurous. No wonder she has so much energy.

"I thought your country was hot. Those Sikhs must sweat like anything. I thought you said your people were clean."

"I don't remember the context in which I said that, but we Hindus are known for being clean in our personal habits, for bathing frequently."

"But no one would say that that Sikh upstairs was clean."

"He was probably going for his wash. Sikhs bathe and wash their hair regularly."

"I thought India was dry and poor, and you had to conserve all the water you could for the crops."

"But it doesn't take much water to wash hair. Our women keep long hair."

"Maybe your country would be better off if you cut off the hair of Sikhs and your women."

"For the Sikh men and our women to wear long hair is a very old tradition. Indeed, we Hindus think that long hair is a woman's crowning glory."

"What good is hair and glory if you've got people starving to death?"

"Not everyone in India is starving. Anyway, it's our culture—our religion, our society."

She looked skeptical.

He searched for some comparison that might make sense to her. "Sikh men are like the Biblical hero Samson. Their hair is a symbol of their power and virility."

"If Samson were living today, he would cut his hair," she declared, and added, laughing, "He would certainly not go around in an English hotel with his hair flying about wildly. Why, the whole floor smells of sweaty hair. You know, I have a nose like a dog."

My father laughed, too.

Breakfast was served, and she attacked it vigorously, but that didn't slow her talking—or, rather, asking question after question about Sikhs, Hindus, India. Asking questions seemed to be her way of carrying on a conversation. "My middle name is Question Mark," she said. He tried to make the conversation personal, thinking that that way she might be able to have more sympathy for the Sikhs. "By the way, my grandmother was a Sikh," he said.

"Then why don't you have long hair?" she asked.

"I'll try to be clearer," he said. "Many Punjabi Hindus have Sikh relatives but remain Hindus. Sikhs are converts from Hinduism—they belong to a different religion."

"How can any thinking person be religious after Darwin?"

"Why not? There are plenty of thinking people who are religious."

"Science tells us religion is superstition. You're a doctor. You're a scientist. How can you not be an atheist? It's all heredity, environment, and experience."

He tried to argue with her, saying that for believers religion was as objective as the table he and she were sitting at.

"They're all barking up the wrong tree."

Mrs. Clyde and my father were at the breakfast table long after everyone else had left. It seemed that whatever he said met with a swift riposte, and that she made no effort to understand his point. She took his most casual remark literally and repeated it to him later out of context. The more he tried to end a subject, to extricate himself by giving short, evasive answers, the more tenaciously she pursued it. In New York, some of her enormous energy had been diverted onto her other friends and onto Mrs. Armer, Berni, and maids, and he could escape to his hotel, leaving her with other people. Now she had no one but him, and he had nowhere else to go, so he had to bear her firepower alone. He felt cornered. As a rule, he was full of energy himself, and very resilient, but talking with her was such an exhausting experience that he had come to feel flattened. I've now known her for three weeks, he thought. However bighearted she is, however eager she is to learn, when it actually comes down to it she has difficulty seeing any point of view different from her own. That may have something to do with the fact that she is rich, and that the rich are not used to having their opinions contradicted or challenged. She behaves as if we were equals, as if we were friends, and encourages me to say whatever comes into my head, but she is my employer, and there is no way I can be her equal. I have to be on my guard and try to please her at all times, however much it goes against the grain. In her presence, I will have to conduct myself according to Bhabiji's saying: "First weigh what you're going to say, and only then say it."

"I hate this hotel," she said suddenly. "I don't want to spend another minute here. I want to move right now."

They had planned to spend only two nights in London, and he attempted to persuade her not to move, since there was just one more night. The time would go very fast, he said. But once she had taken something into her head it was very difficult to get her to change her mind. So he said he'd go out and look for another hotel, and asked her for exact specifications.

She said that she would like them to have two rooms next to each other, possibly with a connecting door, so that if she suddenly sensed a fainting spell coming on and called him he could rush to her side. She wanted each room to have its own attached bathroom, with a shower. If possible, her room should have a balcony or a sitting room with a lot of sunlight. "You know from Old Fields that I'm a sun worshipper," she added.

He realized he had no choice but to do her bidding, and immediately set out to find new hotel rooms, while she went upstairs to her room to try to work on her watercolors. He stopped in at a travel agency, got a list of hotels, and canvassed them on foot. In due course, he took her to see the rooms in a hotel he liked, so that she could judge for herself. but she stepped into the lobby and said she didn't like the look of it—she would never stay there. He couldn't get her to go in any farther. Finally, he caught on to the fact that she would not be satisfied with anything less than a five-star hotel. Hang the expense, he thought. It's her money, and she has the right to spend it as she likes.

He took her back to the club, and, remembering that all the most important Indian princes used to stay at the Savoy, he went there. Apparently, the farmers and automobile dealers of the trade shows had not been interested in staying in such a grand place, and rooms that more or less met Mrs. Clyde's specifications were available. He took them, and by teatime they had moved in.

"The rooms are perfect," she said, and he felt relieved.

Mrs. Clyde didn't want tea in the Savoy, however, because it didn't have "tea music," such as she was used to hearing on visits to Germany. He took her to the Regent Palace, in Piccadilly, which he remembered for its waltzes, and she enjoyed her tea very much. She nodded to the rhythm of the violins playing "The Blue Danube" and ordered a second round of sandwiches and pastries.

They laughed about the pastries they were eating, the Sikh in the club, my father's Sikh grandmother, and why he liked women with long hair, and about how she had such thick hair for her age that most acquaintances didn't believe it was natural until she had them pull it. It dawned on him then that she was just a joyous, outgoing creature, who enjoyed everything—enjoyed her food, enjoyed talking, enjoyed asking questions. He recalled that she had sat in on a couple of philosophy classes at Columbia. She had perhaps learned about the Socratic method there and concluded that it was a stimulating form of conversation. Now that he thought about it, if anyone else had talked about the Sikhs and Hindus the way she did, it might have sounded disrespectful or mean, but with her it was the insatiable curiosity of someone trying to learn new things. He himself was known for being curious about everything, and he could sympathize with her. Maybe everything in her life fell into the category of travelling to new places, having new experiences, having spirited adventures. He reacted the way he did because of something in him—something in the Indian tradition—that made the whole world a system of subservience and dominance, as if, no matter how high you reached, there were always those higher, whom you had to defer to, and defer to completely. Probably her American friends were able to talk to her as equals, in a spirit of fun, but he would always be careful and worried in front of her, fearful of offending her. There was nothing he could do about it.

The waiter brought him the bill, and he paid it, feeling flush. He was in his London, living at the Savoy, having tea with oh-so-familiar music at a place he ordinarily couldn't afford to go to, and with plenty of money in Mrs. Clyde's bank.

MY father and Mrs. Clyde got to Bombay almost a month before the population conference was to begin, so that she could see something of India, as she had planned. But on the way from the airport to the Taj Mahal Hotel, where my father had reserved rooms for them, she saw from the taxi a sight that never stopped haunting her: whole families living in abandoned sewer pipes in a swamp. She kept repeating in the taxi that she wished she'd stayed away from the "poverty, filth, tragedy, hell, heartbreak" that was India. When she reached her hotel room, she choked up with tears in the middle of a sentence and collapsed into a chair. "Those poor people living in sewer pipes!" she sobbed. "To what end? To what end? I don't know why they should be allowed to survive."

My father tried to console her, alternately sympathizing with her point of view and trying to put the poverty in some kind of understandable context for her. "The poverty here is terrible," he said. "But at the same time you should know that the sixteen-mile stretch from the airport to the hotel has some of the worst squalor in India. Not all India is like that."

"It's so hard to bear," Mrs. Clyde said. "I want to go home. I wish all the nations on earth would help to build a great big bomb to blow up this miserable world!"

She had often made this statement before. Still, he was shocked by it all over again, and tried, as he had previously, to tell her that life, with all its joys and sorrows, was better than extinction. But she kept on weeping and shaking her head, saying, "To what end? To what end?"

"Before you run away, we should go and see the beauty of the Moghul monuments, and the boat and mountain life of Kashmir, as we planned," my father said. "India is rich in scenic treasures and spiritual heritage. There is more to the country than what you've seen."

She wiped her eyes and started looking her cheerful self. "It would be wonderful to get out of this hell and see something else," she said.

He thanked his stars that Mrs. Clyde had come to India in October, one of the three or four best months, for a combination of Indian heat and Indian poverty might indeed have driven her back to the United States. They started making plans to leave Bombay after a day or two of rest, my father writing out an itinerary for her and explaining to her the geography of Kashmir, and of Old and New Delhi, where some of the Moghul monuments were situated.

She said she was getting hungry, and he reminded her that, from London, they had arranged to have Om come to lunch that day. Om, my older brother, was studying marine engineering in Bombay. She seemed eager to be finally meeting one of the members of my father's family.

When he saw that her mood had improved, he remarked that he didn't enjoy going anywhere without his wife, his "one and only," and that he was arranging to have my mother join them in Delhi and travel with them in India.

She made a face. He had half expected that she wouldn't cherish the idea. He had noticed that on the whole she did not get along with the women he had met when he was with her, but sought out the company of men, as if she considered women a bore and felt she could have serious discussions only with men. Perhaps women of her class at that time were not interested in serious things, he thought. Perhaps that was why she was drawn to unorthodox women like Margaret Sanger. Still, as a family man, he had always assumed that his wife was welcome wherever he was welcome. And didn't Mrs. Clyde accept the company of

Kitty Martin as a matter of course? My father had even hoped that she might be curious about my mother and eager to meet her.

"How can you possibly pay for her?" she asked. "I thought you were a poor refugee."

"It's true that I can't afford to have her with me in Europe or America, but from what I'm earning from you now I can easily pay for her travels here. Anyway, two can live as cheaply as one in the hotels."

She made a face again but said nothing.

She's so literal-minded that she takes my being an impecunious refugee to mean that I am without any resources, he thought. He recalled that in London she had insisted on paying for a scarf he needed against the cold, saying he should save every penny of his salary or he would starve to death, like many of his countrymen. It is almost impossible to get her to understand that I'm capable of taking care of my needs, the needs of my family, he thought—that, having lived most of my life with a good salary, I cannot suddenly behave as if I were an indigent, with no confidence in the morrow, as if I had no earning power. At the same time, he didn't want to do or say anything to give her the false impression that he was not in any need, and so jeopardize whatever help she might be able to give him. He tried another tack. "The idea of a man going about with a lady who is not his wife will not be understood in India," he said. "A Hindu can travel with a woman at his side only if she is his wife."

She laughed, as if he were making a sociological joke. "Mehta, I'm old enough to be your mother. I'm an old lady and you're my doctor. What's so difficult for anyone to understand about that?"

"But this is India," he said. "My children, in-laws, and relations will certainly not be able to understand our situation."

She was silent.

He pressed home his advantage. "I have not seen my wife for almost a year, and she must be with me."

"But she can be with us only as long as we are in India," she said firmly.

Since his financial situation made the question of my mother's travelling with them abroad academic, he said nothing.

Om arrived for lunch, and spoke of being impressed that his father was staying at the Taj Mahal Hotel.

Mrs. Clyde laughed with pleasure. She seemed her old, ebullient self. They could have been in a luxury hotel anywhere in the world. The three of them went down to one of the hotel's many restaurants and had lunch together. She ordered Indian dishes, ate heartily, and asked Om a lot of questions. When she learned that his real interest was acting and singing, and he had been pushed into marine engineering, she was horrified.

"People have to subordinate their passions and inclinations to the necessity of earning a livelihood," my father said.

"At home, people do what they like and earn a good living," she said.

"But America is very rich. India is very poor," my father said.

"Well, then, Om should come to America," she said.

"But how?" my father said. "You know our resources."

She looked pained, as if she were upset that Om couldn't follow his dream, like an American.

"Also, the American immigration laws are very tough for us Indians," he said, to shift the discussion from something personal to something abstract. "Indians wait for years to go and work there."

She seemed to feel better, and they changed the subject.

❧

WE were in a cabin at an auto camp in West Palm Beach. "Your mother . . . Mrs. Clyde . . . and I arrived back in Bombay . . . a few days before the population conference," my father said haltingly. His voice grew fainter and fainter; he was obviously drifting off to sleep.

I lay very still. I should let him sleep, I thought. But our time is so limited. I have to know what Mamaji made of Mrs. Clyde, what Mrs. Clyde made of Mamaji, whether Mrs. Clyde saw anything about India besides its hellish poverty—whether she came to like India.

"But you haven't told me yet what you did in India the month between your two stays in Bombay."

"Sightseeing . . ." He was fast asleep.

In spite of several conversations in Florida about that month, my father never really succeeded in evoking it for me. Perhaps we didn't have enough time, but I now think it is more likely that for my father Mrs. Clyde in India had been a little too much to cope with. It was one thing for him to be "Mehta" and her attendant in New York and London, and even in Geneva and Cairo, where they had stopped on their way to India, for in those places he was nobody. It was quite another thing for him to be in that subservient position in India, where he was the head of the Mehta clan—the lord of his manor, as it were—and where he had a vast network of friends who admired and respected him, and where he had been master of a huge government department. I didn't get a full picture of what that month had been like until long after Florida, when, some months before Mrs. Clyde died, she allowed me to copy the pages of her diary concerning the time she spent with my father, and gave me permission to use them. (She kept a diary most of her life, but her executors, in accordance with her wishes, destroyed it.) Those pages have proved invaluable in reconstructing this narrative.

29 October
Maiden's Hotel, Old Delhi.

We took the 8:30 A.M. plane for Delhi, arriving at 12:30 P.M. Shanti, Mehta's attractive wife, dressed in Indian costume (they are Hindus), has joined us at Maiden's Hotel. His charming daughter Umi and her nice husband came to call on me in my suite, and I kept them to dine with us.

31 October

A wonderful day full of the beauty, charm, and horror of India. Mehta, Shanti, Umi, and I drove to Agra (4 hours) starting about 8:45 this morning. Part of what we passed looked as though we might be back in Bible days. We saw bullocks (white) in a field, walking up and down a ramp pulling water from a well in a bucket made of a water buffalo's hide. This was emptied into a narrow trough, which ran to where a man irrigated the field by throwing the water about from a broken water pitcher, the kind carried on the head. I photographed the ramp, etc.

We had a rest after a good luncheon at the hotel. Then we went to the Taj Mahal at sunset. Had another rest before a good dinner. Returned to see the Taj in the moonlight before starting the long drive back to New Delhi. Very few were at the Taj at the time. I was able to sing one note under the dome and had it taken up and elaborated, as if by an angel chorus. It is uncanny indeed, and only works well if the note is a high one. Mehta tried, and his note carried on up higher, higher, higher,

1 November
Nedou's Hotel, Srinagar, Kashmir.

We walked to Dal Lake and took a very comfortable ride in a sort of river taxi called a *shikara*. We reclined on a short mattress with a straight back at one end and were propelled by a paddle through a tangled mess of houseboats, *doongas,* and other craft, between appalling banks covered with all manner of dwellings unfit for human habitation.

2 November
Unfortunately, I have what is called "hill diarrhea." I understand that the majority of those that come here are bothered with it. Am eating light. This is the best and only hotel—has practi-

cally no view. The toilets flush only spasmodically; there is very little light anywhere in the evening, due to insufficient current. It is cold at night and there is no heat in the outer dressing room or bathroom. When water runs out of the basin, it runs into an indentation in the floor under the tub, as does the tub water, and from there out through a drain! The towels one would prefer not to touch, and the beds are far from comfortable, with hard pillows! During the day, when the stoves are lit, they give off too much heat.

We took a drive this morning and I made a rough pencil sketch at the lake.

5 November
Maiden's Hotel, Old Delhi.

Am immensely enjoying the comparative luxury of this hotel after the one at Srinagar.

7 November
Imperial Hotel, New Delhi

Shanti had two teeth extracted this morning, and, to my surprise, was able to come to the dining room and eat luncheon with us.

11 November

This morning, I went to the People's House [Parliament] with Shanti and Mehta. An interesting experience. Nehru spoke, but the acoustics there are non-existent.

13 November

Hungry early. Had breakfast in my room. Thomas Cook's and shopping this morning. Wrote Ingles [a doctor who was taking care of Ben Marsh] a brief note.

After luncheon, we got our visas for Indonesia, and I saw the garden where Gandhi was killed when he went there to pray. The spot is marked by a simple stone on which is carved the date and "oh, Ram" in Hindu [*sic*]. That is what he said when he was shot—his last words. (Ram is the name of a god.) The people quietly came to this place and removed their shoes before approaching the stone. One prayed, another picked red blossoms from the hedge nearby, to sprinkle on the stone, as others had done. I saw no woman come, but a small boy came with a man. Such simplicity, respect, reverence, and, I think, affection. I believe it would have pleased and touched Gandhi.

Had made a beautiful dressing gown out of half a bedspread I bought this morning.

14 November

We went to an Indian movie for a while—simple, unsophisticated, and boring from American standards. The music here is so different that I am not able to appreciate or enjoy it. It seems to me to be about halfway between ours and the Chinese.

16 November

Early this morning, Mehta, Shanti, and I drove to Qutb Minar, the famous minaret Tower, one of the architectural wonders of India. It has been called the most perfect tower in the world. It has stood about a thousand years. Afterwards, we visited an Indian village. Mehta and I took a variety of photos, among them ones of "holy men" who were truly appalling.

Aside from Bombay and the trip to Agra, Mrs. Clyde went only to Delhi and Srinagar, but on the whole the Indian pages of the diary bear the stamp of a person who makes a business of being on perpetual vacation. Much space is devoted to straightening out reservations bungled by travel agents; getting visas; going out to airports, for which a lot of extra time is allowed, in case the car has a puncture or there are long lines at the ticket counters; settling into hotels; confirming air tickets for the next leg of the journey. At one point, she decides that she wants to travel home via Thailand, Fiji, and Australia. Reservations have to be applied for, waited for, checked. Some are not available.

Then she hears that Bangkok is hot and humid and full of mosquitoes. She decides that she never wanted to go to Thailand anyway. Now a new itinerary is drawn up, via Rome, Geneva, and Nice, Bermuda and Florida. That, too, is revised, and the trips to Florida and Bermuda are put off until after a rest in New York. New reservations have to be made. And, whichever way she goes, there is always the question of hotel accommodations. Throughout, she observes and comments on the hotel service, the food, the beds, and what she sees on the street below.

From what my family members recall of her visit, her daily routine while travelling was fairly simple. When she wasn't doing watercolors, writing postcards, or shopping, she was taking snapshots of scenes such as porters standing at train stations and men on the roadside cleaning people's ears or performing cataract operations. She looked through American newspapers when they were available, and enjoyed following the adventures of comicstrip characters. She sometimes fell asleep during the day with the newspaper open in front of her, but she stayed awake at night—a night owl, she called herself. She had a friend or two in every port of call. Most of the friends were Americans involved in some kind of "humanitarian" work. She enjoyed surprising them. She hardly ever accepted hospitality from them—it was simpler for her to have them for a meal at her hotel. The talk at such meals was about other friends or about her guests' financial, medical, or family problems—very rarely about what was happening in the world. Letters were forwarded to her from other friends, concerning similar problems, and in response, as often as not, she sent a check, usually earmarked for a specific thing—new dentures or eyeglasses, say—because she liked to feel she was alleviating a particular need. She began confiding in my father and discussing with him the little, specific needs that her guests and other friends, consciously or unconsciously, brought up. He was careful not to curb by word or gesture any of her generous impulses.

One day, he told me, he drove Mrs. Clyde in his car, an old

Vauxhall, to see the house he was building. The second story was being worked on at the time.

"How can you afford to build a house?" she asked. He admitted that he didn't have enough money at the moment to finish it, and she started scolding him for building a house in the first place. He explained to her that because of the way he had obtained the land from the government it was cheaper in the long run for him to build a house than to rent one, and that anyway without a roof over one's head in India one could very easily be sucked down into a vortex of poverty.

She then noticed a man who was camping out on the property to keep an eye on the construction, and my father told her he was the one servant the family still had in its employ.

"What extravagance!" she exclaimed. "A man in your position shouldn't waste any money on such luxuries."

"Here we do not have labor-saving devices like vacuum cleaners, dishwashers, and washing machines, or conveniences like hot running water, supermarkets, and good public transportation—all of which are taken for granted in American cities," he said. "For a man of my class, you might say that a servant, like this car we are sitting in, is almost a necessity."

"But you're a poor refugee."

He couldn't get her to see that, however poor he was, he still had ambitions for his children and family.

"I don't like being here at this house," she said. "Why did you bring me?"

He recalled then that expeditions she made with him to his club and his office, which he had thought would help her to picture his life before retirement, had made her equally impatient. It was almost as if she wanted him to be an orphan, without a family, without a former life, and without ambitions—to be completely dependent on her. He felt discouraged, and quickly drove her back to the hotel.

Later that day, however, when he mentioned the expense of

my education, she seemed very sympathetic. He realized that she had to be able to understand a situation and take an emotional interest in it in order to respond to it—that her sympathy was more easily engaged for someone who was sick or handicapped, who had a particular problem that she thought could be solved with money, than for someone who, like him, was struggling to keep his head above water and to make something of his family.

Throughout her travels in India, Mrs. Clyde was careful to speak to my mother, who knew very little English, slowly and in simple sentences, and frequently complimented her on her small store of English words and phrases. At one point, she admired my mother's Kashmiri shawl and wanted to get one like it. My mother took her shawl off and presented it to Mrs. Clyde. At first, Mrs. Clyde resisted, but then she put it around her shoulders as if she meant to keep it as a souvenir of their friendship. Nevertheless, it was hard to imagine two women more different. My mother remembers that when Mrs. Clyde saw her knitting, sewing, or embroidering in the sitting room of a hotel suite she would ask how she had the patience for such things. When she saw my mother eating pickled chilies in the restaurant, she wanted to know how she could bear to eat such hot food. But her questions were rhetorical. My mother, for her part, found Mrs. Clyde and her ways completely mystifying. Except for her cane, she seemed never to have anything in her hands—no knitting or sewing needle, no embroidery frame. She was supposed to be rich, but she wore costume jewelry, like a poor woman, and, what was worse, it *looked* like costume jewelry. She had creases in her aged face, but she seemed to wander around the world as if she were young. She lounged in the sitting room, not only with her head uncovered in front of the menfolk but also while she coiled strands of her hair around small cylinders—the like of which my mother had never seen—until her whole head of hair was bunched up tightly around her scalp. Then, when she removed the cylinders, she had little curls all over her head, like a schoolgirl. She talked to my father as an equal—as if she were another man—and she talked and talked and talked, seemingly without taking a breath, as if she never stopped to think.

When my mother aired some of her bewilderment to my father, he tried to explain to her that women in the West tended to be more interested in intellectual pursuits than in domestic ones, and did not attach the same importance to gold and silks that women in the East did; that the fairer skin of Westerners tended to wrinkle more, and Mrs. Clyde was, after all, seventy-three; that women in the West, instead of covering their heads, took pride in showing off their hair to men. But he had to acknowledge that when it came to talking he had met few people—women or men—who were Mrs. Clyde's equal.

BETWEEN meals and after meals on that Christmas trip in Florida, in the car and in hotels, whenever my father and I could snatch time for a conversation, he continued the remarkable story of himself and Mrs. Clyde. They returned to Bombay and the Taj Mahal Hotel a few days before the opening of the population conference, on November 24th. My mother was with them, and before they had even settled into the hotel my sister Nimi arrived, covered with soot, having come straight from her job and endured a thirty-hour train journey from Jamshedpur. "The more the merrier," Mrs. Clyde said to my father, as if she felt that with just my mother and my father there she was a third party but with more members of the family around them she could be part of a whole, large Indian family. She greeted Nimi with genuine warmth. Informal, as always, she suggested that Nimi shouldn't stand on ceremony but feel free to unpack and wash up.

When Nimi went off to her room, my father told Mrs. Clyde that he and my mother had just heard through the family grapevine of a boy in the military who was looking for a wife and who happened to be in Bombay just then. "It's very auspicious that we should all be in Bombay at the same time," he said to Mrs.

Clyde. "Who knows? I might be able to arrange for her marriage, and so shed one more responsibility from my shoulders."

"What do you have to do with her marriage?"

"This is India. As parents, we are responsible. In fact, we'd better hurry up. She's almost twenty-five."

"Why, I got married when I was twenty-eight, and I've known women in America who got married when they were forty!"

"Our first daughter, Pom, and our third daughter, Umi, were married by the time they were twenty. That's the usual age for girls from good families here to marry. And Umi has been married for three years now, though Nimi, as an older sister, should have married first. She's already at a great social disadvantage."

"But you told me that she has an M.A. and is self-supporting. Why does she need to get married at all?"

"It's true that she has a job as a social worker, but it has no future—no housing, no benefits. Even as it is, she wouldn't be able to do it without some help from us. This is not America, where women are part of the work force. The Western tradition of single women making their way independently in the world is unknown here. A girl who isn't married remains a lifelong liability to her parents."

"Well, she looks to me to be a perfectly bright, healthy young woman. Why should you have any trouble finding her a husband?"

"I'm no longer in the swim of things. My retirement and my travelling make it hard for me to come to know of boys in the market. And then the boys here nowadays demand big dowries. As refugees, we can't offer much."

Mrs. Clyde listened to him, incredulous. Despite his repeated explanations, she couldn't be made to see why any girl in India first consented to get married, then succeeded in finding a partner, and then went on to contribute so prodigiously to the population growth. She wanted him to denounce the custom at the population conference and launch a campaign to dissuade Indian girls from ever agreeing to an arranged marriage. "Can you think of a better way to control population growth?" she asked.

It took him some time to get her to see that Indian girls and their parents were so deeply conditioned to the custom that the kind of campaign she had in mind would be futile. "Girls are such a burden in our society, and people are so poor, that they marry their daughters off as young as possible," he said. "That's how it is that many women in our country produce children through all their childbearing years."

"Does Nimi know about this military officer?" Mrs. Clyde asked abruptly.

"Yes, we've informed her, but she doesn't take it seriously. That's another problem Shanti and I have."

"Let's invite him to tea here. I would like to have a look at him and see for myself how this whole business works—or doesn't work." She laughed her rich, childlike laugh.

My father arranged for the military officer to come to tea at the Sea Lounge, one of the hotel restaurants, that very afternoon.

At tea, it was quite clear from a few hints the officer let drop that he was looking for an Army wife—one who would fit into the life style of an Army officer. That meant getting along with the wives of his brother officers as part of an official family and living away from him for months at a time, looking after his home and the schooling of his children, while he roughed it in the barracks on the frontiers. What he was looking for was a woman who was as socially graceful as a convent-school-educated girl, which Nimi was, but as self-sacrificing and resigned as a Hindu widow, which Nimi was not.

Although custom dictated that Nimi sit demurely and look pretty and malleable, she took an active part in the conversation, and even made fun of the military officer for his contradictory expectations. "You want a modern, educated girl to take to functions and parties, but you don't want her to be intelligent. That combination is impossible to find."

My mother tried to turn the conversation to the delicious things they were eating, but Nimi, abetted by Mrs. Clyde, pressed on. She didn't see why she should sacrifice her career for him, she said, but perhaps he was prepared to come and live with her among the laborers in the steel plant.

They started discussing Nimi's job, and Mrs. Clyde said that she'd always preferred the Russian economic system to that of the United States, and that what she'd seen in India only confirmed her in her opinion.

After tea, my father escorted the officer downstairs to a taxi. "Are your daughter and the American lady Communists?" the officer asked.

"I don't know about Mrs. Clyde," my father said, "but my daughter is no Communist—she's just a fiery young woman."

When my father returned to the Sea Lounge, my mother, Nimi, and Mrs. Clyde were still discussing the officer.

"He was as stiff as a board, and very conservative," Nimi was saying. "I don't think he'd ever heard of modern, independent women. He's the last person I would ever marry."

Mrs. Clyde laughed and laughed at her outspoken reaction, and said, "You're a girl after my own heart." It seemed that the more outrageous and rebellious someone was, the more Mrs. Clyde liked that person.

My mother quietly remarked that she thought the officer was very handsome, and suitable in every way. He was of the right caste and subcaste, very well positioned to rise in the ranks of the military.

"There's no use building him up," my father said. "I don't think we'll ever hear from him again."

But they did hear from him, for he followed up his visit with a formal proposal. Nimi turned him down flat. My father didn't try to talk her out of it, because inwardly he shared her opinion of the young man. All the same, he worried about the responsibility of marrying her off. He was, however, consoled by Mrs.

Clyde's praise of Nimi's stand: it was all part of her increasing emotional involvement with the family.

Most of the time in Bombay, my father, my mother, Nimi, Om, and Mrs. Clyde went around like a happy family. My father sometimes felt that he was looking after his widowed mother, just as he had actually done for thirty-three years. At a special table my father had secured in one of the Taj Mahal's restaurants, they ate, laughed, and talked about Mrs. Clyde's Indian experiences. Everything about the strange country and its strange customs and attitudes—the condition of the poor, the position of servants, the caste system, the antagonism between Muslims and Hindus, the effects of the Partition—had to be repeatedly explained to her. Whatever her questions, whatever their answers, she always ended up laughing, as if she had never known adversity, as if she asked questions for the sake of asking them. Her laughter touched off laughter in the others. It seemed that the whole point of talking was to try to bring everyone around to her benign point of view—to what she called her "philosophy." She would often finish a discussion with one of her verses from "Horse Sense":

Forgiveness! What nonsense! There's nothing to forgive.
Our thoughts and actions are not free one moment while we live.
Heredity, environment, experience, these three
Give all the freedom that there is on earth for you and me—
Freedom from responsibility.

Or

What is sin? Now at last 'tis known
That what man does he *must.*
Heredity, environment, experience—then dust.

Then Mrs. Watumull, Margaret Sanger, and Georgea Furst arrived for the conference, and my father had to divide his attention between them and Mrs. Clyde. Mrs. Watumull did not like her room. My father, who had made friends with the manager, got him to change it. Mrs. Sanger had had two heart episodes on her way to the conference and needed some medicine, and he got it for her. She also needed some of her notes typed, and he found her a competent Goan typist. (People from Goa, perhaps the most Westernized part of India, tended to have an excellent grasp of English.) Miss Furst didn't know that there was total prohibition in Bombay, and asked for a drink. My father took her on a wild search through the offices and bazaars, in an attempt first to get her a drinking permit that foreigners were entitled to and, when that failed, to get her an unadulterated bottle of gin from a bootlegger.

Finally, the conference started. They all attended the sessions and listened to the reports of delegates from various parts of the world, but Mrs. Clyde was visibly bored. It was soon evident that she was not interested in speeches or in the fine points of population control. The conference was just an occasion to travel and to support the cause of a friend. Still, she did like to be in the middle of whatever was going on.

At one point, Mrs. Watumull was having tea with Mrs. Clyde and my father at the Sea Lounge after a conference session, and she happened to mention his prize-winning population essay.

"I think you told me about your population essay, but I have never read it," Mrs. Clyde said. "I want to see it." She added, "Now is the accepted time."

My father didn't have a copy of the essay in Bombay, but Mrs. Watumull did, and she fetched it.

Mrs. Clyde closeted herself in her room for an hour, then emerged with the essay, saying, "It's wonderful. I have a brain wave." "Brain wave," my father had realized, was her term for a dramatic inspiration, and he prepared himself for anything—anything at all. She went on, "I must have a copy of this essay in the hands of every conference delegate by tomorrow morning."

"Now, now, now," my father said. "That is out of the question. It's almost seven o'clock now."

"There has to be a way," she said. "In this big city, there's bound to be a printer who will help us out."

Once she'd had a brain wave, there was no stopping her. The only idea he could come up with was to take her and the essay to the newspaper offices of the *Times* of India. A man in charge informed them that the printing section was closed, and said they should come back the next day. She was disappointed, but the mere act of having gone there made her feel that the project was under way.

In the morning, my father was tied up with the conference, but Nimi returned to the *Times* with Mrs. Clyde. The manager of the printing section told them he couldn't do the job in a hurry, and directed them to the printing shop of the Commercial Printing Press. It undertook the job.

Back at the hotel, when my father heard the price Mrs. Clyde was paying—a hundred and sixty-six rupees—he said he thought it was exorbitant.

"What is thirty-five dollars?" Mrs. Clyde said. "In America, it would be ten times that."

He guiltily remembered a poor tonga wallah in Srinagar who had taken them from the airport to the hotel and, seeing that one of the passengers was a foreigner, had demanded two rupees. My father had given him a rupee and eight annas, the customary fare, and dismissed the tonga wallah's grumbling as disappointment at not being able to take advantage of a foreigner. But now he felt sorry for the fellow. The extra eight annas would have bought him an evening meal, while it could have meant nothing to Mrs. Clyde. He decided that in future he would be more generous with the money in "the bank," and not try to pinch and save as if it were his own.

The pamphlets arrived the following morning, beautifully printed. My father and mother, Nimi, Mrs. Clyde, and Miss

Furst carried the bundles down to the conference, and Mrs. Watumull had them distributed. Mrs. Clyde was very happy. She felt she had made a valuable contribution to the conference, and was confirmed in this opinion when delegates started lining up to get my father's autograph.

On leaving Bombay, my father and Mrs. Clyde went to Rome, Geneva, and Paris, and then back to London and the Savoy. There he redoubled his efforts to find something else to do, for Mrs. Clyde had paid him his salary and he had some foreign exchange to help get him established. He still had it in mind to move the family to London. Indeed, in New Delhi he had got his friend the British High Commissioner to stamp the passport of each member of the family "For Immigration to England." His Indian medical degree was registered with the British General Medical Council, and its number, 969424, was almost as familiar to him as his telephone number or his club-membership numbers. He now scanned the *British Medical Journal* for advertisements of medical practices for sale and studied the real-estate pages of newspapers. Practices in areas of London like Earl's Court, Islington, and Notting Hill Gate were selling for between twenty-five hundred and three thousand pounds, and houses in those areas for about the same amount. He would require additional money to get himself established, but he thought that by selling everything in India and with some borrowing he should be able to manage. He went to Lloyd's Bank in Pall Mall to explore the possibility of getting a loan. The manager assured him that that would not be a problem. He bought a gray coat, a blue suit, black shoes, a new felt hat, and a new umbrella, and walked the familiar London streets in his new clothes, imagining what it would be like to be a London doctor, with my mother perhaps serving as his receptionist and nurse.

A friend introduced him to an Indian doctor who was looking for an assistant. The Indian doctor at once offered him the job, but the doctor's clinic was forty miles outside London and he wanted my father to begin immediately. My father told the doctor that he wasn't a young bachelor who could just get a room somewhere and start working—he needed time to get Mrs. Clyde back to New York and to go home to Delhi and wind things up there. He had no opportunity to explore other opportunities. After three days in London, he and Mrs. Clyde were on a plane bound for New York.

In New York, Mrs. Clyde wanted him to stay on with her as her guest through Christmas and the New Year. She wanted to do some travelling around the country—to see her brother and sister in Washington, to "motor" down to Florida to see how Ben Marsh was doing. My father asked her if he could fly to California and spend Christmas with me. She reminded him of her brain wave of inviting me to Florida. He wanted to revise the plan. He longed to spend some time alone with me, and help me to sort out my college experiences. He wanted to have a "holiday" from her, because he was feeling the strain of her constant company and the subordination of his will to hers. He was eager to get back to London and set things in motion there. Above all, he wanted to reclaim his independence, to be his own man. He felt he had spent a lifetime pleasing bosses. But he agreed to her proposal, and arranged to move into her guest room while he was in New York, because it turned out that she had no one else to spend the Christmas holidays with. She said she had to see Ben Marsh, who was so sick he might not survive into the New Year, and she said she would be grateful for my father's company. He felt that to say no to her under such circumstances would be letting her down, for he had begun to feel that he wasn't worth what she was paying him, that his medical training was almost irrelevant to his job with her. To compensate, he tried to do more and more for her, but the more he did, the less deserving he felt. It simply increased his sense of indebtedness. He consoled himself with the thought that by my spending Christmas with her in Florida he and I could see each other without his having to spend any money. More important, her meeting me might spark an emotional interest on her part in my education, and eventually lead to some kind of financial help, which would be a great load off his shoulders.

❧

"WHAT did you do after the weekend at Old Fields?" I asked my father in the course of that holiday in Florida. Eager though I had been before the Christmas break to discuss my college problems with him, when it came down to it I was unable to talk about them with him at all. Instead, I kept asking questions about Mrs. Clyde.

"We started out for Florida by way of Washington, and there we paid another visit to Mrs. Clyde's brother, Will."

"What does he do?"

"He doesn't do anything. When he was young, he used to dabble in horse racing and stocks and bonds, I believe. He just lives with Mrs. Hinshaw, his sister, and nurses, in the Mayflower Hotel. Mrs. Clyde had seven brothers and sisters, and he and Mrs. Hinshaw are the only ones still living."

"Are they like Mrs. Clyde?"

"Not at all. Mr. Clyde and Mrs. Hinshaw scarcely ever leave the hotel suite. I don't think that Mr. Clyde even gets dressed; he just stays in his dressing gown all day long. He has fibrillation of the heart, and is afraid of having a heart attack and dying. He doesn't have much energy, and Mrs. Hinshaw doesn't seem to be all there, although neither one of them is much older than Mrs. Clyde."

"Is Mrs. Clyde very close to them?"

"No, I don't think so. Before we went to see them, she noted down the points she wanted to cover. She hardly stayed with them twenty minutes, and after we left she asked me, 'Did I cover all the points?' "

The rich: in the houses we had visited during the summer to try to get scholarship money for me, and on the train that took me to Florida to meet Mrs. Clyde, I had kept wondering, What are they really like? At eighteen, I had a voyeur's interest in almost everything, and I pressed my father, asking, "How were they with one another?"

"I think Mr. Clyde was glad to see Mrs. Clyde, but he was equally glad to see her go. He drinks like a fish—Martinis, mostly—and he knows she disapproves of anybody who drinks or smokes. Mrs. Hinshaw doesn't approve of his drinking, either, and she has a very harsh, cracked voice. The atmosphere in the suite was far from peaceful."

I couldn't imagine that brothers and sisters would behave like that to one another, and I said something about their being very different from us.

"People like us, who don't have money, have romantic longings about it," my father said. "We say that if we had it we would do this and we would do that. But money can be a terrible thing, too. It can lead to drink and divorce and God knows what else. Look at us, father and son. In our society, children are considered continued growth of the parent. We are one and the same in spirit. That's how close we are. But I don't think Mrs. Clyde is very close to her sons, Tom and Bill. She doesn't see them much, and when she does, it's only for a meal or a drive."

GUESSING that another long train journey would be hard for me to endure and that I needed to get back to college to study, Mrs. Clyde wanted me to return to Los Angeles by plane. But we couldn't get a reservation on any flight from Jacksonville to Los Angeles, so I ended up taking a train to New Orleans and a plane from there to Los Angeles. I was back at college by the beginning of the New Year.

It seemed that for days after I left, Mrs. Clyde asked questions about me: How could my father possibly have allowed me to come alone to this country at such an early age? What would happen to me if I got sick? Who would pay the hospital bills?

Who would look after me? How did he think I could possibly
manage to keep up with my studies and compete with people
who had eyes? What use would my studies be to me for earning
a living? What would I do for my summer vacations? How could
he possibly hope to pay for it all? When the questions were about
my habits of work, she would be satisfied with his answers only
until she could think up a new problem and a new question.
When they were about finances, she couldn't be satisfied with his
answers at all.

"What will happen if you should die?" she asked. "Who will
take care of Ved? Where will he get the money even to fly home?"

"I'm not going to die."

"How can you say that? How can anyone say that? Look at
Ben Marsh."

When she returned to Winter Park after leaving me in Jacksonville, she discovered that he had died just a few hours before.
Although Mrs. Clyde had known for some time that he was on
his deathbed, she burst into tears, and for many days afterward
she would suddenly start to cry, thinking about him, and she did
so then.

My father comforted her as best he could. "One has to look
at the bright side of things. If I had thought negatively, I could
not have raised a family at all."

"What's the bright side of having a blind child in college you
can't pay for?"

"Something will turn up. It always does. Just a few years ago,
who would have thought that we would have a roof over our
heads again, and in New Delhi, or that I would get the bank job,
or meet you and be on my feet again, so to speak?"

"But you could die tomorrow."

"I wouldn't enjoy living if I worried about dying all the time."

So the argument went on. Back in New York, my father
made arrangements to sail for England on the S.S. United States
and spend some time looking more deeply into the possibility of
moving to London. The evening before he was to leave, as he was

busy packing in Mrs. Clyde's guest room, she asked him to come
into the living room for a "business talk."

When he entered the living room, he saw that she had spread
all around her her diary, her checkbook, and an assortment of
papers. As soon as he sat down, she picked up the legal pad that
she usually had near her, and said, "I've had a brain wave. I'd
like to make a contribution to Ved's education. Do you know of
a nonprofit organization for the blind through which I could do
it?"

He was thrilled, but also puzzled. The term "nonprofit organization" was unfamiliar to him, but as they talked he came to
understand that she would make a contribution if she could get a
tax deduction for it, and the only contributions that were tax-
deductible were those made to nonprofit or charitable organizations. He mentioned the American Foundation for the Blind,
with which I'd had some dealings.

She placed a call to Dwight Rogers, her lawyer and investment counsellor, and had a long conversation with him, then
turned back to my father. "Dwight is going to look into it, and
he'll have an answer for us by tomorrow," she said. "Now I want
to turn to another matter. You know you are very valuable to me
as my companion-physician." The phrase, though less grand than
"court physician," sounded more friendly to his ears. She said
that it was too bad he lived so far away; she wished he could be
in America all year round.

He said that if wishes were horses beggars would ride, but
that, of course, he had a big family and a lot of family obligations
in India. She said she was a little frightened about not having
some kind of companion for her old age.

He brought up the name of her decorator friend Elizabeth
Osteyee, who sometimes came and stayed with her. Mrs. Oste-
yee's sons were grown up, and she might be free to live with Mrs.
Clyde all year round.

"You know, Mehta," she said, "I don't enjoy the company of
women very much." Also, she said, she didn't want to make a

permanent arrangement with anybody—she could die the next day, and then her estate would be encumbered.

It didn't seem to him a very convincing argument, but then he knew nothing about estates and American law.

"Besides," she said, "I don't want any one person to be living here all the time. I like variety."

As she talked, it became clear to him that she wanted a loose arrangement with him for a good portion of the year. He very diplomatically told her that that would be impossible for him, because he still hoped to practice medicine in London. In truth, he had come to realize that three or four months on the job with her was the most he could ever spend and still keep his mental equanimity. He could tell from her face that she was unhappy. She started looking through her papers, as if their conversation were over. But then she found a piece of paper on which she had jotted down some points, much as she had when she went to see her brother and sister in Washington.

"What about your coming back in June and travelling with me for two or three months?" she said. "I'm sure you'd be happy to get out of that terrible Indian heat."

"Indian heat is something really terrible," he said, recalling that in the British days he and the whole family had escaped as a matter of course to a cool hill station for the summer. But now he couldn't afford to go to a hill station, and the Indian heat took such a toll of his health that he often worried about its shortening his life. Coming out in June would be a godsend, in more ways than one.

"You know, Mehta, every summer I get hay fever. This summer, I'd like to try out the Swiss Alps and the spas and baths in Germany to see if they help in keeping it under control. Maybe going to Bermuda or Hawaii would help. You could accompany me as my companion physician, on our usual terms."

"Whatever you say goes with me," he found himself saying. "But what about my wife, my one and only?"

"What about her?"

"She doesn't like being left alone."

"I thought you said she was looking after the education of your younger children and keeping your home going."

That was true. Someone had to stay at home to look after things. "But she says at our age we should live together."

"How can you? I thought you needed to save money. How can you pay for an air ticket for her, and pay for her hotels in Europe?"

He thought of saying, "Two can live almost as cheaply as one," but then he realized that that was not true in the West. Of course, Mrs. Clyde, as a rich woman, could have invited him and his wife, and if he had been an American doctor he might have insisted that his wife travel with them. But an American doctor would have had some reserves at his back. He would have negotiated from a position of strength. My father had no reserves, nothing at his back, and so he didn't feel he was in a position to insist. He was beginning to realize that his friendship with Mrs. Clyde was of such a nature now that if she said she needed him he could not say no, any more than a practicing doctor can refuse to treat a patient—even a hypochondriac—who comes to him for help. After all, she was just arranging to pay for some of my education. (Years later, when I learned about this conversation from my father, I was horrified at the connection between her offering to give me help and her asking him to work for her. But my father reassured me, saying that if I'd been a witness to the conversation I would have realized that she had already decided to contribute toward my education and was treating the two matters as separate issues—that it was not in her character to make one arrangement dependent on the other.)

"If you agree, I can write a check right now for your return ticket to New York," she was saying. "Now is the accepted time."

"Whatever you say goes with me," he said. As it happened, after a great deal of struggle he had landed himself two lecture assignments. One, with the Associated Clubs of Topeka, Kansas, was a lecture tour of its "knife-and-fork clubs" all over the country from mid-October to mid-November, and the other, with the University of Minnesota concert-and-lecture service, was for a series of lectures from early January to early February of 1954. He had been hesitating about accepting these engagements, not because they would involve a frantic schedule of travel in small planes and buses but because most of the fee of fifty or sixty dollars a lecture would be swallowed up by the airfare from New Delhi to America and back, and he would have no place to stay, nothing to do, between the two lecture tours. He now discussed the whole subject with Mrs. Clyde. She decided that the minimum time he should work for her abroad was three months, and told him that he could stay with her as a guest whenever he was at loose ends in America. Now his airfare to America would be paid, and his board and lodging between the lecture tours would be taken care of. He would be able to save much of the lecture money. It would mean perhaps postponing the London-practice idea. But it was a bird in the hand.

"I may often go to Europe," she was saying. "But I don't want to make any commitments for more than a year, because who knows? I could die tomorrow. And how would my executors know what my arrangements were? Anybody could come and make any claim. I don't want to burden them."

"That suits me very well," he said. "I want to remain a free agent."

She picked up her checkbook to write him a check for an air ticket, but he told her that he could not accept a check from her, because no Indian was allowed to keep dollars in India. It was settled that in the spring she would cable him an open return ticket. She would arrive in Geneva on June 24th, and he would arrange to arrive a day or so earlier, so that he could receive her at the airport.

❦

ON the day my father was to sail for Southampton on his way back home, the telephone rang in my room at college. Instead of just my father calling to say goodbye, as I had expected, both he and Mrs. Clyde were on the phone from New York. My father said in an excited voice that Mrs. Clyde had something to read to me.

"Yes," Mrs. Clyde said. "Your father and I and the lawyers and nice Mr. Barnett, of the American Foundation for the Blind, have been busy working on a letter that will be going out tomorrow. The letter is about you, and I thought you'd like to know what it says." She read the following letter in its entirety:

Old Fields
Huntington, Long Island
New York
January 15, 1953

American Foundation for the Blind, Inc.
15 West 16th Street
New York 11, New York

Att: Mr. Robert Barnett

GENTLEMEN:
I have today asked

City Bank Farmers Trust Co.
640 Fifth Avenue
New York, New York
Att: Mr. John Press

to segregate from my account and hold subject to your orders 80 shares of Montgomery Ward common stock. This is a gift to the American Foundation for the Blind which I hope you will use to assist blind students from India to obtain an American college education.

In using these funds I would be glad if you would help Ved Mehta finish his college education. He is a freshman at Pomona College, Claremont, California, where he is making a brilliant record. He is in great need of financial assistance to that end.

I would suggest that no beneficiary of this fund be given more than $1,500 a year in semi-annual installments. It would be perfectly satisfactory to me if you take no responsibility for disbursing the funds beyond making payments to the Dean of any college where such a student is in residence, considering it compatible with your ideas on this subject, that a receipt from the Dean should be a completely satisfactory accounting for the disbursement of the funds.

With many thanks.

Sincerely,
Mrs. Ethel Clyde

I no longer remember what words of thanks I stumbled through, but I do have a clear impression that she didn't invite thanks in any way. She almost brushed them aside, as if the act of doing something for others were sufficient thanks in itself.

VI

THE HUNGRY I

I T WAS THE BEGINNING OF SUMMER, AND I GOT A FEL-
low-student to drop me with my suitcase at a telephone
booth on Telegraph Avenue in Berkeley. I maintained a
smiling face until he'd driven off, and then I was able to
keep myself on my feet only by leaning against the telephone booth. While I was still standing there, it began
to drizzle. A few days earlier, I had finished my freshman year at
Pomona. Plans I had made to go to Harvard summer school had
fallen through for lack of money, and, with summer stretching
ahead of me, I had no place to go. On an impulse, I had decided
to attend summer school at Cal and had arranged with a fellow-
student to give me a ride there. When we arrived, I had told him
that I wanted to call the person I had arranged to stay with, but
the truth was that I had made no arrangements of any kind. Now
it was late in the afternoon, and, with cars roaring past, I could
hardly think.

Two young-sounding women went by, smartly clicking along
and laughing coquettishly. I imagined that they had strong legs
and pretty, generous mouths, and that Berkeley was full of such

engaging women. I had never lived in a sophisticated American city, and I was excited even as I was terrified. The air around my face felt cold and damp, and I was getting wet. I stepped into the telephone booth with my suitcase and somehow closed the door. The only person I knew in the entire city was Dr. tenBroek, but he was practically everything I aspired to be, and just the thought of calling him made me tremble. Someone began tapping on the glass of the booth. I must really look stupid just standing here, I thought. I picked up the telephone, dropped in a coin, and dialled tenBroek's number. TenBroek answered the phone. After I identified myself, he boomed, "Where are you?"

"In Berkeley," I said, trying to steady my voice. "I'm here to attend summer school."

"I thought you were going to summer school at Harvard. Didn't you write that to me?"

I was irritated at his remembering that, because it meant that I had to stumble through a complicated explanation—how I hadn't found any way to pay for readers at Harvard, because Massachusetts, unlike California, had no state readers' fund for blind college students.

"You're not the first blind student to think that benefits in California are available in the rest of the country," he said. "There's nothing special about Harvard anyway. I should know, since I have a degree from there." He added, "I suppose you are living at International House, and I can reach you there," and then hung up without waiting for any response.

Tap, tap. The wretched person was still waiting outside.

I had never heard of International House, but now I decided that that was where I should try to find lodgings. I got the number from information and dialled it. Yes, it was a dormitory—mostly for foreign students. Yes, there was a room available. And, yes, I could come right over. I got directions—the place was only a few blocks away—and set out.

❧

LIVING at International House was a little like being on an ocean voyage. Among the residents were Scandinavians, Latins, Muslim girls in purdah. Most of them were far away from home and were travelling toward unknown ports. People spent little time in their rooms, which, in any case, were not much bigger than ships' cabins. Instead, they congregated in the lounge, which seemed to be full of people at all hours. It had a heady atmosphere of fast friendships and quixotic romantic attachments.

In the first class of Elements of Economics, which I was taking from Professor Frank L. Kidner, I was able to answer one of his questions. After class, a boy named Jorge came up to me and said, "Haven't I seen you around International House?" (In the account that follows, I've disguised Jorge's identity, and also the identities of many others.)

I almost said, "Oh—you're the bouncing Romeo from Argentina," which was what people at International House called him behind his back. He was famous for never standing still and for picking up practically any girl he wanted to in International House. But I simply said that I did indeed live there.

"I've no head for books," Jorge went on. "Maybe you can help me with 'the dismal science.' "

I felt flattered. But I had to say, "I'm a dismal student of economics—I've never taken it before." From that day on, we were good friends, but I don't think I helped him very much with economics.

A few days later, Jorge and I happened to find ourselves in a nearly empty lounge at International House. "Where are all the girls?" Jorge asked rhetorically. "They must have all run off with Ahmed." He laughed.

Ahmed, who was Persian, frequently complained that he could sit in the lounge for hours without catching the eye of a single girl. He often wished aloud that he had Jorge's thick hair, flirtatious eyes, and boyish looks. Ahmed himself was nearing thirty and was nearly bald. Unlike Jorge, who had come to America as a child, he had been living in America for only a year or two, and didn't seem to be at home in the country.

It was so unusual to find Jorge alone, without a girl, that I found myself saying, "By the way, Jorge, you know so many girls. Do you think you could— could fix me up with a date?" I felt my face flush, but I went on. "During the school year, I don't have time for friendships—I mean, with girls. I have readers from eight in the morning until ten at night." Fearing that I sounded a little pathetic, I added, "I have girl readers—brilliant, and pretty, too—but I don't mix business with pleasure. You know what I mean. When I'm looking for a girl reader, I don't want her to think I'm prospecting for a wife." The truth was somewhat different. I had but to meet a girl, reader or not, and I would immediately start daydreaming about her. Not really as a wife— the idea of a blind Indian man with a sighted American wife was too daunting for me to contemplate—but as someone to touch and to hold. My desire was so urgent and so far out of control that I had only to hear a female voice, in class or out on the street, and my imagination would be off and running. And my imaginings were so wild and disturbing that I would at once be filled with feelings of guilt and hopelessness, as if I had actually tried to do with a girl what I imagined, and she had repulsed me.

Jorge stood up and started bouncing around aimlessly. "You mean you've never been out with a girl? How old are you?"

"Nineteen." I went on, in a rush of honesty, "I've never managed to kiss a girl—I mean a sighted girl." I would have gone on, but Jorge was laughing, not unkindly but merrily. "Don't laugh," I said. "It's always awkward meeting sighted people until they get used to being with me."

"But the expression on your face! You could be pleading for your life!"

I felt hurt, but tried not to show it.

"Let me tell you a story," Jorge said. "There was a cripple— no, a lazy bum—who urgently needed to go to the john. He said to a guy who was going there, 'Go for me, too.' When the guy came out, the bum wanted to know if he had done what he told him to. 'Well,' the guy said, 'after I went, you didn't need to go anymore.' " Jorge laughed.

What is he saying? He's calling you a lazy bum for not asking a girl out yourself. *But I'm working on the problem by asking him.* But it's not the same as asking a girl directly. *But I'm terrified; I need help.* The next time you meet a girl, ask her out. *Oh, no.* Oh, yes.

"You see how it is in this game?" Jorge was saying. "Each man for himself. The next time you're alone with a girl, grab her, put your arm around her, and kiss her. You'll see, she'll like it."

"I couldn't possibly do that," I said.

"I'm telling you, just grab her and kiss her," Jorge said. "Girls like forceful guys."

"Are you serious?"

"Of course, and I should know. Anyway, if you're not careful you'll end up like Ahmed."

"Ahmed comes from a great culture," I said, rising to his defense. As long as I could remember, my father had admired everything Persian—the Persian language, Persian poetry, Persian script. He used to say that the Persians were the Parisians of the East.

"You folks discussing me?" Ahmed said, walking into the lounge. He spoke with a thick accent.

"Ahmed, would you like to go on a date with Ved?" Jorge asked.

"Don't be cruel, Jorge," I said.

"Ved thinks I can get him a girl," Jorge said.

"While you're at it, get me one, too," Ahmed said.

"You kidding? No girl I know will go out with an aging goat like you," Jorge said. "And the trouble with Ved is, he's too serious for any girl to enjoy going out with him."

"The hell I am," I said.

People were now coming into the lounge. At that very moment, a bevy of girls walked past us in squeaking sandals and flat shoes.

Then a girl came in wearing high heels, and her scrapes, clicks, and taps resembled, to my ears, the fanfare for a princess. Suddenly, Jorge was in their midst. Like Ahmed, I was left on the sidelines, breathing in heavy, orangey scent emanating from a girl who had just seated herself nearby and started putting on nail polish. Soon the scent of the nail polish overpowered every other smell around me, and I was a child again, in a shop with my mother, with jars upon jars of sweets, waiting my turn for a bag of orange sweets.

❧

I FIRST met Mandy in History of the U.S.—the course I was taking in addition to economics. She was sitting next to me, and just as the second or third class finished she asked me, "Have you found a reader yet?"

I was so startled and there was such a hubbub—people gathering their papers, getting up, talking, rushing out of the room—that it was a moment or two before I realized that she was addressing me. "Oh, no, I don't have anyone," I said, trying not to sound as desperate as I felt. Then I found myself confiding to her that although I had got readers for economics I had none for history—that the history professor had made an announcement about my need for readers in such a garbled way that so far no one had approached me.

"I'm sure you'll find a reader," she said reassuringly. She had a grown-up voice but spoke like a little girl with a sweet in her mouth, and I found that touching.

She continued to sit there, as if she wanted to talk further with me.

"The reading load in history is so heavy I've already fallen far behind," I said. "I don't think I'll ever catch up."

As a rule, I would not have unburdened myself to anyone, but I was finding that being in a big, new place and longing to make friends had loosened my tongue. I felt reckless, as if noth-

ing I said—or, for that matter, did—could have any conse-
quences. By now, the classroom was empty, and my voice sounded
very loud. I felt awkward being alone with this girl, even as I
was attracted to her. I had an impulse to take hold of her hand,
stroke her face, touch her hair.

Don't touch. How often do I have to tell you not to touch? I was a
child, and my mother had me in tow. She was walking around a
sweet shop, pointing to this and that, and bargaining. I tried to
keep my hands obediently at my side. But my fingers fidgeted
and twitched, and I wasn't able to stop them from darting and
reaching out on little sorties of exploration. I surreptitiously
explored the things piled up on counters and display shelves when
I thought her head was turned. But she caught me. "Don't touch.
How often—"

A few months later, at a school for the blind, I tried to touch
the face of a new teacher to find out what she looked like. She
slapped my hands. "Don't be fresh!" she said. "Keep your hands
to yourself."

The boys in the class cried, "No, Teacher, he's not fresh—
it's just a blindism."

The label, coming from children who were blind themselves,
stung worse than the teacher's slap.

Mandy now stood up. *She's going to leave.* I can do nothing
about it. *Grab her and kiss her.* She may become my reader. I must
maintain a professional distance. *If you don't act now, you'll never
be able to find her.* She's in my class. *But the class is so large, and you
don't even know her name.*

"My name is Mandy," she said, as if reading my thoughts.
"Shall we go?"

I didn't stand up so much as jump up. In my confusion, I
started walking quickly out of the room. I have to prove to her
that I can move about like any ordinary sighted person, I thought.
But why do I care what she thinks? I'd better show her that I
don't. She hurried after me and fell into step. We came out of
the building together, and we found that we were going in the

same direction. I noticed that, unlike other people walking with me for the first time, she didn't seem to worry about me. Yet the path we took was crowded; a number of people were coming and going on it. To dodge them, one of us would sometimes have to fall behind for a moment. Even so, she seemed to understand instinctively that I didn't want her to guide me. She's so natural with me, I thought. We could be two ordinary students.

"I thought of volunteering for your reading job," she was saying. "I could use the money. But, as you can probably tell, I have braces. They don't come off until the fall."

So that's why she sounds as if she had a sweet in her mouth, I thought. She's the first sighted girl to talk to me frankly. Anne Lockwood never talked to me in this way.

"I'm sure you're very sensitive to voices," she went on. "My braces would distract you."

"Heavens, no, your braces don't matter," I said, almost impatiently. "When people are reading to me, I don't pay much attention to their voices. If I did, I wouldn't be able to concentrate on the material."

"Oh," she said, in a small voice, full of surprise and interest. That little word, in that voice, went straight to my heart.

MANDY was reading to me for the second time. We were in one of the cubicles in a library annex reserved for blind students who needed a place to work with their readers. TenBroek had arranged for me to get one. The cubicle was not much bigger than a telephone booth—it had just enough space for two chairs and a built-in desk. Even though our door was closed, we could hear a jabberwocky of other readers in other cubicles. I had trouble concentrating; we were sitting side by side, our knees just a few inches apart, and from Mandy came the faint homey smell of dishevelled clothes—it was the smell of Sunday mornings at home, when we children would sit around on our parents' beds in our mussed-up pajamas and dressing gowns. The same air I'm breathing is going deep inside her, I thought.

Put your arm around her and kiss her. If I as much as touch her, she'll quit. *Maybe she'll kiss you back.* Why take the chance? *You'll be able to taste her mouth.* Kissing is a temporary pleasure. Studying history is a permanent pleasure. *Why can't you have both?* I'll lose her as a reader. I'll fail my course. *Nothing ventured, nothing gained.* Stop it—I must concentrate. *Grab her and kiss her.*

I felt frightened, as if I had actually tried to kiss Mandy and she had spurned me and quit. I heard through a haze Mandy's shy little voice reading Henry Steele Commager's "Growth of the American Republic." She sounded as if she were having trouble getting her mouth around the big words. Her tongue and lips, it seemed, had never adjusted to the braces. I was entranced by the slight, rhythmic clicking sound she made—something between sucking and swallowing.

Mandy stopped reading. "That's the end of the chapter," she said.

I stood up and stretched, and asked her if she would like some water.

"Am I sounding hoarse?" she said.

"No, not at all. I just thought you could use it."

"Sure."

I went out to the hall and got her some water from the water cooler in a flimsy, cone-shaped paper cup, which leaked even as I carried it to her. She drank quickly, her small swallowing sounds at once agitating and exciting me. Because I wanted to prolong the break, I asked her if she came from a big family.

"I have six brothers, and you will laugh when you hear their names—Oxford, Cambridge, Sorbonne, Harvard, Edinburgh, and Trinity. My father never went to college himself, but he named his sons after world-famous universities. He has a mania for education."

"Then he is like Lalaji, my grandfather," I said. "Lalaji died long before I was born, but my father used to tell us that he thought of himself as a 'benefactor of knowledge.' He gave not only my father and his brothers but also every deserving relative the best education he could."

"Your Lalaji does sound like my father," Mandy said. "My father wanted to name me Wellesley, but my mother put her foot down. I was the only daughter, and she wanted me to be named after her."

"What does your father do?" I asked.

"He owns a small grocery store in San Francisco. It doesn't make much money, but he's managing to give us all an excellent education. Oxford is doing a Ph.D. at Cal, and Cambridge is at Boalt Law School here. We all take turns helping Dad in the store. My mother died when I was fourteen. Since then, I've also had to take care of the house." She added, with a little laugh, "But, being the only girl in the family, I have been spoiled plenty."

Mandy resumed reading Commager. She's one of seven, I thought, and I think seven is a lucky number for me. My father was one of seven, my mother was one of seven, and I am one of seven. Fate has brought us together.

It was our third or fourth reading session, and at one point Mandy stopped and asked if I enjoyed going to plays. I told her that I did, but that since coming to Berkeley I hadn't seen any. She told me about a one-act play that students were putting on that evening.

"Are you going?" I asked.

"Yes."

"In a group?"

"No, alone." There was a silence. "Why? Are you interested in going?"

She didn't actually invite me to the play, and I didn't directly ask her to go with me. But somehow it was arranged that I would meet her at the door of the theatre.

At the play, we sat together. I no longer recall what we saw, but I remember that while I was walking with her to her dormitory we discussed the play heatedly, as if we were old friends.

In the doorway, I put my arm around her shoulder in a friendly gesture. Then, on a reckless impulse, I drew her to me and tried to kiss her. I braced myself for a slap across the face, but, to my amazement, she kissed me back.

This was my first good-night kiss with a sighted girl. As abrupt as falling off a cliff, but as long-lasting as a recurring memory. Ah, Berkeley! The place where I had my first real date. Ah, virginal love! The tip of her tongue in my mouth. It filled me with shock and surprise, a sense of discovery and danger, guilt and revulsion. But my tongue almost automatically pressed forward to meet hers, withdrew, and pressed forward again: it made me feel that we were two hungry souls united at last.

❧

"I THINK we left off on page sixty-six," Mandy said, sitting down in the cubicle and opening the book. It was the same businesslike tone she had adopted with me in our history class earlier that morning. "Shall I begin?"

She's pretending that nothing happened last night. She has to pretend, or I won't get any work done. *I think she regrets the whole thing now.* Why not ask her? *I'm afraid she may say, "I don't want to be your girlfriend."*

"Yes, of course," I said, trying to match her tone.

Mandy started reading. My leg, as if it had a will of its own, moved up against hers. I waited to see if she would move her leg away, but she didn't seem to take any notice. I put my hand on the arm of her chair.

She put down the book. "What have I been reading?" she asked.

"I don't know," I said. "I wasn't listening."

We sat there for a moment in silence, the jabberwocky of other readers sounding gratingly loud.

"Can I hold your hand?" I asked weakly. I prepared myself for rejection, but, again to my astonishment, she took my hand in both of hers. "It's impossible for me to go out with you in the evening and then try to read with you the next day," I said.

"It's hard for me to concentrate, too," she said.

"I wonder if other people here get into such situations with their readers," I said, both wanting and not wanting to talk about the problem.

"In my dorm, this place has a terrible reputation," she said. "Girls say blind boys are always pouncing on them. Blind boys sound so desperate."

She knows how desperate I feel, I thought. I regretted that she knew anything about blind people, that in her mind I was one of them, that she knew the reputation of the wretched place in which we were forced to work. I was even embarrassed that she knew how I worked. Now she'll always think of me as a person with special needs and problems, I thought. She'll never be able to think of me as an ordinary boyfriend.

She let go of my hand and said, "We must try to work. You have to get your reading done. I need the job."

"I agree," I said, fearing that if I contradicted her she would quit, leaving me without a reader for the history course. She might even decide not to see me anymore.

She picked up the book and read a few more pages. Then she put the book down and said, "Oh, it's no use—I can't read to you. We should never have gone out. It was a terrible mistake."

"Mistake—how? All we did was spend an evening together. Is that so bad?" I thought it best to play down everything. I took her hand. Instead of withdrawing it, she began to trace some pattern on the back of my hand with her other hand.

I reached over and tried to kiss her.

"No, no—not now, not here." But her words carried no conviction.

I persisted, and she yielded. Our tongues met. I felt a bounding animal exuberance I had never experienced before.

She left to attend a course in English literature. Although nothing was said, I knew she would never read to me again. Kissing her in the middle of the day, in our place of work, had broken the unspoken rule of businesslike conduct. I sat in the cubicle listlessly, worrying that I would fail my history course now that I had no reader.

I have to marry her. But I have no way of supporting her. *I'd have to take her to India.* But she won't fit into our family system. It's just a summer romance. *I've kissed her. I've willfully destroyed an important reading relationship.* But I finally have a sighted girlfriend.

Within a few days, Mandy and I were seeing each other regularly. I was in love, profoundly, and felt I had never been happier.

A DAY or two after Mandy stopped reading to me, I hired Phyllis as a reader. (Phyllis's identity has been disguised.) It happened this way. I met Charlie, one of the regulars in the library cubicles, at the water cooler.

"I only know your reader as a voice through the wall, but she sounds like a real sweet potato." Charlie said gruffly, referring to Mandy. "How did you ensnare her?"

"She's not reading to me anymore," I said. I wanted to tell him the reason, even boast about it, but I felt too shy.

"To find a reader like that and then lose her—what a damn shame. How are you going to get your work done now?"

"God knows. I'm desperate."

I was surprised that Charlie was showing any interest in my

problem. Ordinarily, the library regulars tried to avoid one another, as if they feared that associating with other blind people would diminish them in the eyes of their sighted readers—a fear I had myself.

"If you're really desperate, I may know just the person for you."

"Who? Where?"

"Don't get worked up. Her name is Phyllis. She's here from U.C.L.A. for the summer. She's our age but seems a lot older. She's the only sighted person I've ever heard of who really likes to be around us critters. So much so that most of us avoid her."

"But I'm sure she must have a full reading schedule anyway," I said, discouraged. Readers were in such demand that as soon as it became known that someone was available he or she was spoken for. And people were so possessive about their readers that they generally didn't share them.

"She's not that much in demand. I'm telling you, not everyone takes to her—she gets on people's nerves."

"Why is that?"

"She tries to help too much. She's told me she wants to meet you but she's afraid of you. She says you're too independent and standoffish."

"Tell her I'm desperate for a reader."

"You go sit in your hole, and I'll see if I can find her for you."

In a matter of minutes, Phyllis came into my cubicle. She thudded rather than walked. She was a substantial person, and considerable maneuvering of the chairs was required to get her into the room and get the door closed. When she sat down, I could almost hear her clothes straining and her amplitude settling around her. But her voice was beguilingly light and girlish. If I'd heard it on the telephone or the radio, I would have thought it belonged to a slender, lissome girl, perhaps a ballet dancer.

We talked for a while, and she said she had plenty of time to read to me and could start right then. I gave her the Commager book. She opened it slowly. "I'd like to take the time to read over what you've already read," she said.

It was an unusual request from a reader, and I told her I didn't think that it was necessary for her to take the time to do so.

"I have to read it, or I won't be able to help you," she said.

"I don't need any special help. I just need for you to read."

"Well, wouldn't you want me to go over what I've read with you and help you take notes?"

I was becoming increasingly agitated. I wanted to get on with the book, and thought she was wasting valuable time talking about things that were none of her business. "Don't worry about my notes," I told her. "I type them fast, from memory."

"I like to start things from the beginning," she was saying. "Otherwise, I get lost. If I get lost, you'll get lost."

I could already see why she put other blind people off—she was oversolicitous, almost to the point of insolence. Yet there was something maternal about her, too. I didn't feel I would have to prove anything to her, and that was different from the way I felt when I was with any other girl reader or with Mandy.

"I never get lost," I said petulantly. "But how long would it take you to read what I've already read?"

"Maybe an hour or two—I'm a slow reader."

"Forget it," I said furiously. "Please read."

"O.K. O.K. You're the boss."

From that day on, Phyllis was my slavish reader. She came and went like a cowed attendant. I felt no attraction to her—no fluttering of the heart, no tensing of the muscles, no dream-stirrings in the head. I treated her almost like a machine.

I HAD just picked up Mandy at her dormitory, and we were trying to think of a place to get a quick bite near the campus. She said, "What about the hungry i? I love their chili con carne."

The hungry i, a student hangout and a take-off on the much more famous San Francisco restaurant of that name, where Dave Brubeck played, was not a place I had been to. I would have preferred to take Mandy to a restaurant I knew, where the waiters were used to my independent ways and wouldn't try to push me into a chair; where I was familiar with the menu and Mandy wouldn't have to read it out to me; where, above all, I knew my way to the men's room. I wanted at all times to appear as masterful as the sighted. But I never wanted to gainsay Mandy. Around her, I was always waiting to find out what she wanted to do, so I said, "By all means, let's go to the hungry i. A good bowl of chili is exactly what I feel like, too."

In the hungry i, the waiter did push me into a chair. Immediately, the pressure across my abdomen started building. In any unfamiliar place, I was often nervous and needed to go to the bathroom. For as long as I could remember, I had been embarrassed by this need. Whenever I first went to a restaurant alone, I would try to discover discreetly where the men's room was; it often had a jarring swinging door and a noisy toilet. If I failed, I would control myself until I got home. But in front of Mandy that proved difficult, and there were no clues to the whereabouts of the men's room at the hungry i. Then, too, its chili con carne was so spicy that I kept having to drink water. And afterward we were going to a play, at a theatre where I didn't know my way around any better than I did at the restaurant.

I thought of asking Mandy the way to the men's room, but the mere idea of asking her, and perhaps having her lead me there, as if I were a helpless child, mortified me.

"What's the matter?" Mandy asked. "You look tense."

"I don't mean to."

"Is something worrying you?"

"Well, if you must know . . ." My need was the hardest thing I'd ever tried to put into words. But somehow I did get it out—or, rather, she got it out of me.

"Oh, honey!" she said, full of feeling.

No one had ever used that endearment to me before—indeed, no one had used an endearment to me since I was a child. I had taken it for granted that endearments from the lips of a girl were not in my karma. With a single tender utterance she seemed to eradicate my loneliness and my foreignness.

Mandy reached over and took my hand. Oh, God, she's going to lead me to the men's room, I thought. I was about to yank my hand away, but she flattened it palm up on the table and, with her forefinger, traced a figure.

"This is the shape of the room," she said, drawing a trapezoid. "At the end of this turn here"—she drew a squiggly line—" is the men's room. The tables are rather close together, but I know you're used to managing that."

I felt a surge of gratitude. I also felt an odd sense of apprehension. Her instinctively knowing that I wanted directions instead of guidance—her complete understanding—was awe-inspiring. It suddenly made the idea of kissing her on the mouth seem profane. For a moment, she became like a sister, forbidden and out of bounds.

I got up from the table and, with the aid of the mental map, found my way to the men's room. I stood at the urinal weak and almost paralyzed by the whole ordeal. It was some time before I was able to relieve myself.

WHENEVER Mandy and I were in a restaurant, a theatre, or a concert hall, sooner or later she would say cheerfully "Wash-up time." She would either give me directions to the men's room or, if she needed to go to the ladies', we would walk together, hand in hand. But I could never be as casual about the matter as she was. Sometimes I would sit in anguish for hours, waiting for her to say "Wash-up time." Generally, however, she gave me the feeling that I was in charge. She allowed me to order for her in restaurants, to open doors for her, to help her on and off buses.

When we were walking on the street, she always let me lead her—something that moved me deeply, although it required nothing more on her part than placing her hand firmly in mine and moving naturally, without being nervous about my stumbling or not knowing when to step up or step down. At the end of an evening, she let me escort her to the door of her dormitory, just as if I were any other boy. From my childhood, I'd thought of all sighted boys as swans and myself as an ugly duckling, and I was grateful to Mandy for instinctively knowing that I had an aversion to the subject of blindness, including the word itself. Unconsciously, she catered to my fantasy that I could see. I felt very happy.

Now and then, Mandy unwittingly said something that brought me up short. Once, she came into class and said, "I'm wearing a new dress." She probably wanted merely to share her delight over the dress with me, but I felt inadequate. As a matter of course, a sighted person would have noticed the dress and complimented her on it, I thought. Another time, she was looking through the magazines in the International House lounge and remarked on a picture of the countryside around the Russian River. "It's really beautiful up there," she said. "We should drive out there." I wished I could appreciate scenery, like a sighted person, and could drive her places. Other times, she said things like "Let's go study in the library," or "Let's go to a museum," and then checked herself. Such remarks should have made me happy, because they showed that she often forgot I couldn't see, but they filled me with a sense of hopelessness. She's wasting herself on me, I would think; she should really be going with someone who wouldn't be a burden to her. She doesn't realize it, but she must be going with me out of pity.

I called her "honey" and "sweetie" every opportunity I got, but I noticed that she never called me "honey" after the first time. I rationalized that she was one of those people who object to endearments as unspecific and therefore meaningless, but I constantly wondered how much she really loved me.

One evening, Mandy and I were on a bus. It was crowded, and we were standing together, holding on to the pole, our hands touching.

"Hey, Mandy!" a girl called from nearby.

Mandy turned around and started talking animatedly to the girl. I stood there, hoping that Mandy would introduce me to her, but she didn't so much as acknowledge my presence. Why doesn't she include me in the conversation, I thought. She's afraid that if she does, her friend will look down on her for going out with a handicapped wog.

The friend got off the bus, and Mandy turned back to me. She nervously said something about a store we were passing.

"Who was that?" I finally blurted out.

"Who?" she asked guilelessly.

"The girl you were talking to. Who else?"

"Oh, her—she's Oxford's girlfriend."

"You've known her long?"

"It must be two or three years. Oxford's been going out with her for a long time. Why do you ask?"

"Oh, just out of curiosity."

I felt anger toward her welling up in me, but I excused her, on the ground that anyone would naturally be embarrassed to be seen with me. (In later years, I wondered if she would have been embarrassed about any boyfriend, handicapped or not, because—like me—she lacked self-confidence.)

"Have you ever thought of going out with a blind girl?" she asked one day, out of the blue. It was one of the few times I had ever known her to allude to my blindness.

"What a stupid question. How can I think about anyone else when I'm going out with you?"

"I only asked if you had thought about it."

I dismissed the question, just as I did the whole episode, but it turned out that the encounter with Oxford's girlfriend in the bus was one of several such encounters in which Mandy seemed to deny my presence. Each time, I felt a surge of anger, even as I found an alibi for her. But I never told her how I felt. I avoided confrontations at all costs.

Mandy went home most weekends. At first, I worried that she never invited me to go with her and meet her family. She never even offered to give me her home address or telephone number. But here, again, far from condemning her behavior, I came to condone it, thinking I should be grateful to her for protecting me from her family's ire. Putting myself in her father's place, I reflected that if I had a daughter who had got herself involved with a handicapped person I would vigorously oppose the romance and try to persuade her not to consider throwing away her life on a handicapped person out of some misguided notion that she could make up for the magnitude of his problems. (Coming from a country with practically no tradition of romantic love, I assumed that dating was tantamount to marriage.) Moreover, I told myself that I was not only handicapped but also a foreigner, who, no matter how superficially Westernized, could never have the same grasp of the English language and American customs that an American had. Just as living in a sighted society was making me contemptuous of everything to do with being blind, studying in America was making me contemptuous of everything to do with being Indian. As a freshman in college, I had taken courses in the history of Western civilization, the philosophy of Western civilization, and the classical music of Western civilization. In Berkeley, I was studying Western economics and American history. (Similar courses in Indian civilization were unheard of.) In the light of this Western education, everything Indian seemed backward and primitive. I remember once listening to a record of Mozart and being awed by the dozens of instruments magically playing in harmony, and then listening to a record of a sitar and being filled with scorn for the twang-twang of the gut.

In any event, an unspoken understanding grew up between Mandy and me that I belonged to her campus life—or, rather, to her evening life on campus, since there were long stretches during the day when I didn't see her and didn't know where she was or what she was doing. I assumed she was in the library or seeing her friends, but I didn't want to inquire, for fear of appearing too demanding, and so jeopardizing what little foothold I had gained in her life. All the same, I began to feel that love between a blind man and a sighted woman was doomed, because, although we might forget the world when we were together, sooner or later it would intrude: her father or a brother or a friend would arrive and expose my deficiencies, and she would leave me. I began mentally preparing myself for that day.

WHEN it came to chasing girls, Ahmed had the persistence of a beagle after a hare. Every day, it seemed, he would go up to a different girl in the lounge or the cafeteria and ask her for a date. He became so notorious for this that all his advances were rejected. He would get discouraged momentarily and say things like "What's the use?" but he would rally and soon be back on the chase.

"I sit by these girls and they're all friendly, but when I ask them out they become as cold as paintings on a wall," he once mused aloud. "Is there nothing American women want in their men but looks? Don't they care about souls and qualifications and salary? Here I am, a lover of poetry, well along toward getting a doctorate in electrical engineering, earning the salary of an instructor for my lab work. I have money in my pocket to take these girls anywhere they want to go, and a car to drive them around in. Still, I'm having no success."

"Maybe girls are afraid that they'll get interested in you and then you'll go home to Persia and leave them in the lurch," I said.

"But I'm telling all these girls I want to marry an American and make my life in this country," he said. "I'm telling them I never want to go back to Persia. It's a boring place."

"Maybe you put them off by telling them such things," I said. But I felt I was in no position to counsel anyone about girls, and told Ahmed as much. He, however, wouldn't leave me alone.

"What should I tell them, then?" he asked.

"I honestly don't know," I said.

He went on, somewhat self-pityingly, "Every Saturday night, I'm forced to stay at International House and listen to the radio. I get so depressed that I go out and get drunk. Is that any life for a healthy, educated man of thirty?" Suddenly, he asked, "Does your Mandy have a sister or a friend she could introduce me to?"

Having myself made a similar request of Jorge, I could not very easily turn Ahmed down, so I agreed to ask Mandy, but I tried not to hold out much hope. "Mandy is shy about her friends with me," I said, "and I'm not sure she knows many people at summer school, but I'll ask her."

That night, I tackled the subject with Mandy.

"Maybe I can mention him to my roommate, Bonnie," she finally said. "But she is very particular, and I don't even know what Ahmed looks like."

"Hang it all, the only thing your roommate has to know is that he's a nice fellow," I said. "Do talk to her."

By the next day, Mandy had got Ahmed a date with Bonnie for the following Saturday night. When I told Ahmed the news, he insisted that Mandy and I come along and make it into a double date. I decided that in the matter of girls Ahmed must be as timid as I was. We four arranged to see a play at the university and afterward go and have pizza in San Francisco at a special place that Ahmed knew and wanted to drive us to.

In the International House cafeteria, Ahmed started sitting with me, as if to show his gratitude for my help, and he kept badgering me to arrange for him to have a glimpse of Bonnie— something I felt he should do on his own initiative. He was overwrought, and made such a nuisance of himself that I began regretting I had ever become involved.

Before long, Jorge got wind of Ahmed's date. "Ahmed, you need a connoisseur like me to size her up for you," he said. "I'll tell you what—I have a date with Katherine that night. We could meet you in San Francisco, and the six of us could have a little coffee party." He'd already met Mandy, and he liked her very much. So it was decided that Jorge and Katherine would join us for after-dinner coffee at the pizza place.

On Saturday evening, as Ahmed and I walked over to Mandy's dormitory I wondered how Mandy felt about introducing me to Bonnie, perhaps the first friend of hers I would actually be spending some time with. Ahmed, for his part, was as nervous as a bridegroom. He repeatedly adjusted his tie, straightened his jacket, smoothed his pocket flaps.

Mandy and Bonnie were waiting for us in the foyer of their dormitory. After some confused hand-shakings, we set out for the theatre, Mandy and I leading the way. Bonnie, who had a plump hand and a heavy step, reminded me of Phyllis. I tried not to listen to how Ahmed and Bonnie were getting along, but I couldn't help overhearing that Ahmed was doing all the talking—about his qualifications, his salary, his car. Such things would impress a Persian or an Indian girl but not an American, I thought. Anyway, why doesn't he let her talk?

At the theatre, I got so caught up in the play, a tragic melodrama, that I scarcely gave Ahmed and Bonnie a thought until just before the final curtain, when Ahmed made a real spectacle of himself. He jumped up on his seat and started shouting, "Kill her! Kill her!" He was joined by several members of the audience, who all seemed to have momentarily forgotten that the person whose blood they were demanding was only a character in a play. I was sure that Ahmed's behavior did not endear him to Bonnie.

Our little pizza party went well until Jorge and Katherine joined us for coffee. Immediately, Jorge took Ahmed aside and whispered something to him. After that, Ahmed hardly spoke two words to Bonnie. I had feared that Bonnie might ignore him, but I had never imagined that he would snub her.

The next morning, when I came down to the cafeteria, Katherine, Jorge, and Ahmed were having breakfast together. Jorge was teasing Ahmed.

"How does it feel to be a shepherd?" Jorge was saying.

"It is true I come from a pastoral country, but why a shepherd?" Ahmed said.

"Didn't you have a date with a sheep last night?"

"No more, please, no more," Ahmed pleaded.

"You really matched them well," Katherine whispered to me. "Ahmed himself could pass for a goat."

Ahmed never asked Bonnie out again. I was surprised that he would so easily succumb to a little ridicule.

ONE day toward the end of summer school, three friends of Mandy's—twin sisters and their brother—arrived for a visit from a university in Oregon, where they were students. The twins, Sally and Janet, moved in with Mandy, and their brother, John, took a room in a hotel nearby. Almost the first day they were in Berkeley, Mandy invited me to go with them to a film in the evening. In a sense, I was glad that I was finally going to spend a little time with some of her friends. In another sense, I was apprehensive about spending an evening with not one or two but three strangers. I didn't want to expose myself to their scrutiny and be found wanting.

We all met in front of Mandy's dormitory and set out for the film, Mandy and the two very chatty sisters walking ahead, John and I following. We were late for the film, and were walking fast. John seemed especially clumsy walking with me; perhaps he guessed that if he took hold of my arm I would shake it free— something I instinctively did, to prove that I was self-reliant. As it happened, the sidewalk was narrow, and it was difficult for me to avoid the many iron lampposts. They were so slim that they were hard for me to pick out with my facial vision, and so oddly spaced that I couldn't get a line on them. Sometimes I avoided colliding with one with only an inch or two to spare. Under such circumstances, I would ordinarily have overcome my pride and taken hold of a companion's arm. But John, who was distant and incommunicative, brought out my most truculent side. As a result, I tried to show off to prove to him how adept I was at getting around by myself.

"Hurry up, you're falling behind!" one of the sisters called back to us. John quickened his step. I wished that Mandy was at my side, with her hand firmly in mine. Yet something about the situation—the way she chose to walk ahead with the sisters—stopped me from calling to her.

The wind picked up, and just ahead there were sounds of traffic rushing past. We were almost at the intersection, beyond which was the cinema.

"We can just make the light," John said, and before I knew it he had dashed across the street, alone. I started to race after him. Suddenly, a truck driver gunned his motor. The noise was so deafening that it completely deadened my facial vision. I veered. I slammed into an iron lamppost so hard that it rang like a bell and sent a vibration all the way down my spine. Over the years, I had run into many lampposts, but never before with such a resounding impact. I could feel the left side of my forehead throbbing. Maybe the skin hasn't broken, I thought. Maybe I can slip into the darkened theatre before my forehead swells up and they fuss and feel sorry for me. But even as I stood there, stupefied, the left side of my forehead started rising like dough in an oven. I could feel a trickle of blood dribbling down my face. I knew I should press a handkerchief to the cut and hide the swelling, but for an instant I felt numb, incapable of the smallest action. I hated John for being inattentive, the truck driver for choosing that moment to drive past, Mandy for not walking at my side—above all, myself, for being handicapped.

"Wait."

"Don't move."

"Don't walk."

The voices came across to me through the screen of moving traffic.

"The light is red!" That was Mandy, shouting back to me. She knows that I can tell when the light is red by the way traffic is moving, I thought. Her shout shattered the illusion, which she and I had fostered, that I was as mobile as a sighted person. The iron lamppost will forever stand between us, I thought. I was furious and resentful.

They were now all around me, exclaiming and sighing over me. Mandy gave me a little nudge—of disapproval, I thought. Perhaps she was unhappy because I had pushed away one of the chattering girls, who had tried to get a closer look at the cut, or because the accident had put a crimp in the evening. In any case, I couldn't bear Mandy's disapproval. Tears ran down my hot cheeks.

"Are you all right?" Mandy asked. She held a handkerchief to my forehead. I breathed in the fragrance of her hand lotion.

"It's nothing. Let's go." I pushed her hand aside and started crossing the street, alone.

Following me, Mandy said, "I don't think it's stopped bleeding."

"I don't care."

We entered the cinema, estranged.

In the dark, I finally felt my forehead and held my handkerchief to it. I wanted to forget my throbbing pain and later be able to discuss the film intelligently with Mandy's friends. Maybe I can dazzle them with my analysis of the film, I thought wistfully. Maybe then I can erase the bad impression of me that the accident made. Maybe I can win back Mandy.

I felt for Mandy's hand, and discovered that, in the confusion, I had sat next to John, and Mandy was on his other side. I couldn't imagine why she hadn't asked John to trade seats with her, but then I wasn't doing anything about it, either. Mandy and I had seen many films together, and we had worked out a sort of hit-or-miss method of keeping me oriented about what was happening on the screen. A word from Mandy—when the scene shifted, say—would often keep me from losing the thread of the story. If she got so caught up in the action that she forgot about my needing help, I would prompt her. But now I had John sitting next to me, and, to make matters worse, the film we were seeing had long sections without any dialogue.

On the way back to the dormitory, Mandy's friends never stopped talking about the film. Although Mandy tried to change the subject, and walked with me hand in hand, I felt just as left out as I had at the film. I'm glad that no one has asked me how I'm feeling, I thought, but why haven't they? No matter how good I've become at mobility, there will always be an iron lamppost to humble me. I must look to them like a sulky child.

"Let's not go back to the dorm," Tweedledum sister said.

"Let's stay out all night," Tweedledee sister said.

"Isn't there some place we can camp out?" John asked. "Yes, let's go on a hike."

"I have to sign us in at the dorm by ten," Mandy objected.

"You can sign in and slip out the window," John said.

The three swept Mandy up in talk of breaking rules and going on a nocturnal adventure.

"While you girls are signing in and getting your things together, I'll walk Ved to International House," John said.

"Thank you very much," I said. "I know the way."

"He'll come with us," Mandy said. I was thrilled—but only momentarily. I shouldn't go, I thought. I'll only get in the way of the fun.

They began animatedly discussing where they would go, what they would do, but I scarcely heard them.

At the door of the dormitory, I said good night to all of them. I noticed that Mandy did not press me to go with them, and felt that she kissed me good night rather perfunctorily.

As I set off for International House, Mandy, Sally, and Janet went inside the dormitory, and John began pacing below the designated window. As long as I thought John could see me, I walked fast and purposefully. But when I had turned a corner, and was out of sight, I walked slowly toward Telegraph Avenue, taking small, heavy steps. It's all over, I thought. Lonely Ahmed floated into my mind. In a couple of days, summer school would end, and everyone would be going home for the rest of the summer. I had no place to go, and I had decided to stay on at International House until the fall term at Pomona started, in September. As I approached Telegraph Avenue, I heard distant notes of a violin. The melody was hard to place, but it reminded me of the simple tunes I used to hear in hill stations at night when I was dropping off to sleep. Those tunes were played on a flute, and, depending on shifts of the wind, the notes flickered in and out of my consciousness, making me feel that I would always be at the edge of experience instead of actually having it. But now, as I walked, the violin became more distinct, its music louder and fuller. It drew me to the door of a café.

People were gathered around the door. "What's the song called? Who is playing?" I asked no one in particular.

"Don't know, but the violinist is a beautiful young girl," someone answered.

"Why is everyone standing outside?" I asked.

"The café is closed," someone said. "She's a waitress, and she practices every night after hours."

I stood apart from the group, listening to the ravishing music. I can no more have Mandy than I can watch this girl play, I thought. Mandy has always been unattainable; it was all in my head.

By and by, everyone drifted away, and I was left alone at the door. I felt very tired. I wanted to sit down. Maybe the girl will let me in, I thought.

I tapped on a glass pane of the door, at first tentatively and then frantically, but no one came. I might see Mandy casually tomorrow or the day after, but the yesterday with her is gone, I thought.

With my head down, the hands of my Braille watch pointing to the early hours of the morning, I resumed walking toward International House.

"Hey, there!" a man called from the street.

I kept moving.

"You, there—stop!"

I stopped, but I didn't turn around.

"You are drunk." The man had a half-military, half-prosecutorial manner.

"What is it to you?" I said, and started on my way.

The man gripped me above my elbow, hard. "Wait a minute," he said.

I felt too dispirited to struggle, or even to feel angry.

"Hey, you can't see," the man said. He was suddenly very apologetic. "I thought, sir, you were drunk. I'm a police officer. I didn't know— Where are you going? We are not supposed to, but I'll give you a ride."

I was too weak to decline. The officer drove me to International House in his squad car.

I SAW Mandy once again that summer, a few days after the lamppost incident. By then, her friends had gone back to Oregon. We met for coffee and pastry at the hungry i. She didn't say anything about my forehead, which was still swollen, and I felt thankful to her for not reminding me of the humiliating evening. She said she had to be out of her dormitory by that night, and Oxford was coming to pick her up to take her home. She would definitely come in to Berkeley to see me before I went back to Claremont, and I invited her to visit me at Pomona sometime in the autumn. Outwardly, she and I both behaved as if everything were all right between us. We even laughed about the mismatch of Bonnie and Ahmed. But inwardly I was already mourning the death of our love—my first and last, as I thought of it. I was sure that no nice, sighted girl would ever fall for me again.

"What are you thinking?" she asked suddenly.

"Nothing. Why do you ask?"

"You have a faraway look."

"I don't feel far away." It was a black lie.

"It has been a lovely summer, hasn't it?" she said.

"This is the best summer of my life," I said. Dissembling was becoming so easy.

Then the tone of her voice shifted, and, with it, the ground under my feet. "I hope we'll always be friends," she said.

I felt like screaming. Had we been only friends? Could those kisses be cancelled out so easily? But, as usual, the anger was overwhelmed by sadness at my own unworthiness. Of course, she's right, I reasoned, friendship was all that it could be, and that is what it was all along.

"I'll always have a very nice memory of you to live with," she was saying. "I'd never met an Indian before, never read aloud to anyone before." Thank God she doesn't say "met a blind person before," I thought. Abruptly, she said, "Wash-up time."

I walked to the men's room like a rat through a maze, my cheeks burning with embarrassment at the ease with which she had dismissed the subject of our relationship. So I'm already a "nice memory," I thought. During the evening with her friends, I'd assumed that my relationship with Mandy was over, but now that it actually seemed to be over I was crushed.

I took Mandy back to her dormitory. I kissed her, and I sensed passion in her mouth, as if we were more than friends. Indeed, the kiss revived all the feelings for her that I had been trying to kill.

I thought about asking her where she would be living the following winter, but I couldn't get the words out. When I left her, I wasn't able to take the initiative sufficiently to ask for her home address and telephone number. She didn't offer the information.

As I walked away from her dormitory, I heard the Campanile striking nine, and, in my portentous mood, I felt that it was striking my death knell. I walked to the library, to my cubicle, to Phyllis; I had a reading appointment with her and was already an hour late for it.

"Is anything the matter?" Phyllis asked as soon as I entered. "You look very upset. What's wrong?"

I was afraid that if I opened my mouth I would start sobbing. My head was full of Mandy, and how could I talk about her to Phyllis? In any case, ever since Phyllis started reading to me I had maintained a formal, distant manner with her, even though she had invited confidences by telling me things about herself, such as that she was an only child, that she came from a broken home, that her mother had to make ends meet by working as a cleaning woman.

I sat down and nodded for her to begin reading. Phyllis, however, took my hand in hers—something she had never ventured to do before. I felt too apathetic to jerk it away. She started stroking it.

At first, I found the fatness of her hands off-putting and distasteful, but then a charge of electricity went through me—I felt wild and reckless. Later, I couldn't be sure which one of us had made the first move, but in a moment our mouths were clamped in a kind of desperate, brutal kiss. It was entirely different from the tender, gentle kiss I had shared with Mandy ten minutes before.

It was a long time before we let go. Kissing Phyllis had provided a release for me, like tears after a shock, and brought me to my senses. My formal manner with her clicked into place, and, in spite of her protests, I made her read until the library closed.

At the library door, I curtly said good night and left her. I

was perfectly aware that she was sniffling, but I told myself I
didn't care.

❦

As it turned out, Mandy and I did not meet again that summer. We did correspond for a few months after I returned to
Pomona, but our letters quickly degenerated into polite small
talk, perhaps because she knew that her letters would be read out
loud to me, and I dictated mine, so that I could go over them
and make sure I did not say anything I would later regret. The
following summer, I was making a trip to Seattle, and I stopped
in Berkeley. I arranged to meet Mandy in front of the library.
We had barely shaken hands when she told me that she was engaged
to be married, as if to warn me against bringing up the past. I
tried to rise to the occasion and I gave her my best wishes. Though
a lot had happened to me in the previous year, and I thought I
had long since got over her, I felt a pang. I was determined,
however, not to show it.

We walked around. The day was cold, and I felt irritated
with myself for not being warmly dressed. I suddenly wanted to
go to the bathroom; it seemed an age since she used to say "Wash-
up time."

I started asking her the questions I'd held inside for almost a
year. I knew they came out sounding abrupt, but I couldn't help
it. "Why didn't you give me your telephone number when you
went away for weekends?" I demanded. "Why didn't you introduce me to your family?"

She was taken aback. "You never asked to meet my family.
You never asked for my phone number."

I was sure she was equivocating. "You know how shy I was,"
I said. "If you'd been in India and I had a home there, I would
have invited you, even if you were just an acquaintance."

"I know, I know," she said, in a sinking voice. "Don't press
me. Don't think I haven't thought of it many times."

"I must press you," I said. "I have to know. On one level, you were so giving—you seemed to know everything instinctively. On another level, you held back. You were the first sighted girl who had shown any feeling for me, and I loved you."

She wanted to sit down. I suggested a café, but she just wanted to sit on the steps of a building we were passing. This gave the interview an even more transient character than it already had. "I was—I am—so young," she said. I listened for the clicking sound of her braces, but it was gone. Her voice was bolder, as if removing her braces had unshackled her spirit. "When my mother died, I had to grow up fast in certain ways. But in other ways I became more of a child. You were like no one I had ever met. Don't think that I didn't worry about it. I talked about you at home. Everyone in my family knew that we were going out together. But they were all urging me to break up with you. Oxford actually said I'd taken leave of my senses. I didn't know what to do, and you didn't make things any easier by not pressing me. You could have insisted that you wanted to meet my family. You had the right."

"Are you implying that it was my fault? How do you think I felt when you hardly ever introduced me to your friends?"

"You could have demanded that I behave better, and things might have gone differently between us. But don't dredge it all up now. I'm engaged. I'll always have a nice memory of you."

Her phrase "nice memory" once more made me feel like screaming. There was so much I wanted to ask her—what she was doing, where she would be living, whom she was marrying. But from then on I didn't ask her anything. I just told her that my love for her had been so hedged in by fears and qualms, self-doubt and feelings of worthlessness, that I was never really able to express any of it to her, and that I was able to express it now only because all that didn't seem to matter anymore.

"I'm glad you're speaking out now," she said. "I don't think either of us was ready."

"I think you have a point," I said.

When I left her, I felt sad, and wondered if I should have looked her up at all. But, whatever heartache the meeting had caused, it had lighted up one small corner of my murky relationships. I went to International House in search of Ahmed. I had a score to settle with him. But he and Jorge and many other friends had disembarked, as it were, and scattered. Berkeley was so full of ghosts that I couldn't bear to spend another minute there. I had intended to stay overnight, but I left, and didn't return for nearly thirty years.

VII

SECRET KNOWLEDGE

I REMEMBER TRYING TO DISCOVER HOW GIRLS WERE physically different from boys when I was four years old and my father had returned from England with a doll dressed in Western clothes for my oldest sister. I was allowed to hold Memsahib, as we immediately named her, in my lap. We had run-of-the-mill Indian dolls all over the house, but those were stick figures made of cloth, with saris sewn on, or of clay, with clothes in relief. Even though Memsahib was made of Bakelite and had a cold, grainy surface that made me think of an eggshell, she seemed almost like a person. She was about two feet tall, and she had pigtails tied with little ribbons, legs and arms that could be moved into different positions, and a frock, a petticoat, and drawers that could be taken off and put back on. My sister Pom was very possessive of Memsahib, and would never let me play with her, for fear that I would damage her. She kept Memshib on top of a high cupboard in her room, and when my sister wasn't around I would put a small chair on top of a big chair, drag the chairs over to the cupboard, climb up, and take Memsahib down. I would take off her dress, petticoat, and drawers, and examine her breasts and buttocks. I was struck by the fact that, unlike me, she had nothing between her legs. There seemed to be no explanation for this deficiency, until I grew older, and heard a lot of dirty talk in *gullis* and bazaars about girls. Although my knowledge didn't progress much beyond Memsahib, my imagination ran riot. Then when I was in my teens, many of my images came to cluster around an English dirty word.

Long before I met Phyllis, I often woke up from a dream with the word on my lips, and during the day I would find myself repeating it, half aloud, half to myself, the way my mother used to endlessly chant "Ram, Ram, Ram." I constantly feared that the word would slip out in a crowded room or on a bus, and I would never live down the embarrassment. In fact, I thought the word was going to drive me mad.

Getting to know Mandy had somewhat abated the power of that word. She seemed so chaste, and most of the time it seemed profane to think of her in connection with the word. Moreover, when we were in public together I felt that girls looked at me through her eyes and found me desirable. The feeling lifted me out of the muck and mire that the word represented. Similarly, I often had daydreams about introducing Mandy to my family, perhaps marrying her. But the mere thought of Phyllis filled me with lustful desire. What loomed in my mind about her was her fleshy bulk. (If she had been attractive, I would probably have been too intimidated to feel desire for her.) Perhaps if I could have seen her I would have found redeeming qualities in her looks, but, as it was, touching her had only reinforced my impression of her unattractiveness. I felt that if people saw me with her they would pity me for having no one better to go out with. I certainly couldn't imagine introducing her to my family; there seemed no way she could fit into our home, into our values and aspirations. In any case, kissing her had revived the power of the word with a vengeance. Just the way she kissed me had driven everything out of my head but the word. Thereafter, no matter how hard I tried to repress it, it bubbled up whenever I thought of her. She became a thing to be possessed, experienced, consumed. If I cannot get Mandy to love me and perhaps marry me (permanent pleasure), I thought, then I will have to settle for loveless passion with Phyllis (temporary pleasure).

I cursed the day I first heard the word. At the time, I was fifteen. I was at a school picnic in Little Rock. We boys and girls were all sitting together around a bonfire, drinking Pepsi, 7-up, or Coke out of the bottle. For once, the strict segregation of the sexes in the school—not just separate dormitories but separate dining tables, separate aisles in the auditorium, even separate staircases—was relaxed. At one point, some of us boys struck out toward the bushes along the lake to look for sticks on which to roast the wieners and marshmallows. I tagged along, Coke bottle in hand, behind a tobacco-chewing, country-bred fellow, Oather, who was everything I wanted to be and wasn't. He was American to the core; I was new to the country. He spoke the English language like a target shooter who never missed; I spoke it like the beginner I was, fumbling for every second word. He had a way with girls; I was so tongue-tied in their company that I never got anywhere with them. We were pushing through the bushes, and Oather was telling me which kind of sticks I should be looking for—long, thin, and sturdy, so they could support a good number of wieners and marshmallows. "You know, these blind folks are so clumsy they can no more find flames with their sticks than they can find a quarter at their feet," he was saying. "You'll see—Kenneth will lose his wieners in the flames or set his stick on fire. As for Joe, he probably won't even be able to find the fire—if you put a girl in front of him, he wouldn't be able to find it."

"Find what?"

Then he whispered the word. It was the first time I'd ever heard it used that way, but there could be no mistaking its meaning. The word was susurrant, evocative, and vulgar-sounding. I immediately associated it with the language of secrecy, intimacy, and darkness. Like the schoolboy that I was, I became obsessed with the word from that moment.

At times, the word would remind me of how I used to stick my fingers into my mother's cold cream jar and spread thick gobs of the cream over the tables and chairs, so that they would smell like her. At times, it would remind me of eating a mango—succulent but slippery and thready—or of drinking a cup of steaming cocoa when my mother brought it to me at bedtime. I had but to drink the cocoa and I would be asleep, with the taste of chocolate in my mouth, my fingers still crooked in the handle of the cup. Such memories would suffuse me with a warm, happy feeling, leaving me pleasantly exhausted.

It seemed that everywhere I turned, something or other would call up the word. The most routine gestures, such as inserting a key in a lock, plugging a radio into the wall, even slipping a foot into a shoe, seemed to fill me with aching, longing, and unbearable shame. The word became my guilty secret, and I feared I would never be free of its influence. It came to have such a hold over me that I had but to think of it and my heart would begin to race. The word would pulsate in my mind to the rhythm of my heartbeat, and be amplified until I thought my head was going to split open.

I came to think of it as an epiphany of feminine nature—soft, yielding, accepting, inviting, warm, embracing, comforting, but also sly, elusive, willful, capricious, dangerous, aloof, independent, territorial. My frustration was compounded by an inner sense that there was no relationship between my exalted idea of what the word signified and the base desire it stimulated. The word even became fixed in my mind as an emblem of the mysteries of the English language I wanted to conquer. In retrospect, I can see that the word may have mesmerized me because it transformed something awesome and frightening about women into something familiar and almost touchable. It was also comforting, because it belittled and denigrated something that I felt I could never have but desperately wanted. Certainly it could not be attained, like good grades in school, by hard work—my solution to many problems in life.

❧

"HEY, Mister, your coffee's getting cold," the waitress at the Berkeley fountain said a few evenings after I'd first kissed Phyllis. *So just a nameless mister—a common nobody, with common desires and common longings.* "Hey, Mister!"

I started, on my stool.

"If you let it get cold, it's none of my business," she said, turning her back on me and rattling dishes in the sink. "It's your money." *Strange—in Hindustani, money means semen. Ferocious kiss— still feel her tooth marks. She's available, won't tell anyone, and she is not blind.*

"Miss, you know of a hotel in this area?"

"What kind of hotel?"

"Any hotel."

"There's a big one four blocks down, on the left," she said, over her shoulder.

I picked up the spoon and stirred the coffee, but then I remembered that I had taken no cream or sugar. I put the spoon down.

I took a sip. "Coffee's cold!" I called to the waitress.

"What did I tell you?"

"Can I have a hot cup of coffee?"

"It'll cost you more money."

I put down a dollar bill. "Would you also play something on the jukebox?"

"What? What song?"

"Any song."

The ringing of the cash register, the clink of the change on the counter, the hum and thump of the activated jukebox seemed amplified, as if I had a fever. The word began susurrating in my head. In the jukebox, a car sputtered, turned over, and accelerated to the elemental beat of a drum.

Without waiting for my coffee, I made for the door.

"Hey, Mister!" the waitress called after me. "Your change. Hey, Mister!"

I didn't turn my head.

The way was new to me. It was raining heavily, and the wind was blowing in gusts. I was wearing just a sports shirt, lightweight slacks, and a pair of old walking shoes. I didn't have an umbrella, and rain pelted me from all directions, drenching me instantly. On top of that, people came at me holding umbrellas at different angles and heights, which made walking doubly treacherous. I slowed my pace, stepped aside, ducked, pressed on. Someone shouted at me in a language I didn't understand. An umbrella just missed my eye.

"Watch out!" I yelled. My words were lost in the wind. My spirits sank to the bottom of my soggy shoes.

I was at an intersection I had to get across. I listened for an interruption in traffic or a clicking mechanism that might indicate a traffic light, but I couldn't hear a thing through the din of the rain and wind.

I thought I perceived a break in the traffic, but I hesitated, and the traffic seemed to start up again. I listened; there seemed to be another lull. I made a dash, only to jump back from an onrushing car.

"Can anyone give me a hand? Is anyone here?" I shouted, as if I had never had any training in mobility, hadn't crossed thousands of streets on my own before, had no pride or dignity. The windshield wipers on passing cars seemed to hiss and whirr indifferently. *It's a matter of acceptance. She's the only one around. Beggars can't be choosers.*

I took a deep breath and charged across the street, holding both hands high, like flags. I squelched along in a shiver, my shirt and slacks clammy and weighted with water. Then I was under a canopy, and the din of the rain and the wind seemed to diminish. From the right came the squeak and thud of luggage being loaded into a car. From the left, the whoosh and brush of a revolving door. As it rotated, it threw out little bursts of warm air. The word pulsated to the rhythm of my heart.

"Boy, go in like a knife, or else you'll flop and get a water burn." I was standing on a very high diving board, my toes over the edge, my arms above my head, my body tilted forward, my eyes closed.

I dived into the revolving door, almost colliding with a panel rushing by. Inside was a man behind a desk, finishing up a conversation on the telephone.

"Is this a hotel?" I asked him.

"It's a hotel, all right."

"You in charge?"

"I'm a bellhop." I had never heard the term "bellhop." I wanted to laugh. "I see you're really soaked."

"I need to dry out. I'd like a room for the night."

"You got no luggage?" I could feel him looking me up and down. I had never checked into a hotel before, and his tone seemed to be saying, "No luggage, no room." *You are condemned always to live on the edge of experience, never to have the experience itself.*

"You can't turn me away—I've got money," I pleaded.

"You sure need to dry out," he said, coming out from behind his desk. "Follow me."

I followed him to another counter.

"Would you like me to register for you?" a man behind the counter asked kindly, as if he were used to seeing people in my condition, dripping with water. I nodded. I gave him my name and the address of International House. He told the bellhop to show me to a room.

Later, I couldn't remember whether we'd gone upstairs or

downstairs, taken an elevator or walked along a hall, or even whether I'd tipped the bellhop. All I could remember was that suddenly I was alone in a cocoonlike, carpeted room, free of the tumult of the street, with everything at hand that a person could desire: a bed, a desk, an armchair, a dresser, a telephone. In the bathroom, I took off my wet clothes, hung them up, dried myself with a towel, and washed my face. I went back into the room and got into the bed.

"Heads on the pillows. Hands out of the covers." I was in the orphanage-school dormitory, and the Sighted Master was shouting at us.

I lay there with my hands on top of the blankets, my fingers still, as if years of training had been carried out with this moment of temptation in mind. My head on the pillow was heavy with guilt.

But I turned to the bedside table and picked up the phone and put my finger out to dial. All that I found was a smooth, flat disk. I had never come across a telephone without a dial and wondered if it was a toy. As I was about to hang up in frustration, the operator squawked in my ear, "Number, please."

"Hang up," I said to myself. "Leave her alone. She's not your wife. What would Daddyji and Mamaji think of you? What would Mandy think of you?"

"Number, please. Operator waiting."

For a moment, I couldn't think of the number—I could only recall the pattern it formed on the dial. Finally, I mumbled the number into the mouthpiece.

Phyllis answered the telephone on the first ring, as if she had been sitting by it, expecting someone to call.

"Phyllis?"

Except for that one kiss, I had never paid any attention to her, and I didn't know how to go on.

"Yes, this is me. Always here." She sounded especially girlish and enthusiastic.

"Can you come over?" I said. "I want to see you."

I was sure she'd say no, put up some kind of resistance, not let me go through with what I was sure I would later despise myself for. But she said, "I've been hoping you'd call. I'll be right over. I just have to put something on—I'm sitting here without a stitch."

The picture of her naked excited me. "You're sure it's not too late?" I said, wanting her to have a chance to back out and save me.

"It's only nine o'clock. The night is young. But where are you?"

"Actually, I'm in a hotel."

"That's dandy."

Somehow, that word "dandy" made me hate her, and hate myself for what I was doing. But I gave her the address of the hotel and hung up. I lay with my heart in my mouth, the word throbbing in my head, titillating and disgusting me. Oh, God, I thought. I've crossed the Rubicon. There's no help for me. I remembered what the boys used to say in the *gulli* about how a woman was fashioned: an inverted lemonade bottle—the kind we children were familiar with. Instead of a cap, the bottle—long and thin, with a sloping neck—had a marble stuck in its neck. To get at the lemonade, one had to forcibly push in the marble with a plungerlike bottle opener.

The bellhop had left the key in the lock, and suddenly Phyllis was in the room. I sprang out of bed, naked, and then tried to think how seduction scenes were described in books, but all I could recall was that the man bent down and took off the lady's shoe. I was on my knees at her feet, almost in a gesture of Hindu obeisance. I was fumbling with her shoe when, with one deft motion, she kicked off both her shoes—they were high-heeled pumps. Before I knew it, she, too, was naked, and we were in bed. Suddenly, I was back in my bed at home in India, and monsoon rain was pouring into the room, drenching the carpet and the bedclothes. I was shifting in bed, trying to find a dry patch, but there seemed to be none.

"What's the matter?" she asked.

I feared that if I spoke I might break into sobs.

She started running her hand through my hair. I felt the same charge of electricity as when she had stroked my hand in the library. Our mouths clamped together. *I didn't turn off the light— a real blindism.* Maybe the light was never on. *But what if it was?* Stop worrying. *I should put on my undershirt.* Why? *I read somewhere women like it.*

Her breathing sounded very loud. I was touching her in a way I had not touched anyone else in my life. The matted hair. The weepy eye. The runny nose. The wet lips. Then I was inside the bottle and knocking against the marble.

"Talk to me, talk to me," she was saying. "You're so silent."

"Hold still." I was again at the orphanage school. A lady ghost had got into my bed and was wrestling me. The more I thrashed about, the more I struggled, the more firmly I was being squashed and scrunched and tied up in a voluminous sheet, like dirty laundry.

"I love you," Phyllis said.

"You don't."

"Please don't say that."

Don't touch. I'm parting her and caressing her, I thought. I reached in and pulled out—mechanically, almost as if I were pumping air into my bicycle. At one moment, she was a small, furry, cuddly, quivering being under my hand, and at another she had enveloped me like the velvet blanket on my mother's bed. Her breathing, her moaning, her endearments, her yesses, the immensity of her nakedness engulfed me, broke over me, submerged me, making me writhe and gasp.

I got off the bed. I stood there, feeling small and alone, sadness spreading within me. My unending search, which in a sense had begun at the school picnic, had ended in emptiness.

"The smell—we must do something about it," I said.

She brought out of her bag a tin of talcum powder and gave it to me. Frenetically, I dusted her, the bedsheets, and myself with powder, using up the whole tin. But there seemed to be no way to overcome the riotous odors from the *gullis* of my childhood which had been rising all around us in the hotel room: sweaty tonga horses; milk-laden family cows; unemptied commodes; frying onions; mint and pomegranate-seed chutneys; blossoming sweet peas, marigold, jasmine, narcissus, bougainvillea, queen of the night.

"Excuse me," she said, and went into the bathroom. She turned on the tap, and there was the sound of steady rushing water, uninterrupted by the usual splashing noises of someone washing. I strained to listen.

Suddenly, I was a child. My cousin Ravi and I had our ears to the door to the bathroom off my mother's bedroom. There was the same steady stream of running water. "They're doing it in his room." My father's room was on the other side of the bathroom. "They've left the water running so we won't hear anything," Ravi said. I pressed my ear harder to the door, my heart racing, even though I could no more imagine my father and mother "doing it" than I could imagine them cleaning the commodes. But all I heard was the stream of running water.

And then I was listening at another bathroom door, to the waterfall of glass bangles of Reyshmi, the saucy, pretty daughter of our sweeperess, who came to clean the commodes morning and evening. Reyshmi was my age, twelve or thirteen, but I was forbidden to play with her, because she was an Untouchable.

"If she is an Untouchable, why is she called Reyshmi?" I remember asking my father.

"Poor people often like to give their children names like 'silk.' It must lift their spirits."

"Why is she an Untouchable?"

"Because her life occupation is concerned with feces."

"The other day, Ambu got typhoid from playing with her sweeperess's daughter," my mother said.

The word "typhoid" struck terror in me. One of my earliest memories was of my grandmother scrubbing my hands with charcoal ashes and pumice stone and saying, "If you don't wash your hands after going to the bathroom, you'll die of typhoid." Since then, I'd had typhoid three times, and once I did almost die of it.

I would crouch behind the bathroom door waiting for Reyshmi to come. Every time I heard her bangles in the distance, my pulse would quicken, and blood would rush to my face. She would come to the *gulli* door of the bathroom with a jaunty step—at first with her mother but later alone—singing a love song from the latest film. How different the waterfall of her glass bangles was from the distinctive ping-pang and ringing of my mother's gold bangles when she was fixing her hair, or pulling the end of her sari to cover her head or her shoulder, or sewing or embroidering or knitting or kneading dough or patting chapattis. The sound of Reyshmi's bangles was also distinctive as she lifted the lid and frame of the commode, disengaged the pot, and carried it away. Perhaps because she was still learning her trade, there was a certain deliberateness about the way she did her task. Sometimes, in the middle of it, her bangles would become still, as if she were looking around and thinking how much better was the bathroom, with its marble-chip floor and distempered walls, than the one-room quarters in which her family slept, bathed, and cooked. I wanted to rush in and catch her in my arms and "do it" on the bathroom floor. I didn't care if I immediately died of typhoid. Although I could never imagine "doing it" with my sisters' friends, I had no trouble imagining doing it with Reyshmi. I didn't even think she would scream or protest—just let her bangles shift on her arms as she took off her clothes and lay down then and there, while I locked the doors and turned on the tap. "Yes, Sahib. Yes, Sahib." But something kept me in my place behind the door, immobile as a statue. *"Don't touch."*

Phyllis came out of the bathroom. I started at the sound of her heavy footstep.

"I must go," I said.

"Go where?"

"International House."

"No, don't talk like that. We've got the room for the night. I want you."

"I should never have asked you to come. It was all a terrible mistake." So many things I did that summer seemed like terrible mistakes.

"Don't say that."

"I have to be alone."

She lay down. She reached up and tried to run her hand through my hair. I was sitting on the edge of the bed.

"Stop it. I don't like that."

"But you liked it a little while ago." She went on trying.

I shook her hand off and leaned away. "Didn't you hear me? I don't like it."

"You can't do that—you can't one minute call me to come here, another minute dismiss me: 'Thank you very much. You go now.' I'm not a servant. Is this the way you always behave?"

"What do you mean, always?" I said.

"You're not going to tell me I'm your first." In her voice there was just a hint of irony—something I'd never detected before—and it pleased me.

"You are," I said, as emphatically as I could.

She was silent, and I couldn't tell whether that was because she was surprised or because she didn't believe me. I felt very tired.

"I don't understand you," she finally said.

"I don't understand myself."

I got up off the bed and started toward the bathroom to get my clothes. I felt dizzy and hot.

She gasped, as if I had hit her in the stomach, and sat up. "Don't do this to me. You can't leave me."

I took down my clothes. They felt so clammy that I shivered at the thought of having them next to my skin again.

"You can't go out there—it's raining cats and dogs." *She speaks in clichés. She's so common.* Angrily, I pulled on my wet clothes.

She was sniffling. I told myself that I didn't care. It was the scene at the library all over again. I wanted to be free of her tears, free of her. I wanted to go to sleep and wake up in my clean, dry bed.

She's fat—I hate her, I thought. If only it had been Mandy. But I said, "I'm sorry. I know I seem cruel and heartless, but I can't help it." She was sniffling louder. I headed for the door.

"Wait—wait. Let me come with you. Let me put on my clothes."

It occurred to me that I didn't know exactly where I was in the hotel and how to get out of it—and that before leaving it I would have to settle the bill with the desk clerk. He must have seen Phyllis come up to my room—had probably directed her. I don't want him to think I've been with a prostitute, I thought. We'd better leave together. "I'll wait for you, but hurry up."

She started dressing, but redoubled her crying.

"Please do stop. What would the desk clerk think?"

"I don't give a damn," she said, sobbing.

"I do. I will not have you crying as we walk out." I wondered if her eyes were red and if the desk clerk would know what we had been doing.

She was groping for something in her bag.

"What are you looking for? Let's go."

"My ring. You wouldn't want the clerk to think we're not married."

That word "married," even though it rang false, suddenly brought home to me, as nothing else had, both the enormity of what I'd done and the impossibility of treating lightly what we had done together. I had an awful feeling that this was the beginning, not the end, of something.

I SAW Phyllis several times in several shabby hotels in Berkeley, and when in the autumn she returned to U.C.L.A. and I to

Pomona I continued to see her, meeting her now in shabby hotels in Los Angeles. Every time I saw her, I swore I would never see her again, but after I'd had a good night's sleep in my room the word would throb in my head and desire would return in a rush. I would struggle against the desire and would resist calling her for a day or two, but then I would be on the telephone arranging to see her—usually on Saturday night.

To get to Los Angeles, I would walk to the Claremont bus stop near the railroad tracks, get a bus to the town of Pomona, some five miles away, and wait there until I could get one of the infrequent buses to the city. It would take me the better part of four or five hours in buses to go and come back. Phyllis would meet me at the Los Angeles bus station, which was downtown, in a skid-row area, and we would skulk around, looking for a cheap hotel. There was no way to get a room without lying, pretending that we were husband and wife, that the brass ring she wore on her finger was a symbol of our enduring love. Once in the hotel room, we would tumble into bed like two children roughhousing. I scarcely kissed her; I sometimes recoiled when she tried to be affectionate—tried to stroke my back, for instance. I used to ask myself why I felt so little for her. I wasn't excited by the touch of her hair, the touch of her face, even the touch of her breasts—in novels I had read, people went into ecstasies over such things. All I wanted was to mount her and get it over with. Afterward, my wish to get away from her would seize me so strongly that sometimes I would spend the night with her only because I had missed the last bus to Pomona. I regarded sex as something disgusting and shameful, which could be carried on only with an undesirable person in execrable surroundings.

Phyllis was short, had wispy mouse-brown hair down to her shoulders, a large, athletic-looking face, and fleshy thighs. But what really put me off about her was her fat belly. From my present vantage point, I'm not sure it was so very fat—her belly might have been simply womanly, or it might have seemed very fat to me because I was so thin. I know that long after I stopped seeing Phyllis I continued to feel an aversion to fat women. Now I think that my whole attitude may have had to do with my mother's pregnancy when I was nine or ten years old. I remember I used to like to run into my mother's belly and sort of bounce off it. It was a game we played. Then, one day, I bumped against her and she didn't seem like my mother anymore. She had a sort of football for a belly. After that, I stopped bumping and bouncing against her. I didn't even like being hugged by her any longer.

"What's the matter with you?" my mother would ask.

"I don't know," I would say, wriggling out from under her arms.

I know that around then I developed a fear of being hugged by any of my women relatives—of coming in contact with their bellies.

ONE Thursday afternoon, Phyllis telephoned me.

"Why are you calling me?" I asked. She had never telephoned before. Somehow, it had been understood between us that I was the one who took the initiative in arranging our meetings. She didn't answer me, but I heard her sniffling in a suppressed way. Desire rose within me, and I said gently, "Phyllis, what's the matter?"

"Nothing," she said, catching a sob.

"I'll come and see you Saturday."

"I need to see you now," she said between sniffles.

"You know perfectly well that I can't come to Los Angeles during the week—I have classes and readers. It's only two days till Saturday."

"I'm in Claremont—at the bus stop."

For a moment, I wasn't sure I had heard her correctly. "In heaven's name, what are you doing here?" I said, panic-stricken that people at college would see me with her and guess the nature of our relationship.

"Please. I have to talk to you," she said.

"Has something happened to your mother?" She was about the only person Phyllis had in the world.

"No."

It must be some kind of emergency, I thought. It is just five. If I run to the bus stop, I can spend a few minutes with her and be back for supper at five-thirty. At least, I can keep my appointment with my reader in the library at six. "O.K. I'll be there in five minutes." I hung up.

I bolted out of my room, ran along the hall, jumped down the few steps of the Sophomore Arch, and ran along Sixth Street. I avoided College Way, where I was bound to meet people I knew, and took College Avenue instead, which was practically empty. As I approached the bus stop, I sensed a mass with my facial vision. Thinking it was a tree, I started to go around it, and I was brought up short by her voice. "Hello."

I was so surprised that I almost stumbled and fell down. "I took you for a tree," I said abruptly.

"Can we sit down?" she asked.

I led her to a low wall near the railroad tracks. I sat a little apart from her. She moved closer, oppressively hovering over me. She took my hand. "I'm pregnant."

"You don't say," I said. I was so ignorant about sexual matters that it never occurred to me that she could be pregnant because of something I had done. I thought that pregnancy was a matter of decision, not chance. I fancied that pregnancy required the purposeful dislodging of the marble in the bottlelike structure of a woman, for which mutual agreement was required, and that once the semen was put into the woman the marble sealed it inside her—much as in the lemonade-bottling factory, I imagined, an empty bottle was refilled and the floating marble inside was somehow drawn into place. On this subject, unlike others, I couldn't turn to books for enlightenment: the authorities did not allow any books with sexual content to be put in Braille or on Talking Books. And in the fifties, in Southern California, it was impossible to get a reader to read aloud any book that had sex in it. I remember that I had to pass up a course on the twentieth-century novel because one of the required books was D. H. Lawrence's "Women in Love," which no reader would agree to read to me. The biology course I was taking as a sophomore to fulfill the college's science requirement did not dispel my notion of the lemonade bottle; the simplified facts of sperm and egg seemed perfectly consistent with it.

"It may be your child," Phyllis said.

I almost laughed out loud. I couldn't imagine being a father; I couldn't imagine another me in the world. "How can that be? I can't believe you mean it."

"I'm late, long overdue, and I've always been completely regular."

If she had started speaking in another language, I couldn't have been more mystified. "Late for what? Regular how?"

She said something about her period. I still didn't catch on.

"Don't you know how children are made?"

"Of course I know, but I never agreed to have a child with you."

She started crying. "I'm determined to have the child. It's mine. It's inside me—you can do nothing about it."

There was something about the forceful way she spoke that made me take her seriously, doubt my own knowledge about pregnancy. "Are you really pregnant?" I asked.

"Why do you think I'm here?" There was a new stubbornness in her voice, totally out of character.

"But how could it have happened? And when?"

Sitting there, between a bus stop and the railroad tracks, we discussed pregnancy, and I got a beginner's lesson on how a child was conceived. We must have spent about an hour talking about the subject.

"Why didn't we take some precautions?" I asked.

"We don't see each other very often, and I didn't think it

would happen to me—or maybe I wanted it to happen," she said.

"We are both teen-agers. We have no skills, we have no money. How can I support you and a child?" I thought of Arlie Treadway, from my school in Arkansas, travelling west with his wife, Vernelle, and the baby in the hope of finding a job—a waiflike figure, perhaps fumbling for doorbells and asking if people had a piano to tune, and regretting that he had never finished high school, because Vernelle had got pregnant. I saw before me the image of Abdul, a blind classmate from the orphanage in Bombay, feeling the sidewalk with his foot at every stop and begging for alms: "Sahib, only one anna for bread—I'm blind." I had just begun to lay claim to a better life by being at an ordinary college, with ordinary, sighted students, and it seemed I was about to be dragged down into the vortex of poverty in which most blind people lived.

"I'm not asking for anything," she was saying. "You don't have to do anything for me that you don't want to. I just thought you'd like to know. Say the word and I'll disappear and you'll never find me again."

"I'll do nothing of the kind," I said. The idea that there might be a child of mine in the world who might grow up without my knowing him or her, without my caring for him or her as my parents had cared for me, was horrifying. If that happened, I thought, I would never be able to sleep again, never lead a normal life. "How can I marry you?" I said gently. That word "marry" was one of the hardest words I ever got out. The whole idea of marrying her was preposterous, but I felt boxed in. "We'd never be happy. I don't know that my family would ever accept you. My Uncle Romesh brought home a Christian for a wife fifteen years ago, and she is still something of a pariah—and yet she's an Indian."

"I'm not asking you to marry me. I'm asking for nothing."

I heard a bus coming in the distance. "It's six-thirty," I said, looking at my watch. "You'd better take this bus." I needed time to think.

"Why don't you take the bus with me? We can spend the night in a hotel in Pomona."

"I have classes tomorrow. Besides, I'd better save the little cash I have if you want to see me on Saturday. Then we'll have plenty of time to talk more about this."

The bus was almost abreast of us. It had to be flagged or it would go right by us, but she made no move. I waved at it frantically, and it stopped. She held back. I practically lifted her onto the bus. Then it pulled away before I could even say good-bye. Oh, God, I should have kissed her, I thought. Yet as I thought this I wished I'd never met her, and I resolved never to see her again if somehow the mess could be straightened out. I desperately wanted someone to talk to, but there seemed to be no one in the world who could understand my predicament.

I remembered that when I was growing up my father used to say to us children that if any of us ever committed a crime, even a murder, we shouldn't be scared to tell him about it, that he wouldn't love us any the less for it, that we should trust him to stand by us—help us, not judge us. I wished he were there to advise me, but I thought I would have less trouble confiding murder to him than discussing anything to do with sex. Even he would not understand this, I thought. I felt I had never treated anyone as miserably as I was treating Phyllis. I had just read Martin Buber's "I and Thou" in class, and the notion that one should treat others as one would wish oneself to be treated had had a profound effect on me. I was filled with so much guilt that I kept thinking of "Anna Karenina," my favorite novel, and the image of Anna throwing herself under a train.

"YOU look awful," K said, meeting me on the steps of the library that Friday evening for our usual drive to the nearest ham-burger-take-out stall.

All day, I had been feeling tense and irritable. "I feel awful, but there's no point in talking about it," I said in the car. "It's too late. Nothing can be done."

"You and I don't like to talk about our problems," K said. "But sometimes pain is lessened if one talks about it to a close friend." K had an intense way of speaking, but he tended to use the passive voice and talk in the third person, as if he were speaking about someone else. In most people these quirks of speech would have put me off, but K's Japanese-American speech sounded charming. Indeed, our both being foreigners was one of the things that had drawn us together.

Everything is closing in on me, and soon there will be no point in hiding anything, in living, I thought. "K, I've got a girl in trouble." To my ear, the sentence sounded like something in a novel, but it was the best I could do.

"She's pregnant?" he said, pronouncing the dreaded word.

"Yes."

"I thought you were like me—always wanting girls but never having any dates." K had asked a couple of girls out, but they had turned him down. After that, he had come to think of all girls as unattainable, and had resigned himself to watching them go by from his window in Smiley Hall—a sort of tenement among the men's dormitories—overlooking the main artery of the campus. "Is it a Pomona girl?"

"Oh, no. It happened in Berkeley. It was all a terrible mistake."

"She's not pleasant? You don't wish to marry her?"

"She's fat and unpleasant. I only went to bed with her because I was lonely and curious. I wanted to know what it was like."

We were at the hamburger stall, and he became preoccupied with getting the car into a line of cars ahead of us at the window.

"Have you thought of abortion?" he said as we were driving back.

"What is that?"

"It is an operation for finishing an unwanted pregnancy."

I was taken with the idea, but as I asked him questions I

became increasingly despondent. "Isn't abortion like killing a baby? I couldn't go through with that," I said.

"Among Japanese, precautions are not taken, so when a girl gets pregnant she gets an abortion," K explained. "There's no shame attached to it."

In my head, the word sounded ugly, but K used it like any other word. For a moment, I thought he was pointing a way where there had been no way, and I tried once more to get used to the idea. But then he said that in America abortion was a crime. "You mean one has to go to Japan to have it done? I have no money."

"I think I know someone in the Japanese Family Association who has the name of a doctor in Los Angeles who would do it."

"But then I would be considered a criminal."

"It's not a crime, really. It's just a question of American traditions."

"But couldn't the police come after us?"

"Not you—you're not doing anything. It's the doctor they'd come after, if anybody. And the doctors usually know how to manage such things."

"It's no use, K. I would carry the guilt of killing a baby for the rest of my life."

"Who says it's a baby? At the moment, it's just a piece of protoplasm, a tissue. The Japanese don't feel guilty about such things."

I felt comforted, perhaps because he was telling me what I wanted to hear. I wanted to know much more, but I felt afraid, afraid to know too much. "How do you know so much about it?"

"I learned about it as a boy, at the internment camp."

"And how do women feel afterward?"

"I don't know. It was not much talked about. It was practiced like secret medicine."

"But it must be a much more difficult operation than having an appendix removed."

"How long has she been pregnant?"

"I don't know. What do you mean?"

"When did you start seeing her?"

"A couple of months ago."

"Then she couldn't possibly be too far along. In such an early stage of pregnancy, they don't have to cut her open—they just reach inside and scrape it out."

"But will she be able to have children later on in life?"

"In the camp, the people who got abortions got pregnant again."

I was impressed by his knowledge and experience, and decided to ask a question that had been bothering me ever since my last meeting with Phyllis. "How many times do you have to make love to a woman before she gets pregnant?"

"People at the camp never talked about it, and I don't know that side of things from personal experience. You must know."

I shifted in the car seat. I had never discussed sex with a man before. I didn't want to expose my ignorance any further.

"Do you think Phyllis will be agreeable?" he asked.

"I don't know. But I'm seeing her tomorrow, and I'll talk to her."

❦

IT was Saturday, and I was due to meet Phyllis. I called her. "Where shall we meet?" I asked.

"Why can't we just go to a hotel, as usual?"

"I wish I could, Phyllis," I said. "But the very idea turns my stomach. I'm finished with sex. I'm never going to have sex again. I'll become a monk first."

She was silent at the other end. Then she said, "I don't feel much like sex, either. I don't know why, exactly. Pregnancy is supposed to make you want it more. Couldn't we just go to a hotel and sit?"

"You know it would never work."

"I know," she said.

It seemed to me that for the first time since I had known her we were speaking the same language.

"What do you want to do, then?" she asked.

"I don't know. I have to think." It was a phrase I found myself saying all the time now. But when I did try to think I felt inconsolably sad, as if something within me—something that kept me wanting and struggling, working and hoping—were dying. "Let me call you back."

"When?"

"In an hour or so."

As soon as I'd hung up the telephone, it rang. It was K. "I have the name of the doctor," he said.

"Oh," I said.

"You don't need it? Was it just a bad scare?"

"No, that's not it."

"Then?"

"Well, I have to get her to agree to it. Even if I got her to agree to it, how would I get her there?"

"I can drive you there."

"But what if something happens to her on the operating table? I've heard of people who never come out of general anesthesia."

"I don't know if she would get anesthesia. That requires another person, and these doctors work alone. But if something happens I'll drive her to the emergency room of a hospital."

"But she might die."

"I never thought of that." He sounded flustered.

"Anyway, I have no money."

"Well, then, there's no way." He seemed at a loss, as if he hadn't envisaged difficulties, and they suddenly seemed too much for him. "So what will you do, then? Marry her?"

"Maybe. And drop out of sight of my friends and family."

I CALLED Phyllis back and said, "I think instead of my coming to Los Angeles you should come to the town of Pomona and check into a hotel."

"It's safe? No one will see us?"

"Safe enough—it's an emergency situation."

"We'll spend the night in the hotel, then?"

"Oh, no. I'll leave you in the lobby and go back to Claremont."

"I want you to stay with me," she said, crying. Since she had told me about her pregnancy, she seemed to cry every other moment.

I changed the subject. "By the way, I want you to meet a college friend of mine."

"Oh, yes? Who?" Her crying stopped abruptly. She sounds excited—just what I expected, I thought. She sees this as a first step toward the end of her isolation from my normal life.

In the evening, I took a bus to Pomona and met her at the bus station. I prevailed upon her to take a single room in the hotel, and insisted on waiting in the lobby while she took her things to the room.

As we were leaving the hotel, I tried to think of something to say that would smooth over the awkwardness of our new arrangement. "It's nice not to have to lie about getting a double room," I said.

"Why don't you marry me and make an honest woman out of me?"

Just a few hours ago, she said she wanted nothing, and now she's thinking of marriage, I thought. I can't cope with it.

She took my hand and, as she often did, clutched it and started nervously running her thumb back and forth across my knuckles. My hand was so alert to interpreting signals that her idle fidgeting irritated and confused me. My mother also had a clutching, nervous hand, and it always made me feel the same way. But with my mother I would calm myself by recalling how capable her hands were. She knitted socks and sweaters and scarves for all seven of us children, sewed our clothes, cooked our meals, washed tubfuls of our laundry. She was capable of doing the work of three servants. I had always imagined that my wife would be able to do all the things my mother did, and also read and write elegant English and do all the worldly things my father did. And now, of all the people in the world, here was Phyllis—a slow, common girl who couldn't hold a candle to my mother or my father— almost proposing marriage to me.

"Stop it," I said, pulling my hand away.

"What's the matter? Don't you even like holding my hand anymore?"

It's best to humor her, I thought. "It's just that my hands have been feeling a little sensitive lately," I said.

We walked into the soda fountain where I'd asked K to meet us. The majestic notes of Mozart's "Haffner" Symphony rang out from the radio. "Do you like Mozart?" I asked her.

"I've only heard the name."

"Do you know the music of Bach or Monteverdi or Bartók?"

"No. Why do you ask? Are you giving me a test, or something?"

I wanted to lash out at her with "Philistine! Ignoramus!" As a college sophomore, I could think of no words more damning than those two. But I bit my tongue, as I was taught to do from childhood when I got angry, and said in my politest voice, "Oh, no. I was just curious."

I thought of the bearded man in the wintry St. Petersburg station, full of foreboding for Anna, and felt that nothing mattered anymore.

Phyllis took my hand again. "My mother has two rooms. We could live with her in the beginning. You wouldn't mind a little squeeze." She pressed my hand.

"Don't talk such rot," I said.

She went on, as if she hadn't heard me, "I can get a job, like my mother, and go to school in the evening. And you could read books at home and listen to the radio."

"Phyllis, please stop it, or I'm leaving."

"Don't be upset. I'm just looking ahead."

"My friend K is coming to pick me up and take me back to the college in an hour or so."

"You haven't told me anything about your friends. You don't tell me anything," she said in a complaining voice.

"I know, I know," I said, and abruptly asked her if she knew what abortion was.

"I'm not having it. I'm too far along to take a pill, or anything like that, and I'm not going to go through an operation—for you or anyone else in the world. It's my child. You can't make me do it."

"Phyllis, I don't want you to do it," I said. And I didn't. But I was soon debating the pros and cons of aborting, as if we were discussing an abstract issue that didn't concern us. Was the embryo a child or a piece of tissue? Weren't the rights and wrongs of abortion as relative as anything else? If the Japanese did it as a matter of course and Americans didn't, didn't it just mean that Americans were superstitious? Why bring another unwanted baby into the world, when half the babies in the world were starving? "Isn't it better all around if one can choose to have a child instead of being forced to have one because someone got pregnant?" I said.

"But you're talking about my having an abortion. I'm not having it. I know you don't love me. The minute I have an abortion, you'll never see me again. I'll lose you forever."

Until that moment, I hadn't imagined her actually going through with an abortion, but now that the subject had become an argument between us she struck me as unreasonable. "If you don't think I love you, why do you want to have my child?"

"I'm going to have the child even if that's all I'll ever have of you. You can't talk me out of it."

❧

"WHAT did you think of her?" I asked K as we were driving back to the college after dropping Phyllis at the hotel.

"It is touching to see the way she looks at you. She's very much in love with you."

"I wish she hated me."

"You mustn't think bad thoughts."

"Didn't you think she's very plain?" I wanted to say "fat" but said "plain" in deference to his kindly nature. Somehow, I felt the need for a visual confirmation of my impression of her.

"She's a mature-looking lady," he said.

I couldn't coax him to say anything more. "Did you like her?" I finally asked, in frustration.

"I liked her, but there wasn't much time for me to get to know her."

"Can you imagine us together, even for a moment?"

"Why not?"

"I always imagined myself with someone like Johnnie," I said, "although, of course, I don't stand a chance with her."

"Johnnie is a very good-looking dame."

"K, you're a real friend." I was glad he was being so honest with me.

"I always hope to be of good service to you."

❦

"WHEN you were talking about abortion, didn't you say you knew of a doctor?" It was Phyllis. She was calling me from Los Angeles, and she sounded frantic. Her voice was unnaturally high and squeaky.

"No, I don't know any doctor. K has the name of a doctor. Why?" It seemed impossible that in the twenty-four hours since I had seen her in Pomona she could have decided on her own to have an abortion, without talking to me and taking my feelings into account.

She didn't answer my question directly. "Can you give me K's number?"

"You can't just call him like that. He's my friend, damn it."

"I need help," she said, breaking down and crying. "I'm under a terrible strain."

I gave her K's number and then asked her again why she needed the name of the doctor. But she hung up while I was still in the middle of my question.

I was stunned and livid. While I was debating with myself what I should do next, the telephone rang. It was Phyllis. "K has agreed to make the appointment and drive me to the doctor," she told me. "He said he'd wait for me while I have the operation and then drive me home." Her voice sounded unnaturally happy, almost ecstatic.

"You can't be serious. I can't believe that you'd go through with it."

"I'm very serious. I have no choice."

She became incoherent, and it was some time before I gathered that she had gone to see a doctor to get a pregnancy test and had discovered that she had been pregnant longer than she'd thought—longer than we had been seeing each other. "I didn't tell you—I didn't think it was right—but before you came into my life I slept with Ahmed several times," she said.

"Ahmed! Not Ahmed, the Persian student at International House?"

"Yes, that Ahmed."

"You mean the baby might not be mine at all but Ahmed's? Is that what you're telling me?"

"Yes."

"I didn't know you even knew him. He never mentioned you."

"Why should he have?"

I remembered the surprising way she had kicked off her shoes in the hotel. I should have known that there was another man before me, I thought. Imagine his not telling me. But then I told myself I was no better; after all, I, too, had kept her a guilty secret.

I still had trouble believing what she was telling me, but I said, "Have you talked to Ahmed? I'm sure he would want to marry you and keep the baby."

"Ahmed's the last person I'd think of marrying. He's a brute and a hog."

I couldn't imagine how Ahmed could have behaved any worse than I had, what he could have done to Phyllis that made her hate him as much as that, but I was so dumbfounded by the astonishing turn of events—of all people, Ahmed!—that the whys and wherefores didn't seem to matter. I concentrated on the central point—that she was not pregnant with my child, and that if she had an abortion it had nothing to do with me. God is great, I thought. I don't have to choose between killing myself and marrying her. I've sinned and learned my lesson. I'll never do it again.

I felt a powerful release, as if I were suddenly rich and could do anything I liked in the world.

"I'm sorry I didn't tell you that I knew Ahmed, because I knew you two were friends," she was saying. "But I just couldn't."

"Please don't apologize to me about anything," I said. "Does K know about Ahmed?"

"No. He mustn't, or he won't help me."

"As his friend, I have to tell him, but I know he won't be any less willing to help you."

"I also need your help. I need four hundred dollars urgently. Can you lend it to me?" She was pleading, entreating me.

"I don't have it, or I would give it to you. I'm just getting by. Why not ask Ahmed?"

"That hog! I would rather die than ask him for a penny."

"What did he do to you?" I was getting interested in spite of myself.

"Please don't ask me any questions about him. I don't

want to think about him. People usually have something put away for a rainy day. You must know someone who can help. I can't put off this operation. I'm already further along than I should be."

"Money is Ahmed's obligation," I said angrily. "I shouldn't be expected to assume that responsibility. In fact, you shouldn't go through with the operation without talking to him."

"Please don't bring him up. I'm begging you for help."

That word "begging" melted my anger. I confessed to her that my father had salted away a few hundred dollars in the bank for my summer expenses, since I couldn't go home to India and my scholarship and grant money did not provide for vacations. I told her that I had given my father my word that I would not touch the money for any other purpose. All the same, I would give her everything that was in the account.

"You'll really lend it to me?"

"I'll give it to you."

Sometime later, she was importuning me to go to the doctor's with her. "I want you to be there during the operation."

"God, no, Phyllis. Anything but that."

"I want you to be there in case something goes wrong. I'd like to see your face before I die."

"You're not going to die. You're being melodramatic."

"It does happen. Women do hemorrhage to death."

She's right, I thought. Who knows what kind of doctor this is? I had a vision of the operation being botched, the doctor disappearing, Phyllis dying, and saw myself being arrested on the spot and charged with being an accomplice in the crime. "I'll do anything, Phyllis, but not that."

"Please, please."

"I'll think about it," I said, and got off the telephone as quickly as I could.

❦

IT was Saturday again, the day of the operation. The campus had a ghostly, deserted quality. A sense of foreboding hung over it, and there was so much smog drifting in from Los Angeles that my eyes wouldn't stop running.

"I don't think you should come," K said as I walked with him to his car in the parking lot. "If something should happen to her and the whole thing becomes public, your college career will be ruined."

"I feel I am abandoning her. I'm not taking responsibility for what I did with her."

"But you didn't get her pregnant."

"I might as well have. Since Ahmed is out of the picture, she doesn't have anyone except me."

"You're right. But, as your friend, I must ask you: Are you prepared to lose face?"

I knew what he meant. We had a similar expression in Hindi— "to have one's nose cut off"—and that was about the worst thing that could happen to a person. "No, I don't want to lose face, but there isn't much risk of that, is there?"

"It is for you to judge."

That's true, I thought. If it comes out that I slept with Phyllis, I'll be drummed out of college. Just the other day, the college chaplain said, "Woman is always the temptress, and man has to resist."

"But what about you, K?"

"I have no involvement with her. If the police come, I could say in good conscience that I was just helping her."

It didn't sound very convincing, and I said as much.

"Besides, I have a car, and I can drive."

God damn it, everything in this country comes down to eyes and cars. I wish I'd never come here. I yielded.

The moment K drove off, I was sure I should have gone with him. But now there was nothing to do except return to my room and wait. "What is the Trinity?" Mr. Gleason had said to us in the freshman course in the history of Western civilization. "How can the Father, the Son, and the Holy Ghost be three figures but one Godhead, I ask you. Are they one or three? And what is the Holy Ghost? Can you see Him? Can you touch Him? Can you hear Him? Can you smell Him? What does it mean to say Christ rose from the dead? Do we have scientific proof that anyone has ever risen from the dead? What does transubtantiation mean—how can the bread and wine of the Eucharist be transformed into the presence of Christ? Do you people really think you are eating the body of Christ when you bite into the Communion wafer? Or drinking Christ's blood when you drink Communion wine?"

The people in the class had seethed with resentment and anger. It seemed that everybody wanted to talk at once.

"For hundreds of years, wars were fought over the answers to these questions." Gleason had pressed on, raising his voice above the stir.

During the course, I had decided that I was a rationalist and an agnostic. But now, as I thought about Phyllis and the operation, I remembered a Christian nurse I had had in a hospital as a small child. Under her influence, I had started thinking of myself as a Christian, and every night for months I had repeated an evening prayer she taught me:

> Heavenly Father, Thou wilt hear me.
> Bless Thy loving child tonight.
> Through the darkness be Thou near me.
> Keep me safe till morning light.
> All this day Thy hand hath led me,
> And I thank Thee for Thy care.
> Thou hast clothed me, warmed me, fed me.
> Listen to my evening prayer.
> Let my sins be all forgiven.
> Bless the friends I love so well.
> Take us all at last to Heaven,
> Happy there with Thee to dwell.

I hadn't thought of the prayer since I was six or seven. Now it came to me unbidden, and I found myself saying it over and over.

In my room, I waited for the phone to ring. I'd avoided asking K for the doctor's name and address, in case I should be accused of complicity later. I should have asked him at least for the phone number of the doctor, I thought. Then I could have called. I didn't know how well founded my fears were, but I didn't want to take a chance. After all, I was the one who had, in a sense, got the doctor for her.

In some part of my mind, I must have feared the worst all along for Phyllis. Am I too cautious or is K too reckless, I wondered. If it had been Mandy in trouble, there was no way I would have let K go alone. Anyway, I would have married her and brought up Ahmed's child as my own. I got a splitting headache, collapsed on the bed, broke into a profuse sweat, got a stomachache, threw up. The hours went by, and still there was no word from Los Angeles. *A broken and contrite heart, O God, shalt thou not despise.*

When K did call, I was so overwrought that I had difficulty catching what he was saying. No, she hadn't died. No, the police hadn't come. He couldn't call earlier, because the doctor had only a makeshift clinic, with no telephone. He had spent the whole time sitting in a little waiting room, not knowing any more than I did. No, there had not been an anesthetist or nurse.

"So you don't know how the operation went?"

"The doctor said the operation went fine. At the end, I went in to help him carry her to the car. I'll never forget the basin of blood on the table."

In the next couple of years, I talked to Phyllis from time to time, but I never saw her again. Indeed, I turned a deaf ear to her pleas to see me. I often reflected on how lonely she must have been—she never confided in her mother. I felt sorry for her, I felt guilty about her, and in a sense I felt responsible for her—she was the first woman I'd known—but I wouldn't see her. Perhaps

I was afraid she would become dependent on me. Perhaps I was afraid of slipping back into the old, sordid pattern.

The last time we spoke was in 1956. She had got her degree and was going to New Mexico to work with American Indians. Long after I lost all contact with her, I kept dreaming about the basin of blood, until I thought it would drown my very soul.

VIII

A LOVE
LETTER

MORE SELECTIONS FROM MY JOURNAL, THIS TIME FROM
my sophomore year.

❧❧❧   September 22
❧❧❧ Everyone here is reading "The Prophet" and is under the
❧❧❧ spell of it. Don Stackhouse, who has transferred to Stanford, writes that before he read it he was clutching at straws,
trying to find a reason to live. He says that reading it has made
the past seem less shadowy and the future less bleak. I've read the
book, but it doesn't speak to me.

October 23
I presided over an International Relations Club dinner in honor
of Orozco's "Prometheus" mural in Frary Dining Hall. Painted
in 1930, the mural was Orozco's first commission in the States,
and is one of the few outstanding works of its kind west of the

Mississippi. The new Mexican consul general attended. Guests included President Lyon, the professor of Latin-American civilization, the chairman of the Art Department, a professor of art at Scripps College. Reporters from Los Angeles covered the event.

November 10

I.R.C. panel discussion today on "Socialism: What Else?" I represented India, Gerhardt Vehlhaber Germany, Frank Tysen Denmark, Jim Kostoff the U.S., and Uka Ngwbia Liberia. We provided a maximum of knowledge and entertainment.

December 1

The fraternity rush season has begun, and I'm afraid I won't be invited to a rush party. How I long to join a fraternity. They're like college clubs, and British clubs were one place where Daddyji was always the first Indian to be accepted. I suppose I get my social ambition from him.

Perhaps half the men here are in the half-dozen fraternities. (Unfortunately for the girls, there are no corresponding local sororities.) These fraternities are not as pernicious as national fraternities at other colleges, where people live and eat together in their fraternity houses. Here the fraternities only have individual rooms in the basements of men's residence halls. Also, as one fraternity member put it to me, "unlike national fraternities, our fraternities have no restrictions on the membership of Jews and Negroes." But then we have no Negroes here.

December 5

I didn't get an invitation from Nu Alpha Phi. But then I never stood a chance of being a Nappy—I don't have a Nappy voice or handshake, I'm not a popular guy with girls, I'm not Ghost material. I've only been invited to the Alpha Gamma Sigma rush party.

December 11

I got a bid from Alpha Gamma. It's one of the two least socially desirable fraternities. Alpha Gamms are the also-rans, not the college leaders. It's a nice fraternity nonetheless, with earnest, pleasant, hard-working guys in it.

A lot of brothers taunting pledges in Frary Dining Hall, and sounds of thwacking outside as pledges in the Frary courtyard are paddled for the fun of it. All in good spirits, no one paddled very hard, I think. But then it's just the start of Hell Weekend.

December 12

Hell Weekend rules for pledges, or worms: All of us worms are to address the "actives" as "esteemed masters." When we are swatted, we are supposed to say, "Thank you, Esteemed Master. May I have another?" We worms are supposed to keep asking for swats until the esteemed masters are tired. We worms are to carry with us at all times for the benefit of our esteemed masters: a cigar; a bottle of Orange Julius; a cube of ice; shoe polish and rag; matches; chewing gum; cigarettes; work gloves; a hand towel; a grub hat; two raw eggs; Life Savers; a surprise goody (to eat); a live worm. We have to learn the Greek alphabet and live in the "dungeon" under the frat room until called, and then crawl out on our hands and knees. Thank goodness, not all these rules are observed.

December 13

This evening, some of us foreign students spoke on how we viewed the manners, social customs, and morals of the U.S. Finally, I had a chance to let off some steam about the temporary pleasures of dating.

December 15

We all met in our frat room in the basement of Clark Hall—comfortable easy chairs, a pool table, individual paddles of brothers hanging on the walls. We new brothers were presented with diploma-like certificates giving us all the honors and privileges of the fraternity, signed by the president and secretary. There was a lot of ragging, lots of threats—not so much to humiliate, I think, as to evoke general laughter. We new brothers were given ordeals. Roland Summit was asked to make a map of the sprinkler systems of the Marston Quadrangle. I think the older brothers plan to ride around in cars watching the new brothers do these silly things. I wish the brothers had picked on me, but they left me alone.

December 16

I'm getting tired of snacks at the Sugar Bowl, which is run by two quiet ladies who live together. If I had a car, I would go to Stinky's. Girls who read to me in the day go to Stinky's for hamburgers in the evening. It sounds so exotic and social. I just have to hear "Stinky's" to feel left out.

ON November 3rd of my sophomore year, I wrote a letter to Mr. W. T. Jones, one of the two or three of my Pomona professors I admired most, setting forth reasons that I wanted to transfer to an Eastern university. He was my philosophy teacher, but that academic year he was on leave to the Naval War College, in Newport, Rhode Island. My letter went, in part:

As you know, for quite a while I have been contemplating the possibility of going East, to Harvard, Yale, Princeton, or Cornell. One of the reasons that made me hesitate in entertaining this thought was the dread of being in an "impersonal institution." To evaluate what an "impersonal institution" means, I attended the University of California at Berkeley this summer and stayed at International House. I found that the cross-section of people that I met there compensated me considerably for not being at a small college like Pomona.

If I may enumerate, there are five reasons I feel that in the long run it would be to my advantage to transfer to a larger university:

1. Since I have already spent three years in the southern part of the United States and will have spent two years on the West Coast by the end of this academic year, I feel it would be worth my while to get to know the eastern part of the United States before I return to India.

2. I left India when I was only fifteen, and because of the lack of proper educational facilities for the visually handicapped there I had a very sketchy education. Consequently, I was never able to acquire knowledge of the history and culture of my own country, which other children do as a matter of course at school. This I feel to be a serious gap in my education, for in the last analysis I will have to earn my bread in India. By transferring to one of the universities in the East, I will be able to take some courses in Indian history and culture, which are not available to me, of course, at Pomona.

3. I would like to take a semester or two of Sanskrit. The nationalistic tendency in India will increasingly require an understanding of Sanskrit, which is the foundation of a number of Indian languages. By the way, my knowledge of Hindi, Urdu, and Punjabi is limited to speech only, because there was no Braille system for writing them when I was growing up.

4. As you know, the thing I want to do most after graduation in America is to attend Oxford and get a degree in jurisprudence, which will give me the best chance of a livelihood in India. My financial means are so meagre that the only way I could go to Oxford would be by receiving some kind of financial aid from a university or foundation. I feel that this would be easier in the East than at Pomona, if for no other reason than that the larger universities in the East have greater financial resources and contacts.

5. This reason is very tangible. It is valid only if some of my father's assumptions and mine are right about my future in India. I am bound to encounter some kind of opposition to making my livelihood there

because of my handicap, and maybe even because of my Occidental education. We think that my chances for a livelihood might be improved if I had a degree from a very well-known American university.

Before I can transfer to any of the universities mentioned above, I will need some type of financial aid from them, because the states in which they are situated do not have a reader's fund, as California does.

Whenever Mr. Jones commented on my papers, he numbered his points, as if he felt that reducing thought to numbered items was the clearest way to think. I was so much under his influence that in those days I numbered practically everything I wrote. Consequently, I had difficulty putting into words the many more reasons that I had for wanting to leave Pomona.

When I first got to Pomona, I had been excited by its exhortation that all who entered the college should be "eager, thoughtful, and reverent." After a while, I had come to balk at the emphasis on reverence—which, possibly rooted in the Congregational foundation of the college, often seemed to give the place a predominantly Christian outlook. I remember that on Sundays there was a lot of going to church, and that there were a lot of church suppers. In fact, it seemed that many people, both students and teachers, were not only reverent but pious. They appeared to believe that they had better values than, say, people at state universities, and that they shared their values only with people at a few top-notch small liberal-arts colleges or with old, famous New England universities with Christian antecedents. Pomona people talked as if they had a special place in the world as the torchbearers, as the "elect," as the leaven in the lump. Sometimes the college seemed to feel that it was a bastion of Christian civilization, and the barbarians were at the gates. (On the Pomona seal were the words "Our tribute to Christian civilization," and children of Pomona College alumni were called "tributes." The idea of a "tribute to Judeo-Christian civilization" seemed unheard of. I don't remember many Jews in either the faculty or the student body.)

At Pomona, not only did people seem to be cut off from the

world; people went around thinking they were the center of the world, and no one at the college challenged that assumption. The possibility that excelling at Pomona might have little to do with excelling anywhere else seemed never to be raised. People apparently thought that part of the college's virtue lay in its distance from the surrounding chaotic society. True, one day they would be in the middle of that society, and then they would certainly have to participate—make a contribution, help change it—however difficult that might be. It was best, then, to store up knowledge and virtue and acquire values at Pomona for that later time. Thus it was not so much that people were politically unconscious as that they were consciously holding politics in abeyance, had deliberately placed a moratorium on it. (Such overt political consciousness as existed was limited mostly to the Young Americans for Freedom—the conservative Republicans, the supporters of Nixon and Senator William Knowland.) At the time, there was no good newspaper published in Southern California, and a lot of students came to Pomona as non-newspaper readers and stayed non-newspaper readers.

In any event, I found the atmosphere at Pomona parochial. For instance, Anne Clark, perhaps the brightest student in our class, who was one of my readers, would skip over long passages in the "Iliad," an assigned book, because, she said, they were "too gory" to be read aloud. Perhaps because I had grown up in the cosmopolitan British Empire and had lived through one of the most politically intense moments in Indian history, and perhaps because in all of Claremont I was the only Hindu, the only Indian, the only blind person, I found the atmosphere of the place stifling in all sorts of ways as time went on. I felt that if I got to a large, cosmopolitan university I would be back in touch with the wider world. I would find more kindred spirits, and feel less isolated.

Mr. Jones' reply to my letter about transferring, dated November 9th, took up my points one by one:

Though I shall be sorry to see you leave Pomona, I am obliged to say that I think your decision to go elsewhere to complete your B.A. is sound. I will comment on each of your five reasons.

1. I agree that there will be a real advantage for you to get to know another part of this country, and despite the levelling influences of radio and TV, there are still significant sectional differences.

2. and 3. These seem to me important considerations. You certainly should know more about the institutions and history of your own country, especially if, as you say, there will be a prejudice against you because of an Occidental education.

4. I just don't know about whether there are greater possibilities in the Eastern universities for financial support. There are certainly larger funds, but there are also greater demands. What this adds up to for you, I don't know.

5. This seems to be a minor matter; if the other reasons did not on the whole point up to a move, I would not consider reputation very seriously.

Mr. Jones suggested that I write long letters to the four universities, giving my background and my plans, and emphasizing my reasons for wanting to transfer and my need for financial aid, and that I then apply only to the universities that seemed most responsive to my letter. He said he would, of course, be glad to write recommendations for me. President Lyon, the deans, and my other professors also supported my decision to transfer. Mr. Mulhauser said, "You've probably already got as much out of Pomona as you can. Staying on here, and moving in lockstep with your classmates until graduation, may just be stultifying for you."

I wrote the long letters to the four universities, and got strong responses from Harvard and Yale. I applied to both, telling them that I was planning to be in the East after Christmas to be with my father, and asking if it would be possible to set up an inter-view during the Christmas holidays. I was granted one at Harvard on December 21st with Mr. David Henry, the associate director of admissions, and one at Yale on December 22nd with Mr. Arthur Howe, Jr., acting chairman of the board of admissions.

A thirteen-hour flight got me to Boston on the day of my Harvard interview. I took a taxi to Cambridge, and checked into the Continental Hotel. It was expensive, but it had the advantage of being close to Harvard Square. After Arkansas and California, the accents and rhythms of speech I heard around me sounded so cosmopolitan that I felt I was back in the Raj. I felt very much at home. This is where I belong, I thought. The Arkansas school and Pomona were just way stations on my journey to Harvard.

THE December wind was blowing hard. It was my first expe-rience of a New England winter. I had no coat or hat, scarf or gloves. In fact, I didn't own any of them; in Southern California one scarcely needed a jacket. I was wearing the only good wool suit I had. I felt frozen and exposed. Harvard Yard was deserted, as if the university were already shut down for Christmas. More-over, the terrain was unfamiliar, and walking difficult. By asking one or two strangers who were running past, I found my way to Mr. Henry's office in University Hall. I was a few minutes early for the interview, and as I waited I tried inconspicuously to warm my hands under my jacket, so that I wouldn't have to give him a cold hand to shake.

I heard my name. I jumped up. It was Mr. Henry. I gave him my hand—still cold. He took it, in a warm, friendly, alert hand. We exchanged some amenities, and I followed him into his office and took a chair, all the while listening closely to his voice. He seemed about thirty, and came across as an Eastern version of the prep-school type we had at Pomona—someone who was perpetually young, and was so much at ease with himself that he put other people at ease. Next to him, I felt very old. I had come prepared to talk about my reasons for wishing to transfer, about my need for financial aid, about my essay on our flight from burning Lahore during Partition, which I had written as part of my Harvard application. But Mr. Henry didn't give me a chance. He started asking me questions about how I had managed to travel alone from California, and how I had found my way to University Hall. It turned out that he had never met a blind person before, and he was wonderstruck that I could follow him from the waiting room to his office and find a chair unassisted, and that I could talk to him as naturally as if I could see. At first, my answers were offhand—I wanted him to get off the subject of blindness—but his interest seemed so genuine that I was soon explaining at some length about facial vision. He was incredulous.

"If you don't believe me, come out with me sometime and we'll go bicycling," I said, surprised at my own boldness.

He wanted to know more about my bicycling, and I told him about our family's compound in Rawalpindi, where I had taught myself how to ride a bicycle. He seemed spellbound, and that added to my enjoyment of describing things to him.

"Do you know anything about Harvard life?" he asked.

The phrase sounded exotic, and it was now my turn to be spellbound, as he described the college's house system, its "tutor and tutee" meetings, its cultural activities, the kind of people who thrived at Harvard—the best students from traditional preparatory schools. It was clear that his loyalty was to Harvard College, as opposed to the university at large; he seemed to take it for granted that the college was the crème de la crème of the various constituents of the university, and he soon had me feeling that I would never be a Harvard man unless I went to Harvard College.

I asked Mr. Henry what my chances of getting into the college were, my heart racing uncontrollably.

"You should be a shoo-in," he said.

I wasn't sure I had heard him correctly, and said as much.

He referred to my academic record at Pomona and my unusual background, and repeated the term "shoo-in."

Soon Mr. Henry had a course catalogue in hand and was helping me decide which professors I might study with—Daniel Ingalls, William Langer, Archibald MacLeish, Albert Guérard. Some of these were legendary names at Pomona. I was so impressed and awed by everything Mr. Henry was telling me that Pomona, by comparison with Harvard College, seemed like just a high school. I've always wanted to go to Harvard, I thought, but I'm now ready for it in a way that I wasn't two years ago. Because of good teaching and small classes at Pomona, I'm better prepared. Because of the Southern California climate, I'm healthier.

I didn't want to spoil the buoyant atmosphere of the interview, but years of disappointment had made me wary of believing that something pleasant was likely to happen to me. So I reminded Mr. Henry that I could not possibly come to Harvard without financial aid to pay readers—a point that I had dwelt on in my application to Harvard.

"Financial aid for transfer students in their first year is not common," he said. "We don't like other colleges to think we are trying to lure their good students away from them. But your case is very different. Your college authorities are enthusiastic about your transfer from Pomona, and your scholarship is not for ordinary Harvard expenses but for paying your readers."

I could not have argued my case better.

"I'm sure that in your case satisfactory arrangements will be made," he continued. "If we want someone at Harvard, we don't let anything stand in our way."

He wanted to introduce me to the dean of admissions, Wilbur Bender, and we went upstairs to his office. Mr. Henry filled in Dean Bender—a hard-driving, gruff fellow—on our conversation. Dean Bender made kind noises about my admission and about financial aid for readers, and asked Mr. Henry to show me one of the houses where I might live.

As I walked around with Mr. Henry, I could sense that he was watching me, as if to convince himself that I had facial vision, and to understand how I used it. He seemed full of boyish wonder at my sureness of step—as natural to me as to a yak on a slippery slope. While we were inside University Hall, I was able to perform with a certain amount of aplomb, but outside, in the bitter cold, my step was a little less sure. Nevertheless, since the path was familiar to me I walked it without so much as touching his arm. Especially at corners, the cold wind cut through me, but he was so busy watching me that he seemed not to notice that I was ill-prepared for winter weather.

After crossing Massachusetts Avenue, we went into Adams House, and Mr. Henry showed me an impressive suite on the ground floor, near the main entrance. He then took me around the House, which seemed like a little college within a larger college, with its own special character and charm.

Afterward, Mr. Henry left me on Massachusetts Avenue. As I walked along the avenue toward Harvard Square, the phrase "shoo-in" kept drumming in my head. I'm going to be a Harvard man, I thought, As always, Daddyji is right—we Mehtas make a good personal impression. He'll be so proud of me.

At Harvard Square, I fancied for a moment that Mr. Henry was still with me and was going to put his hand on my arm and help me across. I stiffened with anger. I suddenly felt tired from the effort of having to prove to him my ability to get around. On an impulse, in the renowned manner of the great Harvard man George Lyman Kittredge, I held out both my arms and marched across, heedless of whether traffic was moving or not, assuming that it was the motorists' responsibility to look out for me.

"How did things go at Harvard?" my father asked, in Punjabi.

"Couldn't have gone better."

"And at Yale?"

"If anything, better still." After Harvard, I had gone to Yale and been interviewed by Mr. Howe. He, too, seemed certain of my acceptance.

"As I always say, we Mehtas carry our luck with us," my father said. "We always make a good personal impression." I could feel him looking at me closely. "But why does your face look so drawn?" he asked, sounding suddenly anxious, and moving closer to me in the back seat of the car. It was just after Christmas, and we were in Mrs. Clyde's car, driving along the Merritt Parkway in Connecticut. "I hope nothing has been worrying you."

"No, nothing," I said. It's an out-and-out lie, I thought, but how can I tell him about the strain of travelling alone, of having to prove myself at these interviews? How can I tell him about Phyllis's operation? I continued to feel haunted by the whole sordid experience. I felt I would never get over it.

"I'm glad to hear it," my father said brightly. "Your face certainly looks a little fuller. You must be eating well and keeping fit."

"Of course I'm keeping fit," I said rather testily. He had managed once again to put me on the spot. The truth was that since I stopped seeing Phyllis I had started having attacks of abdominal pain. Hardly a week went by without them. I took it for granted that they were psychosomatic and would go away. But they had persisted, and were no less debilitating for being recognized as perhaps psychosomatic. I saw no point in worrying my father by mentioning them, however. I thought that if they didn't go away soon I would have myself examined by a doctor, like any other adult. At nineteen, I was constantly preoccupied with being independent.

"I like the sound of you two speaking Indian, but, Ved, you shouldn't tire your father out by talking to him," Mrs. Clyde said from the front seat. Although her remark struck both my father and me as silly—far from exhausting my father, our talks always exhilarated him—we immediately fell silent. We were constantly on our guard against displeasing Mrs. Clyde in any way.

Ever since my father came back to America, a few months earlier, to do his lecture tour of "knife-and-fork clubs," one of our greatest wishes had been to be together at Christmas, but we couldn't justify spending the money it would cost to make that possible. All his hard-earned income was barely enough to meet the basic needs of the family. Then, one day in November, Mrs. Clyde paid me a surprise visit at Pomona. She stayed for a couple of days, to get a good look at the place where I was studying. She asked to see my schedule of classes and readers, and told me that I was working too hard. "You're just like your father," she said. "His schedule of lectures also sounds really tiring." She announced that she wanted to treat my father and me to a "good rest" over the Christmas holidays at Old Fields. After she left, she sent each of us a round-trip air ticket. But, as in a fairy tale, she attached a condition to her gift: that I come to Old Fields only for the week after Christmas, though my father would be there the week before as well. Her explanation was her often repeated complaint that our talks tired my father out. Perhaps she had formed this impression because she herself was such a non-stop talker, often saying the same thing over and over again, that after spending a few hours with her most people looked tired. In any case, because of the condition she imposed, my father had flown to New York the week before Christmas, and I had stayed on at Pomona for a few days before my Harvard and Yale interviews, and had spent Christmas Day itself with Norman and Ellen Cousins, friends of my father's, who lived in Norwalk, Connecticut. The next day, Mrs. Clyde had driven over from Huntington with my father and her driver to pick me up. We were now on our way to Old Fields.

"Mr. and Mrs. Cousins seem like such hospitable people,"

Mrs. Clyde was now saying in the car. She asked my father how he had met Mr. Cousins.

"I met him in India, when he came to interview Prime Minister Nehru," my father said, "He is the editor of the *Saturday Review*. I showed him some of Ved's letters home, and he asked me, 'Why doesn't Ved write a book about his struggles and experiences?' Ved must have got a good few tips about writing during his stay with Mr. and Mrs. Cousins."

I was embarrassed that my father had brought up the subject of my writing a book—a word I could scarcely use even just in my thoughts. I always thought of what I might write as a "narrative" or a "story."

"Not really," I said. "But he did once ask me how I spent my summers, and I told him that I generally went to summer school. He suggested that I set aside next summer to write."

"As I always say, 'like me, like my book,'" Mrs. Clyde said. Since my first meeting with her, I had read her book "Horse Sense." "I had a lot of laughs writing it. But how can you write a book without seeing?"

I bristled. "Why? Blind people have written books," I said, although I had no confidence that I myself could ever write a book.

"But how?"

"Just the way he writes letters," my father said. "He can type it out."

"No, that's not quite accurate," I said, getting involved in the discussion in spite of myself. "Nowadays, I dictate everything, so that I can read it over and revise it. I developed this system when I got to college. There's no other way to write papers."

"You see, he has to pay readers, amanuenses, and typists," my father explained to Mrs. Clyde.

I was now embarrassed that our conversation had taken a financial turn, in case Mrs. Clyde thought we were asking for help.

"I can't possibly think of writing anything," I said quickly. "These are the years I must concentrate on my college studies."

"You take it from me, one day he's bound to write a book," said my father, who was never one to give up on anything.

"If Mr. Cousins thinks you could write a book, he must be right," Mrs. Clyde said. "And he can get you the money to pay help."

Neither my father nor I replied to this.

"Why can't Mr. Cousins get you the money?" she insisted.

My father said that his relationship with Mr. Cousins was not of a kind that would allow him to appeal to him for money, no matter how good the cause.

"As I always say, 'now is the accepted time,'" Mrs. Clyde said. "If you can't afford both to go to college and to write a book, you should give up college. Some of the greatest people didn't go to college. Did Churchill go to college? Did Jesus?"

"But we are Indians, and we believe that knowledge is salvation," my father said. "The more education Ved has, the better equipped he'll be to deal with life." He thought that by shifting the ground to our culture he could duck the issue.

"But Churchill—" she started.

"I'm not Churchill," I said.

"But I would trade my B.A.—if I had ever got one—any day for 'Horse Sense.' What might be wrong with the two of you is you've got a lot of education but no horse sense." She gave one of her loud laughs, as if to say, "Contradict me if you can." We had long since learned that there was no point in contradicting her.

It was my last day at Old Fields. My father and I were sitting with Mrs. Clyde on the glassed-in porch off her bedroom, trying to catch the morning sun.

"What plans have you made for the coming summer?" she asked me.

"I haven't made any plans yet," I said. Every time I thought about the approaching summer, I got a sinking feeling. The routine of studying was the only way I knew of keeping homesickness at bay.

She turned to my father. "How much have you put aside for him for the coming summer?"

"Nothing to speak of. The summer is a long way away."

"But how do you expect the child to eat? He'll starve and die."

"He won't starve and die as long as I'm alive," my father said. "I've always managed, and I will manage again."

"But if he doesn't have money how will he eat? And if he can't eat of course he'll die. Why wouldn't he?"

She had such a literal way of thinking that we both found ourselves laughing. She joined in our laughter.

She picked up her legal pad and pencil. "Well, how much would it cost for you to spend the summer writing the book?" she asked.

I was taken aback. I hadn't given any thought to the matter. "I don't have the slightest idea," I said.

"You must have some idea," she said, "or how could you think of writing a book?"

I wanted to say that the idea was my father's, not mine, but I was afraid of starting an argument. She asked how much it would cost me for room and board, and how much for an amanuensis. I gave her the best estimates I could, and they came to about a thousand dollars.

"You mean you could write a whole book on a thousand dollars?"

"No, I didn't mean that. I suppose I could start something and see how far I got in a summer."

By the end of the day, she had talked to Dwight Rogers and drafted the following letter to the American Foundation for the Blind:

GENTLEMEN:

I have instructed Eastman Dillon & Co., 15 Broad Street, New York City, to segregate from my account and hold subject to your order 18 shares International Paper. These shares are a gift to the American Foundation for the Blind with my best wishes for ever increasing success. It is my hope that it will be used for the benefit of some blind student from India. Mr. Norman Cousins has suggested that instead of attending summer school Ved Mehta devote next summer to writing and the development of his, in Mr. Cousins' opinion, marked literary ability. In order to follow this suggestion, Mr. Mehta would require the assistance of a reader-secretary, etc., and would have living expenses to meet. These would cost about one thousand dollars. I should be glad if you were to decide to make it possible for Mr. Mehta to follow Mr. Cousins' suggestion.

Sincerely,
Mrs. Ethel Clyde

While I was delighted that she was making it possible for me to spend a summer writing, I was terrified at the prospect. How did the whole business of my writing a book get started anyway, I wondered. It was one of my father's typical ideas—like the one that I would grow up to be another Caruso, combining Eastern melodies and Western harmonies, when I had neither the voice nor the talent nor any knowledge of Western music. But, in contrast to how I felt about singing, I myself secretly wanted to write the story of my life. I thought it would be cathartic. There was something challenging about writing a book—something not generally associated with blind people. Anyway, a book would help me define myself, and could win a place for me in the wider world. But there was all the difference between dreaming about writing a book and sitting down to write one. I had one of the worst attacks of my recurring abdominal pain yet.

As I thought about writing the narrative, it became clear to me that writing about myself would mean confessing very personal things. I couldn't think of anyone better for such a delicate, intimate job of amanuensis than Johnnie Johnstone. For one thing, no one had a more sympathetic ear. But, more to the point, I thought that telling her the story of my struggles over days, weeks, and months might—just might—make her fall in love with me.

I had never stopped being in love with Johnnie since I first heard her kind, open-hearted, pensive, beguilingly reticent, slightly ironic voice. There was lively but genteel laughter in it, and, at the same time, the ever-present undercurrent of sadness, which made me find her both amusing and touching. In fact, I felt about her voice the way I thought I would feel about her eyes if I could see—it was a window to her soul. Her diction was as clear as limpid water, and there wasn't a hint of self-consciousness or pedantry in her speech. She was extremely intelligent but always tried to hide it, so that boys wouldn't feel threatened by her. She was also an outdoor type. I thought of her as an exalted, unattainable being, who was good at everything. Next to her I felt like a dullard, who stuck to his room and the library. It was no accident that I had got to know both Mandy and Phyllis when Johnnie was home for the summer, and that both relationships were short-lived. Indeed, I later thought that Mandy and Phyllis had been only surrogates for Johnnie, my true love.

Johnnie and I were often in the same courses and read the same books for our classes, so when she was reading to me we shared a spirit of camaraderie, of common enterprise, of trying to puzzle out things together—the meaning of this passage, the significance of that symbol. So I mostly saw her in the context of work. In class, she might come and sit next to me; if we ran into each other at the Coop, we might have a Coke together. But we always talked about books or professors or classmates; she never talked about whom she was dating, what parties she was going to, what she was doing with her weekends. It was as if she had instinctively decided that I didn't belong to that side of her life—the very side that I really wanted to belong to. I often wondered if she ever thought about me when we weren't together, as I did about her—if I appeared in her dreams, as she did in mine. But I never dared ask her. In the year and a half I had known her, I had not had the nerve to so much as whisper a word about my love to her. I had simply assumed that all true love was selfless and required lifelong sacrifice and silent devotion, that it was doomed and I must resign myself to going through life alone, my love unrequited. I had consoled myself with the thought, however, that as long as she went on reading to me I had the sound of her voice to sustain me from one reading session to the next.

Lately, Johnnie had been reading to me—for an English course—tales of knights errant jousting for their ladies and going on quests for the Holy Grail. I had been inspired by the tales, and had started having all kinds of bizarre fantasies about her setting me ordeals for winning her. In one she banished me to a forest, where for years I had to live on roots and berries. But now I saw in the book project a glimmer of hope—hope for my love. Also, since I would be going to Harvard in the fall, I felt that sooner or later I would have to declare myself to her, take my chances on all or nothing. Otherwise, I would live with a sense of regret all my life, wondering what would have happened if I had made my feelings known to her.

Soon after Mrs. Clyde's gift came through, I stopped Johnnie a few minutes before the end of a reading session, told her about the project, and broached the subject of her being my amanuensis for the summer, at the same time apologizing for the strangeness of the idea.

"Gee, Ved, writing a book with you—I'd like nothing better, but I'm afraid I couldn't possibly do it," Johnnie said. "I have to go back and be with my mother in Seattle."

"I'll come to Seattle and we can work there," I said, without a moment's hesitation.

She seemed startled. "Seattle? You don't know anyone there. How could you possibly manage alone?"

"I know you. I'll get an apartment."

"Have you ever lived in an apartment by yourself?"

"No."

"What would you do for food?"

I was stumped for a second. I had never so much as boiled an egg. But I had eaten alone in restaurants, and I said, "I'll eat in restaurants."

"But you've never been to Seattle. How will you find your way around?"

"Perhaps you could show me about once. I learn very fast. Besides, I'll be working all the time."

"If that's what you want to do, I'll be happy to do it." Her voice suddenly became animated. "You'll dictate and I'll write. We'll be working on an actual book—think of that! And if you got a real apartment, with a kitchen, I could cook a little bit for you, and we could have lunch together—break up a long day of work with lunch, you know." She now threw herself into the spirit of the idea just as she had at first resisted it.

In all the time I had known her, I had never had so much as a sandwich with her, and the thought of standing around the kitchen while she cooked—in an informal way, without the time limit of a reading session—took my breath away. I'll be eating with her, perhaps sharing an apple or a peach with her—just imagine!

I realized in a flash, as when the meaning of an elusive dream suddenly becomes clear, that I couldn't write the narrative with anyone but her. Not only did she have an understanding heart but she was the only person whose literary judgment I trusted—who could tell me after a paragraph whether it was sense or nonsense. Above all, I had to have the feeling that I was addressing my words to her. In the course of the summer, I would have a chance to prove my worth to her. Then I remembered Richard Hungate, the most sought-after man in our class, whom she was dating, and realized, with deep sadness, that I could never measure up to him. I felt depressed, but told myself there were instances in books of perfectly sensible, desirable women falling in love with hunchbacks and the like.

"No, I really couldn't accept the job," she said now.

"What? Why not?"

"I couldn't accept money from you, and I need to earn money over the summer to help pay my tuition."

"But how would my paying you over the summer be different from my paying you for reading now?"

"It's different because it's not schoolwork. I just can't have you come all the way to Seattle because of me, and, on top of it, pay me. You know, the train to Seattle is quite expensive. And an apartment won't be cheap, either, especially since you'll have to take a furnished one. I just can't have that."

I almost told her about Mrs. Clyde and her gift, but I felt shy. It would mean explaining the unusual relationship between my father and Mrs. Clyde, her wealth, her interest in me and my education, Mr. Cousins' role—things that I could scarcely verbalize to myself. But if I can't bring myself to tell her about Mrs. Clyde, I wondered, how am I going to be comfortable dictating my life story to her?

"The money part you honestly don't have to worry about," I finally said. "I have a cache of a thousand dollars that I can use only for this project."

"Oh, how interesting!"

"My only problem is where I'll stay when I first arrive in Seattle," I said, to get away from the subject of money.

"Oh, that's not a problem. I'll write and ask my mother if you can stay with us until you find a place," she said matter-of-factly.

The thought of meeting her mother was so staggering that I

felt an attack of abdominal pain. I put my handkerchief to my face and pretended I had a sneeze coming.

❧

THE attacks had started early in November. Now it was March, and they gave no sign of abating. I finally got myself to the college clinic. I was seen by one of the college doctors, a bumbling, good-natured, slow-witted man, who examined me as I stood in his office, feeling my abdomen through my shirt.

"A case of common indigestion," he said.

"That can't possibly be right," I said. "I've had these pains for a few months."

He pushed his fingers up into my ribcage.

"Ouch!"

"It hurts, doesn't it? You probably have a lot of gas in there. Just watch your diet and eat bland foods for a while."

I did what he told me, but the pain persisted, and a couple of weeks later I went back to the clinic.

"Where, exactly, do you think you feel the pain?" he asked, this time sitting me down.

"Lately, it seems to be localized on the right side of my abdomen."

"Then it's definitely a case of appendicitis. You'd better go to Pomona Valley Community Hospital and have yourself an operation."

The mere thought of going through an operation, without family or friends around—a little like the way Phyllis had—was unsettling.

"Can the operation wait?" I asked. "I don't want to miss classes and fall behind in my studies."

"On second thought, maybe it's not appendicitis at all," he said accommodatingly. "It could be your pancreas—or your gall bladder. Let's get some X-rays done."

"Will they cost a lot?"

"As a foreign student, you're covered by the college health-insurance policy."

He gave me a slip of paper, and I went to the hospital in Pomona and had the necessary X-rays done. A few days later, the college doctor informed me that they had turned up nothing. "The pressures of college work can bring on such pain," he said. "Try to forget it."

But the pain didn't go away, and a few weeks later I went back to the clinic once more. This time, the doctor had me get a stool test done, after which he informed me that I had intestinal parasites. I took the medicines he prescribed, but with no better results.

Around that time, I was reading Marcus Aurelius's "Meditations" for a course, and had come under the spell of his philosophy of endurance, temperance, justice, and wisdom, and his example of total immersion in work and duty. His principle of stoic endurance had a special effect on me, and I began to regard my abdominal pain as my own test of stoicism. "Hundreds of years ago, Sophocles and Marcus Aurelius, and recently Arnold Toynbee, have given expression to a single truth, that man grows through suffering," I wrote to my father. "This truth has been enshrined in art, music, literature—in all of human experience. I articulate this lofty sentiment because it is a tenet of my credology." ("Credology" was a word I had just come across, and I used it at every opportunity.)

❦

MORE journal entries from my sophomore year.

January 21

Daddyji writes that my little sister Usha has got some skin affliction called leukodermia. Although she's only lost pigmentation on two small spots on her face and neck, people have already started shunning and pitying her. The prettiest of the Mehta

333

sisters, she's now thought to have no chance of marriage. What a blighted country we come from, where such attitudes are possible.

January 22

I won third place in impromptu speaking in a contest of twelve colleges. I must try to do more public speaking next semester and improve my technique.

January 26

We are in the throes of final exams for the first semester. We Pomonans look down on Stanford because it has a quarter system, which means that for Stanford students Christmas vacation is for fun instead of study.

February 12

Today, President Lyon announced at the college convocation that I had led all the Pomona sophomores in grades. Daddyji will be so proud of me.

February 14

I've felt close to Jacqueline Horner ever since my freshman year, when a picture of her reading to me appeared in the Los Angeles *Examiner*. I thought I'd impressed her with my speech on Hinduism at tonight's church supper, and afterward made bold to ask her for dessert and coffee at the Sugar Bowl. She said her father had warned her against dating men who didn't have trust funds. She said that she wasn't saying I had designs on her assets, but that she'd feel happier keeping things platonic. This is a new twist in my career of collecting rejections.

February 16

Sister Nimi writes that she has decided to perpetuate her friendship with Mahesh and get married to him. Mahesh is assistant director of Audit. But Sister Nimi says he's interested in many other things besides accounting—gardening, carpentry, bird-watching. From her description, he seems to be the type of person that I would be charmed by. How I wish I could attend her wedding.

February 18

Daddyji writes from Europe that although he has only met Mahesh once, he has known Mahesh's family for many years and is thrilled. He says that, after all, Nimi is twenty-seven, which is very old for an unmarried Indian woman.

February 19

I wish to be envied for having not just any girl on campus, which I might be able to pull off, but the belle of the campus. I feel that Johnnie's perfection could compensate for my imperfection.

February 20

To celebrate my being first among the sophomores, K and I drove to Los Angeles and had our first expensive meal.

March 1

I got a letter today from Dean Bender. He says he thinks Harvard can make arrangements to get me a scholarship to pay readers, but I have to decide immediately between Harvard and Yale. In other words, they don't want to put in time on my behalf if in the end I wouldn't be coming there. Mr. Howe is still eager for me to come to Yale, because they have a special fund for political refugees that could be used to assist me. But he wants me to take the college-entrance tests for transfer students. I've explained to him several times that these tests are not appropriate for me—I was not born in this country, and they don't have proper Braille copies for blind people. But he's adamant. He thinks I should do exactly what every other transfer student has to do, and not ask for special allowances if I want to come to Yale. I don't know what to do.

March 7

Each new brother has to present a paddle, to be hung in the frat room for posterity. A paddle must reflect his personality. Many new brothers have been working on their paddles for days. I myself have now spent a good many hours sanding, staining, and shellacking my paddle—giving it a rich gloss. Roland Summit helped me write my signature on it. It's the most revealing thing I could think of to put on my paddle.

March 8

I have withdrawn my application to Yale. After thorough consideration, I decided to stake all my chances on Harvard. It was disheartening to take this action after spending so much time in completing the papers for Yale. Howe seemed genuinely disappointed, but he forced my hand by insisting that I take the college-entrance tests for transfer students. Now I just hope I'll get into Harvard or I'll really be crushed.

March 9

Aside from the Nappies, we Alpha Gamms are the only fraternity with a cabin. It is a great allure, because brothers can drink there with their girls. But what good is a cabin to me? I'm afraid to go up there without a girl and be stranded and have nothing to do.

March 10

On his "See It Now," Edward R. Murrow exposed McCarthy for the horror he is, in his own pictures and words. Herb Garelick, David Shapiro, K, and I sat in front of the television, completely mesmerized. Edward R. Murrow should run for President.

March 12

This year, we are representing Pakistan at the Model U.N. What irony! I prepped the delegation on the splitting of the subcontinent. People didn't even seem to know that Pakistan consisted of two halves, separated by hundreds of miles of Indian territory. I told them that we should do our best to antagonize India, which, as the leader of the Arab-Asian bloc, refuses to play the game of power politics—a game at which Pakistan has proved so adept. We decided that our women delegates would wear saris and the men would wear Western garb, as officials in Pakistan do.

April 19

I've finally heard from Harvard. Dean Bender is prepared to admit me, but he wanted to know if I would still like to come there if Harvard was not able to give me a scholarship to pay for readers. Transferring to Harvard without a scholarship to pay readers would mean that I would be constantly aware that the book I was reading was costing me money that I would need for clothes and food. Without hesitation I wrote to him today that I would not. The Clyde fund and what Daddy could supplement would barely cover the cost of tuition, board, and room. For me, it would be like going to the university without being able to study.

April 20

Today was Sister Nimi's wedding and *doli*—imagine, such a modern girl being carried away in a bridal palanquin.

April 22

Mrs. Watumull writes that she is eager for me to go to Harvard, but, as much as she and Mr. Watumull would like to help me with a grant to pay readers, their foundation is simply not in a position to give me further assistance. She reminded me that she had made this clear to Daddy when she originally gave me the grant enabling me to go to Pomona.

May 3

Usha was a slip of a girl when I left, and now she writes that she's wearing saris.

May 31

Sister Nimi was the only Mehta girl who ever held a job. But now she's married and living with Mahesh and her mother-in-law, far from her family and friends. She was such a fiery girl, but her letters have become so tame. Something seems to happen to Indian girls when they get married.

June 2

I still have not heard from Harvard about a scholarship for readers. It seems that Dean Bender and Mr. Henry go on being worried about my ability to get around Harvard, "adjust to a new environment." I don't know what it'll take to convince them that I want to transfer. I've written them yet again telling them that readjustment and "reorientation" will not present a problem for me.

June 7

I'm off to Seattle to work with enchanting Johnnie on my narrative. I'm full of trepidation. This is a new word I've learned from reading Virginia Woolf, and it expresses what I'm feeling exactly.

JOHNNIE received me at the train station in the rain, and we took a taxi to her house. She showed me to a room in the basement, where I could stay until I found a place of my own. Her father, who worked in the traffic department of the Southern Pacific

Railroad, arrived, and she went upstairs to greet him. Seattle seemed to be a wet place, with a perpetual chill in the air. I couldn't stop trembling. My two years in sunny California have destroyed my tolerance for cold weather, I thought. I'd better get a grip on myself, or I'll look like a Nervous Nelly to Johnnie's parents. I tried to relax my muscles, and breathe slowly.

"Come up and meet Bob and Betty!" Johnnie called down to me.

I had never heard Johnnie refer to her parents as Bob and Betty before, and was surprised. But then I remembered I'd heard her speak about her parents only three or four times in the two years I'd known her—and then mostly about her mother.

I climbed the stairs, trying to master my nervousness. I followed Johnnie to the back yard, and there she introduced me to her parents. We all sat down, and Mr. Johnstone said, "The lights of the town of Kirkland look especially pretty on the lake tonight."

Without meaning to, he's calling Johnnie's attention to my not being able to see, I thought, and I said, "I thought Johnnie told me your house had a view of Mount Rainier."

"Mount Rainier is part of the Cascade Range, but it is to the south and we're facing east," Johnnie said. "Mount Rainer always seems to be surrounded by clouds. We only see it when the sun comes out, which is rarely."

Wanting to get onto a different subject, I remarked that calling parents by their first names was something unheard of in India. "It sounds so progressive."

"I suppose her calling us by our first names is a sign of the times she grew up in," Mrs. Johnstone said. "In those days, we parents wanted to be pals with our children."

"We still do," Mr. Johnstone said.

Johnnie laughed.

"Also, I think Johnnie first started calling my husband Bob because he was not her natural father," Mrs. Johnstone said hesitantly. "Her real father died in a car accident when she was not even two. When Bob and I got married, she was just short of four."

So Johnnie grew up without her own father, I thought. Maybe that's why she sometimes sounds so sad. I wanted to hear more about Johnnie's father, but I didn't know how to ask about him. So I said, rather awkwardly, something about how euphonious the name Johnnie Johnstone sounded.

"I gave Johnnie my name and brought her up like my own child," Mr. Johnstone said.

"Bob adopted her just before she started going to school," Mrs. Johnstone said. "So she's always been a Johnstone to her school friends, not a Turner."

Mrs. Johnstone stood up, and said that some time back she had seen a recipe for lamb curry in the newspaper. It had looked complicated and challenging, but she'd cut the recipe out and tried the curry. She and Mr. Johnstone had liked it so much that she had decided to make it for my first meal in Seattle.

I said I was honored.

She and Johnnie went into the house. Within a few moments, the smell of spices drifted into the back yard. I began to relax and feel more like myself.

※

IN the morning, after breakfast, Johnnie and her mother started pulling weeds in the back yard. I asked them for the number for a taxi, so I could go look for an apartment.

"Do you think you can manage on your own?" Mrs. Johnstone asked.

"He's very independent," Johnnie said. (She remembers that she was so used to my stubbornly doing everything for myself that it never occurred to her to come looking with me.)

I was so hell-bent on getting out of the house without a fuss that it was not until I got into the taxi that I wondered if I should have asked the Johnstones for help. The only lead I had was to try the housing office of the University of Washington. But before the morning ended, with the help of a student escort from the office I had found a place to live. It was cheap, small, and easy to take care of, and it had all the essentials—a bed, a table, two chairs, a stove, and a small refrigerator. Moreover, it was within reach of many student-type restaurants and a laundromat, and was near the university library. (There was a lot of political stuff about the Partition that I needed to check for my narrative.)

I went back to Johnnie's house for lunch, and after that she and I got into a taxi with my suitcase. She was coming along because I wanted her to see her place of work. It was Friday. The arrangement was for her to begin Monday morning at nine and work eight hours a day, six days a week. I proudly gave the driver my address, feeling very much a man of the world, especially since Johnnie was there to hear me.

"The apartment is so dark and damp," Johnnie said as soon as we walked in. "Why did you decide on a basement apartment?"

"It was cheap and efficient and near the university," I said, with a sinking heart. Above all, I had wanted her to like it.

"Good writing has certainly been done in garrets," she said cheerfully. "This isn't a garret, but maybe this is as close as you can get to one in Seattle."

❧

JOHNNIE arrived at nine on Monday, bright and energetic, her hair audibly bouncing on her head—or so I imagined.

"I hope you didn't have too much trouble getting here," I said, not knowing quite what to say.

"Not at all. It's a very easy half-hour bus ride from my house."

She drew a chair up to the table, which I'd put in the middle of the apartment, and started rearranging the sheaf of blank paper and my college dictionary and thesaurus. I sat down across from her. "What are we going to write today?" she said.

I had an almost paralyzing dread of writing and of Johnnie's sitting in judgment on what I wrote. I had an attack of abdominal pain. The pain was so excruciating that I could hardly keep my face from contorting. I had spent all weekend worrying about how to keep the pain secret from Johnnie. I was afraid that if she found out that on top of everything else I was sickly there wouldn't be the least hope of her ever falling in love with me. I'd come to find any physical infirmity embarrassing—not only my own but that of anyone else. It was part of my fantasy that I had no physical imperfection—that, in fact, I could see. Besides, I was afraid that if she came to know about my attacks she would feel responsible for getting me to a doctor. There would be more X-rays and tests, and maybe hospitalization. That would mean the loss of valuable working time, and, for Johnnie, a loss of income she was counting on for college the following year. I was sure she would never accept money from me unless she had done a good day's work for it, and if she didn't make enough money she might have to leave me for another job. I couldn't allow my personal problem to compromise the professional nature of our relationship, which I felt had to be pure—especially so since I felt guilty about my secret reason for hiring her in the first place. But how was I to go about hiding the pain from someone who was as sensitive as she was and who would be closeted with me in one room, day in and day out, from nine to five?

"Do you have any letters or papers?" she asked helpfully. "We could go through them, and maybe that would get you started."

I told her that in the spring I had written to various English and American schools, such as the Perkins Institution for the Blind, with which I had carried on voluminous correspondence from India about the possibility of admission. I had asked them if they had our correspondence on file, I told her, and had requested permission to see it. But I had mostly got perfunctory replies, saying they had very little or nothing.

"Didn't you save any of their letters to you?"

"I had them all on file, but when I finally got to America I burned them. I didn't want to carry around the miserable record of my rejections."

"What did the letters say?"

They had been afraid that by admitting me they would be contributing to my "cultural maladjustment," but I couldn't tell her that—couldn't bring myself to utter the dreaded phrase. It had continued to determine my fate. Against the advice of the authorities, I had come out of my country in what they called my most impressionable formative years—and now, as they had predicted, just five years later, at the age of twenty, I felt that I belonged to neither East nor West, to neither India nor America. Often, when I got depressed, I would think back to the letters and wonder if the authorities hadn't been right after all. Yet how could I tell her any of that? I wanted her to think of me as strong and manly, well adjusted and in command. I couldn't even bring myself to tell her about my journal, which I had typed myself on and off since I had come to this country, and which I had with me; the mere thought of exposing to her scrutiny my private maunderings in mangled English was mortifying.

"Those letters said a lot of different things," I told her.

"Maybe it's just as well that you don't have documents. You might end up writing an essay, and what you really want to do is write a story. I suppose you'll have to rely on the inside of your head, like other writers," Johnny was saying.

The inside of my head. *It's an autobiography. Begin with birth.* I can't think of more than a sentence about that. Who can? *Begin with going blind. That's an important theme.* I don't know much more than that I had meningitis and lost my sight. What else is there to say about it? *Begin with your father.* I wish he were here to give me the background. I don't know any of the facts. *Just write your memories of him, memories of your mother.* I need more information, more guidance. *Just begin, begin anywhere.* Johnnie won't like it. She'll laugh at me. *You have no choice.* I can't. *Just start writing a scene.*

I looked at my watch. A good hour had gone by, and I didn't have a single sentence on paper. The idea of sitting there, letting her see that I was not in command, not to mention spending Mrs. Clyde's money without having anything to show for it, began to prey upon me.

"My father came home one day and shouted at my mother, 'Your superstitions will be the end of our family!'" I began. Johnnie's pen moved in abrupt motion, as if in syncopation to my words. "He had a fierce temper, and she had long since learned to bear it silently. She now said nothing. 'Don't you have a tongue in your head?' She started weeping. 'Whatever you say,' she said, still not knowing whether she was doing the right thing in opening her mouth."

I wrote on, mesmerized by the sound of my voice, with the illusion that I was alone in a padded room, and there was near-silence to encourage my thoughts. Johnnie wrote so quickly that now and then the pen seemed to fly off the page and then return to it with a little tap, as if she were trying to discipline it. In college, when Miss Rietveld was not available I often had to dictate to people who interrupted, shifted in their chairs, shuffled papers, tapped their feet, chewed gum, smoked cigarettes, played with their hair, coughed, chattered on—assaulted my ears in a hundred ways. I would tell them that such sounds were as jarring to me as having someone constantly flash light in their eyes would be to them, but saying that would only start an argument. They would want to know what I was trying to do—stop them from breathing and living so I could get my work done? I should learn to adjust. In contrast, Johnnie was so quiet and attentive that I was aware of her presence only from the reassuring sound of her pen forming words on the page. Even if I hadn't been in love with her, I could have embraced her for her instinctive understanding of my needs.

"He finally sat down and started unlacing his shoes," I wrote on. "She heaved a sigh of relief. Another storm had passed." As I continued with the scene, which my mother had often enacted for us to tell us what a fierce temper my father had in the early years of their marriage, things came rushing to mind which I hadn't even known I had inside my head. The pain of dictating abated, my face relaxed; I forgot the sound of my voice and entered a trancelike state, as Johnnie's hand and pen, somehow magically moving to my words, thrilled me, making me feel I'd taken command of the narrative and, by extension, of her sympathies.

By the end of the week, I was freely uttering the phrase "cultural maladjustment" and writing anecdotes irrespective of how they made me look in Johnnie's eyes. My reticence about the work yielded to the necessity of working.

❧

I OFTEN used to imagine what I would be doing if I didn't have the pressure of Johnnie's constant presence, if I could write by myself. I imagined that I would spend much of the day in bed, daydreaming, reading, sleeping, fretting about not writing, waiting for inspiration, making frequent trips to the refrigerator, inventing errands—generally avoiding sitting down to write. But with Johnnie there, her pen poised, waiting for my words to write down, I had to supply the words: my pride was engaged. If for five minutes I couldn't think of something to write, I would think: I'm stupid; she'll think I'm stupid. I would almost feel the tightening of the screw—one more turn, I thought, and I will die for the lack of anything to write. Then, suddenly, the words would come tripping out of my mouth, and soon I would have a sentence, a paragraph, sometimes a whole scene. Yet my having managed to get through an hour offered no assurance that I would be able to get through the next. The whole process was mysterious. The psychological insecurity actually seemed central to the process—it drove me on. I came to think that my only hope of conquering Johnnie's heart lay in sheer exertion and total discipline. Sometimes, in the middle of a sentence I would get an attack. I would cover my face with a handkerchief, as if I sensed a sneeze coming or needed to blow my nose. The attack would pass, and I would doggedly go on dictating.

During the two and a half months Johnnie worked for me, I tried to keep to the invisible professional line that had been put in place the first day. Although she cooked dozens of lunches for me—mostly hamburgers—and I dictated hundreds of pages to her, our relationship remained essentially formal, confined to the work at hand. I felt honor-bound not to compromise my work and her good opinion of me. I kept my fantasies about her to myself.

The hardest part of the day began at five, when Johnnie left. The evening stretched ahead of me, empty. So did Sunday. I would long for the company of my college friends. I wished I were in Claremont, in Berkeley, in India—anywhere but in godforsaken Seattle, where, aside from the Johnstones, I knew nobody. Johnnie herself was new to Seattle and didn't seem to have any close friends—at least, she never mentioned them. In any event, I wanted her to have a complete break from me: spending eight hours a day six days a week immersed in the details of my life was enough.

As soon as she had closed the door behind her, I would slump on the bed, my arms under my head, exhausted by the effort of trying to impress Johnnie. I would mentally clock her bus ride home, imagine her in her hillside house, puttering about in the kitchen, or tending to flowers and weeds in the back yard, or looking at the lights on the lake, and I would get depressed about lying in my one-room utility apartment, as inert as a vegetable. I would, however, stay awake by force of will, because I had a rock-firm conviction that if I didn't have a good dinner and an uninterrupted night's sleep I would not be able to write the next day. So, no matter how tired I felt after two or three hours of lying about, I would comb my hair, put on a tie and jacket, and go out to one of the two or three restaurants nearby, where the waiters had come to know my independent ways. I would usually be given the same table and have more or less the same dish of fish or steak, finish off with fruit salad, and return to my apartment. Now and then, I would come upon some festivities in the streets—there was an annual Sailors' Snake Dance, for instance—and would join in. But sooner or later I would be shouldered aside, as if I were only in the way of people's revelry. And usually I just went back to my apartment, read, and fell asleep. In the morning, I would shave and dress, have a glass of milk and a plain doughnut, and wait for Johnnie.

THE abdominal attacks became more severe, and I was sure that their severity was connected with the pressure of writing. When I embarked on the project, I hadn't realized how difficult it would be to wake up every morning to a blank page and a blank day, with Johnnie there as a witness. Once I found out, it never occurred to me that I could drop the writing or take a holiday from it. Anyway, holiday to do what? "In life, there is only flight or fight," my father used to say. "And Mehtas are not quitters." During the first few weeks in Seattle, I ignored the attacks. Then, by making discreet inquiries at the university, I learned of a well-known specialist in gastrointestinal disorders, a Dr. Mills, and went to see him after work. There were more tests, and his diagnosis was that I still had several kinds of intestinal parasites. He gave me strong medicines, and they did succeed in controlling the severity of the attacks, but they also made me drowsy for a good part of the day. I kept on hoping the attacks would go away, but they didn't, so I went back to Dr. Mills. "Tell me the very worst, Dr. Mills," I demanded. "I've seen many doctors and had all kinds of tests and X-rays, and they've done me no good. I want to know if I'm going to have these pains for the rest of my life."

He laughed. He had a friendly office, and he radiated competence and efficiency. He was also very kindly; he refused to accept payment from me. "Of course you'll be rid of the attacks," he said. "You have no parasites now. But I think the trouble is that all of us have been going at this piecemeal. What we need to have done is a full-scale barium-enema study. If that doesn't turn up anything, you'll have to enter a hospital for a few days of observation."

But my remaining time in Seattle was short, and I asked him if the study he recommended could wait until the autumn, when I would be back in college.

"It's a standard study; it can be done anywhere," he said.

"THIS is a letter from Dean Bender, at Harvard," Johnnie said. "I hate to read it to you."

"Oh, no."

She read the letter. It was pleasant and polite. They wished they could agree with me that I should come to Harvard, but I had to remember that I was blind, and it would be difficult for me to adjust to a new environment. They realized they had admitted me in April, but their admission had been contingent on giving me financial aid for my readers. That was simply not possible. The committee on admissions had my best interests at heart. He and Mr. Henry had enjoyed meeting me very much. They wished me well.

I sat there, numb. Just the night before, I had written to my father that I was sure to go to Harvard—that the committee on admissions couldn't keep me dangling on a string until August and then reject me.

"What are you thinking?" she asked.

"Oh, nothing," I said, trying to sound normal. So I'll have to go back to Pomona, I thought. I have to put the best face on it, and tell her it's all for the best. She knows that I like the

California sun, that it's an advantage to stay in a place where one has friends and knows professors.

"Isn't it too bad?"

"Not really. It may be a blessing in disguise." That was a cliché my father often used.

❦

As I was dictating to Johnnie about my bicycling in Rawalpindi, she asked, "You really can ride a bicycle?"

"Of course I can. I have sometimes ridden around Claremont on a bicycle late at night."

"But how?"

"Maybe you and I can go for a ride together, and I'll show you," I said, but then I thought that by making such a suggestion I might have overstepped the bounds of our relationship, and I added, "I mean, if I'm riding on streets where there's a lot of traffic, I like someone to go ahead of me. It's easier that way." And then, as I started imagining going bicycling with her like any ordinary person, I began to fret that if she came up with a couple of bicycles and expected me to ride one in town I might take a spill and disgrace myself, so I said, "Of course, I prefer to ride where there's not much traffic."

So far, she has known me only in the context of reading or writing, I thought. If she does come bicycling with me, she may see me in a different light. An outdoor girl like her needs a demonstration of physical prowess. After all, she goes hiking in the mountains practically every Sunday. I found myself boasting, "You know, I used to ride without hands, sometimes with my little brother Ashok on the handlebars."

It was clear that she was impressed. But she said, "I don't know anybody here who has a bicycle."

"Maybe we could rent a couple," I said.

"I don't even know where we could rent bicycles."

"Maybe you could ask your parents."

She said she would, and I continued dictating the bicycle section.

🌣

My opportunity to show off came a couple of days later, almost at the end of my stay in Seattle, when we found out about a place near Green Lake where one could rent bicycles, and about a bicycle path around the lake. We decided to knock off on a Friday afternoon and go bicycling.

The bicycle path proved to be very narrow, but I had no difficulty riding on it. I sat straight in my seat, my hands resting lightly on the handlebars. Johnnie rode just a few feet ahead of me, talking to me as naturally as if we were in my apartment. I raised myself on the bicycle and put on some speed. I wanted to pass her and give her a demonstration of how well I could handle a bicycle.

"Hey, are you trying to race me, or something?" she said, putting on speed herself.

Perhaps because it was a weekday, the path seemed fairly free of bicycles, and I shot past her, saying, "Why not?"

She laughed and raced after me, but I pedalled hard and managed to keep ahead of her. I felt rejuvenated. For once, I was not cooped up with her in a confined space, with a strict regimen. I was out in the open; the air was misty and fresh.

Johnnie passed me. "How do you feel?" she asked.

"I feel there's nothing between the lake and Puget Sound except the two of us."

She dropped back, as if she were embarrassed by what I had said. I slowed down, and soon we were riding side by side.

"You know, Green Lake"—she was out of breath, almost panting—"is a great place for water recreation. People over there are riding on a water cycle."

Oh, God—no matter how well you learn something, there's

always something better to learn, I thought. "I want to try one."

She wasn't sure it was such a good idea, but I cajoled her, and soon we were both on the water, riding in tandem on a water cycle.

I couldn't get over the ingenious contraption under us—pontoons on either side, a handle and a rudder for steering, and paddles that somehow turned and propelled it forward. I found it much harder to bicycle in the water than on the road, and after a few minutes I felt exhausted. I give up, I thought. I'll never be a match for the likes of Richard Hungate. What's bicycling compared with playing baseball or football or tennis or cricket, or even water-cycling?

It was getting near five anyway. We paid for the water cycle. She walked with me to the door of my apartment, then hurried away to catch her bus.

❧

A COUPLE of days after the Green Lake outing, we went to "Uncle Vanya," which was being performed at the Showboat, a paddle-wheel steamer that sat on concrete blocks in Portage Bay and was used as a theatre.

On the way, I held her hand. It was her right hand, the hand that had taken down my words the whole summer long—the words really addressed to her heart.

We were on the bridge leading to the boat. We were early, and the bridge was empty. I walked with a jaunty step. The bridge had a little give to it, which made me feel lightheaded, as if I'd left Seattle and its concerns behind. I felt reckless and happy, and I decided to tell her what had been in my heart for nearly two years. I felt I owed it to my love for her to take the gamble, seize the moment; God knew when I would get another chance, when I would be alone with her again without a desk between us. In any case, her job with me was nearly over. She had made the money she needed for her college year. If my telling her made it impossible for us to work together—well, that would not be the end of the world for her.

"Johnnie—" I began. Her hand stiffened. I broke off. I swallowed hard, and said quickly, "Isn't it interesting that Chekhov should have been trained as a doctor?"

The summer—the summer with Johnnie, the summer of writing, the summer of being marooned in a city of lonely sailors, as I thought of it—came to an end at that moment on the bridge, with the stiffening of her hand. Somehow, at that moment I sensed that my dream that one day I might be able to make her love me would always remain a dream. I felt sure that when we got back to college she would not read to me and would generally avoid me—and, indeed, that was what happened.

Years later, when I quizzed her about why she had reacted so strongly to the mere utterance of her name, which I must have spoken a hundred times a day, she told me that on this occasion she had detected a difference in my tone. "I knew your voice to be friendly, and, when I was working with you, to be irritated and scolding at times. But the voice I heard on that occasion seemed to be colored by an emotion for me that I didn't even realize you had in you. Your tone was suddenly tender, dreamy, rash, almost delirious. You seemed to be on the point of making a declaration. Until that second, I hadn't so much as suspected that you had any special feelings for me. I had taken it for granted that our friendship was based on a common interest in writing, in literature, in intellectual things, and sensed that you were about to introduce something extraneous to that. 'I won't have this,' I said to myself. 'Helping him with a literary enterprise is all that I ever agreed to. Now he seems to be wanting to change the rules of our relationship.' I felt terribly disappointed in you. I wondered if it was always going to be impossible to be simply good friends with a man. The moment was so overwhelming that afterward I could never be the same with you. I felt I had sort of lost my innocence. For months thereafter, I would think about that moment and wonder what I could have done differently, so that you would never have had those feelings for me."

Now that I was quizzing her, I wanted to know, as the final clearing up, one more detail. I had long since come to terms with the reality that telling her my story had made no impression on her heart, that the exertion to keep her pen moving, to dazzle her with bicycling and water-cycling, had left her cold. But I had gone on wondering if there was something I could have done and had left undone that might have made her fall in love with me, and I put that question to her now.

"No, there was nothing you could have done." She was firm on that point. And then she said something that gave the whole summer with her a strange twist. "Taking down your story, far from making me fall in love with you, made me turn away from you as someone who might have been a close friend. The moment on the bridge was just the coup de grâce. You see, working for you was a disturbing experience in a way. You had set out to write this book and, over the summer, had achieved so much— completed almost half of it in the space of a couple of months. I felt I could never have achieved what you had, and that made me feel bad about myself, and put a distance between us."

Now that we were talking, she asked me, in turn, what I had had in mind, and how I had felt after she all but checked my declaration.

"I had no particular speech in mind. I had counted on the spirit of the moment to pull me through—to help me to declare my feelings for you. When I sensed that you didn't want me to go on, I fell apart, like a kite that breaks up before it has even caught the wind."

"And then what happened?" she asked. "Do you remember what you said?"

"You mean on the bridge? I said, 'Isn't it interesting that Chekhov should have been trained as a doctor?' That was the first thing that came into my head. You see, doctors were very much on my mind that summer." The tightly guarded secret of that

summer was, of course, pointless now, and I told her about the
terrible stomach pains I had had in Seattle.

"What a good actor you were," she said.

🌸

AFTER "Uncle Vanya," after Johnnie left me at the apartment
to take the bus home, I went out into the city and wandered in a
daze from bar to bar, ordering Cokes and leaving them mostly
undrunk. Some lines of an anonymous Urdu poet kept repeating
themselves in my head:

> Sigh I did not, nor did I reproach.
> Neither did I use my tongue.
>
> Even then I could not conceal my love.
> Whenever someone spoke your name
>
> I held my heart
> And controlled myself

At one point, I followed some sailors to a cavernous dance
hall, where sappy music was dripping out of the loudspeakers.
The sailors "rented" women clustered around the door, who were
strangely called "taxi dancers."

Mindlessly, I followed their example, and, for two dollars,
rented my own taxi dancer. She stood there, passive, perhaps
wondering how I was going to manage on the dance floor. I firmly
put my hand on her back; I took her other hand and raised it,
and turned her around to face me. She was very round at top and
bottom, like a barbell—the shape of the city itself—and was the
biggest woman I had ever put my arm around. The melody echoing in the dance hall was in four-four time, and I started doing
the foxtrot. She danced close to me, as if she thought I had rented
her only to feel the press of her heavy, large body. I pushed her—

almost like a stalled car—around the dance floor for a couple of records, then paid her the two dollars and went home.

❧

I REGULARLY wrote to my father about the progress of the narrative. He was travelling in Europe that summer with Mrs. Clyde as her "companion physician." On July 12th, I wrote:

Half the time I've been in Seattle it's been raining. Instead of depressing me, it cheers me up—it seems like a perfect inducement to stay inside my apartment and work. So far, I've finished ten chapters of the narrative. At this speed, Heaven knows when I will ever see the end of the first draft. Sometimes I feel exultant and may overvalue what I have done; at other times I feel humble and may undervalue what I have done. I can hardly wait for you to read them and tell me what you think.

I had got the ten chapters typed, and I sent them to him with the letter, thinking that he was my best reader and critic, not only because he appeared in every chapter but also because he was the head of the Mehta clan, whose members were an integral part of my story. Anyway, he himself was a natural storyteller, and was an adult witness to events I was writing about from a child's perspective.

A month went by, and I heard nothing from my father. Then, on August 25th, a day after "Uncle Vanya" and a few days after the Harvard rejection, which I still hadn't been able to tell him about, I received a thick envelope from him in the morning mail. In it were the manuscript, with all kinds of marginalia, pointing out certain inaccuracies and errors in emphasis, and a twelve-page critique. After Johnnie finished reading it, we sat in stunned silence. One long section of the critique had to do with the portrayal of him in the early years of his marriage to my mother, in the first two chapters. His comments on the two chapters were so devastating that I decided that the whole enterprise was a mistake. If I couldn't even get his character right—the character of the man I loved most in the world—what chance had I of getting anything else right? I thought that I simply didn't have enough factual information, literary background, writing skills, or emotional maturity to write a book. In undertaking the project at all, I had just been carried away by Mr. Cousins' enthusiasm and by the lure of Mrs. Clyde's benefaction and Johnnie's companionship.

It would be bad enough to read it myself, I thought, but having to have her read it is unbearable. I wanted to die.

"Oh dear," Johnnie said, finally. "It looks as if you'd have to do a lot of work."

"It's all worthless," I said.

"Maybe you shouldn't look back. Maybe you should finish the book first."

"I don't see how I can. If I'm on the wrong road, there's no sense in going on."

I wanted to make it up to my father, and I spent the rest of the day trying to write a letter of apology to him. But everything I wrote sounded like gibberish. Finally, I sent him this confused, contradictory letter, with the manuscript of twenty-four additional chapters I had written, which I felt he should read, if only as an indication of the hard work I had been doing over the summer:

DEAREST DADDYJI,

I read today your letter with your twelve-page comment on my manuscript. I feel very remorseful about the shallowness of my understanding of various matters. Much of my misunderstanding can be attributed to the young age at which I left India and my lack of education in that country.

But no such excuses seem to lessen the grief I feel for grossly misrepresenting certain important phases of our Indian life, which, in spite of my meagre knowledge, I've tried to present to the reader in order to give him a background not only of the family, which in itself would be interesting, but also of our country. In endeavoring to tell a good story, in a style to enlist the sympathies of the reader, certain very important facts seem to have been perverted. If I had been an experienced writer I perhaps would have handled the material much better. I mean, I would have tried to preserve the facts as they really were instead of twisting and manipulating them to suit a form—to present contrasts, to invoke readers' sympathies, and to use all the other techniques that writers indulge in who are more concerned with exercising their imagination to the utmost than with presenting factual material.

The worst thing I seem to have done is misrepresent your character—and there is perhaps no father who has done more for his children than you. You have the most understanding nature. You have always been an example to us children. No amount of dogged perseverance and determination would have got me anywhere without your example.

Now that I look back on the first page of my first chapter, in which I have given you such unjust treatment, I feel very much grieved. I knew when I wrote it, it was absolutely antithetical to your character, yet, intoxicated by the pen, I let the pen have its way. My intention was to begin in that dramatic way and then disclose your character gradually, to present to the reader the full impact of your magnanimous character by contrasting it to what Mamaji says you were when she first married you. I started out that way because I feared conveying too soon the great affection I feel for you. In my immature and inexperienced way, I hoped that the reader, through the course of my narrative, would feel toward you the same affection that I did, not by the picture I painted of you on the first page but by each action, each incident that bears the imprint of greatness, magnanimity of understanding, and love. Those were my aims, but they had terrible results. Read the enclosed material more as a fictional account—for that's what it sometimes turns out to be—than one which contains nothing but unvarnished truth.

This summer has taught me one thing: I do not have enough factual material to write a book. Perhaps ten years from now, I might have. Even if I did have it now, I wouldn't know what to do with it. I am reminded, however, of a saying by Strachey, who has written a beautiful essay on autobiography. He contends that no autobiography is true, it is only what the writer chooses to think of his past at the time he is writing. This is about the only comfort I can derive at present about the state of my work.

Just read the enclosed chapters through and do not try to criticize or edit them, for I will have no time to think of all this for quite a while as soon I will be engrossed in my studies. Whenever God wills and we meet, we can discuss at length all the manifold problems which have resulted from such an endeavor.

With love to you and Mrs. Clyde,
Affectionately yours,

Ved

It was the fifth of September. In the ten days or so since I posted my remorseful letter to my father, I had received two hastily written letters from him in response, along with the manuscript of the twenty-four chapters, which had very few markings on it. In his letters he said that the twenty-four chapters as a whole seemed altogether more successful than the first ten, and that perhaps his reaction to the first ten chapters had been so negative because he had received such a shock, reading about people and events he knew so intimately. He said the shock had worn off and I shouldn't think of abandoning the narrative under any circumstances. He did, however, continue to worry about how various family members would react to their portraits in it, and therefore did not want anyone else in the family to read it until he and I had a chance to meet and go over the manuscript sentence by sentence. He also felt that the portraits of my mother and of him in the first two chapters were so far off the mark that he didn't see how those particular chapters could be salvaged. The tenor of the letters was optimistic, and he seemed to be saying that we had both overreacted in the first instance. But I was not reassured. He's just being fatherly, I thought.

I had managed to bring the story up only to 1949, when, at the age of fifteen, I left India to study in the United States; perhaps as much as half the narrative still had to be written. I was so battle-weary that I couldn't imagine ever picking it up again. But I wanted a record of what I had done that summer, and wanted to have something to show to Mrs. Clyde. I therefore quickly revised the whole manuscript, in line with my father's comments, and got it retyped—it amounted to two hundred and sixty double-spaced pages. I airmailed the typescript to my father, with a list of a hundred questions of my own concerning various people and events. At the same time, I sent carbon copies of the typescript to Mrs. Clyde and to my freshman-English teacher, Mr. Mulhauser, who used to say that writing was harder than digging ditches.

❦

MORE selections from my journal:

September 6

I am on my way back to California from Seattle and am staying with my cousin Surinder and Jackie in Eugene, Oregon, for a couple of days. It's odd to see Surinder with an American wife and fussing so much over a cat, like an American. The cat smells something awful, and the smell pervades the whole house. But Jackie says he smells of sunshine and Ivory soap.

September 7

I've done nothing but eat and sleep. There seems to be nothing else to do at Surinder and Jackie's. I'll be taking a train today to Los Angeles. I have to start getting ready for college. Luckily, the college has made me a Pomona scholar and granted me an additional few hundred dollars, which, combined with the money from the Clyde Educational Fund, will mean that my junior year should be free of financial pressure.

September 10

I'm spending a few days in Long Beach with Herb Garelick. Most of our time is spent sitting on the beach and listening to the waves and to old people getting together and gabbing in what they call a "spit and argue club."

September 12

My spirits degenerate when I'm not working. I just have to read a letter from home and I start to cry. I remain a very sentimental person—all the education in the world cannot change that.

September 21

Usha writes to say that she and her college friends have been at National Cadet Corps Camp and are leading a very military life. She wears bush shirts and khakis and heavy boots, and is busy from reveille until prayers in the evening. She is learning how to shoot. The country must really be going crazy when they teach people like my little sister to shoot.

September 23

I'm back at college. Somehow, writing this summer made me feel very close to everyone at home, and now I feel cut off again. Here I can't speak to anyone about my home or my country. It seems people have no point of reference, and even if you can get them interested, there's so much to explain.

September 24

Daddy writes, in his usual fashion, to say that my not getting into Harvard may be a blessing in disguise. It enables me to stay in a place that I know and where I'm known. But I wonder if he's saying all that he feels. Certainly I didn't tell him all that I felt.

September 25

I'm thinking of buying myself a car. Except for a few Hollywood brats who have flashy cars, most people here seem to have very standard, straightforward four-door or two-door Fords or Chevrolets, just the most basic cars. Many of them have old, beat-up cars with some character. Indeed, most cars have fins—finny ends.

October 2

If now I often fail to write to the family, it's because of the gulf that time is creating between them and me. The images that I had from their voices have grown dim, yet the feelings and thoughts I have for each member of the family have not suffered. They retain their freshness still. Writing this summer has given me not only the keen satisfaction of reconstructing half-forgotten events and personalities dear to me but also new confidence in my ability to revitalize those precious memories. The happy days, with the sprinkling of a few sorrows, buttressed by my family's love and affection, will always remain dear to my memory.

October 3

This year looks as if it would be harder than the previous two years of college in terms of the volume of reading and the student competition. I'm taking courses in Roman history and the philosophy of history. Both have extensive reading. In my contemporary-literature course I will be reading such great authors as Molière, Goethe, Dostoievski, Tolstoy; in my philosophy course, such great philosophers as Descartes, Hume, Kant, Hegel, Schopenhauer, Marx, Engels; in my intellectual-history course, Voltaire, Adam Smith, Shelley, Wordsworth, Henry Adams, Spengler, and Toynbee. In my intellectual-history course I will also be studying the impact of great political figures in Europe and America since 1750, and taking cognizance of ideas of nature, reason, romanticism, classical liberalism, evolution, progress, and, finally, anti-intellectualism, as an ironic end to the course.

October 4

On a dare, I borrowed a Model A truck from Hugh Wire's brother and drove by myself from Sixth Street to College Avenue. People were shocked that a blind person should drive a car alone, but there was no traffic on the street, and, with the windows open, it was almost like riding a bicycle. After all, I grew up around my father's car, and used to drive it a bit in our compound. It's really time I bought my own car.

October 5

Many professors here, though good teachers, are not well known. Each of these has one book to his credit—a Ph.D. thesis, revised and expanded. Many of them are preachers who missed their calling. But Mr. Jones is different. He's written a huge textbook on philosophy, which is used widely.

Perhaps because Mr. Jones is a philosophy teacher, he has an open, receptive mind, and I've been talking to him about my wish to become a writer—not an Indian writer, not a blind writer, just a writer. He agrees this means I have to experiment with writing as if I could see. After all, I live in a visual world, assimilating visual impressions through my four senses. Some of the best work of Beethoven was done when he was deaf. Milton, too, did some of his best work after he went blind. I must, however, be careful to use the passive voice, write like a historian, who writes of things he has not witnessed with his own eyes.

Jones agrees my experiment will meet opposition—people are generally made uncomfortable by the unexpected. I had best confine my experiment to this journal for the time being. If my experiment is successful—and it may take years or decades to know that—the people will come around.

October 6

Mr. Jones, who has a courtly manner, is rotund, with a round body and a round face. He's amiable and jolly and laughs a lot. He's very easy to listen to—there's no hemming and hawing in his lectures, and his accent is an engaging mixture of Southern and Oxonian. He comes across as direct, human, perhaps the least posed of all the professors here.

He always addresses us students as "Mr." or "Miss," as if he thought that will help us act older and more mature.

October 7

Mr. Gleason, my history teacher, has huge eyebrows, from under which he looks down at us. He's so shy that if you ask him a question he is apt to lash out at you as if you had invaded his private domain. He often contorts his body when he lectures. In fact, he seems always to be twisting himself around the lectern. Once, when he was walking around the classroom, he twisted himself around the radiator and got his foot stuck in it. He didn't acknowledge it, perhaps didn't know it himself. The pacing of his lectures is slow, as if over the years he'd calculated the time it takes for students to take notes and had made allowances for that. He seems to have read the same lectures, with the same jokes and the same pauses—and perhaps the same contortions— for more than a decade. It sounds as if I didn't like him, but I actually love him.

October 10

Johnnie has grayish-green eyes and pink, round cheeks. She is quick to blush. She has a big but controlled smile, which shows her white teeth. Her hair is dark, with bangs in the front and cut just below the earlobes in the back. She dresses neatly and sensibly, and with an eye for color.

October 11

I've decided to quit Alpha Gamma. It turns out that it's more important to me to be accepted than to belong.

The only sad part is that if I should ever start going steady with a girl I wouldn't be able to pin her and have all my brothers serenade her with a love ballad in front of her dormitory.

October 14

Many bright students at the moment are down on Mr. Jones and are all flocking to Fred Sontag, a new, young instructor in philosophy who's a doctoral candidate at Yale. He seems to be encouraging students to speculate as if they were the equals of the great philosophers they are studying. He seems to teach Plato's dialogues almost as if they were written today, in Californian English. No wonder students find Mr. Jones' historical, almost analytical approach to philosophy cold.

October 23

Chester Horton, the president of the Dads' Club, stopped me to say he was disappointed that he had not received a letter from my father to read at the Dads' Club's annual party for Pomona fathers today. But even if Daddy had got Horton's request, how could he be expected to know how seriously people take the Dads' Club here?

November 1

K was extremely upset that the entire time he was talking to Crane Brinton, our visiting professor from Harvard, the professor seemed to be paying little attention to him.

November 9

Edward Weismiller has a sweet, young, long-suffering voice and is very much the tortured poet. He sighs heavily and always manages to convey that he himself is a poet—almost in competition with the poets he's teaching—which gives a nice edge to his poetry-reading in class.

He is smooth, energetic, and sort of polished-looking. His skin is of a slightly darker tone—maybe he maintains a good suntan. He dresses less formally than the other professors—sometimes he even wears open shirts.

November 14

My two vices are buying books and classical records. If I could see, perhaps I'd buy even more books than I do.

November 15

It so happens that lately I have got in the habit of dictating my journal entries, because I can write better if I can read and revise. But I have decided that I will go on typing some of the entries myself, for otherwise I'll never have time enough with the secretary to do anything else.

My experiment is going great guns. I usually rely on casual remarks of friends and strangers to construct my own composite. It is amazing what delicate and discreet use of detail can do for a piece of writing. Images give precision to thought.

November 26

So many bright people in my class under the influence of Sontag seem to be turning religious this year. They all seem to be reading papers at evening meetings—Anne Clark, Ann Moseley, Hugh Wire, Marjorie Baer. The papers seem like a mishmash of religion, philosophy, and existentialism.

November 27

I've acquired a 1948 Chevrolet sedan for four hundred dollars. The circumstances for purchasing this car were so favorable that I could not resist the temptation to buy it. It is in good condition and should not be too great an expense. I have acquainted Dean Beatty with the situation, so it won't affect my financial aid adversely. I chalk up my owning of the car to another insatiable thirst for experience, wise or unwise.

Owning a car will not solve my dating problem, but might alleviate it. I've noticed that even when girls own their own cars, they expect the man to be in the driver's seat. I suppose for my car to be really useful I'll have to find a girl who's prepared to let me sit in the driver's seat but help me drive.

November 29

I just got new tires and seat covers for my car.

December 1

President Lyon has blond hair that curls in a tight, even, wavy pattern and is combed straight back. He's polite, very genteel, so proper. One can imagine him extending the tips of his fingers for a handshake and saying something like "So kind." He seems to regularly give a moral address in the weekly assembly with *x* number of points. Generally the message is "Be good, be better, be even better than that." But he's very lovable.

December 2

Pomona is a very homey place. Because of the climate, the windows of the classrooms are often open, and you can hear the sound of a lawnmower in the distance. And Betty Peterson has taken to knitting in our classes. She's making a dress for herself.

December 3

In our class is a girl named Diane Pardue, who is so, so Southern California. She is very muscular and always has a great tan. She has very blond hair, very short and swept back. She wears a lot of makeup and puts polish on her fingernails and toenails. She wears an ankle bracelet. She's so bright and glamorous and wonderfully glittery. She's out of place because most of Pomona women don't expose their bodies or wear much makeup.

IN September, when I got back to college, Mr. Mulhauser sent word that he would like to talk to me about the narrative. I was both terrified and elated, as when he used to call me into his office to go over papers I had written for him. He would spend half an hour or more going over five or six pages, sentence by sentence, now ridiculing my use of some pretentious word, now laughing in a good-natured way at my sentence structure. He seemed more literary, more interested in the style or meaning of what we wrote, than any other professor I'd had as a freshman or a sophomore. The meetings were gruelling, but I invariably came away edified.

"While there may be sentences here and there that need to be tightened up, certain transitions between chapters that need to be worked on, as a whole the work is impressive," he said after I sat down. He was shuffling the pages of the manuscript. In class, he usually followed up his praise with criticism, and I braced myself for it now. He went on, "Who knows? You may make money hand over fist." He lit a cigarette. "Seriously, what I like most about the work is its tonal organization."

Mr. Mulhauser had always stressed in class that we should try to find out the meaning of unfamiliar words and phrases and then practice using them ourselves. Now I asked him what he meant by "tonal organization."

"By tonal organization I mean that the reader is presented with fluctuations of emotion." He talked and smoked at the same time. "The author structures the material according to, for instance, contrasting tones. Take the manuscript at hand. In one chapter a reader is made to feel sad when he sees this little boy, the protagonist, being sent off to a school for the blind. He may protest in his heart, but he is made to see that it is inevitable. In another chapter, a reader is made to rejoice as he lives through, with the boy, a sister's wedding. A reader may flinch from certain marital customs, but he is fascinated by the exotic goings on."

His use of terms like "work," "reader," "author," and "protagonist" seemed to raise my manuscript to the level of a real book. I had trouble giving any credence to what he was saying, and told him as much. "The only organizing principle I was aware of using was that of chronology," I said. "Anyway, it's all inaccurate and misleading." I told him about an idea I had recently had. "The first two chapters are so bad that I think that my father should write them. If the narrative is ever published, I'll just write an introduction explaining why I felt my father was better suited to doing that."

"What a strange idea." He seemed to be gazing right through me.

"But how can I write about events that happened before my conscious memory?"

Mr. Mulhauser laughed. "But it's your book," he said.

"The reader must have a correct picture of my father and mother. My father knows the family background much better than I do."

"Whose idea was it that he should write the first two chapters?"

"It's my idea."

"You seem afraid to take responsibility for your own writing. I don't think you realize what you've accomplished here. I agree that the first two chapters are weak and will require working over, but they succeed in establishing your parents as symbols of two Indias, one modern, one ancient. That's no small thing."

"But there is a gap between how they really are and the way I've portrayed them."

"But why does it matter? You can tidy up the facts here and there, but the general portrait, I'm sure, is accurate. It rings true to the spirit of their description later in the manuscript, and that description is affectionate and loving and human. Your father probably expects social history, but you're writing autobiography. What matters in your case is not so much facts as memories."

It was my first experience of writing something private and exposing it to what amounted to public scrutiny, even if the scrutiny was that of my beloved teacher. His praise, deserved or not, was making me shy, and I implored him to give me some definite criticism.

"Oh, I could make many criticisms. The narrative veers from indirect speech to direct speech for no reason, and the writing throughout is flat. It's clearly written by somebody whose English has not yet hit its stride. But I think you should be careful about letting anyone tamper with the manuscript, even your father. You should make changes only with the guidance of an expert editor at the publishing house that is interested in publishing the book. I suggest you show your book to Crane Brinton."

"But why Mr. Brinton?"

"I'm surprised that you ask such a question."

I myself was surprised at my question. A few weeks earlier, the arrival of Mr. Brinton as a visiting professor had created a great stir at the college. He had studied at Oxford as a Rhodes scholar and was a long-time professor of history at Harvard. And both Oxford and Harvard had a special magic for us. President Lyon, it seemed, hardly ever spoke at a public meeting without mentioning his days at Oxford as a Rhodes Scholar, or the half-dozen other Rhodes scholars who were on our faculty. Similarly, Pomona professors who had gone to Harvard were loud in praise of their university. We students had flocked to Mr. Brinton's course on the eighteenth- and nineteenth-century intellectual history of Europe with high expectations. But (except for the dramatic opening sentence of his first lecture: "Ladies and gentlemen, the rate of copulation among human beings has been constant throughout history") he had disappointed everyone. Indeed, his lectures were so casual and offhand that it was hard to take them seriously.

"I know that everybody complains about his lectures," Mr. Mulhauser was saying now, as if reading my mind, "but Brinton is famous and has a lot of connections. He might help you find a publisher for the book."

I came away from my meeting with Mr. Mulhauser intoxicated. Something I had created had been worthy of his time and attention. The manuscript may not be a way of winning the love of a girl, but it's a way of winning the respect of a professor, I thought.

As a result of talking to Mr. Mulhauser, I suddenly discovered feelings of possessiveness toward the manuscript, like those of a parent toward a child, and had what I can only call a literary awakening—a surge of confidence in my narrative, and, by extension, in myself. I felt I now had plenty of ammunition to do battle with my father. I wrote to him:

I don't want you to write the first two chapters of the narrative after all. You see, it is too much of a united work to bear any changes in one chapter without endangering the appeal of the rest. Indeed, if you try to make any substantial changes in any of the chapters you might run the risk of disturbing the tonal organization of the narrative. I want you to think of the book as a reader, not as a father. Facts are all well and good, but the book also has to be true to the spirit of my memories, experiences, and impressions—right or wrong. Indeed, I don't think I should be reluctant to publish the narrative because all the facts are not there—because the inclusion of some of the facts has been sacrificed for the sake of a good story.

The reader does not want the social history of India but the impressions of a boy, writing a book at twenty, looking back and reflecting upon his past. A certain amount of reconstruction of facts, therefore, is expected in autobiography—indeed, in any history or social history. Even in history, there is always the problem of exactly what happened and what the interpreter thinks is the significance of those facts. What might make a book good for American and English readers might not make it good for Indian readers—and I'm, of course, writing for the Western reader.

Reading the letter today makes me realize that I had only substituted the views of my new-found literary father for those of my actual father.

I GOT an appointment with Mr. Brinton and went to see him. "Sit down, sit down," he said, in an urbane manner, his voice somewhat metallic, like the sound of his name. He immediately started talking about some motor trips he and Mrs. Brinton were taking in order to study the terrain of the Southwest. I had barely got a word in when he was shaking my hand and ushering me out, probably thinking I had come merely to make his acquaintance.

I quickly told him about the narrative, a copy of which I was clutching in my hand.

"You've written a book, an autobiography, and I was going to talk about Rousseau's 'Confessions' in class today—what a coincidence!" he said. The sentence was disquieting in many ways. A "book" suggested something finished and whole; "autobiography" suggested an assertive, self-aggrandizing act. Nothing could be further from Rousseau's "Confessions" than my narrative, which I imagined was more about India, about politics and social life, about my family, than about me. "I'd be glad to read it."

I handed over the manuscript and left.

A few days later, Mr. Brinton telephoned and asked me to stop by his office. Unlike Mr. Mulhauser, in talking about the book he scarcely mentioned the content but instead dwelt on its commercial prospects, which he thought were considerable. "Who knows? This book could make you a good bit of money. It could launch you on a career in journalism. Edward Weeks, the editor of the *Atlantic Monthly,* is coming to speak at the college assembly in a few days. He's a friend. I'll introduce you to him. Maybe he can help you."

For years, I had toyed alternately with the idea of being a journalist and the idea of being a lawyer, but lately I had decided that I would rather be a college teacher. As a teacher, I could pass my years in the only setting I knew besides that of my home and family. Teaching would be a vocation of lifelong study, and studying was second nature to me. Even as I showed my manuscript to professors, my hope was not so much that they could help me get it published as that they could help me get to Oxford or Harvard after my graduation. I said as much to Mr. Brinton in a fumbling way.

"Harvard's degree is even more exportable than Oxford's is nowadays," he said, "A published book should certainly help you get a Harvard association. Yes, Harvard would be a possibility."

❦

MR. WEEKS spoke at our assembly on the eleventh of November. He talked about the need for a new generation of storytellers, saying that storytellers generally started out writing about their own experiences, in the style of an author they especially revered. He recalled that when he was a high-school senior he wrote a short story for the yearbook about a runt of a boy, who suffered indignities because of his size. "Of course, I didn't invent a thing," he said. "Every word was autobiographical." In style, he went on, the story was a "shameless" imitation of George Ade—his literary hero at the time—whose stories he used to read regularly in *Cosmopolitan*. In writing an autobiographical pastiche he was in good company, he thought; Hemingway had started out by writing about himself in the style of Ring Lardner.

Although it was hard for me to imagine that the charming, urbane, dignified speaker on the stage had known misery in his boyhood, he struck a sympathetic chord in me. It rose in a crescendo when he quoted Hemingway as saying that the best training ground for a writer was an unhappy boyhood, and also when he closed by saying that the new generation of storytellers would enhance a new international humanism, cutting across national boundaries and realizing that "what men have in common is so much more important than that which divides them."

After the assembly, President Lyon gave a special lunch for Mr. Weeks, to which he invited a few distinguished professors and a few students—including Johnnie and me—who were interested in literature and writing. Mr. Weeks's laugh, something between a giggle and a chuckle, and often quite raucous, would erupt in the room as if he found everything amusing. Sometimes a laugh was provoked by a student's comment, like "Pomona is the Oxford of the Orange Grove." At other times, it seemed to rise unbidden, as if he were tickled by some private thought.

During the general conversation, Charlie Stivers, an English major, whom everyone considered the most promising writer in our college, said he was working on a story that he would like to submit to the *Atlantic*.

"We would probably publish your story in a section of the magazine called 'Atlantic Firsts,' where we publish young writers who are making their début in print," Mr. Weeks said. "One of the bonuses of giving lectures around the country is meeting young blood and having a chance to read young people's writings." He had a hoarse, adenoidal voice, and constantly cleared his throat.

There was a silence, as if he were waiting for more students to speak up.

"Ted," Mr. Brinton said, breaking the silence with his slightly metallic voice, "we have here a blind Hindu student who's written some pretty interesting stuff about growing up in India."

I wonder what Johnnie's thinking, I thought. She probably thinks I am good at telling anecdotes but am not a real writer, like Charlie Stivers and Bob Towne and Doug Grayson.

"Ved's a junior, who's been taking my intellectual-history class. One or two other professors who have read the manuscript think, as I do, that if he finishes it he might have a salable autobiography on his hands."

I should have been pleased that Mr. Brinton had brought me to Mr. Weeks's attention, but instead I was upset. My secret love letter to Johnnie was in danger of becoming public property. Moreover, the room was full of the college's would-be writers and poets, who stood out as members of an exclusive literary fraternity. Unlike me, they all took creative-writing courses, and often wrote college shows and acted in them. I wasn't even in the English Department—I was a history major—and I spoke English like a foreigner.

"That sounds very exciting. Would you be able to spare a few minutes after lunch? Perhaps we could go somewhere and talk about your manuscript."

I was so busy thinking about Mr. Weeks's voice—open-hearted, warm, accepting, enthusiastic, cultured (a little like a male version of Johnnie's)—that it was a moment before I realized that he was addressing me, asking me to spare him a few minutes. "Yes, of course," I stammered.

❦

PRESIDENT LYON conducted Mr. Weeks and me to a private reception room after lunch.

"How long is your manuscript?" Mr. Weeks asked when we were left alone.

"Two hundred and sixty typed pages."

"That'll make a good two-hundred-page book. If we rush, perhaps we could get it on our spring list. We might be able to publish parts of the book in the *Atlantic Monthly,* which would give it a good send-off."

I was astonished. He knew scarcely anything about the manuscript, and yet he was so accepting of it. Once again, I wondered how it was that I had got nowhere with Johnnie, to whom I had spoken the whole manuscript aloud. How did men get through to women? Was the language of eyes all that counted? But then I thought that I had always had more success with older people than with my contemporaries—with my father rather than with, say, my sister Umi.

"I'd like to take your manuscript with me," Mr. Weeks was saying. "I could read it over the weekend and get back to you on Monday."

The thought of picking up the threads of the narrative suddenly overwhelmed me. I'm not the writing type. Mr. Weeks is wasting his time with me. He should talk to Charlie Stivers and Bob Towne. "I couldn't possibly give it to you," I said. "It's rough and only half finished."

"That doesn't matter. I'd like to see it anyway."

"My father wants me to rewrite the first two chapters and revise everything else."

"What possible objection could he have? I'm sure you write about people affectionately."

"He doesn't like certain things I've said about him and my mother, and he's also worried about what the different relatives will think when they read what I've said about them." Suddenly feeling that Mr. Weeks might lose interest in the manuscript, I added that I had recently written a letter to my father that might bring him around.

"I'm sure he'll come around. When do you think your father will be able to give you his revisions and you'll be able to revise the manuscript?"

"It's hard for me to do much during the school year."

"How old are you?"

"Twenty."

"There's a great deal to be said for publishing a youthful book when the author is as young as possible. I think the sooner we can get your book into print, the better."

Mr. Weeks was the first professional literary man I had ever met—someone who, I imagined, concerned himself daily with the meaning of life, with the grace and the meaning of words. Somehow, I thought of Mr. Cousins as a journalist, a sort of unofficial statesman, rather than as a literary man. Yet the writers I had read about had all had terrible struggles writing. For them, writing seemed as painful as pulling teeth. In contrast, whenever I read Mr. Weeks's column in the *Atlantic Monthly,* "Peripatetic Reviewer," I got the impression that for him writing was a breeze. He came across as someone writing in a relaxed manner, perhaps in his dressing gown and slippers. In any event, his manner was so direct and friendly that I found myself talking to him as naturally as I might talk to a friend of my father's.

"My narrative is written very simply," I said apologetically. "I wrote it straight out, so it's written the way I talk."

"Hemingway has made simplicity in writing a virtue. And

his style of writing is most prevalent these days and enjoys the greatest merit."

"But Hemingway writes a sort of prose poetry. My writing is very prosaic."

"The simpler the better. Many writers feel that way about their first books. Anyhow, there's much interest in the Orient nowadays, and yet material on it is limited—we recently published articles in the *Atlantic* on conditions in your homeland by Dr. Carl Taylor. We got a very enthusiastic response from our readers. There's a great need for people from the Orient to interpret their cultures for us Westerners. If we got your book out, you'd have a leg up to be an intermediary between the two cultures. With the book as a string to your bow, you'd be in a good position to go into the journalistic field and do very well. In other words, you'd be off to the races."

Mr. Weeks's speech was rich with persuasive images, and everything he said made good sense. The early publication of the book could ease my financial burden, perhaps even pay for my graduate education. Anyway, it could certainly open journalistic doors, as he said. He himself had great connections in that world. Even though I couldn't imagine working on the narrative during the school year, I told him that I would try to get the revised manuscript to him by January 1st.

"I'll set aside the first weekend of the New Year to read it, and send you a critique that Monday," Mr. Weeks said. "If we got the completed manuscript by next September, we could publish it around the time of your graduation, when you'd still be only twenty-two. Boy! Wouldn't that be nice. I think the college would make a fuss over it, and I think it would generally get quite a reception when people stopped to think that you'd published it at such an early age."

I knew that Mr. Weeks was an angler; his "Peripatetic" column often dealt with fishing. I felt like a trout at the end of his line—the more I thrashed about, the more firmly his hook seemed to sink into me. He was slowly pulling me in, his every remark turning the reel and shortening the line. I was in his boat. He had cut the line and dropped me in his bucket. I felt that there was nothing in the world better at that moment than to be his catch.

Someone I had barely met was charting my future, plotting my career. I would never have Johnnie's love, but I would have a consolation prize in the book.

"I'll try to finish the book this summer," I said.

(I should mention that Mr. Weeks published an account of this meeting in his book "In Friendly Candor." He places our meeting in 1953 instead of 1954, and thus has me a sophomore instead of a junior, and has me dictating the book during the summer of my freshman year rather than the summer of my sophomore year. He also says that he took the manuscript with him after our meeting, and there are other factual inaccuracies, but in spirit our accounts agree.)

That night, I typed a letter to my father. After describing my meeting with Mr. Weeks, I wrote:

If you are interested in going ahead with this lead and following it through to its logical end, do let me know immediately, even by cable, for I have to give Mr. Weeks an answer. I would suggest that you write me detailed notes on how I might rewrite Chapters I and II. Perhaps your notes for each chapter could be twelve or so typewritten pages long. I could then use these notes to write up the chapters in my own style, so that they would conform with the rest of the narrative. I hope all this does not put too much of a burden on you. If you find the work I've asked you to do difficult, you can let it all go and I will write the two chapters up the best I can. But I must hear from you immediately, because I must make secretarial arrangements for Christmas vacation so that I can revise the script in light of any corrections and suggestions you might have and get it retyped for Mr. Weeks.

I do not want to do some of this work at the expense of my studies, however. But Mr. Weeks contends that finishing the book should be my priority, since it is more likely to meet with success if it is published at my young age. Would you rather have me ask for an advance from Mr. Weeks to cover secretarial help or would Mrs. Clyde be willing to put up more money? I ask this since accepting money from Mr. Weeks would mean that I would become beholden to him.

In a year and a half, I will be through with college. Then I will have to choose my definite field. If this book is published in some form or other, it will be a good start to a literary career. It will help me to make connections in the literary/journalistic field, in which I am likely to be perhaps the least handicapped and the most independent. But then again maybe I'm better suited for college teaching, which is what I really want to do. For that I would have to go to graduate school, however, and for that I would need a lot of money. Earnings from the book would be most helpful. It just might be all this is a childish intoxication from meeting Mr. Weeks. Of that you are the best judge.

My thoughts were as confused as the letter. I wanted my father to give me material for chapters, but I didn't want to burden him. I was exhilarated by my meeting with Mr. Weeks, but I didn't want to be beholden to him. And so on. The truth was that in my heart of hearts I knew that I needed a block of several—maybe many—years to write the book I wanted. Yet the meeting with Mr. Weeks had started an irresistible momentum.

ONE of the first things I did when I got back from Seattle was to follow up Dr. Mills' suggestion that I get a barium-enema study done. I went to see a Dr. Lewis Vadheim, in the town of Pomona. He examined a thick file of reports of tests, X-rays, and doctors' notes that I had been carrying from doctor to doctor, and arranged for a full-scale study. In late November, he gave me his diagnosis, which was that my appendix was swollen and should be removed.

"Is it an emergency? Does it have to be done right now?" I

asked. When I was small, Sister Umi had had an attack of appendicitis and had been rushed to the hospital for an operation.

"No, but you shouldn't delay it unduly."

I told Dr. Vadheim that I was prepared to get the operation done just after Christmas, but I remained confused by the various diagnoses; for instance, I didn't know whether I had ever had intestinal parasites. I asked him if he would write to my father, as one doctor to another. I could no longer keep the attacks secret from him: since I was a minor, Dr. Vadheim would require my father's permission for the operation.

Dr. Vadheim dictated a long letter to his secretary, which went, in part:

The results of the barium X-ray study were negative, however, except for a rather peculiar-appearing bulbous appendix that was visualized. It is the feeling of our radiologist that this represents a dilated appendix with a constricted neck, which contains either a fairly large, non-opaque calculus or represents a mucocele of the appendix.

Although your son does not always localize his pain and tenderness to the appendicial area, and most of his symptoms seem to be those of an irritable bowel, it may contribute considerably to his distress. In any event, it is our feeling that Ved is going to have acute difficulty with his appendix at some time in the future. We feel, certainly, that there is a 50% chance that he will be relieved of his symptoms by appendectomy. If you are in agreement with our conclusion and will send us a written consent to perform appendectomy, we will be very happy to proceed with the operation. It would work out best for Ved's schedule if such surgery could be performed on or about December 27, 1954.

Partly because of money and insurance problems, the operation was not performed until March. No one knew about it except my chief amanuensis, Miss Rietveld, who dealt with most of my correspondence. After the operation, unbeknownst to me, she wrote the following letter to my father:

March 13, 1955

DEAR SIR:

By this time you have the cable that I sent you yesterday at Ved's request. He called me just before the operation and I went to the hospital as he came out of the anesthetic. Dr. Afflerbaugh performed the operation, and he tells me that it was successful and Ved is doing well.

At the hospital I found Ved listening to a Talking Book of Tolstoy's "War and Peace." He was not very relaxed, and talked about wanting to be in classes again tomorrow, which is, of course, out of the question. I hope we can get him to relax a little. When he was a freshman and sophomore, I urged him to try for good grades, but now his record is so well established that he need not work quite so hard. But he continues at the same pace and will accept nothing but the highest standards for all his work.

But I wish you would advise him to build up his physical strength and enjoy life a little more this spring. He has many friends here and they would enjoy him very much if he had just a little time to give them. The International Relations Club, to which he actually gave life, would be very pleased to see him once in a while, too. I am telling you this in confidence as you will know how to tell him these things much better than I do.

I will write you again tomorrow or the next day about his progress.

Sincerely yours, and Ved's friend and well-wisher,

Harriet Rietveld

I was in the hospital for two days and in the college infirmary for three. The stitches were taken out on the sixth day. The doctors reported that my appendix was unusually long—some eight inches—and that they had found a stone at the base of it. I concluded that the pain had been caused all along by a chronic case of appendicitis. In any case, I was finally free of the pain that I had lived with for over a year.

❧

THE January date for sending my manuscript to Mr. Weeks came and went. I held it back until I could meet with my father and go over it. In February, he wrote, from India, that he was soon coming to Southern California; Mrs. Clyde had invited him to join her in late April in Long Beach, where she would be going, with Dr. Martin, to attend the third annual meeting of the American Academy of Nutrition. It seemed that Dr. Martin wanted her to take an interest in the work of the academy, and she wanted my father to advise her on the worthiness of the cause. He said that she and Dr. Martin had arranged for him to present a couple of papers on nutrition in India at the meeting and to be the main speaker at its closing banquet. "This means we'll be able to spend a good few days together and go over your manuscript," he wrote.

After the meeting, my father and Mrs. Clyde came to Claremont and took up residence at the Claremont Inn for ten days. But when they had been there barely a day the telephone rang in my room and I picked it up to hear a friend say, "Ved—Ved, K is dead. He shot himself five minutes ago."

"Shot himself?" I gasped and sat down. Just a few months earlier, a friend, Don Stackhouse, had killed himself. And now—K.

That night, I went to bed beside my father at the Claremont Inn.

"Ved," he called over to me from his bed, "if you ever feel completely licked"—the slang ill became my father's English—"promise me one thing."

He paused, as if to find out whether I was listening. I was, intently, but I was so overwrought that I couldn't bring out the simple word "What?"

"Promise me that you will write to me first to pour out your heart, and then wait for my reply before you do anything foolish."

In my sorrow, I found it comforting that he thought I was not above doing something "foolish" myself—that he didn't think

K had done something totally inconceivable. Yet he seemed to be asking so much. It wasn't just that he was living in India and I in America but also that I was twenty-one, and the emotional distance between us, which I had first sensed in adolescence, had now widened to a gulf. It was impossible for me even to think of talking to him about K's suicide or much else that was painful in my life now. I especially feared that if he ever found out what K had done for Phyllis and me he would be my severest judge. Still, it was my father asking something from me. I could not withhold the promise, even though I knew I could never honor it. I already feel licked, the way K must have felt, I thought. "I promise," I said.

My father pressed his advantage. "I'd like to understand how you two became such good friends. You tell me he was six years older than you. Didn't you say that his parents were migrant laborers from Japan and that he himself was a houseboy for a time? His background seems to have been very different from ours. I don't mean to sound snobbish, but he must have come from different stock. How interesting that, of all the wonderful people you must have met at Pomona, he became such a good friend of yours. I have to say, at the risk of sounding callous, that people who take their own lives must have a screw loose somewhere. But then Japanese go in for suicide. It's part of their culture. In our culture, a person who commits suicide is thought to be reincarnated as a crow, shunned by birds and people alike, condemned to squawk all day long, knowing neither peace nor rest."

I understood that my father was saying these harsh things not because they represented what he felt or thought but because he hoped that by saying them he would loosen the hold of my friendship with K and thereby diminish the grief I was feeling. There were many points in his speech that I wanted to respond to, but I couldn't bring myself to say anything. In any event, I didn't want to burden my father with my troubles. In a few days, he would be going to Europe and from there back to India. What could he possibly do for me from halfway around the world, when he could do so little for me while he was lying in the same room?

"Maybe you don't want to talk about it now," my father said. "You must have a lot to think about." In a few moments, I heard his heavy breathing—he was fast asleep. I was glad that he was understanding enough to leave me alone with my thoughts.

If I'd been up to confiding in my father, I would have told him that any thoughtful person would have been drawn to K. He had poise and dignity; he was sincere and cheerful, and had a persevering nature. But I was drawn to him for my own reasons. He was more mature than the other students, and in many ways I was, too. Like me, he had a mixed cultural outlook, and, again like me, he had had a sketchy education, which made him determined to get the most from his time at college. There were many other similarities in our circumstances. In fact, even my struggle over my narrative had a counterpart in what K went through just before his death. I couldn't help wondering whether, if he had got even a small portion of the encouragement I had, he would have killed himself. I recalled how deeply he had been affected by the legend of Prometheus. Indeed, the Orozco mural must have had some special meaning for him. The night before his suicide, several students saw him standing in front of it and staring at it, as if he were trying to commune with it, divine its inner meaning.

ALL the time I knew K, he worried about money. He worried that his widowed mother had to go on working to help pay his college expenses. "Fruit packing is seasonal employment, so most of her income comes from working in the onion fields," he said. "I hate to see her pulling onions day after day. She's such a frail old woman." He smoked a great deal, and worried about the expense of his habit. Sometimes, to get cigarette money he would have to make a special trip to Los Angeles to see one of his sisters, who worked there as a secretary. "She has got so used to my turning to her for cigarette money that when I go to see her she just slips it into my pocket, so that I won't feel embarrassed," K said once. "In Japan, a man would never accept money from a sister. You know, I should be helping my mother and sisters, and I'm not giving any of them a cent."

When I returned to Pomona from Berkeley for my sophomore year, K was returning for his senior year. The first time I saw him, he told me, "The whole summer vacation, I pulled onions alongside Mother for eight, ten hours a day. It's terrible work. I told her that I don't want her to work anymore—that the moment I graduate I'm going to get a job and support her." But he was a history major and didn't see how the degree could help him earn a living. "I like history," K told me. "It allows you to jump out of time and place. But how can it enable me to support myself? People say I could work for better Japanese-American relations. But I know nothing about Japanese history, literature, philosophy—I can't even read Japanese. All my courses have always been in Western civilization. There isn't a single course given here in Japanese—and even if there were I don't think I have the intellectual capacity for starting on a whole new culture at my age."

All along, K had thought that he'd like to teach history in a public high school, but when he discussed the idea with Henry Cord Meyer, the professor he admired most in our department, Meyer said, "In the first place, you can't teach in public school here without teaching credentials. To get them, you would have to take a whole year of education courses after graduation. And I don't need to tell you that education courses are a complete waste of time. In the second place, even if you got teaching credentials you would have trouble getting a job. Public schools are looking for all-American teachers, and as soon as they know you're a Japanese-American they'll have no interest in you. Private schools don't require teaching credentials, but they have their own snobberies that will stand in your way. K, you have a good mind—you should go straight for a Ph.D. in history. That way, you'll be able to teach in a college, and you won't encounter prejudice. I'll help you get fellowships to good graduate schools to see you through."

Although most better students at the college went on to graduate school or a professional school, a Ph.D. was about the last thing K had considered going in for. But after his talk with Meyer he said to me, "If he has that much faith in me, I can't disappoint him." He felt that Meyer knew better what he should do with his life than he himself did. K assumed that because Meyer was a student of the struggles of minorities in nineteenth-century Europe he was an expert on the problems of Japanese-Americans.

Almost as long as I had known K, he had been under the spell of Meyer's personality, as I myself was under the spell of Mulhauser's, Jones', and, indeed, Meyer's, at various times. At Pomona, it seemed that almost every student was under the spell of some professor, who encouraged him and became his champion for college grants and prizes and graduate school. K once wrote to Shinn, at Reedley, describing Meyer:

The man's joie de vivre has a tremendous impact on students who have the luck to draw him for Western Civilization or who elect to take Europe Since 1815, despite warnings from veterans that it stands with Jones' History of Philosophy course as about the most formidable in Pomona's curriculum.

It must be plain to you that I number myself among the fortunate to have been associated in my small manner with Dr. Meyer.

K was also enthralled by Meyer as a teacher. His letter to Shinn continues:

Meyer's lectures show concentrated preparation. He spent thirty to forty hours preparing for a forty-minute lecture on Germany as he witnessed the country in 1952–53. He checked his own impressions with statistics and what other people had said about it. He has a beautiful command of the English language and uses sharp, vivid, "catchy" nouns.

He doesn't restrict himself to facts—he describes states of mind. He uses gestures and modulation of voice to overcome his natural hoarseness. He frequently uses pictures, posters, and excerpts from primary sources; he also frequently assigns maps. In this he's very much like you were in History 8AB at Reedley.

He often invites us to his home, where he meets us at the door dressed like an Austrian, in an embroidered jacket and leather pants, his clothes accentuating his tall, gangling figure. An incongruous figure, he bounds around making us comfortable on antique chairs while we listen to Edith Piaf on the record-player and spill coffee on his rug.

I can recall waiting outside his office for forty-five minutes one time while he talked to a freshman who couldn't see that Joe McCarthy was anything more than what he said he was: a super-patriot, a guardian of America and the American way of life, a super-sleuth, pure as the driven snow. Perhaps Meyer was a bit out of line in trying to change the boy's mind, but he told me later that he had encountered similar young men in Germany in the thirties who thought Adolph Hitler was the savior of Germany and the German way of life.

Following the Ph.D. conversation with Meyer, K seemed to forget his urgent need to get a job after graduation. He began applying to several history Ph.D. programs, and Meyer wrote letters for him. In K's year, there were only a couple of other serious students the History Department was sponsoring for fellowships. One of them got a big fellowship to study in the East, the other a big fellowship to go abroad. But K got only one acceptance, and that was from the Claremont Graduate School, next door, and Pomona agreed to pay his tuition of five hundred dollars toward an M.A. degree there.

Meyer and others tried to console him by telling him that doctoral fellowships were a little like a lottery, and he should not pass up the chance to go to graduate school. But K was devastated, and didn't see how he could possibly go there, since he didn't want to keep relying on his family to help pay his room and board. Then he heard that there was an opening for the job of resident assistant at Smiley Hall. He had always lived in Smiley, and the job provided free room and board for a year in return for assisting its majordomo. K applied for the job and was interviewed for it by Dean Beatty. "He talked so fast that I just couldn't communicate with him," K said afterward. "Words came out of my mouth, but feelings and responses didn't. I just didn't seem to belong in his office."

I remember telling K that he shouldn't worry—that all interviews go badly, and that it wasn't as if Dean Beatty were meeting him for the first time. Indeed, K did get the job. He thereupon accepted the offer of admission to the Claremont Graduate School. But soon he was fretting about his mother's reaction to his plans. "If I were going for teaching credentials, I think she would understand and would be prepared to sacrifice for another year to help me get on my feet. But, as it is, she's going to ask me what good is an M.A. degree, and I have no answer."

"Maybe you can teach in a junior college, like Ridgeway Shinn," I said.

"No. People tell me that there is just as much prejudice against Japanese-Americans in junior colleges as there is in public high schools."

I suggested that maybe he should postpone his plans to go to Claremont Graduate School, but he felt that the arrangements were too far along for him to withdraw.

In 1954, K graduated cum laude, and he temporarily forgot his misgivings and apprehensions amid the general jubilation. He told me that his sisters, who came to the ceremony, were proud that they had helped in their small way to put him through college. (He didn't introduce me to them.) His mother, who didn't come, sent a message that she was delighted that her son had won a degree from an American college. Mrs. Lundstrom wrote him a letter, beginning "Dear George," in which she said that all her confidence in him had been justified.

When K returned in the autumn, he told me, "I have done something very wrong. I didn't tell Mother that I'm a graduate student. I've led her to believe I'm getting my teaching credentials. She's very upset I'm still in school, but now she's expecting me to be through in the spring and start teaching in the autumn. I don't know how I'll ever be able to tell her the truth. When I saw Mother pulling onions again over the summer, I knew I should have gone for my teaching credentials after all."

I reminded him that teaching credentials no more guaranteed a job than an M.A. degree did.

"Even if I hadn't got a teaching job, at least Mother would have known I'd tried," he said. "After all, I'm the only man in the family. If I were in Japan, I would be the head of the household, and I would have to support not only Mother but my sisters, too."

He said he had told his sisters about his plans, and they had agreed to keep their mother in the dark. The youngest sister, who was waiting to go to college right after K finished, had told him, "I don't care if I never go to college, if you can get a Ph.D. No one in all our ancestry has ever got a Ph.D. You'll be the first."

"Your family probably loves to sacrifice for you," I said, but he could not see it that way.

"I am caught in the choice between my duty to Mother and further education," he said.

K had imagined that graduate school would be different, but he did not feel different from the way he had as an undergraduate. He was living among undergraduates at Smiley Hall, and the graduate school seemed little more than an outpost of Pomona. Anyway, it was small and devoted most of its resources to education courses for teaching credentials. He also found he was taking courses mostly with professors he had already studied with at Pomona. Indeed, only one of his professors, Henry Cooke, was a member of the graduate-school faculty, and he was the weakest teacher K had. On top of everything else, Meyer was away on a year's leave, at the University of Wisconsin. As time went on, however, K seemed to get interested in the material he was studying. He took heart from the comments of his professors on his work. He started corresponding with Meyer, and Meyer wrote that Wisconsin had an excellent graduate program in history, and that he could help him get a fellowship there for the following year. K began talking as if he were convinced all over again that he would go for a Ph.D. and that he had the intellectual ability to earn it. He applied to Wisconsin, among other places.

At the beginning of the second semester, it was announced at the college convocation that I had led the Pomona College men in grades. K made a big fuss about it, and proposed that we celebrate the event with dinner and champagne in Los Angeles. Since K was poor, I had taken it for granted that the dinner would be my treat. We did have a bottle of champagne opened, but we could get down only a few sips—neither of us had ever taken an alcoholic drink before. Then, when the bill came, he insisted on paying it. I argued and protested, but he took the bill, saying, "I knew you wouldn't feast as well if I told you I would pay."

A day or two after the dinner, he came to my room and announced, "If I get a fellowship for next year, I'll turn it down. I'm never going to go for a Ph.D.—I don't have the intellectual capacity for it. History is too difficult. I should never have gone to graduate school." He continued, rather sheepishly, "This semester I've already substituted some education courses for some history courses. I've applied to Claremont Graduate School for a renewal of my tuition fellowship to get my teaching credentials."

I was taken by surprise, even though he had changed his mind about the Ph.D. and his abilities many times before. "Lately, things have seemed to be going so well for you," I said.

"They weren't. I just didn't want you to know."

I tried to say something optimistic. "You can get teaching credentials first and go on for a Ph.D. sometime later," I said.

"I'm much too old for that," K replied.

Nothing I said seemed to lift his spirits.

In April, K heard that his tuition fellowship from the Claremont Graduate School had been renewed. He was also given assurances that his resident assistantship would be extended for another year. He was now all set to get his teaching credentials. Then he heard from Wisconsin that he had been accepted in its Ph.D. program and awarded a teaching-assistant fellowship of a thousand dollars. He immediately turned down the fellowship, but he couldn't bring himself to write to Meyer. "The terrible thing is, Dr. Meyer has backed me to the hilt," K said. "When he finds out that I'm giving up, he's going to feel badly let down. He's going to say, 'Why didn't you make up your mind before I put myself out for you?' He'll never want to help me again."

"Meyer knows about your financial situation," I said. "When you explain it all to him, he'll understand."

"He'll never understand. He's finished with me," K said. He was resigned to getting his teaching credentials, but he was as unsure as ever what use they would be in landing him a job. He went to see the dean of the Claremont Graduate School to find out if there was any way of getting teaching credentials by going to summer school. "He said no matter what I do there's no way it can be done," K explained. "I'll have many more education courses to take after this semester. I'll need another year here. How am I going to explain that to Mother?"

Back in February, at the beginning of the second semester, K had started thinking about a topic for the thesis he was required to submit in order to receive his M.A. He had considered writing on the problems of minorities in Europe, but he decided against it, because he didn't know any European languages. In any case, with Meyer away, he felt there was no one he could work with on the topic. Then he recalled that a year earlier he had heard a lecture on the idea of progress in the eighteenth and nineteenth centuries in Europe, given by Crane Brinton. Brinton had made the subject sound very simple. K now settled on it as the topic of his thesis. When I came to know about his choice, I tried to warn him off it. "The topic is probably too big for most Ph.D. theses," I told him. "You should choose something very small and manageable. Don't be fooled by Brinton. I took his course in intellectual history, and he has a very conversational way of lecturing. He can make the most complicated ideas sound easy."

"But my thesis might be the last big academic paper I'll ever write," K said. "I want to make it really impressive."

Enthusiasm had a way of running away with K, and he was so fired up by the topic that there was no restraining him. I counted on his adviser to veto the topic, however. Then, as luck would have it, he got Gleason for his adviser. It was common knowledge among students in the History Department that Gleason and Meyer were at war, and had little time for each other's protégés. Gleason, who never let one forget that he had got his degrees from Harvard, was a stiff, shy New Englander. Meyer, who had got his degrees from the Universities of Colorado and Iowa and from Yale, was a folksy Midwesterner. In any event, it seemed that Gleason had given K a green light, perhaps without giving the topic—or K's ability to handle it—much thought. "If you want to get your degree in June, get your thesis in by May 2nd. That's the last possible day," Gleason told him, and sent him on his way.

Once K got down to his research, he discovered that there was perhaps no subject on which there was more material in the library than the French Revolution, and he imagined that every book on the revolution had an important reference to the idea of progress in the eighteenth century. God only knew how many books there might be in the library with discussions of the idea of progress in the nineteenth century. "The library is like a forest," he told me. "I don't know where to begin. I could read for the rest of my life and still not get it all done."

I told him he should go to see Gleason and try to change his thesis topic, but he found the prospect of backtracking humiliating, and also thought it was too late in the day to find a new topic. I told him that he should not lose sight of the fact that he was only doing an M.A. thesis, and should not permit himself to get swamped by the research. He would agree with me when we were together, but then he would go to the library and start looking at the catalogue cards and taking books down from the stacks, and get overwhelmed all over again. Weeks went by, and he still hadn't written a word. He was not one for making outlines or thinking through what he wanted to say. He always had trouble putting his thoughts down on paper; he was a fast typist, and relied on thinking at the typewriter. Whenever I stopped by his room in Smiley Hall, he would be sitting at the typewriter, hammering away furiously. He kept at it, but he never seemed to get beyond the first page of his thesis. He started saying things like "I'm a moron" and "I'm not fit for anything."

"You work too hard," I told him once. "Leave the thesis alone. Go away for a couple of days—to the beach or the mountains. Just go away from this room and from this typewriter."

"When I go home in June, I must have the degree to show Mother," he said. "If I don't have anything, I'll never be able to look her in the eye again."

It was nearing the end of March, and the college was about to close for spring vacation. I told K bluntly what I had so often hinted at: "I would like to meet your mother and your sisters." I thought I might take some soundings and perhaps try to explain K's situation to his family. "Why haven't you introduced me to them?" I all but invited myself to his home.

"Because"—and he stuttered—"I am ashamed of the way we have to live. I couldn't let you see our house. We are so poor. Mother—"

I protested. "Do you think that matters?" I said. I reminded him about my own parents and how the Partition had left us almost penniless, but it seemed there was nothing I could say to make him see that around me he didn't need to be ashamed of his poverty. I got up to leave.

"I want you to know that you are my best friend," he said, in a strangely shy voice. He's lonely in a way that most students here aren't, I thought.

We saw each other so often that as a rule we did not shake

hands, but this time he put out his hand. I took it. Slight of build, he had small, thin hands, but he generally had a strong handshake. This time, his hand was cold and a little limp.

K came back from spring vacation with a draft of his thesis. He showed it to Gleason. Gleason told him that it was labored and confused, and the style needed a lot of work, and he intimated that perhaps K should think about getting teaching credentials after all. Cooke, the other thesis reader, had more or less the same opinion. K was stunned. I read the thesis and tried to help him revise it. But it seemed that short of rewriting it there was no way for him to fix it. Around the middle of April, he came to my room and said he scarcely had the beginnings of a second draft. "There's no way I can get it done by May 2nd."

"Why don't you get an extension until the middle of June?" I said. That was the time when the degrees were to be conferred, and I thought that if he got his thesis in under the wire he could still get his degree.

K lost his temper. "You're just like the rest of them—you don't think much of my intellect."

"That was the last thing I had in mind," I said. "I just wanted you to have a few extra weeks to work on your second draft."

K ran out of my room angrily, even before I had finished my sentence. He telephoned me a few minutes later to apologize, but also to say that he would not ask for an extension.

As it happened, during the fortnight before K's thesis was due I didn't see much of him, because of my father's pending arrival and visit. I hadn't seen my father for almost a year and a half, and so that I could take some time off to be with him I missed breakfasts and lunches and spent every spare moment studying. Somehow, I didn't run into K. I was so preoccupied that I neglected to call him, and it didn't register with me that he hadn't called me. Except for Christmas and summer vacations, this was the longest we had gone without seeing each other.

I met my father in Long Beach and returned to Claremont with him on the evening of May 1st. I remembered that K's thesis was due the next day, and I called him.

K answered the phone. "Hello?" His voice sounded distant and shaky.

"I'm sorry I've been out of touch, but Daddy's been here. How's it going, K?" I said.

"Badly, very badly," he said impatiently.

I waited for him to go on, but he didn't. "You're exaggerating," I finally said.

"I can't have it ready by tomorrow," he said.

"Damn it, it's still not too late to ask Gleason for an extension. I'm sure if you asked him he'd give it to you."

"He's counting on my handing it in tomorrow."

"Gleason will understand." There was a pause. That made me wary. "K, give me your word that you will call Gleason right after you hang up, and try for the extension. Promise me."

"If you say so, I will," he said in an offhand way. "I want to see you very much. May I come over now?"

"I'm not in my room. I'm staying with Daddy at the Claremont Inn. I'd like very much for you to meet him. Let's have dinner together tomorrow." He was silent. "K, are you there?"

"Yes." All of a sudden, I felt guilty for having put him off. "I guess that's all," he said faintly.

"I'll come by tomorrow and then we can make arrangements for our dinner together," I said. I reminded him about his promise to get the extension, and we hung up.

The next day, I stopped by his room twice, but he wasn't there. The second time, I pulled out a piece of paper from an overflowing wastepaper basket, sat down on his bed—which was strewn with papers—and was about to type out a note to him when I noticed that there was a half-typed sheet in the machine. I didn't want to disturb the typing, and decided to call him later.

Afterward, I telephoned him a couple of times, but there was no answer. That evening, I went to the college to pick up a change of clothes and to try to find K and get him to come to the Claremont Inn for dinner. Just as I entered my room, the telephone rang, and I heard the news that K had killed himself.

IT was the day after K's death, and people kept calling me at the Claremont Inn, wanting to talk about the suicide. There was a call from one of K's education professors at the graduate school. "Have you seen the newspaper accounts of Kaizo's death?" he asked.

"No, I haven't," I said, and he told me of reading that around nine in the evening K had put on several layers of clothing and got into bed in his room. He had put two pillows against his chest and stomach, and had fired twice with a semi-automatic pistol in the region of his heart. The sound of the shots, though muffled by the padding of clothes and pillows, had been clearly heard by a student named Bruce Prestwich in the next room. He had run to K's room and found K lying in the doorway, murmuring, "I shot myself. . . . This is the way it should be." Prestwich had telephoned for a doctor and an ambulance, but K died before any help could reach him.

"I know Bruce's mother well," the professor said. "In fact, it was from her that I heard about Kaizo—she called me this morning. She says Bruce is so upset that she hasn't dared talk to him about it. It has been very hard for the boy. He has had to give statements to the police, and fend off newspaper and television reporters. I didn't know Kaizo very well, but he must have been an odd duck. You must have heard that just the night before he shot himself a few students saw him staring at the mural of Prometheus they have there at Pomona."

"I did," I said.

"That's the last thing you'd find me doing if I were contemplating taking my life," the professor said.

No sooner had I hung up the phone than it rang again. It was Dean Beatty. "As you were his closest friend, I wanted you to know that the Japanese Family Association has taken the responsibility for all the funeral arrangements," he said. "Kaizo left a note saying that his sister in Los Angeles should be the member of the family to be informed, and that the conveying of the news to his mother should be left to her. This was done. His mother and sisters came to the college this afternoon. I took them to dinner at Frary Hall. When they left, I felt comforted by the deep resignation of their own spirit. They made me feel, without saying so, that Kaizo was entitled to his life and to his death— that he had returned to his Japanese fathers."

"Did K leave any other notes?" I asked.

"He left a couple of other notes, which he wanted us to mail. One was for Mr. Meyer. It was just a torn piece of paper on which Kaizo had scribbled 'Forgive me.' The other was a postcard to Mr. Shinn. It said, 'Mr. Shinn—I can't explain everything. Lately I've been so depressed—I've made many terrible mistakes. Forgive me. Kaizo.' "

"Was there a note for me?" I asked, my hand trembling.

"No—probably because he had just seen you."

But he hadn't seen me, I thought.

"Did he ever talk to you about killing himself?"

"No."

"Do you know why he might have done it?"

"I can't say that I do. I mean, not really."

"Kaizo must have known we all liked and respected him," Dean Beatty said.

But he was so lonely, I thought.

"From what Gleason and Cooke tell me, he must have felt very deeply his lack of adequate knowledge of philosophy and literature for writing on the topic that he chose for his thesis," he continued. "But he was entirely capable of finishing his thesis well."

However, he himself wasn't sure, I thought.

"He may have been too conscientious, perhaps oversensitive. He sought perfection in the Oriental manner," Dean Beatty said.

Anyone would have been overwhelmed by the subject, I thought.

"But he kept his sorrow to himself and resolved that the only way left open to him with full self-respect, and in full harmony with his Buddhist ideals—and his cultural conception of himself—was to end his life. Cultural maladjustment was at the heart of his problem. But, as I was saying, we can take solace in the fact that Kaizo has returned to his Japanese fathers."

As I hung up, I thought of how K's friendship had been a light to me. The light might at times have been shaded or obscured, but now it had gone out. I was left to find my own way through the darkness of his death. I tried to think of K as I knew him. I thought of his small, thin hands and his small physical stature. But instead of hearing his familiar soft-spoken voice I heard a deeper, judgmental voice, blaming me for not being more supportive—for not making a point of seeing him during his last, desperate days. Dean Beatty seemed to have worked out to his satisfaction why K had killed himself. Tomorrow, there would be other analyses, and I could not help feeling that many of them would arrive at the same conclusion of cultural maladjustment— the very fate that had been predicted for me by Western educational authorities when I was trying to come out of India for an education that was not available in my country.

The authorities had said that after my schooling in England or America I would feel maladjusted whether I lived in India or in the West—would feel that I belonged neither to its culture nor to mine. At the time, in my childish enthusiasm and optimism, I was not able to grasp the importance of what they were saying. Later, I had often had occasion to think about their forebodings. Wherever I was, at the Arkansas school or at Pomona, the more I became adjusted outwardly to Western values, the more Indian I felt inside. Every step I took toward successful adjustment seemed to open up a steeper precipice ahead, making me more fearful of a misstep. When I was leaving high school, Mr. John Ed Chiles, who had played a role in my education akin to that of Mr. Shinn in K's, had said, "You came to us as raw material and we are sending you to seek your destiny as a finished and guaranteed product. Do not fail us." I, however, felt anything but a "finished and guaranteed product." Both K and I, in our different ways, had looked to education as a means of escaping a miserable fate. But I wondered whether, if I should fail Mr. Chiles and all the college teachers who had helped me, I would have the inner strength to go on. I wondered whether, along the way, school authorities had predicted a sad life for K, and how well he could have assimilated American values while holding on to his Japanese principles—if that was indeed what he was trying to do. I wondered whether what had finally killed him was the difficulty of holding on to a code of dignity and honor amid the jangling small-change opinions of parochial men about the predicament of someone with a mixed heritage. I wondered whether their opinions, even if they were correct, indicted him or them.

My father probably felt that K was cowardly to take his own life, that K's was hardly the way to help his mother or improve Japanese-American relations, that it was selfish for him to leave the weeds of maladjustment growing when he might have helped cut them. My father would not want anyone to consider himself responsible for K's losing his grip on the sickle, for leaving him to find his own way in the weeds growing faster and faster around him, making a morass from which, as K saw it, there was no escape except one. I wondered if the path taken by K was one I myself might have been headed toward until I began my writing with Johnnie. Without my realizing it, that piece of writing had given me some degree of self-knowledge. It had initiated the long process of weaning me from the values of my father, and had brought me out of my lonely, childish world into the bigger world that included Mr. Weeks.

IN Claremont, Mrs. Clyde kept my father busy. Dr. Grenoble Knight, the president of the American Academy of Nutrition, wanted her to help the academy establish a nutritional sanatorium, and I remember that my father had to go on a day trip with Mrs. Clyde and Dr. Martin and his wife to inspect the site. Also, because my father hadn't been to Claremont since I entered college, a considerable fuss was made over him. He spoke at the assembly; he was entertained by the Lyons; and there was hardly a day when a professor or a friend didn't come and have a meal with us. As for me, I was mourning the death of K. But still, somehow, we put in work on the manuscript, early in the morning or late at night.

I would faithfully type out my father's suggested changes, along with the page numbers, on the typewriter that Mrs. Clyde had given me. But later, when he reviewed the changes, he almost invariably wanted to drop them, saying that they were only in the nature of background and were not important. He told me to disregard even the notes he had given me for the first two chapters, and to rewrite them as I wanted to, and I decided I would try to do that over the summer. In the end, all the objections I'd worried about for almost a year amounted to no more than half a dozen minor corrections in the entire manuscript.

Years later, I came upon a copy of a letter he had written to Mrs. Watumull around that time, which went, in part:

We went over the first part of Ved's autobiography, 34 chapters. His is a moving story and true to facts although at one or two places I do not agree as to his conclusions or reactions to the situations where I am personally concerned vis-a-vis my wife (I do not think she will agree, either), but those are Ved's impressions of the time and I do not feel justified in criticising these, although it perhaps affects my ego adversely.

Before my father left Claremont, we talked about my plans for the coming summer. "I wonder if you shouldn't pass up Harvard summer school and instead spend the summer finishing the book," he said. I had applied to Harvard summer school—among other reasons, to get a taste of the university to which I had not been able to transfer—and Harvard had awarded me a scholarship. "I should warn you, though, Mrs. Clyde will not help further with the book," my father continued. "She feels that she has done her part by giving you seed money. But if you want to write I'm sure we can come up with the money, since the book is bound to be a good investment in your future."

I thought of K, constantly fretting about his due date, and shook my head. "I'm definitely going to Harvard summer school," I said. "I may not feel emotionally and intellectually ready to go on with the book for years, and even if I did finish it while I'm still young it would be only an outline for the full-scale autobiography that I eventually want to write."

"Whatever you say goes with me," my father said.

I felt he had given in to me too easily, and felt a need to explain myself. "This semester, I took my first writing course, and it has brought home to me how little I really know about writing. I don't think I rewrote a single sentence when I dictated the narrative, but now I can hardly write a simple scene without rewriting every sentence ten or fifteen times, and it still doesn't sound right. I'll have to read a lot and write a lot before I can go on. Being at Harvard is just what I need. I'll be taking a course in the twentieth-century novel and another in short-story writing."

"You're the best judge," he said.

I still felt a little guilty about getting my way, and told him that I was sending the manuscript to Mr. Weeks, and that being in Cambridge would give me the additional advantage of being near the *Atlantic Monthly* offices in Boston. I would make a point of seeking out Mr. Weeks and getting his advice on how to shape what I had written and how to go on. "If he likes the manuscript, maybe I could finish it the following summer," I said. I felt that it was almost incumbent on me to go on with the book—however inadequate it might be—in order to come to terms with K's story, with my own story and life. The narrative was no longer just a letter to Johnnie; it had another purpose.

As soon as my junior year ended, I flew to Cambridge, and arrived there on June 7th, a month before the start of summer school. From the listing at Phillips Brooks House, Harvard's social-service agency, I got myself a month's sublet at 48 Boyleston Street, and then I hired a Harvard student as an amanuensis and started rewriting the first two chapters of the narrative. I called Mr. Weeks, and he invited me to lunch. I met him in Boston, at the homey converted brownstone where the *Atlantic Monthly* has its offices. We went together a couple of short blocks to the Ritz-Carlton. He had the light step of a slender man, and walked as if he liked the world and thought that the world liked him— and I had second thoughts about my priggish notion that all good writing came out of suffering. He also didn't nag me about how I managed to get around by myself—as Mr. Henry had, for example. He took it for granted that I knew what I was doing, and that made me feel close to him.

At the Ritz, as soon as we had sat down he said, "I haven't had a chance to read your manuscript yet, but our managing editor, Nancy Reynolds, has. She's very enthusiastic. After lunch, we'll have a conference with her, and she'll tell you what she thinks. When do you think you could wind up the story and have it in tip-top shape?" He had a way of talking that made writing sound easy, and also made me feel grown-up.

"I think Henry James says somewhere that it takes a writer

months to acquire a sense of form but years to put it into practice," I said, trying to sound literary. "I find that my style is changing so fast that I'm worried that there may be a gap between the style of the Indian sections and that of the American section."

"I think when you get down to it you'll find that the writing will go as smoothly as it did last summer," he said, sounding ebullient, as always.

After lunch, we walked back to his office, which was enormous—it had once been a ballroom. The room overlooked the Public Gardens. "There's some kind of endowment to take care of the Gardens, so I have plenty of flowers to look at every day," he said. He gave his familiar laugh—a cross between a chuckle and a giggle. "I think of them as my private grounds." He asked his secretary, Virginia Albee, to call in Miss Reynolds for "the conference on the Mehta book."

Miss Reynolds, a tall, stately woman who sounded as if she were in her late twenties, came down the hall, her heels echoing loudly against the wooden floor.

"Nance, shoot," Mr. Weeks said as soon as she had sat down.

"The chapters are very short, and that gives the book a sort of episodic quality," she said.

"I agree with you," I said. "I constructed each chapter around an incident. I think it would be quite easy to combine chapters, organize them around three or four incidents."

"That's one thing out of the way," Mr. Weeks said.

"I wonder if the stuff about Partition, the British leaving India, and the establishment of the new Indian government needs to be in the book," she said. "It seems to slow down the story. What would you think of eliminating it?"

Horrified, I turned to Mr. Weeks. "Partition and its aftermath form almost half the manuscript."

"Eliminating it can't be right," he said.

"I wonder, though, if the story wouldn't have more punch if it were simplified," Miss Reynolds pressed.

"But what story?" I asked, incredulous.

"The story of your blindness," she said. "As I was reading, I kept wondering why you barely touched on it, whether it shouldn't be the central theme of the book."

"But it's not central to my life," I said truculently. I appealed to Mr. Weeks again. "The book is supposed to be about Indian family life, Partition, the last days of the Raj, about so many things. Blindness is an incidental theme."

"Nance, I think the more themes the better. They're bound to enrich the book," Mr. Weeks said. "Anyway, in such matters the author should be the court of last resort. It's his book, after all."

As had happened with my father, my victory had come too quickly, and I suddenly found myself saying that I could make blindness the central theme of the American section—something I'd never intended to do.

"It's hard to work with a manuscript until it's all in," Miss Reynolds said.

She had a point, and I at once felt that I shouldn't have submitted the manuscript until I had finished it—that the whole purpose of sending the manuscript to Mr. Weeks had been put in doubt.

"I think if we had a good detailed outline of the rest of the book we should be able to begin working with you on what you've already written," Miss Reynolds said reassuringly.

I said I would write one for her, and hoped that Mr. Weeks would be able to read the manuscript himself sometime soon.

❧

A WEEK or two after the meeting with Mr. Weeks, I sent him the following letter.

July 7, 1955

DEAR MR. WEEKS:

As there was some confusion regarding the purpose of my handing the manuscript to the Atlantic last time, on Miss Reynolds' suggestion I'm outlining in the most succinct way what I want to do with the unfinished narrative. First of all it is unfinished.

What I really want to know from you is whether the book is worth working on. I have no money at all to continue it myself. (As I have to work with a secretary all the time, writing is an expensive proposition for me, and, again, as I am supported all on scholarship, if I don't attend school I have to work.) If you happen to think the book is worth working on, then I should like to know if some kind of an optional contract *could* be arranged or a grant made.

I never make a paper outline and have carried the outline of the whole book in my mind.

Here I gave an outline for twenty-one chapters, and I concluded:

The book will not end on a pessimistic note, but the optimism will be implicit insofar as adolescence is over, although by no means are all problems solved.

In general, in these last few chapters I want to capture the emotions and feelings of blind people, and talk in a restrained way about the things I got in America which I could have got nowhere else, even in my own loving home. It is only one person experiencing the generosity of a whole nation, and from one viewpoint.

I didn't hear from the *Atlantic Monthly* for more than a month. It was just as well, because I was soon involved in summer school. For all the worries of Mr. Henry and Dean Bender that I would have great difficulty adjusting to a new environment, I found Harvard as easy to manage as Pomona—in fact, in some ways easier. The Phillips Brooks House quickly provided me with readers and secretarial help. The new, air-conditioned Lamont Library had special individual reading rooms on the top floor set aside for blind students. Also, the courses were on the same academic plane as those at Pomona. And I found it easier to make friends in Cambridge. People were much more cosmopolitan, and accepting of people's differences. When I'd been at Harvard scarcely a week, a group of Radcliffe and Harvard students invited me to go with them to Tanglewood, and I had a wonderful weekend of sleeping out in the open at night and listening to music during the day.

The only surprise was my room in Weld Hall—usually a freshman dormitory for men, which was being used to house summer students. The room was large and, except for a bed, bare. It had two huge walk-in closets. There was no way I could make it feel like home with the forty-four pounds of belongings that the airline had allowed me to bring along.

TOWARD the end of my stay in Cambridge, I had another meeting with Mr. Weeks. By now, he had read the manuscript, and he was enthusiastic about it. He gave me some notes he had made on the book:

I feel that the early chapters of your book will be the better for amplification and for the addition of more personal material and incident. The reader should be *made* to share in the full force of your deprivation. We should share in the difficulties of your first groping and adjustment, and you should identify for us those members of your family who were most helpful and sympathetic and endow them with the individuality which they possess in your mind. I don't think this revision should interfere with the forward progress of your book and I am confident that you can give the early text the additional animation it needs at some later stage. By Chapter 15 you have hit your stride, and your style has movement and plenty of incident. If the balance of the book continues at this pace, I have hopes that it will be acceptable and do well.

"Is there anything we can do to help you finish the book?" he asked me.

I told him again that my main problem was money for secretarial help.

"We can arrange to advance you five hundred dollars—two hundred and fifty this year and two hundred and fifty next year," he said.

I was overwhelmed. I had earned money only once before, when I was sixteen and had a summer job in an ice-cream plant. I couldn't imagine anything better than getting paid for something I'd written—except, of course, Johnnie's returning my love. But then, I thought, the trouble with love is that it involves the will of another person, whereas writing is something I can do myself. That was the beginning of writing's taking a place in my life, almost as if it were a person, with its own consuming demands.

It took me years to realize that in a sense the letter had all along been to myself, since even in loving Johnnie I had been looking at my own reflection.

IX

MAGNETIC POLES

M RS. CLYDE READ THE MANUSCRIPT OF THE INDIAN HALF of my young autobiography and, as a result, got interested in her own family history and antecedents—for the first time, it seemed. She began her researches with the earliest member of the family she knew anything about— her paternal grandfather, one Thomas Clyde. She had heard that he was probably born in Belfast. She went there in June of 1955 with my father, who was again travelling with her as her companion physician, and called at the office of the registrar of births and deaths at the city hospital. But she discovered that the hospital records started only in 1864—long after her grandfather would have been born. She had heard that he was married in a Presbyterian church in Philadelphia, and so she went to the oldest Presbyterian college in Belfast and secured a list of the oldest Presbyterian churches in the city. She then made the rounds of the churches on the list, but did not find any record of

Thomas Clyde in the archives. She came to believe that perhaps he hadn't been a Presbyterian after all, and had only been married in a Presbyterian church. Anyhow, she got discouraged and abandoned her researches, and never returned to them.

In my own efforts to find out something about the Clyde family, I came across a woman named Martha Knight—the wife of Mrs. Clyde's nephew George Hill Clyde—who had managed to collect considerable material about the family. It appears from this material that Mrs. Clyde's grandfather Thomas Clyde was born in Ireland of Scottish-Irish parents. He was orphaned when he was very small, and, at the age of eight, was sent to America to live with the family of his uncle, also named Thomas Clyde, who was a grocer in Philadelphia. The uncle gave the boy the common-school education of the day and then put him to work in his grocery shop.

The younger Thomas Clyde, while still a child, was one of the first people in America to board the first iron ship ever built— it came to this country from Britain in the eighteen-twenties. In 1832, by which time he had become an American citizen, he got a job as overseer of a stone quarry in Ridley Creek, Pennsylvania, on the Delaware River. The quarry furnished big slabs of stone under contract to the government, which was constructing a breakwater on the Delaware River at Cape Henlopen. The slabs were carried to the site in the quarry's sloops. Clyde did so well that before long he was able to buy a quarry of his own on the river, and he began furnishing stones from it to the government not only for the Delaware breakwater but also for many other such public-works projects. Then he began thinking of shifting out of the business of supplying stones, and getting into the more profitable business of building and owning the vessels that carried them on the waterways. In 1839, there arrived in this country an important Swedish inventor and marine engineer named John Ericsson, who had won a prize in England for his invention of the screw propeller for the locomotion of steamships. Previously, most people had assumed that steamships could be driven only with side wheels, at least in harbors and rivers, which had shallow draughts. Clyde was apparently the first American to see in Ericsson's invention the promise of a cheaper, safer, steadier, and speedier method of locomotion on water. He associated himself with John Ericsson and built several small experimental steamships with the screw propeller, for use in inland waters, and was thus able to demonstrate that such ships could dispense with side wheels. In 1844, he built the John S. McKim, a large wooden oceangoing ship driven by screw propellers, and so founded the Clyde Steamship Company, with headquarters in Philadelphia—a company that was to grow into his shipping and railway empire, and was to help change the face of America from Faulkner's "markless wilderness" into a commercial landscape of coal and iron.

Thomas Clyde continued to put down new keels and build new ships, and in due course he held an interest in most of the steamships plying between the major ports along the Atlantic coastline. With John Ericsson, he pioneered in the construction of iron and steel ships, and chartered some of these to the United States government during the Civil War; one of them was the celebrated Monitor, which vanquished the Confederate Merrimac.

By the time Thomas Clyde died, in 1885, his interests extended beyond shipping into railroads, real estate, and banks and insurance companies, and he had in his employ thousands of people, who were devoted to him: he had kept open for as long as ten years the payrolls of ships lost at sea, and made monthly payments to the widows and orphans of the missing sailors.

In 1837, Thomas Clyde had married Rebecca Pancoast, a woman from a distinguished Quaker family. (They were, however, married in a Presbyterian church, just as Mrs. Clyde had heard.) Thomas and Rebecca Clyde had six children—William Pancoast, George Washington, Benjamin Franklin, Margaret, Annie, and Thomas—and the eldest son, William, who was Mrs. Clyde's father, surpassed even his father as a shipping magnate.

William Clyde was born in 1839. After spending a year at

Trinity College in Hartford, Connecticut, and then serving with the Philadelphia Grays during the Civil War, he joined his father in the business. In 1870, he became president of the Clyde Steamship Company, and in 1872, by which time the company was operating freight lines between Boston, Philadelphia, and Baltimore, and two combined passenger and freight lines between Charleston and Galveston, he moved the offices of the company from Philadelphia to New York City. In 1873, he became president of the publicly held Pacific Mail Steamship Company, whose main business was carrying United States mail, under contract, on the Pacific Ocean.

In 1865, William Clyde married Emmeline Field, whose ancestry could be traced back to Sir Thomas Mowbray, first Duke of Norfolk; on back to William Mowbray, one of the twenty-five Barons of Runnymede who signed the Magna Carta; and back still further, to the Norman Conquest itself. William and Emmeline Clyde had eight children: Marshall Hill (1865–1946), Thomas (1867–1937), William Pancoast, Jr. (1872, died at birth), Emmeline (1874–1915), William Pancoast, Jr. (1876–1967), Mabel (1878–1959), Ethel, our Mrs. Clyde (1879–1978), and George Washington (1881–1944). William Clyde attended the Episcopal church, voted Republican, and was a leader in many humane and charitable causes. He was a member of several New York social clubs, a couple of yacht clubs, a shooting club, and a salmon club. When he died, in 1923, at the age of eighty-four, he left a mansion he had built at 5 West Fifty-first Street to his wife, along with its contents, and the residuary estate equally in trust for his children.

The Clyde Steamship Company was one of a handful of family-run steamship lines to survive into the twentieth century. But in 1906 William Clyde had sold it to Charles W. Morse, who consolidated it with its competitor the Mallory Line. In 1928, the Clyde-Mallory Line was merged into the giant Atlantic Gulf & West Indies Steamship Corporation, which had already absorbed several other nineteenth-century family-run shipping companies.

The corporation was for all practical purposes put out of the shipping business during the Second World War, when the United States government first chartered and then purchased outright many of its ships. At the end of the war, the government offered to sell the ships back to the corporation, and even pay half the cost of reconverting them to coastwise service, but in the era of road transportation the inducement was not enough.

❧

MRS. CLYDE had shown little interest in her family. Once, when I tried to draw her out on the subject, our conversation went like this:

"Were you born in New York City, Mrs. Clyde?"

"No, in Babylon," she said cryptically.

"Babylon where?" I asked.

"Where do you think? Babylon, Long Island."

"What were your brothers and sisters like?"

"Oh, Lord, you want to know that, too? There were eight of us, but one brother, William P., died soon after he was born. He was the second- or third-oldest. I don't remember. I wasn't around then—I came later. The only ones that were still around when I met your father were Will and Mabel."

"What was your father like?"

"He was a very stuffy man. My cousin Louie Runk and I lost our religion after we read Darwin's 'The Origin of Species.' My father used to say, 'A woman without religion is a pretty cold object.'" She laughed her hearty laugh. "But he was also fearless. I remember that a client of the Clyde lines sent his hound dog from down South to New York and the dog didn't arrive. The owner wrote to Father that he was coming to New York to 'get him.' Father went and met him, and faced him down. He told him, 'Any time you want to "get" a man, don't notify him first, or he'll have the police present.' That was characteristic of him."

"And your mother?"

"She didn't go to college, or anything like that. She had a lot of children. She was a gentle type of person. Sweet, but nothing very definite or striking one way or the other. Everyone thought her to be a little crazy in the head. But then all the Hills—her mother's family—were a little crazy in the head."

"Did you grow up in New York City?" I asked.

"I didn't go to school, if that's what you mean—or hardly ever," she said. "I think I was sent to boarding school for one year, when I was about fourteen. I was up in New England somewhere. Until that time, I studied at home. I was a very delicate child." She laughed, as if she had trouble picturing herself as delicate.

"How did you spend your time at home then?"

"A lady came and read Chaucer aloud to me. I gave her a hard time. I also travelled a lot. I remember that when I was a little girl I saw Queen Victoria in London, going past in a big coach, and I've been travelling ever since. I used to go on cruises, but I was never on one of the Clyde lines. Never in my life. But I met my husband on one of my cruises."

I knew from an edition of *Who's Who of American Women* that she had married Ernst Gottfried Vollmer in 1907, and I asked her now about her husband.

"Why do you care about him? He's dead, and I didn't like him anyway. Can you imagine me being married to an officer in the Kaiser's Guard?"

"How old was he when you met him?"

"Do you realize that you're asking me about someone I knew forty or fifty years ago? All I remember is that when I told my father I was going to marry a German he laid down two conditions—that I wait a year, and that I learn German. I had always been the rebellious, nonconformist type. They used to call me the black sheep." She laughed. "But I decided that my father's conditions were not unreasonable, and went along with them. While I was waiting a year and learning German in Europe, my father went to see Gottfried's superior, to try to get him to dissuade Gottfried from marrying me. The superior said, 'You are a very lucky man, Herr Clyde, to have your daughter courted by Gottfried. I wish Gottfried would marry my daughter.' I got married hastily, in a civil ceremony in Potsdam, but Father didn't consider me really married yet. He wouldn't let Gottfried and me hold hands. So we went to London and had a real, proper church wedding for him. That wedding, too, was hastily arranged— Lady Stratford had to go out and buy flowers for the church at the last minute. We were married in a church with two dogs outside, very near what is now the Westbury Hotel, where I like to stay when I can't get rooms at the Savoy."

"After you got married, where did you live?"

"Oh, in a huge palace of a house in Potsdam. But we weren't very happy. Gottfried was always shocked by me. He once asked me to bring him his slippers. I said, 'I'll bring one if you bring the other.' I once put on his uniform during a parade and stood out on the balcony. The officers passing below saw my uniform and saluted me, and I saluted back. That really shocked him. He was a very striking man and had many girlfriends, and our marriage broke down early. I remember at the outbreak of the First World War we were here in the United States. He wanted to go back to fight in the German Army. We had to fake or steal a passport for him, secretly buy German money, and smuggle him out of America. He was killed in 1916. I was never meant to be married to a German, or maybe to anyone else. If he hadn't died, I would have divorced him. After my marriage, I'd taken on German nationality, but since Germany had become America's enemy I wanted to become an American citizen again. There was a long legal fight, which I won. And that's when I took back the name Clyde. I never liked being called Frau Vollmer anyway. Who would? Since I was going to live in America, I wanted my boys to grow up with an English surname. I took back my maiden name, but I couldn't get rid of the 'Mrs.,' because of my boys."

"Were your sons born in Germany?"

"Yes. Bill was born in 1908 and Tom in 1912. But they got

their schooling here in America, at Choate. Then Tom left Princeton after two years to go to Wall Street. Bill went to Williams and Columbia. But his main interest was always flying planes. Poor boy, he was heartbroken during the Second World War, because they only let him fly transport planes—they wouldn't let him fly on the front line, because his father had been a German."

"Toby is your only grandchild?"

"Yes. But don't ask me any more questions. I'm an old lady, and all that is in the past now." She picked up the newspaper.

EVERY year or two for about twenty-five years, almost up to Mrs. Clyde's death, my father would find himself meeting Mrs. Clyde in Europe or America, in the most ad-hoc way imaginable, and would end up doing whatever she took it into her head for them to do for a few months—often from spring to fall, the period when she suffered from hay fever—and then he would return to India to recuperate from his job with her and devote himself to family concerns. As I write, I have at hand the sections of Mrs. Clyde's diary recording the months that he spent with her during the years from 1953 through 1956, when I was an undergraduate at Pomona. These pages throw some light on the kind of person Mrs. Clyde was and the kinds of things she and my father did together in those days.

She writes that on June 24, 1953, my father arrives in Geneva in good time to receive her off the plane from America. He conducts her to the hotel she knows from previous visits, and they settle in. Over the next few days, she takes a stroll and eats some delicious meals. She shops for silk chemises and looks up a couple of old friends. She notes that he has some tooth trouble and has to make visits to the dentist. She drives in a hired car to a sanatorium in Thun in search of a hay-fever cure. But Dr. and Frau Waerland, who supposedly have the cure, are at another sanatorium, in Bad Soden. She unhurriedly makes her way there, by car and train. She checks into the sanatorium and, under the guidance of the Waerlands, begins a treatment of diet, exercises, and inhalations of "atomized" air containing certain medicaments. (Although my father doesn't really believe in the cures, and the life of the convalescing rich isn't natural to him, he more or less has to do whatever she does, including taking the cures. He finds himself developing a medical interest in them, however, because my mother has been asthmatic for most of their married life, and the Waerland cure has to do with allergic and respiratory problems.) Mrs. Clyde takes a day trip to Bad Ems to look into some respiratory appliances being made there, and to look up an old friend, Otto Mock, who is a doctor at the Bad Ems spa, and his wife, Marga.

She flies back to America and divides her time between town and country, between Gramercy Park and Old Fields. She calls this friend, sees that friend, meets her sons, has her hair done, goes for dress fittings, watches birds, does her exercises, writes letters. There are bills to be paid, house chores to sort out, doctors to be visited—for internal examinations, for blood tests, for cardiograms. She experiments with organically grown foods. She goes on expeditions to see Lady Wonder (a horse that reads minds and types) and to visit a freak museum that has on view a twenty-six-inch full-grown woman and is showing a circus of trained fleas. Her hay fever comes and goes. Every day, she checks the pollen count in the newspaper. She starts making plans to be someplace where ragweed doesn't grow, thinks that Bermuda doesn't have any ragweed, and goes there for ten days.

The next June, she returns to Europe and Bad Ems, where my father receives her. She takes the full spa cure—regular daily mineral-water baths, nose and mouth inhalations, ingestion of special mineral waters, "fango" mudpack treatments, and massages. She takes advanced German lessons and makes my father take beginners' lessons. She visits churches, tastes local wines, has tea and cakes, and goes to outdoor concerts staged daily for patients taking the cure. She has some trouble with her neck and shoulder and intensifies the fango treatments. She tries some homeopathic medicine for her hay fever. She mentions that my father is having dental work done and has developed some ear and arm trouble. (The life of a convalescent has its own dynamics, and he, too, develops some symptoms. Having them treated gives him something to do, makes him participate in the business of the cure.) She takes a train to Geneva, but her luggage is misdirected to Basel. She goes to Basel and holes up for a night there. She returns to Geneva and, after some difficulty, finds accommodations in a good hotel, and they settle in. She visits an exhibition of watches and jewelry. Her wristwatch bothers her arm; her wedding ring constricts her finger. She gets rid of both, buys a watch on a chain, and feels "freer." She takes a lesson or two in French. She gets a bad knee, and for a spell has to walk with crutches—a situation that requires special attention from my father. She takes a train to Paris and from there flies to London. Then she goes back to the United States by sea, and he flies back to India. The next two years are much the same.

At one point, she flies to London. At her behest, my father follows up a story in an English newspaper about some allergy treatment and therapeutic hypnotism. She goes to see the Changing of the Guard at Buckingham Palace. ("One wonders that the people are willing to be taxed for this daily pageant.") She tries out Indian restaurants, and goes to a magic show called "Mysteries of India and the Orient." She stops in at a newsreel theatre to watch newsreels about the Grace Kelly–Prince Rainier wedding and the Bulganin-Khrushchev visit. She begins taking a new, "snuff-like" medicine for her hay fever. She has an evening at the theatre, seeing Vivien Leigh in Noël Coward's "South Sea Bubble." She goes to the Royal Academy Annual Exhibition, and comments that she hates modern art. She goes to an exhibition of Grandma Moses paintings. ("As an American and as a human being I am proud of Grandma Moses.") She takes a tour of the Thames Valley.

She goes back to Bad Ems. The Mocks have dubbed a corner

of their garden Ethel's Corner, and in it they have set out some furniture she has presented them with. She often has tea there. She makes another gift of two thousand dollars to the American Foundation for the Blind for me, to be dispersed over two years, for reader and vacation expenses for further education. She goes to Bad Nauheim, but finds its custom of ringing church bells for weddings and funerals irritating—they seem to ring all day long, starting at seven-thirty in the morning. ("As this is a health resort, especially for the heart, there appear to be many deaths to judge by the number of times one hears those noisy bells and the few weddings seen. A poor 'ad' and poor psychology for Bad Nauheim.") She flees from the bells to Frankfurt. She comes upon an article in the *Reader's Digest* called "He Never Asked That a Thing Be Easy" and is deeply impressed by it.

Although every page of Mrs. Clyde's diary is dated, the diaries as a whole have a timeless quality, a little like that of Mann's "The Magic Mountain." Despite all the time she and my father spent together, she seems to have known as little about him as she knew about the foreigners around her; it's as if she were leading him through some intricate social dance. Indeed, when she was abroad she lived among foreigners like a prototypical American tourist—untouched and unscathed, unknowing and innocent.

It seemed to my father that since he and Mrs. Clyde had very little to do they bickered about nothing. Once, in Bern, he recalled, they were walking to see some bears living in a pit, for which, it was said, the city was named. They passed under an arcade. "How dumb of them to have this cover overhead," she said. "It cuts off all the sun. What do you think made them put it there?"

"Rain," he said.

She seemed put out. "You must always say 'I think' before you speak. You should say 'I think it is because of rain,' because how can you possibly know?"

" 'I think' goes without saying," he said.

"But you didn't say 'I think'!"

He felt checkmated, and decided there was no point in arguing, but she kept on with the subject all the way to the bears in the pit.

That night, as he was dropping off to sleep, it occurred to him that what she might have been complaining about was that he wasn't making himself clear enough to her, and thereafter he always made an effort to preface possibly controversial opinions with "I think." But she didn't seem to appreciate his effort, and often complained that he wasn't clear enough. Years later, he realized that what she had really objected to was his laconic answers, as if he weren't doing his share of carrying on a conversation. Both she and he were great talkers, but in her presence he soon came to talk less, because everything he said seemed to get him into hot water. He would therefore simplify things for her benefit or sometimes try to divert her to forestall further questions, only to arouse her curiosity. She ascribed this increasingly laconic conversational style to his foreignness or, as he grew older, to the onset of deafness on his part. As for him, he tried to carry the burden of conversation whenever he thought he could safely do it without involving himself in a dispute.

In addition to accompanying her everywhere and performing all sorts of personal services in the manner of, as it were, a gentleman-in-waiting, my father had many medical duties to perform for Mrs. Clyde. He had to monitor her pulse, her blood pressure, and her weight daily, consult with her doctors, review prescriptions—generally oversee the health of his patient. I used to hear from him regularly, and had several opportunities to observe for myself the personal side of his work for her, but I often wondered about the medical side of it. A long time afterward, I came upon copies of letters he regularly sent to Mrs. Clyde's New York doctors from Europe to bring them up to date on the latest treatments she was trying out. My father used the full force of his scientific training and his spirit of inquiry to investigate whatever treatment she took it into her head to pursue; the following letter is typical of the painstaking lengths to which he went to serve her.

25 September 1954

DEAR DR. MARTIN,

When I reached Europe early last June I learned from Mrs. Clyde of her "exciting" discovery in Europe a month earlier of the name and address of a physician, R. Sr., who had been practising at Bad Ems. He had treated her for asthma 44 years ago. For some time past she had been thinking of his old technique, which had cured her permanently of asthma, and she hoped that that very line of treatment might be the answer to her present trouble; namely, hay fever. Mrs. Clyde had made inquiries about Dr. R. Sr. and discovered that he had died some years ago but that his son, Dr. R. Jr., was now practising at Coblenz (about 25 kms from Bad Ems) as a specialist in ear, nose, and throat. As you know, Mrs. Clyde has a standing spa physician, Dr. Mock, at Bad Ems. She had asked him to make an appointment for her with Dr. R. Jr. This had been done and Mrs. Clyde, with her niece Miss E., who is a German-speaking American, had seen Dr. R. Jr. He had explained to them the line of treatment his father had followed with Mrs. Clyde and other patients; namely, titillating the mucous membrane of the nose with a probe having at one end an olive-shaped knob of the size of a large pea, which was vibrated by a vibrating machine, the strength of which was controlled manually and determined for each patient as required. He impressed upon them the great success which his father had achieved with this line of treatment, saying, however, that, of course, all patients did not benefit equally well from it. Thereafter Dr. R. Jr. had proceeded on his two months' vacation.

I had a number of questions on the technique and its results. What anatomical, physiological, pathological, reflex, or psychological changes were to accrue from such a mechanical procedure? I was particularly anxious to exclude the possibility of any pathological changes which even remotely may take place at the junction of the skin and mucous membrane in the anterior nares, especially in a person of advanced age with a history of cancer in the family. I was therefore anxious to get some references and to find some authorities on the subject to whom I could refer to be on the safe side. But I could not find a physician either at Bad Ems or at Coblenz who was practising this technique. I wondered why, if at one time such a technique was in vogue and produced good results, it was abandoned.

In the interim, Mrs. Clyde ordered a custom-made probe from a surgical factory in Bad Ems. When we returned to Bad Ems on 24 July Dr. Mock started the nose-vibrator treatment as suggested by Mrs. Clyde. He followed her instructions to use cocaine (actually novocaine was used) for the first two treatments, and to limit the time to one minute in each nostril to begin with, the strength and time to be increased gradually. The first treatment given by Dr. Mock was for a minute on each side with one turn of the knob of the vibrator's regulator. Dr. Mock planned to titillate not only the anterior and middle nares but also the posterior nares, for which he thought that a probe with a much smaller knob should be made. But Mrs. Clyde definitely remembered that Dr. R. Sr. had only titillated the anterior portion of the nose and the idea to treat the posterior nares was given up. Dr. Mock gave a second treatment on the third day, this time for one and a half minutes on each side with one and a half turns of the regulator. This proved to be a little too strenuous, and gave Mrs. Clyde a slight headache and earache, which lasted for a day or so. Taking all the pros and cons, Mrs. Clyde decided that she would rather get the treatment from the specialist—namely, Dr. R. Jr.—when he returned from his vacation. She contemplated undergoing the full treatment of 10–12 applications by him, and both Dr. Mock and myself were to familiarise ourselves fully with the technique, which perhaps even Mrs. Clyde herself could follow as it was presumed that the patient could follow the technique without any harmful effects.

While we were waiting for Dr. R. Jr.'s return, Mrs. Clyde decided to visit the French Riviera. On our return to Bad Ems, we stopped in Coblenz and had an interview with Dr. R. Jr. I went with Mrs. Clyde to see Dr. R. Jr.; so did Mrs. Mock, as Dr. Mock was too busy to come with us.

In reply to several questions Dr. R. Jr. gave the following answers: The patients were given treatment from 3–5 minutes in each nostril. He showed us a flexible wire with cotton wool at the end which he used. He used a vibrator over which he held the wire. It was the same machine that his father used. He controlled the strength of the vibration by the pressure of his hand on the wire. He used novocaine for the first two or three treatments. He just used cotton wool at the end of the wire moistened with olive oil or liquid paraffin. In case the mucous membrane was swollen, he used adrenaline or privin before the treatment. He treated mostly the anterior and middle nares, very seldom the posterior nares. He was quite sure that any intelligent patient could treat himself or herself at home without any harm. The only contra-indications to the treatment were polypus and sinusitis. The patient's own reactions and complaints were his determining factors as to the time and intensity of treatment. No physiological or pathological changes could result from the treatment. 10–12 applications would sufficiently thicken the mucous membrane. Two to three times a week was the line of treatment he followed. His father was the only physician who had used this line of treatment on several hundreds of cases during his 35 years of practice. The records of these were lost as their home was bombed during World War II. As regards his own records, he is a very busy specialist and cannot find time to compile a scientific paper for publication, though he hoped that one day he would do so. His father had used the same technique and apparatus as he was using. He could not say why other physicians were not following this line of treatment. He could not refer to any medical authorities. Treatment should preferably be undertaken by a physician, and he would send the directions for him and the patient to follow. He would write these out in German and have them translated into English by his daughter in Hamburg, and would in due course send them to Mrs. Clyde in Bad Ems.

The first treatment, a demonstration, was given by him with the vibrating machine and the olive-shaped probe which Mrs. Clyde had taken with her. It was a fairly rough handling and the treatment which was to have been for two or three minutes in each nostril had to be curtailed to less than a minute in each, as Mrs. Clyde showed signs of distress.

The whole interview had more of a social character than a scientific one between one doctor and another. In the presence of Mrs. Clyde and Mrs. Mock, many points raised could not be pressed home for a definite answer.

No sooner had we started on the homeward journey than Mrs. Clyde, with her usual intuition and decision of character, had come to a conclusion—"no more treatments" for her until she knew more. Moreover she found certain discrepancies in the statements of Dr. R. Jr. between her first interview and our second interview. This was disturbing to her, and as she wanted precise answers to her many questions it was decided to have a third interview with Dr. R. Jr. In this interview, only Dr. Mock and I would discuss the scientific aspects with Dr. R. Jr. and if possible experience for ourselves the reactions to the actual treatment.

Dr. Mock and I interviewed Dr. R. Jr. as agreed. Mrs. Clyde and Mrs. Mock accompanied us to Coblenz but only joined us after the interview. At this interview, Dr. R. Jr. took quite a different position from the second interview. Consequently, I wrote down what he said and read it to him lest I had misunderstood him. The following are his statements: "Only a specialist should undertake such treatment because he understands the nose and can find the most sensitive spot. It depends upon the spot to get the effect. . . . If any complications occur, the specialist can handle them. . . . One must observe the nose for the effect. . . . The nose is a very delicate organ. . . . The experience of the specialist is very important in treating such cases. . . . I can see from the face of the patient as he enters my office whether the treatment is doing good or not. . . . In cases of asthma the results are better in women as they are more sensitive. . . . After the climacteric the gynaecologist must always be consulted for any harmful effects." He agreed that there was a possibility, though a very remote one, that in a person of advanced years with a history of cancer in the family, changes could start resulting in malignancy.

All this was so different from the previous interview that I was totally nonplussed. No sooner had we joined Mrs. Clyde and Mrs. Mock than I read out to them what I had taken down as above. The new stand of Dr. R. Jr.—for instance, that only the specialist should tackle the mucous membrane of the nose, and that if any complications arose the specialist could be counted upon to deal with these—sorely disappointed Mrs. Clyde, who had gone to the very source for her idea at such expense and inconvenience, and who had offered herself as a guinea pig for the benefit of others.

I must confess I had not let my skepticism get the better of me at any stage. I was anxious to discover a new line of treatment, for I have at home (India) my wife and sister-in-law suffering from asthma. I thought I could perhaps introduce the new method for their relief and for the relief of many other patients in India. I was naturally cautious and asked searching questions, but I continued to keep my mind open. In the end I was disillusioned.

The above account is self-explanatory, and you, Dr. Martin, may draw your own conclusions from it.

> With kindest good wishes,
> I remain,
> Sincerely yours,
>
> A. R. Mehta

Reading such reports, more than thirty years later, still distresses me. I suppose I'll never really get over my father's being caught up for most of his retired life in the nonsense of a rich hypochondriac. Indeed, in hundreds of letters he wrote to me, and in many conversations I had with him about Mrs. Clyde, he expressed regret that after retirement he had never taken up the challenge of doing something that was more in his professional line. At the same time, he maintained that there was no feasible alternative to working for her. He constantly sought and followed up other leads, he said, but none of them seemed to hold a promise of setting the family on its financial feet. He would point out to me that his meagre financial resources made it impossible for him to pull up stakes in India and set them down in the West, for instance, and yet no sooner had he said this than he would get to wondering whether he was right, and start dreaming about what else he might have done. In fact, often when we met during those years he would begin questioning and wondering and dreaming in this vein, as if he longed for release from his financial dependence on Mrs. Clyde but found no way to go about getting it. Ever since, I have more or less carried on with myself the debate he carried on with himself: Was there no feasible alternative to Mrs. Clyde or did he take the easy way out? Did he forfeit the chance to venture out on his own or did that chance never exist? I'm also bedevilled by other questions, which I could never bring myself to discuss with him. Was the burden of my education responsible for his finding himself in such a fix, or did my being in the West and needing him actually give him a certain goal and purpose in his post-retirement years?

Such questions of character and motive are hard to assess from this distance.

Could a man of his experience and worldliness not have found anything better to do than to work as a companion physician to a rich American lady, whose ways of dealing with him he sometimes found irksome and perhaps humiliating?

If the situation with Mrs. Clyde had been presented to him as a long-term affair, he would have rejected it out of hand. He would have preferred staying in India and being "master of my fate and captain of my soul," as he liked to say, and somehow carrying on like other refugees in his position. But, as it was, he would wake up one day in India and find a cablegram saying, 'What about meeting me in Europe on such-and-such a day?" The arrangement gave him an illusion of freedom of action. It nurtured his hope of finding something more professional to do. Meanwhile, the arrangement grew and developed, almost by itself, without either of them ever deciding upon what it turned into. And it wasn't always a job. In America, he was, of course, always her guest, and after the first few years they were on a first-name basis.

Somewhere along the way, he must have caught on to the fact that she wanted constant companionship in her old age. It must have been obvious to him that she was lonely and would go on needing him if he gave in to her demands. After all, she was getting older, and she didn't seem to be close to her family.

But she had lived most of her life as a single woman, and seemed to be used to it. Anyway, when he met her she was in her seventies and it was by no means clear to him that she would go on wanting to travel year after year. After all, how many women in their seventies and eighties—nay, nineties—pick up and go, the way she did, and invite someone halfway around the world to join them?

Still, he must have gathered fairly soon that she had a particular fondness for having him around.

But he kept on running into dozens of other friends whom she'd taken on trips to Europe, Bermuda—wherever. He always felt that they were better suited to travelling with her than he was, and that she probably preferred them to him. They were all Americans; they were altogether more on her wavelength.

Then why did she keep on coming back to him, again and again?

It might have had to do with his dashing presence, the figure that he cut in the world. In some part of her mind she perhaps hankered after the glamour she had known as a girl and as the wife of an officer in the Kaiser's Guard. And then my father, as a doctor, moved on terms of equality with all the European physicians who were always treating her or whose treatments she got interested in. Many of them deferred to him.

Then why wouldn't he have done something else in the first place, like setting up a private medical practice, and not needed to depend on Mrs. Clyde?

Set up a private practice *where?* In America? At that time, the American quota for Indians was so minuscule that it would have taken him years of waiting to be admitted, and, once he had been, he would have had to pass a battery of tests before he could be licensed. And how could he have supported himself and his family all that time?

Why not England, then? In those days, it was easy for Indians to immigrate there. He was already a member of the British Medical Association. And how avidly he studied the advertisements in the *British Medical Journal* of private practices for sale!

But after the Partition it would have meant being uprooted a second time in the space of very few years—uprooting his younger children in the middle of their schooling. And then there was the whole question of which culture they would belong to, live in, marry in, get jobs in. There was also Mamaji's well-being to think of. Two of my sisters were married and settled in India, with children. All her friends and relatives were in India. How would she survive socially in England without knowing much English? And then there was her asthmatic condition—could she really tolerate the cold, damp English climate? Anyway, he felt that without a cushion of capital for a new life in another country the move was too hazardous.

What about the money he was starting to earn from Mrs. Clyde? Wouldn't that have been capital enough?

All the money he ever earned from Mrs. Clyde got spent as it came. He never asked for and never got an increase in his salary. And, remember, she paid him the seven hundred dollars a month only when they were travelling outside the United States. This money went a long way toward paying the bills in India, but it never did amount—never could have amounted—to much in the West.

Then was he not in earnest about settling in England at all?

Until retirement, except for three years or so in the West, his whole life had been spent in India. India was reality; settling in the West was maybe just a dream. He kept on postponing the move, procrastinating. Some of that was in character, but some of it also had to do with the difficulty of his circumstances.

Why couldn't he have set up a private practice in India?

There were some problems with that, too. In the India in which he had grown up and spent his working life, working for the government was the most highly respected thing you could do. The public sector dominated every aspect of the private sector. And very few of his contemporaries who had retired from the government were able to make the transition to the private sector. They simply couldn't adjust. For them, it was like moving from being members of the nobility to being commoners. And they preferred the fate of impoverished nobility to that of the money-grubbing world of the common man. Yet it had less to do with conscious snobbery than with a certain way of living and being. For instance, even the idea of sending your friends—people of your caste and subcaste and group—bills for services rendered was repugnant to an ex-government servant. In fact, many Indian doctors in private practice tended to treat their friends free of charge. And then there was the psychological aspect of his own age, which can't be emphasized enough. Every working day of his life, he must have come across evidence of how young the average Indian died compared with the average life span in the West. In part through his efforts, that average age had been raised, but when he retired it was little more than thirty. To reach the age of fifty-five in that kind of environment must have made him feel that he was really living on borrowed time. On top of everything else, the fact of retirement itself must have taken a heavy toll. He had been a very active man, with an important place in the world, whom the country had put to pasture—discarded, as it were—to wait for his own death.

Was the whole idea of private practice just a dream?

Maybe so. It's not clear whether, deep down, he had the confidence actually to see and treat patients. After all, his entire adult life had been spent in administration, in preventive medicine, in controlling and fighting epidemics. He'd hardly ever given an injection himself or written a prescription. His medical knowledge of the treatment of individual patients was no doubt very rusty. He would almost have had to go back to the university and bone up.

But a man of his knowledge of both the East and the West could surely have found some other avenue of work related to medicine?

It wasn't for lack of trying. He looked into lots of things, like being an Indian representative of an American chemical or pharmaceutical company. His lengthy correspondence with several drug companies survives, but none of them wanted him. Perhaps the truth was that he didn't have a head for anything to do with business. He had romantic ideas about chasing money but no head for making it.

Could he have done more lecturing in America?

He used to wonder about that. But he claimed he missed his chance when he bungled an interview with a top-flight lecture agent, Lee Keedick. He balked because the agency wanted a thirty-per-cent commission, and he walked out, thinking that he would be his own agent. He used to say he was always penny-wise and pound-foolish. After that, the only lecture agencies that were interested in him were small-time bureaus in places like Kansas and Minnesota, and the lecture fees didn't amount to much more than fifty dollars. Anyway, the question comes up—lecture on what? He wasn't a scholar, he wasn't a writer or a politician, he'd never given any lectures before. He didn't have a name. About the only credentials he had for lecturing were that he had a personality, was born in India, and had general knowledge about the country—and how much mileage could you get out of that?

Is it the case, then, that he really could not have done anything else?

Maybe. Most of his life was spent in a society that had practially no mobility, where people's destinies were fixed, almost like little planets. It must have been hard for him even to contemplate the idea of a career very different from the one he knew.

But the career with Mrs. Clyde *was* very different.

He just fell into that.

Did he like Mrs. Clyde?

Yes, very much. She represented to him everything he'd always thought America was: generous, openhearted, accepting, ingenuous, and rich.

Then it must have been good for him in some way to be with her. There must have been many positive things about their relationship.

Yes, there were. Being with her in Europe and America provided him with an escape from the demoralizing, brutal Indian reality. Thanks to Mrs. Clyde, for a few months of the year he had the luxury of living in five-star hotels in cool climates, eating light, healthful meals, being free from petty Indian jealousies and backbiting—living in clean and restful conditions. A lot of the time, they were in Germany. He loved and admired the Germans, for their industry, their cleanliness, their manners, their technology—all the things in which he felt Indians were deficient. Next to England and America, there was no place he'd rather have been. Being with her must also have provided him with temporary relief from daily family cares and wants. It probably prolonged his life by twenty years or more. The truth may be that he was always pulled by the magnetic poles of East and West—his Indian background and a deep attachment to his mother and his family, on the one hand, and his Western education and his love of the Western life, on the other. The job with Mrs. Clyde allowed him to divide himself between the two worlds and be nourished by both, as if he were a man of private means.

So I keep on debating, as it were, the ifs and cans and might-have-beens. In retrospect, my father's association with Mrs. Clyde seems inevitable. But then in retrospect things always do.

X

FACE TO FACE

WHEN I GOT BACK TO POMONA FROM CAMBRIDGE FOR my senior year, I felt lost. Every time I passed under the window of K's room—something I couldn't help doing a dozen times a day, to and from classes, the library, and Frary Hall—I would hesitate, half expecting K to call down to me to wait for him, as he had done daily so that we could walk together. Also, my studies didn't have their old meaning. And the high grades for which I'd worked so hard and all the honors—standing first among the sophomores, standing first among junior men in the first semester, and, most recently, being nominated as a junior for Phi Beta Kappa—seemed empty, for it seemed to me that K had failed academically and died because he had pursued knowledge for its own sake, while I had succeeded academically and survived because I had concentrated on results. I thought that in an ideal college the students would not be rushed through learning and rewarded for a storehouse of carefully arranged and neatly labelled packets of facts, as they were at Pomona, but be given time for reflection and rumination, for the development of the sensibilities, for the cultivation of critical thinking, and for self-expression. I let up on my rigorous study schedule and took long walks, during which I imagined that I was communing with nature, like the Romantic poets. Wherever I went, I also listened for human situations, which I tried to turn into short stories, a little in the manner of the later Tolstoy. By no means did I wish to abandon my studies—my interest in literature, history, and philosophy was as strong as ever. I simply wanted to study the subjects in my own time, in my own way, without the constraints of assignments and examinations. Like Tennyson, I yearned not for knowledge but for wisdom.

SOME more entries from my journal—this time from my senior year.

October 19

It seems library-living has got to us. No one in our class actually wants to go out into the world and work. Our entire class seems to be aiming for graduate or professional school.

October 20

Thanks to Sontag, students in our class who are only average in English, say, have suddenly discovered they can be fine metaphysicians. In his courses, people are studying harder, getting better grades, and getting more encouragement than they have ever known before. As a consequence, they are raising their sights. People who were talking just last year about teaching in high school are talking now about going to graduate school and becoming professors of philosophy. It's a sea change in the expectations of our class, and it's a tribute to Sontag.

Although I haven't taken any of Sontag's courses, I've heard him in public discussion groups, from which it's clear that he appeals to students' deepest wish to be discovered, to be pronounced brilliant. Unlike other professors, who inform students, he seems to want to *know* them. While he seems to pursue their opinions by asking questions, his underlying, unstated question always seems to be "Which one of you is the smartest?" That gives his performance a lot of drama.

Sontag's approach is enhanced by his height—over six feet, I believe—and by thinness, a mocking tone of voice, and his dark-brown eyes. They have deep circles around them, which make his gaze especially searching.

October 24

I was distressed to learn from Daddyji's letter that he has been confined to his bed for three weeks with influenza, and that floods have almost reached our house. I cannot take seriously his comment that his age has made him absent-minded. Sixty is by no means old age. Winston Churchill is still going strong. In fact, he wrote his Second World War series in his seventies.

October 27

I simply must know some Latin if I'm going to get to Oxford, but it is one of the hardest subjects I have ever taken, and my Latin professor at Scripps is going at a speed that is leaving us gasping. I am spending almost two hours a day at Latin outside the class.

November 4

After I don't know how many letters to and from Oxford, I have my admission to Balliol College. It's conditional on my getting money to support myself there for two years, but it is an unequivocal "yes."

January 1

I just heard that Ed Taylor got a Rhodes. Everyone says that this was Pomona's year for the Rhodes. President Lyon says I would've got it if I had been an American citizen. C'est la vie.

January 8

Johnnie has applied for a Woodrow Wilson Fellowship. She says if she gets it she'll go to Cal to study English as a graduate student. She's also applied for a Fulbright to go to France. If she doesn't get either fellowship, she says, she might teach high school or grade school. If that fails, she says, she might get married to someone at Stanford business school. And she's in earnest about it. So that's what it all comes down to—and she's writing perhaps a brilliant essay on Joyce, Woolf, Galsworthy, and Bennett.

January 10

Richard Hungate and John Peck, the two most eligible men on campus, seem likely to marry girls from U.C.L.A. and Whittier. Pomona girls are pretty upset about it.

January 24

I've got the money—I'm going to Oxford! Unbeknownst to me, Mrs. Watumull suggested to the Hazen Foundation that it give me a fellowship. The president of the foundation writes to say they will do it. Such a thing could only happen in America. I can't believe my good luck.

March 8

Daddyji has arrived in Germany to take up his assignment with Mrs. Clyde. He writes to say that he has also been engaged for a lecture tour in the United States this autumn. So I'm bound to see him in England sometime in late summer. Hurrah!

April 6

Today received a great piece of news—Harvard has awarded me its national prize fellowship of $2,200 a year for three years to do a Ph.D. in history. But, alas, I prefer the Hazen Oxford alternative and have so written to Dean Reginald Phelps of the Harvard Graduate School. I've asked him, however, if I could come there after doing a second undergraduate degree at Oxford.

April 12

I presented a paper to the California Council for the Blind in Fresno on the dismal selection of Talking Books by the Library of Congress. The paper was so well received that Dr. tenBroek asked me to join the council as some kind of executive. But I told him that I'm not interested in doing work for the blind in any shape or form. I want to be totally assimilated into the sighted world.

April 15

Dean Phelps writes that Harvard cannot postpone my fellowship or promise that they will give favorable consideration to my application after Oxford, but he's hopeful. That's enough for me.

IN the middle of my senior year, when I stopped in at the Religion Department after lunch to pick up a book, Mary (her name has been changed), who was working there as an assistant, asked, in a rich Southern accent, "You're really from India India?" As she got the book for me, she went on, "What are you doing so far away from home?"

I gave her a brief, reticent answer—I'd never met her before— and turned to leave.

"Not so fast," she said, a little imperiously. "Where I come from, gentlemen don't just give ladies the brushoff unless they are downright rude—and then they're not gentlemen." She laughed. Her laugh was girlish, but rich and full.

"You must be new at the college," I said, turning back to her. She sounded young and pretty and flirtatious.

"New as a penny," she said, and added. "You mean everyone here knows you except for poor old me?"

"Where in the South do you come from?" I asked.

"Fresh from Nashville. This is my first job and my first time away from Tennessee."

We talked a bit about being away from home. Then she asked abruptly, "Are you going to invite me for a Coke at the Coop or run out of here like a wild man?"

Left to myself, I probably wouldn't have had the courage to ask her even to have a Coke with me, although it was more than a year since I'd had a date and I was starved for feminine company. In fact, with her I felt even more shy and formal than usual, because she was clearly older and not a fellow-student. But as we left the office together for the Coop I felt elated at having met her.

At the Coop, Edward Weismiller was sitting with Charlie Stivers at one table, going over a short story with him, and at another table Dick Thomson was interviewing students for a piece in *Student Life*. Mary and I sat down near the back.

"Pomona seems like such a special place," Mary said. "You're so lucky to be going here."

"I don't know about that," I said, hedging.

"I get the impression that everyone here is always busy, busy, busy," she said. "Even when people are having fun, they seem to do it in a busy way. Now, at Vanderbilt, where I went, people worked, but they also had a lot of fun." Such commonplace observations coming from someone else might have made me cringe, but from her they sounded original, as if a particularly keen outside observer were evaluating Pomona students.

"What did you do for fun at Vanderbilt?" I asked.

"Sometimes nothing more than sit in a swing in the gallery and get into a brown study," she said, mysteriously.

"I've come across 'brown study' in novels, but what is a gallery?"

"I thought you were going to ask me that," she said. "That's why I used Southern words. I heard you like to write, and I know that writers like words."

I had to tease the meaning of "gallery" out of her. She finally said, "It's a porch."

As a rule, I hardly spent more than five minutes in the Coop—its atmosphere of group life made me anxious—but that day I must have spent the better part of the afternoon there; I even stood up my reader. I couldn't get enough of Mary's languid voice, her Southern drawl, her quaint speech—her unhurried Southern ways. As she talked, I mentally compared her with the girls I'd known—girls I'd dated or tried to date. She's not timid, like Mandy, I thought. She's not desperate, like Phyllis. She's a prize, like Johnnie. Of course, she's not as intelligent as Johnnie, but then Johnnie never took a real interest in me. But Mary seems to be interested in me as a man, as if I could see. She is natural, accepting, self-confident.

"Have you ever been to the South?" Mary was asking me.

"I went to high school in Arkansas."

"Heaven alive! Then we have a lot to talk about."

I was no longer in touch with any of my Arkansas school friends; hardly any of them had gone on to college, and our different concerns and the geographical distance had drawn us apart. At Pomona, to have spent some time in Arkansas was infra dig, so I'd done my best to outgrow my Arkansas past. In fact, I'd come so far from it that I found even my Pomona present parochial and was dreaming about a glamorous Oxford future. Listening to Mary talk, however, made me almost homesick for Arkansas, homesick for my high-school friends, and made me realize for the first time that I had an American past. Her excitement made me suddenly value Arkansas, and, by extension, myself—even if fleetingly.

I told her a little about Arkansas. Before long, I was confiding to her that I felt tongue-tied around women but that she was different. As we were saying goodbye, I invited her to have coffee with me at the Sugar Bowl that evening. To my delight, she accepted.

❦

AT the Sugar Bowl, almost before we had sat down and ordered apple cider Mary said, "I hope you're a Christian. You know, I couldn't be dating someone who isn't."

The word "dating" took my breath away, because it meant that she thought of us as having a continuing relationship rather than a casual friendship. In my Indian way, I immediately began wondering how she would fit into our family system. But her statement about Christianity gave me pause. Lately, as I had endured sorrows that did not admit of rational explanations, I'd been turning to God. I was drawn, however, not to Hinduism— it seemed to me as absurd as the clay figures of the gods and goddesses, with their multiple heads and arms, that my mother worshipped—but to Christianity, for, in addition to having roots in my childhood, it now seemed as inspiring as the Western history, philosophy, literature, and music that I was studying. Although I was by no stretch of the imagination a practicing Christian, I felt I had to give Mary an unequivocal answer if we were to go on seeing each other, so I said boldly, "Of course I'm a Christian."

"I love getting all dressed up and going to church," she said. "I like to sing in church. Do you?"

"Well, my voice isn't trained for Western singing," I said, and I tried to turn the conversation from church and singing to Indian music.

"But which church do you belong to? I like Mr. Rankin's sermons, don't you?"

"I do," I said. Although I'd scarcely heard Robert Rankin, the chaplain of the Associated Colleges, preach, I reasoned that I might as well have, because over the years I'd had many conversations with him about Hinduism, Christianity, and Zen Buddhism.

"What do you like most about being a Christian?"

The question was so unexpected that it took me a minute or two to formulate an answer. "Reading the New Testament," I finally said, a little lamely, and I added, "I can't imagine anyone studying English literature and not being interested in the Bible."

"But a believing Christian has to go to church and be on fire with faith," she said. "I don't feel alive unless I've heard a sermon every week."

Oh dear, she's going to ask me to go to church with her, I thought. The very idea filled me with dread. I'd scarcely been to a religious service since Arkansas, where we students were required to go to the church of our choice, and I'd chosen the Episcopal church. I remembered how self-conscious I would feel when the minister asked the congregation to turn to this page in the prayer book or that page in the hymnal, and people around me would raise their voices in prayer or song while I, not knowing the words, stood there with a blank face and empty hands. If I tried to mouth the words by following my neighbors, I would always be a syllable or two behind. That didn't matter so much with sibilant words like "trespasses," but short, single words like "done" stuck out, exploding in my ear like firecrackers. Sometimes I would doze off during the sermon and keep waking up thinking that it was over and people were standing up and I alone was still sitting.

"I don't often go to church here," I said.

Because I couldn't bring myself to tell her everything that terrified me about church, I merely said that it was difficult for me to walk into church alone.

"Yes, I thought I hadn't seen you in church," she said. "Let's go to church together next Sunday."

There was no help for it——I'd brought the situation on myself—so I agreed. "It's a date."

That Sunday, I was in turmoil as I went to church with Mary, but she hardly seemed to notice my faltering singing and praying. She and I joined other couples in the vestibule, waiting to shake the minister's hand, and afterward we all discussed the sermon. Until then, I'd scarcely been aware that there was a social dimension to church.

❦

MARY had a car, and she went everywhere in it. It was a Buick, and I soon learned to recognize the soft purring of its engine. Sometimes when I was walking on the campus, I would hear it beside me. "Hey, there!" she would call out. "Can I give you a ride?" At first, I resisted, partly because nothing on the campus was very far from anything else, but also because I didn't like being seen sitting next to a woman behind the wheel. She wouldn't take no for an answer, however, and I soon grew to like riding around with her—especially because she had such a relaxed way about her. She would drive with one hand on the wheel and the other holding my hand, and she'd call out greetings to friends along the way, sing, and, if I had a few extra minutes before a class, race out of town and zoom along Route 66 in a spirit of pure devil-may-care, and somehow get me back just in time.

Mary liked to go to films. One of the first ones we saw together was "Rebel Without a Cause." At one point, when James Dean and his rival were playing "chicken," she burst into tears. I was both touched and overwhelmed. I tentatively held a handkerchief to her eyes, fearing that she would brush it away, but she took my hand and guided it. Her goodness is worth all the intelligence of Pomona girls, I thought.

After the film, she invited me to her home—a cottage, where she lived alone. She made tea and had me sit next to her on the sofa. I took her hand. She started caressing the back of my hand. I leaned toward her, wondering what she would do if I tried to kiss her. Then I felt frightened and brusquely drew back. She's too tall, I thought. She's at least two inches taller than I am. I can be attracted only to shorter girls.

"What's the matter?" she asked.

"Nothing."

"But what are you thinking?"

My thought struck me as so absurd that I quickly said, "I'm thinking about you." The remark sounded obviously false.

"Silly Billy." She leaned toward me. She touched my face. Our mouths met. I was surprised by how natural it felt to kiss her.

❧

UNLIKE many of the Pomona women, Mary seemed full of transparent feminine charm and wiles. She paid a lot of attention to dress, used hand lotion, and wore perfume during the day as well as in the evening. At first, I found her scent overpowering, but soon accepted it as a part of her personality. Although, unlike me, she drank coffee and occasionally smoked a cigarette, she felt guilty about doing so. "Oh, Lordy!" she would say. "If people down home saw me drinking coffee or smoking, they'd be right well scandalized. I'll have to give them up before I go home to Nashville."

At the time, I was reading the Existentialists, and used to agonize about who I was, why I was here, where I was going. The few times I mentioned such concerns to her, she brushed them aside as the worries of a man who had not yet fully discovered the joys of faith. She often spoke of people who read a lot and thought a lot as too intellectual; they were not ladies and gentlemen, she said. All this was contrary to everything I had ever thought. Indeed, I couldn't imagine anyone's being too intellectual.

"Don't you ever wonder if your faith is true?" I once asked her.

"Do I wonder if my name is Mary?"

Once, when we were around some of my intellectual friends,

she dropped the fact that she'd been elected homecoming queen at Vanderbilt.

"How corny!" one of them said, laughing.

I squirmed, but she wasn't fazed. She simply said, "To be elected homecoming queen, you have to be pretty and popular. Now, I ain't saying I'm pretty, but, boy, I was sure popular."

I felt a surge of pride in her for standing up for herself.

Mary tended to be late, so when we were going to concerts or plays on campus I would make it a point to arrive early at her cottage and would wait downstairs while she finished dressing upstairs. I found myself mesmerized by sounds of her opening and shutting drawers, brushing her hair, trying on shoes. The walls and ceiling were so thin that I had the illusion I was in the room with her. If I tried to hurry her along, she would call down, "Don't you know that women are always late?"—a remark that reminded me how little experience I still had of women outside my family. I would begin to fret that she might throw me over for an experienced, sighted man. Then I would hear her running down the stairs with a light, eager step. Soon I was breathing her fragrance and feeling her kiss. She had generous, warm lips; and if, in my shyness, I was a little stiff, she would take my face between her hands. At such a moment, everything—grades, Oxford, money, sighted men—would suddenly fall away.

There were many things I did for the first time with Mary. We went to a football game. We went grocery shopping. We would walk down the crowded aisles wheeling the cart, as if we were a married couple. Then I would daydream about one day having a wife and pushing our child in a perambulator through a park, and I would feel weak all over with excitement and fear.

Mary often cooked dinner for us, and she didn't let me just stand around the kitchen but put me to work peeling and chopping, washing and stirring. She sometimes put a bite of something in my mouth to see how I liked it. I felt I had never been so intimate with anyone.

Whenever Mary sensed that I was self-conscious about my blindness, she would involve me in an activity—washing her car, for instance. Sometimes she would even ask me to help her select her clothes for an evening. With someone else, that would have made me even more uncomfortable about my blindness, but not so with her. She would describe the colors of various outfits so simply and vividly that I had the feeling I was seeing them for myself. Nor was that feeling a total fantasy, I thought. After all, I'd been able to see until I was almost four. I felt that the experience of those years must have been preserved somewhere in the depths of my mind.

One evening, as she ran down the stairs with her usual eager step and I stood up to kiss her, she stepped back and said, "You didn't even notice that I have a new dress on."

It's hopeless, I thought—I remembered a similar experience with Mandy. She should be going out with someone who can see and admire her.

"I did notice," I said truculantly, trying to bluff my way out of the miserable situation.

"Then why didn't you say something?" It was uncharacteristic of her first to confront me and then to needle me. I felt as though I had walked into a door that had been shut in my face. I wanted to rush back to my room and nurse my hurt in private.

"I always have the sense when I'm with you that you can see me, and you can tell the color of my clothes by the feel," she was saying.

I was four, and was back in Lahore. My mother was flipping the light switch faster and faster, asking me, as her breathing got harder and harder with asthma, "Can you tell? Is the light on or off?"

"I can't tell."

"Look. Open your eyes. On or off?" *Click click click click click.*
"Off."

Her breathing was harder now, "Try again." *Click click click*

Five clicks. "On," I said.

"You sure?"

"Yes."

"Then you can see a little."

"Yes."

"Try again." *Click click click click click click click.*

"Light or dark?"

Seven clicks. "Dark," I said.

"Oh, loving God, you have heard my prayers." The wheezing subsided, and she was bending over me and kissing me, with her tears and hair falling over my face.

"Of course I can see you," I now said to Mary.

"Red must feel different from blue."

"Sometimes," I lied. I took the sleeve of her dress between my thumb and forefinger and felt it carefully, putting on a look of deep concentration. She favors whites and pastels, I thought.

"What color?"

My pulse quickened. She is going to catch me out, I thought. I'll lose her.

"It's emerald green," she volunteered. "It brings out the color of my eyes."

The moment of reckoning had passed, and I sighed with relief. She took my face in her hands. "You can tell everything. I bet you even know how I look on a particular day."

"Sometimes."

"Then the blind can see. God has His own mysterious ways of compensating for everything."

The focus had shifted from my abilities to those of the blind generally. And when it came to them I was as brutally honest as though I were not one of them. "They can do nothing of the kind," I said.

"Well, you may not always know exactly how I look, but you always know how I feel."

"That's the Gospel truth." I hadn't used that phrase since Arkansas.

I recalled one of my father's beliefs—that I could be happy only with a Christian girl, because Christians were taught love and compassion, while Hindus were taught merely fate and duty. I decided to throw myself on her compassion. "Mary, I can't tell how you look on any day. There's no way I can tell colors."

She was silent for a moment, but then she said cheerfully, "Then we'll just pretend you can."

I wanted to go on, but she shushed me, and I let the matter drop. After all, I rationalized, I live in the seeing world, and I lead my life as if I could see. Why should I make such an issue with her of the whole question of seeing? I could not, however, I realized now, keep on pretending that I was a Christian. Ever since I lied to her about being a Christian, I'd been having nightmares. "Mary," I said, "you should know that I'm not a Christian. I'm drawn to the religion, but at present I'm nothing."

"You think that's big news to me?" she asked haughtily. "Everyone at the college knows you're one of the cynical intellectuals. But Mr. Rankin has his eye on you. He will make sure that you find Jesus."

As I was about to protest that I was not a cynic, but that I wouldn't be ready for Christianity for a long time, if ever, she took my face in her hands and said, "You bad boy, you. I could tell you a thing or two about me that would shock the daylights out of you."

I felt her warm lips on mine, and words didn't seem to matter anymore. We walked out of the cottage hand in hand.

A few lines from "Love's Labour's Lost," which had made a great impression on me when I first read the play, came into my head:

> From women's eyes this doctrine I derive:
> They sparkle still the right Promethean fire;
> They are the books, the arts, the academes,
> That show, contain, and nourish all the world.

❧

ONE evening, after Mary and I finished a meal that she had prepared, she surprised me by asking me to do the dishes—something I'd hardly ever done before. I set about scraping the food off the pots and pans with as much enthusiasm as I could muster, but I found it hard going. Mary had a habit of being profligate in her use of such utensils, so there was a little mountain of things to be washed. Also, I couldn't be sure I had scraped something clean without running my fingers over the greasy surface. After a while, I said, "Mary, why don't you wash and I'll dry and put things away?"

"Down home, ladies slave over the stove, and gentlemen clean up," she said.

Curse down home, I thought, and I started piling the plates in the sink, making as much noise as I could.

"Now, you be careful with those pretty dishes," she said.

I applied some soap to the sponge, telling myself she was only treating me like an ordinary man, and that was what I wanted.

"This doesn't look very clean," she said, picking up a plate I'd washed. She put it in the sink for me to wash again.

"Mary, please take over," I said. "You can do it in no time."

"Can't have that, now. Down home—"

"I know."

Later that evening, after I'd finished the dishes, we were sitting on the sofa. I took her hand and leaned toward her to kiss her.

"No, no, no," she said.

I couldn't tell whether she was miffed at me for not doing the dishes with better grace or was just being coquettish. "I think we are going too fast," she said.

She is right, I thought. We have known each other for only a couple of months. But my hand went cold; I thought that all was over, and a feeling of my own worthlessness gripped me. I always felt that one misstep would be the end of a romantic relationship.

"I'm not ready to give you all you want," she was saying.

"I don't think I've ever asked you for anything," I said.

"You need a woman around, you need a home. And me? I'm just trying out my wings. I want to go back to Nashville in June, get my own apartment and a job, and have fun for a few years."

"But that's all right," I said. "I plan to go to Oxford. All I want is to continue as we are and then see what happens. But don't put a stop now to something that I've really had for only the first time."

"But you're not a Christian."

"I don't know myself exactly what I am."

She waited for me to go on, but I didn't know what else to say. She dropped my hand. There was never any hope of anything coming of it anyway, I thought. I was about to get up and leave. Suddenly, she nestled close to me and put her head on my shoulder. She touched my ear. "I never noticed before that your ears are so close to your head," she said. She had a way of raising my spirits just when they were at their lowest.

I reached to kiss her. She pulled away. The windows in the cottage were loose, and a little breeze rattled through them, disturbing the stillness of the evening. "You are a Hindu cynic, and I am a Christian," she said, with a sigh.

"Just say you are a Christian, Mary, and leave it there," I said, my spirits sinking again.

"Then what are you?"

"When we met, I thought the Christianity of my childhood was returning, but now I've gone back to being an agnostic. That's what I've been all along."

"I am one of those people who have to have faith in order to be alive. I shouldn't be dating anybody who doesn't have faith."

It was true—it was hard to think of Mary without faith. In

fact, I felt that if she had not been religious she would not have gone out with me in the first place. All the same, I needed time to think. I mustn't say or do anything that might precipitate a break. I stalled. "I suppose you'd want me to be not only Christian but also Baptist."

"I couldn't marry anybody who wasn't a Baptist."

The word "marry" had never been uttered between us. I could scarcely say it inside my head. I mostly thought of marriage and a wife in the abstract—never in connection with a person I knew. Now Mary had brought the idea of marrying her out into the open. And, however intimate we were, the idea of having her—Mary—around me all the time and letting her see how inadequate I was, see that I wasn't even able to read or write without assistance, was frightening. I abruptly stood up and walked to the window.

"If I didn't think that deep down you were Christian, I wouldn't be going out with you," she said. "I've known all along that you have a cynical side to you. That's the side that I've been praying to change. I've been praying right along that you will join my church."

"And come and live with you in Nashville, Tennessee?" I said sarcastically.

"No. I thought you were going to go home and live in India."

"Then why do you care whether I'm Christian or not?"

"Because, silly, I want the best for you, as I want the best for myself."

I felt so confused that I wished I'd never met her, never held her, never gone with her to films, to dinners, to church, to concerts, to parties, to grocery stores. She had immeasurably enriched my life, but, as I now saw it, at the enormous emotional cost to me of inevitably losing her. I was no more ready for her than she was for me, but in some part of my mind—perhaps because of my Indian background, in which men didn't get to know women outside of marriage—I had us established as a permanent couple.

"Mary, it does no good to talk about such things," I said. "I'm still searching for God."

"You just think too much," she said. "You talk as though it were an act to believe in God. I wonder if you'll ever be ready for God."

I flung the window open, and the room suddenly lost its intimate, enclosed feeling. It became cold and drafty.

"Come here and sit beside me," she said, and I did. "I could not be close to anyone who I thought was rejected by God."

"You think that there is no salvation outside Christianity?" I thought it was best to make the conversation less personal.

"None, as far as I know." It was the first time she had qualified her faith—yielded some ground, as I saw it, by admitting that there might be a place for a nonbeliever in her world. "I am willing to change for you," she said, "but only so far."

"So you do understand. You do allow for my confusion."

"How can I understand? Do I ever argue about who my father is? Then how can I about God?"

"Mary, we are so happy together, except when we talk about religion." I took her hand. "You don't know how much you mean to me." She snuggled closer.

When I left her, it was three o'clock in the morning. Outside, the air smelled of rain, and before I'd gone very far it was drizzling. The *plop-plop* of the raindrops on the branches and leaves of the eucalyptus trees accentuated the silence around me.

❧

A FEW evenings later, I dropped by Mary's house on my way back from the library, and found a man I'll call Bud sitting in my exact spot on the sofa, with Mary beside him. Bud and I knew each other slightly, and we awkwardly shook hands.

"All gentlemen telephone before they call," Mary said, without showing any embarrassment.

I thought of saying that I had never had to telephone before, but instead I left as soon as I gracefully could. The next evening, I asked her about Bud, and found out that she had been dating him off and on for over a month. At first, I thought of berating her for her duplicity, but then I told myself that any sighted girl in her right mind would prefer a sighted man to me, and Bud was not just any sighted man—he was a model Pomona man. He played football, sang in the college glee club, and was a Nappy, standing out even among his fraternity brothers for being "happy, helpful, and hopeful." On top of that, he was a Ghost. I told myself I should be grateful for having had any attention at all from a girl whom Bud found desirable. My anger gave way to sadness.

After that evening, Mary started putting me off when I asked her for a date. I knew I should stop asking her, but I couldn't bring myself to do that—especially since she was her usual loving self when we did see each other. So I pretended that I didn't know that she was going out with Bud, even as I both dreaded and longed for the day when she would come right out and tell me that Bud had supplanted me in her affections. She made no move to tell me, however.

One evening, as we were walking to her cottage after a church supper, I couldn't contain myself any longer, and burst out, "How can you possibly date both Bud and me?"

"Down home, ladies have lots of suitors," she said, as calmly as if we were discussing the supper menu.

"You didn't have any other suitors when we first started seeing each other."

"Not true. For a couple of years, I've been corresponding with two boys in the Navy who've been wanting to marry me. Until a lady gets married, she can have as many admirers as she likes. You know that."

I felt a pang. She was never mine completely, and now I've lost what little I had of her, I thought. If she only wants a good time, she can have a much better time with Bud or the two sailors than she ever can with me. "How will you go about choosing among your suitors?" I asked wearily.

"Whoever deserves me will win my hand," she said, and she asked me if I wanted to hear about her sailors.

I nodded, in spite of myself.

She started describing them, making one sound more alluring than the other, thereby turning my concern into a game. She was so beguiling that I was drawn into the game as if I had no personal stake in what she was talking about.

We were at her cottage, and sat down on the front steps. It was a warm evening with the pleasant scent of eucalyptus in the air.

I made a case for the sailor who seemed to have the better worldly prospects.

"You talk as though I were looking to buy a house," she said.

"That's the way marriages are made in India," I said gravely.

She blew up. "What's the matter with you? Aren't you jealous? Don't you care about me at all?" To my amazement, she began to weep. She went on murmuring, "You don't care, you don't care."

"I do," I said, clumsily putting my handkerchief up to her eyes. "I've been devastated by your carrying on with Bud."

"Then why haven't you said anything about it?"

"I hate scenes, and, anyway, I know my place."

By the end of the evening, I had concluded that although she might be out for a good time—indeed, was leading us all on without knowing it—her feelings for me were every bit as genuine as I had originally assumed them to be.

WHEN I telephoned Mary one evening to see if she was free for dinner, she said she wasn't, but invited me to stop by after dinner for a snack when the library closed. I was touched by her remembering that after I'd spent an evening in the library I was always hungry. When I stopped by, I had trouble thinking of something to say; we hadn't seen each other for almost a week, and the ground of our relationship seemed to be giving way. "It's my birthday," I blurted out. I hadn't planned to tell her that.

"You're kidding. How old are you?"

"Twenty-two. But I don't feel different from the way I felt when I was eighteen."

"I don't feel a day over eighteen, either, though I'm twenty-five."

Mary had not previously revealed her age. Whenever the subject came up, she had dismissed it with some such remark as "You should never ask a lady her age." All along, I'd known she was older than I was, but I was taken aback to learn that there was such a big difference in our ages.

"Why didn't you warn me?" she was saying. "I would have had a birthday cake with twenty-two candles if I'd known. I would have made the cake myself, as big as a tray. I would have had a party for you. It's not too late. Let's call up Jean and Jack and Nicholas—"

"I just want a quiet evening with you."

"Why didn't you tell me?"

"Since I left home, I haven't mentioned my birthday to anyone."

"Why not?"

"I don't know, myself. Perhaps I don't want to be pitied for being so far away from home. It's absurd, really. I don't even read the letters I receive from home around my birthday until after it's over. I don't want the person reading them to me to feel obliged to make a fuss."

Mary walked into the kitchen, and I followed. She looked in the refrigerator. "I don't have a treat in the house."

"Don't you have some bread?"

"You know I always have bread."

"Well, then, let's have cinnamon toast and tea, the way we used to do when the library closed."

"What a fun idea," Mary said.

She put some slices of bread in the toaster and started opening and shutting the kitchen cabinets.

"What are you looking for?" I asked.

"Just because you're a birthday boy doesn't mean you have a right to all my secrets." Mary laughed.

We sat down at the kitchen table for our cinnamon toast and tea. It turned out that she had stuck a couple of little candles in candleholders into my piece of toast, and now she ceremoniously lighted them. "Hurry up. Blow them out, and be sure to make a wish," she said, holding the flames up to my face. They felt very hot.

I was a little boy, and my mother was standing at my bedside, saying, "Wake up, wake up." When I sat up, she held something near my face. "What is it?" she asked, her breath coming hard.

"It's a flame."

"Can you see it?"

"It's very hot," I said hesitantly.

To my relief, she didn't press me. "Child, blow on it and make a wish."

"Why?"

"It's your birthday!"

I blew on the candle but couldn't think of a wish.

"Now you'll grow up to be a sahib like your daddy, and ride a blue horse like a rich man," she said.

That was the last time I'd had candles for my birthday. On later birthdays, I'd just had sweetmeats, like everybody else. But when my birthday came I sometimes thought of the flame in my mother's hand, and my cheeks would feel hot—just as they did now. And I also had the illusion now that I was not only feeling the heat of the flames in Mary's hand but actually seeing the orangey-yellow flicker, just as my mother had wished me to. But the flames in Mary's hand were burning low. I made a silent wish: "I want us to be together like this forever and ever." At that moment, I would have given everything—my ambitions and all—for my wish to come true, and, by extension, my mother's wish for a full and rich life for me. I took a deep breath and blew out both candles.

"Honey, after I make a wish I always pray," Mary was saying. "Then the wish always comes true."

Automatically, I started praying: "Heavenly Father, let us remain like this always." If her God can move mountains, He can do anything, I thought—make me her husband, a Christian, and a professor overnight.

Mary bit into her cinnamon toast and took a sip of her tea. "What did you wish?" she asked, and immediately added, "Don't tell me, or it won't come true."

The precaution is academic, I thought, coming back to earth. The wish is totally absurd. It was nearly the end of March, and in June she would be finishing her job and returning to Nashville, while I, as soon as I had graduated, would go to Cambridge to spend the summer working on my manuscript. And from there I would go to Balliol College, Oxford, where students living in college were required to be single and be part of a mostly male society. Anyway, I had scarcely enough money to get myself to England, never mind paying for her to come with me.

"You know how to do little things and do them beautifully," I said.

"On your birthdays, you must feel especially homesick," she said.

"I do, but I generally keep my homesickness to myself." I mechanically repeated one of my father's sayings: "What cannot be cured must be endured."

"Soon it will be seven years since you saw your mother, won't it?" she said.

Her simple sentence—the fact that she had added up in her

head all the years I'd been away from home—affected me deeply.
I found myself talking freely to her, in a way I hadn't talked to
anyone since I came to America. "I used to think that the longer
I stayed away from home the less I would miss it," I said. "But
it hasn't worked out that way. I miss it more and more. I sometimes think that if I hadn't been able to see my father in America
I might not be alive today."

"Fiddlesticks! You intellectuals can really be morbid."

I laughed. "We Indians have very closely knit families. That's
our whole world." I told her about my brothers and sisters—
about Pom and Nimi and Umi and Om and Usha and Ashok.

And she talked about her father, who was a florist, and her
two younger sisters and baby brother. She said she wished I could
see their pictures.

I told her that sometimes I wished I could see pictures of my
own family, to refresh my memory.

"But you must remember their voices."

"Voices fade very quickly. In fact, I think their voices faded
in my head within a few months of my reaching Arkansas. After
I'd been there a few months, they sent me a record they'd made
at a carnival in Delhi. The voices already sounded so different
from the way I remembered them—I couldn't believe my ears.
And the record was so bad that I couldn't play it more than two
or three times. Since then, I haven't heard the voice of even one
of them."

"Why don't you telephone?"

"It takes hours to get through. Then, it's a radio connection
and they say you can't hear very much, and it's very expensive."

There at the kitchen table, we talked into the night, remin-
iscing about our homes and families, my eyes once or twice filling
with tears.

"You ought to share more," she said at one point. "You
shouldn't hold back so much. Maybe if you talked more about
your family to someone, it would help."

I noticed she said "someone," not "me," but it didn't seem

to matter. The mere act of talking had released a surge of energy. I felt capable of love—not love that wanted and hankered but love that accepted and gave. I felt that instead of trying to reclaim an old relationship I was on the threshold of something new, something fresh.

"I love you," I said. With surprise, I realized that in all the time I'd known her I hadn't said that to her—or, indeed, to any woman. My pride had always got in the way: I was loath to declare my feelings before I had a guarantee of complete acceptance. But it no longer seemed to matter whether she loved me or not. I loved her in my new way.

She put her warm hand on my hand, which was resting on the kitchen table. "Will you believe me if I tell you I like you better than any other gentleman?"

"I do," I said, smiling at her use of the word "gentleman."

We embraced. We let go.

"I need you badly," I said.

"Or someone like me," she said, with a laugh.

"Or someone like you," I echoed, remembering Bud and the sailors, my ambitions, and the studies ahead of me.

"We have only a couple of months here," she said. "Let's pretend there are no differences between us."

"Let's," I said. I took both her hands and concentrated on her gentle, soft voice, on her beautiful Southern drawl, on her enchanting, girlish laugh.

When I walked back to my room late that night, I felt happy. At that moment, Mary seemed to me Lahore, home, church. She was also that violin player in the small café on Telegraph Avenue in Berkeley, but she had opened the door and invited me in. She had served me tea and cinnamon toast, comforted me, and sent me on my way.

❧

IT was the day after I finished my final examination—the last requirement for my A.B. degree—and I was leaving Pomona and Claremont, my home for four years. I had decided not to stay around for the Commencement exercises, which were almost a week away. Although I was afraid that my professors, President Lyon, and Miss Rietveld—all the people who had helped me so much through the years—would be disappointed not to see me march with my class in cap and gown, and accept the degree in person, I simply couldn't afford to lose a moment in getting to Cambridge: I had to hire an amanuensis while students were still looking for summer jobs, and start my writing. Besides, I had no family to take pleasure in the ceremony, and I certainly had no heart for the succession of pre-Commencement class dances and parties getting under way. I didn't even say many formal goodbyes, though it made me sad to think that my friends would find me suddenly gone. Ever since being shipped off before I was five to a school more than a thousand miles away from home, I had found goodbyes excruciating.

Almost the last thing I did in Claremont was to go and say goodbye to Mary.

"I can't tell you how much it's meant to me to know you," she said at the door as I was leaving.

"Mary, knowing you has made me feel less lonely—made me believe in a more gentle life than I had ever thought was possible for me," I said haltingly.

"Don't be sad," she said, taking my face in her hands. "God willing, we will see each other again soon." She kissed me, and disappeared into her cottage as fast as the blowing out of a candle flame.

When I returned to my room, I found that Mrs. Thind had arrived to drive me to the airport.

I had already sent my books and records by sea to Oxford; had sold my phonograph and tape recorder to a fellow-student, since the electrical voltage in England would be different; and had discarded many of my California clothes, which were unsuitable for the cold English climate. Mrs. Thind wanted to know what I was doing with my bookcase. I'd built it with planks and heavy glass bricks, which I'd framed in wood, and it was the only piece of furniture I owned.

"I'll leave it behind, I suppose," I said. "It's not of much value."

"I'd like to have the bookcase," she said. "I want it because you made it."

I was flattered. We dismantled it, and lugged it, along with my small suitcase and my little Swiss typewriter, to my car, which I hadn't been able to sell. Mrs. Thind, who had come to Pomona by bus, got in the driver's seat. She had kindly agreed to dispose of my car after I left.

We drove out through the familiar college gates and were off.

"Next time I see you, you'll be an Englishman," Mrs. Thind said at the airport, as I thanked her for all she'd done for me in California.

"I don't know about that," I said.

"Well, anyway, come back soon," she said. (It was fifteen years before I got back to California and saw her again, and longer still before I saw Mary, who by then was the wife of a successful Nashville stockbroker and the mother of two teen-age children.)

I ARRIVED in Cambridge on the morning of June 4th, and, with my suitcase and typewriter, went straight to the Phillips Brooks House. Through the people there, I was offered a one-room apartment on Massachusetts Avenue near Harvard Square. It had belonged to an elderly widow who had recently died, and it was so musty and full of dust that as soon as I walked in I had a fit of sneezing and coughing. It was also cluttered like a Victorian curiosity shop, and, oddly, every inch of wall space—over the bathtub, over the bed, over the table—seemed to be taken up with shelves of the *Reader's Digest*. But it was only fifty dollars a month. I immediately took it. The same day, through Radcliffe, I got in touch with an amanuensis—Grace Kestenman, who had just finished her junior year there and was looking for a summer job. I hired her on the spot, to work from eight to five, six days a week, for a monthly salary of a hundred and twenty dollars.

I quickly settled down to a daily routine of writing. Fortified by breakfast of a sugar doughnut and orange juice from a corner drugstore, I would start dictating to Grace, my head full of scenes that I feared would vanish if I didn't get them down on paper in a hurry. I had worried that I couldn't pick up the threads of the narrative without Johnnie, and Johnnie's hand to take down my words. But, perhaps because I was already so far into my story, it seemed almost to write itself. Anyway, I was now writing the American section, right up to leaving Pomona, and because it was so much closer in time it was more vivid in my mind than the two Indian sections, now awaiting revision.

Grace, who was quiet and reserved and smoked a lot, seemed a little dazed by what she'd got herself into—something she tried not to show. But, in her way, she entered into the spirit of the project.

"I mustarded my roll," I dictated on the first morning.

She stopped writing and said, "You can't say that in English."

"I can, too," I said. "Don't you say in English, 'I buttered my roll'?"

"Yes, but we say, 'I put mustard on my roll.' I know it's not logical, but it's correct."

Though I wasn't totally convinced, it was her version that went into the draft.

We worked so hard that during the two months or so we sat together in the small, cramped room I didn't get to know much about her. When we might have talked, during our lunch hour, from one to two, she would go off, saying something like "I simply have to have a break and see my friends and get out in the world, or I'll go nuts." I would eat a cold meat sandwich in five minutes and be ready to go on working, but I would have to wait until she got back, at two. Grace would leave promptly at five, and I would put my feet up and think about scenes for the next day. I would work myself into a feverish state over things I wanted to write about, and then start worrying that if I fell asleep I would forget them all.

Once a week, I would take the subway to Boston and go to the offices of *The Atlantic Monthly*. With some apprehension, I would give what I had written that week to Miss Reynolds. She would then tell me what she thought of the previous week's copy and make suggestions for revising the two Indian sections. During one of my first visits, she told me that she went over my manuscript every day early in the morning, at her family's house in Wellesley, and mentioned often seeing a hummingbird flutter outside the sunroom window when she looked up from her work. After that, I liked to think that the hummingbird, fluttering outside Miss Reynolds' window, was keeping a watch over my manuscript, and that as long as the bird was at the window the fate of my book was secure.

Every week or two, Mr. Weeks would take me out to lunch at the Ritz-Carlton and would want to know how I was coming along. "While Ved was studying at Harvard, he made frequent trips to our office to go over his manuscript with my assistant, Nancy Reynolds," Mr. Weeks wrote in his book of reminiscences, "Writers and Friends." Actually, I wasn't studying at Harvard that summer. "He came in by subway, and only once did I see him fall. He was late for lunch, and I had gone down to our steps to await him. I saw him in the distance, but he had no way of knowing—nor I—that the pavement across Commonwealth Mall had been dug up, and that on the inside of the curb there was a deep depression, into which he pitched. He brushed himself off, turned back to the Ritz-Carlton to wash up, and then unperturbably skirted the pit to our meeting."

I finished the manuscript on August 3rd, got it retyped, and took it in to Mr. Weeks for his reading and evaluation, and went to New York for a few days to see some of my father's friends. Back in Cambridge, I waited for word from Mr. Weeks. On the morning of Tuesday, August 14th, I finally got a call from him. He said that he had read the entire manuscript and wanted to read to me a memo he had written about it:

First of all I want to compliment you on the admirable progress which has been made with this material in such a short time. After dipping into the first two sections for a quick look at what had been done there I gave my close attention to Section 3 and have now given it something in excess of eight hours of careful scrutiny.

The American chapters have been written with vitality, with burgeoning confidence, with good humor and a most sensitive appreciation of character. "A Donkey Among Horses" is the most revealing to those who dwell in the sighted world, just as "Mary" is the most touching emotionally. At the same time, there are passages of understatement where you do less than justice to the experience. This is particularly noticeable in your account of your first days in New York. You hardly spend an adjective in your description of the subway; the odors which must have assaulted you on your visit to Coney Island you never mention; your ascent of the Empire State Building is something we would all like to hear you talk about. Finally, after having told us of your long fast on the plane because you did not know how to manipulate your knife and fork, you owe it to the reader to explain how much the di Francescos were able to guide you in your table manners. You could hardly have lived on meatballs and spaghetti for an entire fortnight.

Your chapter on mobility and facial vision is so remarkable that it leaves me wondering why you have said so little about the impact upon you of your visits to various parts of this country. The air of Cape Cod must have felt very different to your senses than the hush of the redwoods; the Grand Canyon should have given you a different kind of prickle than whatever sensation you got on the roof of the Empire State. Again, you say that you thumbed your way but you never reproduce any of the conversations or acts of kindliness which must have fallen to you as they befall every hitchhiker.

Finally, there are gaps and shortcomings in Chapter XXX which I think I can make clearer to you in the course of our luncheon. My plan of operation would be for you to work for the next forty-eight hours on the revision of Section 3, then have a talk with me on either Thursday or Friday, in which we compare notes on Section 1, and that we should meet again on Monday, August 20, for a checkup of Section 2. This would mean that the book would be retyped and then sized up for spring publication.

As soon as we hung up, I set to work, did all the revisions in forty-eight hours, showed them to Mr. Weeks and Miss Reynolds on the sixteenth and the seventeenth, and handed in the manuscript for another retyping.

On Monday, the twentieth, I had my final lunch about the book with Mr. Weeks. He seemed excited. "My boy, I think I have a title," he said. He and Miss Reynolds and I had been thinking of titles all summer long. Miss Reynolds had apologetically suggested "My Odyssey." I'd been able to come up with nothing better than "Crossing the Bridge." "The problem of the title must have been pressing on my mind," Mr. Weeks was saying, "because I woke up at two last night with the words of Paul's First Epistle to the Corinthians echoing in my head, as if they had actually been spoken to me: 'For now we see through a glass, darkly; but then face to face.' "

My heart sank. I thought the title he had in mind was "Glass Darkly," and I was about to protest that any reference to darkness would perpetuate the myth that the blind live in permanent darkness. But he said, "Listen to it, how nice it sounds—'Face to Face.' "

At that moment, I could have embraced him: he seemed to make the book exist by the mere act of naming it.

"When will you be publishing the book?" I asked.

"You know I'd like to publish it, and Nancy would like to do it, but it really depends on what our friends at Little, Brown say. And, of course, they haven't seen a word of it yet." Mr.

Weeks started explaining to me the business arrangements between the Atlantic Monthly Press and Little, Brown, and how the editorial decisions of the joint company were made, but I soon stopped listening. Whichever way the editorial decision goes, I thought, I have finished a stage of my life. I have really finished with what I started out to do in America.

At lunch, the words of Paul kept echoing in my head, as if I were trying to fathom their meaning, accustom myself to them as a definition of my young life: "But then face to face; now I know in part; but then shall I know even as also I am known." "Then" seems to refer to the end of life, I thought. But my life is just beginning.